Racehorse Breeding Theories

by Frank J. Mitchell, Ph.D.

In Collaboration with
- Steven A. Roman, Ph.D.
- Rommy Faversham
- David Dink
- Jay Leimbach
- Ross Staaden, BVSc., Ph.D.

The Russell Meerdink Company, Ltd.
Neenah, Wisconsin, 54956 USA

Publisher's Note:
The facts presented and opinions expressed in this book are those of the various authors. The authors and publisher shall have neither liability nor responsibility to any person or entity with respect to the information presented herein. While the book is as accurate as the authors can make it, there may be errors, omissions or inaccuracies.

Library of Congress Cataloging-in-Publication Data

Racehorse breeding theories / [contributing editor, Frank J. Mitchell et al.].
    p. cm.
  Includes index.
  ISBN 0-929346-75-0 (hardcover)
  1. Race horses--Breeding. I. Mitchell, Frank J., 1959-
  SF338.R233 2004
  636.1'22--dc22

                    2004001372

Cover design by Bosetti Production, Art & Design

Published by
The Russell Meerdink Company, Ltd.
1555 South Park Avenue Neenah, WI 54956 USA
(920) 725-0955
www.horseinfo.com

Printed in the United States of America

Table of Contents

Acknowledgements

This book would not have been written but for the prompting of Jim Squires, breeder of Kentucky Derby winner Monarchos. Those who view the breeding of a great racehorse as a blending of art and science will find a bit of both between these covers.

The Blood-Horse, *The Thoroughbred Times*, Keeneland Library, the Breeders' Cup and Bloodstock Research and Information Services have been instrumental in providing data, background information and photographs.

Working in collaboration with the many authors and contributors to this book has been a privilege. Collectively we thank all those breeders, analysts and theoreticians who have gone before and given the historic perspective needed to pursue the future of the breed.

The knowledge and fearless persistence of the staff of The Russell Meerdink Company, Ltd. was essential to bring this project to a successful conclusion.

Foreword

Is horse breeding art – the human effort to imitate, supplement, alter or counteract the work of nature? Or is it science – the observation, identification, description, experimental investigation, and theoretical explanation of natural phenomena?

When so confounded by such mysteries, there is no one better to turn to than the great Albert Einstein, who believed the mysterious to be "the most beautiful experience of man and the source of all true art and science."

If you didn't know better, you'd think he might have spent his life trying to raise race horses, before turning to the easier challenge of formulating the theory of relativity.

Strange as it may seem, this esteemed scientist had the same regard for mystery as the less-esteemed but similarly inclined trainer of Triple Crown Winner Seattle Slew, the legendary Billy Turner. You can't set out to breed horses like Slew, nor to buy them, Turner maintained, "they just show up."

In no position to argue with either after 25 years of arranging equine mating in pursuit of great athletes, I remain resigned to the notion that the secret of horse breeding is and should remain a beautiful mystery. The minute that it becomes an exact science I am both out of my league, and as they say, "out of here."

That does not mean I do not thirst for every piece of scientific evidence, every theory, personal experience or even unfounded rumor floated in the history of the world that might help me raise a better horse. This means not resting until every word of this text has been devoured, for the great secret undoubtedly is so tightly woven it can only be unraveled one tiny thread at a time through a lifetime of work.

A quarter of a century of personal unraveling has yielded only a few precious strings to which to cling: one, that genetic traits can indeed persist through many generations, not just two or three; that mating solely or even mainly on the basis of pedigree without physical consideration of the two animals is idiocy; and that the importance of females has been and continues to be vastly underestimated in the equine world.

Most important is that breeding horses cannot be pursued as either science or business. No amount of money can buy this elusive treasure. Breeding the best to the best and hoping for the best is a good idea, but if it worked only the wealthy would breed Kentucky Derby winners. No, breeding horses is pure art, and must be approached as the painter does a masterpiece – one small stroke at a time. Passion – not the pocketbook or social standing of the breeder – is more likely to be the very heart of the secret. As I read somewhere – probably in French literature – "Art is the accomplice of love. Take love away and there is no longer art."

Jim Squires
Two Bucks Farm
Versailles, Kentucky

Preface

In a book about breeding the Thoroughbred, any number of voices can be heard. In addition to information from the best-known commentators of the day, breeders of the blooded horse have received a long and mixed history from those who came before. Frequently this is passed on as oral history, from fathers to sons and also from mentors to their assistants, who go on to become trainers, breeders, farm managers, and sometimes even journalists.

This way of passing on information — partly learned and partly intuitive — is one of the reasons that horse racing is such a tradition-bound sport. Both on the farms and on the track, there is the sense of those who came before, who broke the ground, who learned things about management and horses, and who sent along their wisdom to the succeeding generations.

Without them, racing would be a sport without a foundation, without a sense of what it is. So it is not without some trepidation that I undertook to produce a book on one facet of this important and fascinating business that we love.

This task is daunting because in this book, I address the major systems and approaches that breeders use in trying to fashion the fastest horse possible, and the variety of approaches alone is a commentary on the importance that breeders place in their horses and in trying to breed a top racer.

For most owners, breeding Thoroughbreds is one of the least frequently rewarding pastimes to be involved with, but when the payoff comes, what a thrill it is. A breeder may spend many years and many dollars before coming up with the horse he has been aiming for, but when that horse arrives and stands in the winner's circle, what breeder would count the cost?

In addition to time and money, producing a good Thoroughbred requires patience, insight, perseverance, enthusiasm, hope, and a sprinkling of good fortune. In other words, breeding the racehorse is a character-building enterprise.

With all these factors, the new owner-breeder approaches Thoroughbred racing with an awesome responsibility: to absorb this wealth of history and information and then turn it to good use in the production of top athletes. Since breeding and racing are most certainly competitive endeavors, a breeder can expect only a limited assist from his colleagues. They are in the game to succeed, as well, and giving away the game is not the way to the winner's circle, especially at the highest levels of the game, where the stakes are the most critical.

And yet it is significantly in response to this dilemma of needing information and understanding in a competitive environment that this book is undertaken.

Understanding all the information in these chapters is not necessary to breed a good horse. Some have succeeded with little more to recommend them than ownership of a few mares of nondescript family and performance. Yet the great horse came, and they enjoyed the fruits of an unearned blessing.

For most of us, however, the more information and the better approach taken will yield more and better results. In keeping with this view, this volume offers a wide and various assessment of the major breeding systems or theories, as well as history and background to breeding and genetics themselves.

The various chapters include a brief background and history of the breeding theory under appraisal. Then the meat of the chapter is a detailed description of the theory.

These range from relatively technical explanations to some livelier and more journalistic accounts that help to highlight the approaches that can be taken with a particular theory. The writers attempt to give the readership all information they need to implement the theory and make it a part of a breeding program.

The chapters also attempt to verify the relative scientific validity of the theories and approaches. This more than any other factor sets this book apart from other attempts to offer breeding theory to owners and breeders, because I ask, "Does this really work, and if so how often has it been proven to be effective?"

Not surprisingly, not all theories are created equal. Some are fascinating, others moderately useful, and a few as worthless as corn shucks. Considering that theorists tend to be in love with their theories, there may be some differing views on the efficacy of some of these approaches.

Clearly if one of them was the silver bullet for exploding all the mysteries and problems of breeding slow horses (a goal at which most of us are successful), we wouldn't be reading about it in this book. The originator would be out sweeping all the major stakes and accepting his trophies and rewards.

Instead, theories offer a tool that may give an incremental edge to the user. This is said with entire candor, because the first lesson to learn in breeding horses is that it is the toughest game in town. And getting an edge, even if only an increment of five or 10 percent, is an advantage not to pass over lightly.

As a result, many breeders use a number of approaches in their program and then try to assess their overall success. This is probably the only systematic way to judge which theories are effective for particular breeders.

Those in certain locales and with a fixed level of competition may find success with differing theories or approaches because they are the only breeders utilizing that method in their area. This, along with the skill and intuition of the breeder, are only some of the intangibles that come into effect with a breeding program.

The importance of using a program is hard to overemphasize. Without guidelines or a regular approach, how is a breeder to know when he has it right? A program allows the breeder to assess what works and what doesn't, and over time, the best approaches for individual breeders will assert themselves.

Introduction

Humility, perhaps, is the first requirement for someone wanting to breed the Thoroughbred. That may sound peculiar, considering that many breeders are frequently anything but shy, but loss is the norm with horse breeding and racing, and anyone who can't take the punishment had better choose a less damaging pastime, such as collecting stamps.

So in breeding blooded horses for the infinitely pleasing sport of racing, it pays to know what the game is about, lest it catch the unassuming breeder broadside athwart the temple and flatten him.

As a result, I have a few things to say about the past (from whence breeders and horse breeding have come), both in this introduction and in the several chapters on this endless fascinating topic of breeding fast racehorses.

Not surprisingly, there are many things we can learn from those who came before. Both the horses they bred and the practices they engaged in tell us that the sport was of no less importance even a hundred years ago. Men of importance, great wealth, and no mean intellect have found horse racing and also the breeding of their own stock an immense pleasure and an extraordinary challenge.

Therefore I do not propose that I have all the answers. Rather to the contrary, I am willing to declare that I have very few of them, with occasional fleeting glimpses of what might work in different situations and in different times.

As this amounts to a confession of humility, I will also declare that breeding good Thoroughbreds has fascinated me from a very early age. As I could not then admit that the practice of breeding such splendid animals was the result of barbarous chance, I began to search for understanding of the systems that went into the Thoroughbred.

This book is a chronicle of much of that journey, taken by myself and by many others over the centuries that the Thoroughbred has existed. When we see that first Thoroughbred who takes our imagination, he is standing in a beam of light, and there is something magical about his presence. Finding such a thrill in an animal is important for us as human beings, but once we've found a treasure in the racehorse, isn't it our next impulse to want to recreate this marvel for ourselves and others?

That or something similar to it has been the goal of generations of horse lovers and breeders. In retrospect, there is an accumulation of information from history and tradition, from science and science-related inquiry, from analysis of data and its application to practical breeding for the best. In the lengthy history of this accumulation, there is dross aplenty but also nuggets of value from many different sources.

In the early decades of the Thoroughbred, the spirit of breeding and racing was more restricted and only a relative few could reasonably participate. The Sport of Kings was for the nobility and or the very lucky, and their aim was winning the Plates and Cups offered by the King and his noblemen. But late in the 19th century, the models of science began to have an influence on the way people thought about breeding.

As Mendel discovered some of the elementary principles of genetics and Galton began to interpret them, the economics of industry began to play an associated part in changing racing and breeding. Great new wealth was created as growth in European countries, and also in North and South American countries — mass production, factories, and systemization — began to open the sport to many who had no history with racing or the horse.

Although some who benefitted from the new wealth of a century ago were long associated with horses, many others were not. They knew that Thoroughbreds were the best horses, the bloodstock of the titled elite and privileged. Therefore, if the nouveau riche wanted to be like the established gentry, they needed Thoroughbreds as well.

The changes in economy brought about changes in society and also in farming because the horse is a reflection of the culture that breeds it. Where once the most commercial aspect of Thoroughbred breeding was for a major Kentucky breeder to ship his yearling crop to New York and sell them at the sales grounds to would-be racing men, the approaches to auction and to promoting bloodstock became much more familiar to us in the opening decades of the 20th century.

As one would expect from a time and society that gave the greatest credit to men and considered that succession from father to son was of the primary importance, the concept of the male line had an early and still lingering fascination for some breeders.

Lending overimportance to the male line led commentators at various times to harken back to an older day when the line in question was dominant. For instance, Roamer, writing in the *Thoroughbred Record* of May 15, 1926, commented: "There is a bare possibility Wise Counsellor may be the instrument to revive the glories of the Glencoe line. There is no more representative American racehorse in the country today, as a glance at his bloodlines speedily discloses . . . One must go back six generations in the top line of Wise Counsellor's pedigree before a foreign horse is encountered, Glencoe, and in the bottom line of his pedigree we do not find an imported mare until we come to his 15th dam, the famous Cub mare, foaled in 1762 and imported by Col. James Delancy."

Roamer, while reminiscing, also shows more than a little national bias. At a time when the U.S. was a fresh player as a world power, many people were highly jealous of our accomplishments, as horse breeders or anything else. And who can blame them in a society so young that many could nearly remember its beginning?

If America scarcely had a history at the turn of the 20th century, racing has never lacked an appreciation of one. Just as the original racing men and horse breeders valued their family traditions and history, so they esteemed their horses in pedigree and in tales of courage and obstacles overcome.

Roamer wrote about the romantic and improbable backgrounds of Wise Counsellor. He noted that "Wise Counsellor's history is one of the romances of the turf . . . His dam Rustle was one of a lot offered by Dr. W.C. Gadsby of Kirkwood, Missouri, at the annual vendue of the Kentucky Sale Co. at Lexington, Ky., December 2, 1920. Rustle was then fifteen years old and while she had been bred that spring to Mentor, it was questionable if she was in foal. There was no demand for her, and she was sold to Mr. Thomas Bradley for $100, proved to be in foal and dropped a colt the next spring which made turf history as Wise Counsellor. Mr. Bradley raced Wise Counsellor at two and he won some $33,000 in his colors. Prior to the Kentucky Jockey Club Stakes, Wise Counsellor was sold to Mr. J.S. Ward for some $66,000, so Mr. Bradley and his brother, who had taken a half interest in Rustle, previous to Wise Counsellor's birth, received a return of approximately $100,000 on an outlay of $100."

The history of such horses is important to the sport, as they help keep hope alive and engender enthusiasm for the difficulties all breeders encounter. But history, the romance of the turf, and colorful anecdotes have limitations when applied to breeding. They can't be tested or reproduced in any useful way. A breeder cannot go out and buy an apparently barren mare for $100 and expect to have any success.

But the beginnings of scientific understanding led many breeders and thinkers about horse breeding to try to find methods that were capable of reproducing the successes they saw around them. Among these, nicking was probably the strongest element of the majority of breeding programs at many times in history.

In effect, the breeders tried to reproduce the best horses of their eras by reproducing their pedigrees. Sometimes they would use half-sisters or half-brothers to great horses, and then others would try a granddaughter of one with the grandson of another. As expected, the potential for genetic variation is very high the farther away one goes from the top stock.

In addition to nicking, the breeding theories of this sort that have survived to this day include Dosage, which tried to reproduce a certain "dose" of blood or create a particular aptitude in a mating; inbreeding, which seeks to concentrate desirable traits by repetition of ancestors; and a few other concepts that have not stood the test of time by capturing the breeders' interest.

As a fuller understanding of genetics and its applications came around, eugenics led the field among applications of scientific knowledge to breeding horses. Breeding the best to the best has held true and sound, in the face of many ingenuous nay-sayers, but around the world, many of the best operations for breeding racehorses are founded on this seemingly simple principle.

In fact, the president of one of the most successful international breeding and racing operations recently remarked to me, "It's easy to breed good horses. Just take a top racemare or producer and send her to the best stallions in the world. Then just about one out of every four or five will be a stakes winner, and maybe one in every 10 or 20 will be an absolute world-beater."

Sounds simple, doesn't it?

It is, if a breeder has the stock to begin with. If not, then the game is up for the eugenics approach.

But, as can be seen by thinking about the quotation above, there is genuine scientific thought going on in these applications. Breeders using the method of breeding the best to the best are accounting for the quality of the horses involved, then applying statistics to estimate the likelihood of a successful outcome, and doubtless using this scale as an indicator of when to sell an animal or when to buy one that stands out from the crowd.

In moving breeders to an understanding of statistics and their proper application to breeding horses, nobody ranks higher than Joe Estes. A great editor and a blunt and incisive writer, Estes was the most important thinker about breeding for more than 30 years. And as editor of the *Blood-Horse* magazine, he had a bully pulpit to express his views and bring a pragmatic dialog about breeding into the public arena.

In keeping with our notes about Wise Counsellor above, Estes wrote a commentary about the stallion in his *Blood-Horse* column of Sept. 16, 1939. In it he recommended that major Thoroughbred breeders send top-class mares to the stallion because Estes had the "conviction that Wise Counsellor has a unique genetic constitution, with more characteristics favorable to the production of racing success than any stallion which has stood in this country for many years."

The basis for Estes's comments was not a hunch or a marketing ploy. He had begun to appraise stallions using statistics, and his conclusion was that "at the least Wise Counsellor has not yet been given the opportunity he has earned." Estes recounted that from his first 10 crops, Wise Counsellor had sired 92 percent starters, 79.5 percent winners, and 11 percent stakes winners.

No wonder that Estes was all torn up over Wise Counsellor. The stallion, from the most marginal mares, had extraordinary statistics for starters and winners. Judging the results from his mates, it's amazing that he managed to get as many as 11 percent stakes winners.

The consideration of quality is important in any breeding operation, and this led Estes to call for a better book for Wise Counsellor. He also acknowledged the stallion's shortcomings: "His pedigree is unfashionable. His foals are only occasionally exceptional as to conformation. They are almost entirely sprinters. A big majority of them are selling platers."

Few writers are bold enough to call a spade that specifically, but Estes was. And he concluded that "There is probably not a stallion alive today which would have got better performers out of the mares which produced these foals."

Judging from Wise Counsellor's comparable index measuring the quality of his mates, Estes's conclusions went largely unheeded, and the stallion's statistics remained essentially unchanged through his final crops just a few years later.

Regardless of the outcome with Wise Counsellor, Estes's work was a major step forward in analytical research into pedigrees and performance. Not coincidentally, Estes made many of the other significant steps that have come and been published for public understanding.

His work has been of sufficient and lasting value, and The Russell Meerdink Company, Ltd. published many of his principles of breeding in a slim volume with information from some of the great researcher's public speeches.

Not only did Estes examine particular stallions, but he put the question of stallion assessment on a firm scientific foundation by using complete data from a stallion's (or a mare's) career and by insisting on the importance of control groups.

This last consideration was an immense improvement because it requires that all classes of horses be part of the research project. All too often, research is done with only a limited group of horses (typically stakes winners), and then conclusions are drawn on the basis of common names in pedigrees. Unfortunately, with some naive researchers, no thought is given to whether the population as a whole carries these names in the same proportion as the elite group used for "research."

Estes's understanding of these basic tenets of statistics has allowed his work to stand the test of time and prove of great worth even today.

Furthermore, by using control groups and working up a database, Estes was able to work out averages for the breed and statistics encompassing the results of entire racing years that stretched over decades. These deep databases allowed him to produce the average earnings index, which measures the earnings of a stallion's progeny against the average purse money earned by all racehorses in a given year.

By creating an index of earnings, Estes was able to rank stallions in a meaningful way by their progeny earnings, without dramatically skewing the results due to a single big winner or multiple large crops of minor winners.

While these changes in evaluating stallions were a major improvement, Estes's application of indexing and breed averages was probably even more important for a proper understanding of broodmares. Traditionally, there has been a prejudice against high-class racemares as producers. Some of them stank. Unfortunately, they are much more visible than no-account mares who produce nothing, and the notion arose that the top racemare was an inferior product as a broodmare.

Estes took issue with this as soon as he began to work with statistics seriously in the 1930s. His numbers told a much different story than the anecdotal information. In an article from the *Blood-Horse* from March 3, 1962, Estes produced a table ranking the breed average against several groups of mares. Estes was right. The better the group of mares, the better their overall producing records, with the breed averages at the bottom.

Has our understanding of statistics and breeding the Thoroughbred improved since Estes? Well, not much.

There can be no doubt that information is much more widely available than it was 30 and 40 years ago. It is cheaper, and more people have access to it. But relatively little important work has been done to advance our understanding of pedigrees and bloodstock.

The expansion of science has made an impact on our understanding of conformation and the physics of a horse's motion. With these last, the scientific study of biomechanics and cardiovascular function have made contributions to the way trainers work with horses and also the way the marketplace evaluates them.

In breeding fast horses, we have moved through a century of changes and fascinating animals. Breeders have expanded their repertoire from a consideration of historical issues and sire-line data to include various approaches made feasible by an increased understanding of science. From these varied approaches and theories, the contemporary breeder can pull out the information that best fits his program and try to mesh together the many pieces of the puzzle in the attempt to breed the best horse possible.

CHAPTER I

The Origins and Genetics of the Thoroughbred

To pinpoint the genesis of the fine-blooded racing Thoroughbred is far from the simplest puzzle. In most histories of the breed, three founding fathers — the Byerly Turk, the Darley Arabian, and the Godolphin Arabian or Barb — are mentioned as the stallions to whom all present Thoroughbreds trace in the male line. This is true, but a quick look through really old pedigrees, however, shows that these three were by no means the only stallions used in the early days of the breed.

The Markham Arabian, for instance, was imported into England for King James I in 1616, and many other stallions and mares from the East and from the Mediterranean region in general were brought into England to "improve the breed of horses."

From the many horses used in the formation of the breed, most were quickly weeded out in the selection of good racing types and have no significance historically or genetically for the Thoroughbred.

But looking at extended pedigrees does reveal some surprises. For instance, when Lady Wentworth produced her *Thoroughbred Racing Stock*, the most common names appearing in the pedigree of English Triple Crown winner Bahram were not the "founding fathers." Instead, relatively unknown horses such as Darcy's White Arabian, the Morocco Barb, and the sire of Old Bald Peg were repeated in the pedigree more than 100,000 times apiece. The primary reason for these names to appear more often is that they are older, and when they show up in the internal lines of descent, they are multiplied more times in the course of an extended pedigree.

The horses above, along with dozens more with lesser representation, show that the origins of the Thoroughbred are significantly older than the three surviving male lines. In addition, the foundations of the breed — both its quality and its existence as a light-horse breed descended extensively from Eastern sources — are much deeper than many references lead us to expect.

This concentration of genetic material for the purpose of running has allowed the Thoroughbred to be the most significant factor in the development of other light breeds of horses used for sport and recreation. The Standardbred and Quarter Horse, in particular, owe a great debt to certain strains of Thoroughbreds which found their truest expression in other fields of sport.

From this thumbnail sketch of the Thoroughbred's origins, I would like to draw a few conclusions. One is that the vast amount of genetic material from previous generations is gone with the wind. While many thousands of horses lie in only a single generation at the far reaches of a pedigree, the horse standing before you today possesses exactly the same number of genes as ONE of all those thousands of forebears. All the other genetic elements are gone.

Second, the importance of the male line is highly overemphasized. Male-line descent has been much more important in human society for legal and sociological reasons, but its significance to horses is primarily the importance that we humans have placed on it. I certainly have nothing against the continuance of particular male lines, and they might actually be a good thing since they encourage variety in breeding. But as we begin an understanding of Thoroughbred breeding, let's quickly work to separate the importance of the male line from the importance of great stallions. As far as it goes, their influence can be carried on through collateral lines of the pedigree, even if their sons are not successes at stud.

Third, the concept of the Thoroughbred as a hybrid is incorrect. Although some very sensible people have latched onto this, in the strictest sense, the Thoroughbred is definitely not a hybrid. A hybrid in this sense is a cross between two species, such as the horse and the donkey, and the resulting offspring is almost always sterile. Obviously, this is not the case with the Thoroughbred. In a more general sense, however, the Thoroughbred is a breed with a closed stud book of fairly long history, and as a result, crossing strains, especially those that have several generations' separation, may result in something approaching "hybrid vigor."

I will expand these thoughts into more detailed discussions after surveying the prospects of genetics to contribute answers to the questions of breeding and racing horses.

CHAPTER 2

Genetics and Gene Mapping

Since the purpose of this volume is not to chronicle the Thoroughbred's history but to illuminate such as can be said about breeding the racer, I am skipping lightly across the stepping stones of this fascinating brook leading to the main river of our inquiry.

The genetics of the Thoroughbred is a subject that is absolutely central to breeding the racehorse, but unfortunately, we don't know everything about the horse's genetics at this point. Indeed, we know very little about the horse's genes, but in the words of Dr. Gus Cothran of the University of Kentucky, "Our work in mapping the genome of the horse is going well, considering what we expected just a couple of years ago."

The advances in technology and in the known genome of other species the past two years have significantly enlarged what Cothran and his colleagues are able to map out for the horse. He continued by noting that "We have about 800 genetic markers mapped and are expecting quite a bit in the next couple of years. We are going to be seeing things we wouldn't have dared hope for. There's now talk of sequencing the entire horse genome because the map is going to be much more detailed than we anticipated in '95."

Cothran and other researchers into the genome of the horse have been aided by the rapidly accelerating work of others in the field of gene mapping. He noted that "We've been able to ride on the coat tails of other species, especially the human genome," in blocking in chunks of the genome and speeding up the process of the map.

This is important progress. Even the gene map is important, but talk of sequencing the genome could be even more significant to breeders and researchers, since the genome sequence fills in the dots on the larger map.

Cothran's progress offers hope for breeders in a number of areas, although the applications for this information are far from developed. He said, "We are just in the stage of building the map and just beginning to use it. It is going to be quite useful."

Although breeders might start seeing stars in hope of using these technologies to breed a better and faster racehorse, Cothran said that the likely applications are more general, at least for the immediate future.

The most likely immediate applications are for "using the map to see whether a suspect gene was responsible for a particular disease and for creating tests to check for its presence in individuals." This holds out hope that certain diseases, and possibly also some weakness or faults, can be eradicated by careful use of the genome in test-case situations.

"In the case of wondering about passing on known defects," Cothran said, "the map is at a point of usability for finding characteristics and already is at a stage for detecting a very small number of known defects. A small number of tests is possible now."

Defects that plague a large portion of the horse species would be the most likely to receive immediate attention because the developers would see those problems as the ones most likely to give them a large return on their research and development. And Cothran said that testing in this area "will be the thing that increases the quickest." Clearly, economic considerations will lead the development and implementation of this research, at least for the immediate future.

Unfortunately, the likelihood of applying gene mapping to questions of breeding is probably a ways off. Cothran said, "The case of choosing this mare to mate with that stallion is more problematic simply because there are so many more factors in getting a good racehorse or athlete."

Rather than curing a disease or finding a mutant gene that causes a problem, breeding a racehorse calls a multitude of genetic and environmental and psychological factors into play. "Racing performance is such a complex thing," Cothran said, when compared to genes that relate to specific traits or problems. He said, "We can look at a mare and stallion and say that these parents have a high possibility of producing a good runner, but other factors have a lot to do with it, too."

Even so, Cothran believes that "there will be more application that way as our knowledge increases," although it may not be what breeders are wanting to hear. He said that "DNA parentage verification is about the only gene technique being used for Thoroughbreds, but I believe that some tests will become available and may have some usefulness."

That is certainly less than many breeders are hoping for from genetic research, but it may be all we need. Do we really want or need for the game to be entirely predictable? I doubt it, and if it became so, where would the fun and excitement go?

Whereas many breeders consider that genes entirely determine what the Thoroughbred will become on the racetrack, Cothran tempered that perspective, noting that "single genes have a limited influence on the eventual outcome in most cases."

This is virtually the death knell for those theories believing that a single gene or a single factor is responsible for a racehorse's ability. Single genes do not create or entirely control organs, structures, or functions. In a fruit, researchers estimate that several hundred, perhaps several thousand, of genes are involved in determining size alone. How many different interrelationships and gene codes are involved then in an animal as complex as the horse?

To develop this line of reasoning, Cothran went on to say that "conformational traits are not usually controlled by a single gene, but bleeding might be something we could address by a process of weeding out."

Trainers across the country might hear that and say, "I can control bleeding. Can you give me a way to tell if the critter is fast or slow?"

But again, the answer is more complex than the question because racing is not a simple thing. Cothran said, "I know there's interest in looking for performance characteristics, but not all of them are genetically controlled, and not all are controlled by breeding. If a couple of genes were responsible for muscle quality, for instance, you could produce offspring with optimal muscle, but they might have poor minds or develop other faults that would limit or prohibit their use in racing. That's why it's so much of an art. There are so many factors responsible for producing the successful athlete — environment, training, health, psychology" — that breeders underestimate their own sophistication in producing good athletes. They are not made with a cookie cutter.

Even among the best breeding operations, the reliance on probability is an important factor in breeding because if the top breeder gets 50 high-quality foals annually, he can expect to have a respectable number of them survive the rigors of training and the uncertainties of fate to be competitive at the top level of sport.

A sensible approach and a reasoned practicality are necessary for any successful breeder, and Cothran threw in a comment that ought to make anyone think long about his operation. He said, "Most studies of racing ability find that its heritability is about 30 percent, and that's not surprising, when you consider what it is."

Racing ability is not a genetic trait like coat color. So it does not transmit from parent to offspring in the same way that a purely genetic characteristic would do. Athletic ability in the Thoroughbred is the result of many traits, many factors, and many relationships among the horse and his caretakers, health, environment, and so forth.

Take the case of Stymie, for instance, as an example of the variety of factors that go into making a horse successful. This colt was not well-pedigreed. He did not inspire much confidence among his trainer or owner early on, and was a minor claimer at one point in his career.

The noted trainer Hirsch Jacobs claimed him, however, and as part of the Jacobs training and racing stable, the colt improved. Stymie did not improve immediately nor indicate that Jacobs was gazing into a crystal ball when he claimed the handsome chestnut.

Instead, Jacobs ran him back in claimers. The chestnut showed some ability, winning four times in 28 starts at age two, but even three more victories from 29 starts at age three did nothing to say he would become one of the best horses in training. If 57 starts in two seasons of racing cannot find the best form of a horse, how is racing ability quantifiable?

Stymie's physique held part of the answer. He needed to grow and strengthen, and when turned out in late 1944, at the back end of his three-year-old season, the son of Equestrian improved significantly from the rest and came back a better horse.

In Stymie's case, physiology and environment made a difference in the horse. Although photos show him rather light and spare as a three-year-old, Stymie developed and became more powerful and more assertively masculine in appearance as he aged. His balance also improved, as he added weight both through his neck and shoulders and also strengthened across the loins and through his hindquarters.

Stymie was lightly built as a three-year-old. His immature physique compromised his racing ability.

Stymie is a positive example of how changes in environment or in physiology can make immense improvements in the success of a racehorse.

At the same time that other factors play a large role in how a racer performs, "there is a big genetic component," Cothran asserted. "But it's spread pretty evenly throughout the breed."

This isn't terribly strange, since there are relatively small differences among most Thoroughbreds. The breed, for the most part, stands between 15.2 and 16.2 hands, which is a reasonably small variation. And there are many other points of similarity, such as circumference of the cannon bone below the knee, which point out that the breed has homogenized more today than a century ago, when more versatility was required or expected of horses.

Photo Courtesy of the Keeneland Library, Morgan Collection

Stymie at age four, after he had matured and improved his balance. He became one of the leading runners of the mid-1940s.

Today, the distances run are almost all between six and nine furlongs, and the natural variation in the breed is quite capable of supplying the small number of horses that can race competitively at distances beyond a mile and an eighth.

Such realizations do not mean that inquiry into genetics has no place in breeding horses or that it will have a minor role in the future. Cothran said, "We are right at the start of being able to ask questions that we couldn't — even a couple of years ago. It's asking the right questions and setting up the most productive projects that will determine the good results. Scientists doing this need to ask breeders, vets, and so forth what they believe is important. Then it's a question of who pays for it. Costs, even for things that are quick and easy, are too large for labs to bear without some way of seeing an eventual payback. So we'll need to look at some avenues for consistent funding for the benefit of everyone."

Male-Line Descent

Although human beings have arranged their transfers of property and power through lines of male descent, there is no reason to apply this too literally to horses. Genetic descent comes through all the contributors in the pedigree, with the contributions of some being weeded out for good cause or by chance, but not by sex.

With human beings, the inadequacy of male-line transmission has caused repeated problems, particularly in monarchies. The likelihood that more than two or three generations of a family will produce a man with the skills needed to run a country — medieval or modern — is slim. The outcome for political institutions is typically rebellion, repression, war, and pointless misery for all.

Horses don't wage war, but their lines of descent rarely last for long without some degeneration. In fact, it is very rare for any male line to have a leading sire in three successive generations. Then after a generation or two off, some of them can pick up again and regain an important position at the top of the breeding heap.

For the entirety of the breed, there are three stallions' male lines still in existence. The Byerly Turk is surviving by a faint thread, and with the near-sterility of Precisionist, the best of this line's American descendants in decades, the Byerly Turk/Herod line is essentially done. Among the best breeding stock, there is a small percentage of male-line representatives from the Godolphin Arabian or Barb. This fine little horse was an immensely successful sire, and for a time, he was as important as any other in his international influence, but with the rise of Bend Or, the Darley Arabian began a century's ascent to complete dominance, and the Darley Arabian/Eclipse male line is almost certainly going to be the lone line of descent at some point in this century.

That the breed is tending this way in male line is not surprising, as the male line is the most competitive spot in a pedigree. The stallion who gets the best winners gets the best mares. That's the way it is, and that's the way it should be. The only alternative is to breed to middling stallions for generations in hopes of getting a supreme animal. This has actually been attempted a few times with success.

Breeding solely to hang onto a male-line influence is very limiting, however, and the economics of breeding and owning racehorses makes it feasible for only a very few owners to attempt.

Furthermore, passing out of the male line does not end a horse's genetic influence. Genes are passed on randomly from all parts of the pedigree, through both the sire and the dam. As a result, it could as easily be the sire line's genes that fail to dominate or that fail to be passed on in the colossal lottery of genetic succession.

Genetics and Probability

This last consideration brings up the subject of probability and its importance to an understanding of breeding, bloodlines, and theory. The likelihood that something will occur or its frequency of occurrence is known as "probability," and it is important to understand this as a breeder progresses with a program.

The most basic element for understanding probability in some context is to have a control group or population survey. This allows a researcher (or breeder) to distinguish between good results that occur by accident (even a blind squirrel will find an acorn occasionally) and good results that follow a pattern and are repeatable. Out of the annual mass production of the breed, the repeatable patterns are less common than incidents of sheer good fortune, but the breeder with a practical grasp of his business is looking for the second option.

The first step, then, is to select a control group and begin to understand the normal patterns of occurrence in horse breeding. These random studies have been done several times by researchers, and the results are published in the fine print among the stakes results in the *Thoroughbred Times* magazine.

By looking at the norms of the breed, all parties can see what can occur randomly in the Thoroughbred. For instance, regardless of quality, about 70 percent of all

AVERAGES FOR THE BREED

Averages for the Breed statistics are designed to give the reader a baseline to evaluate the performances of contemporary racehorses, sires, and dams. Statistics shown in the column on the left below reflect the worldwide performances of all named foals born in North America between 1987-'96. Statistics in the column on the right reflect the same data for foals by the top 1 percent of all sires by total earnings for the same decade. All statistics are based on data in the Jockey Club Information System's worldwide database. The Jockey Club database includes complete records for racing in North America, England, Ireland, France, Germany, Italy, Puerto Rico, Japan, and United Arab Emirates for some, but not all of the years covered by these statistics.

Statistics below are designed to give a snapshot of what an average "good" horse should accomplish.

	Foals of 1987-'96	Foals by top 1% of sires
Number of Foals	399,121	
Starters/Foals	69.4 %	85 %
Winners/Foals (Starters)	46.1 % (66.4 %)	65.5 %
Repeat Winners/ Foals (Starters)	35.1 % (50.5 %)	53.4 % (62.8 %)
Stakes Winners/Foals (Starters)	3.4 % (4.9 %)	9 % (10.6 %)
Graded SW/Foals (Starters)	0.8 % (1.1 %)	3.5 % (4.2 %)
Grade 1 SW/Foals (Starters)	0.20 % (0.29 %)	1.1 % (1.2 %)
Stakes-placed /Foals (Starters)	5.3 % (7.6 %)	11.8 % (13.9 %)
2-year-old Starters/Foals	34 %	46.8 %
2yo Winners/ Foals (% 2yo Starters)	11.3 % (33.3 %)	18.6 % (39.8 %)
2yo SW/Foals (% 2yo Starters)	1 % (3 %)	2.4 % (5.1 %)
3-year-old Starters/Foals	59.9 %	76.8 %
4-year-old Starters/Foals	44.6 %	56.8 %
5-year-old and up Starters/Foals	27.6 %	35.9 %
Average Career Starts/Foal	14.7	18.4
Average Career Starts/Starter	21.2	21.7
Average Win Distance in Furlongs	6.82	7.24
Avg Win Distance on Turf in Furlongs	8.29	8.47
Average Earnings/Starter	$33,877	$78,776
Average Earnings/Starter Male (Female)	$39,967 ($27,569)	$98,212 ($58,264)
Average Earnings/Start	$1,596	$3,630
Average Earnings/Start Male (Female)	$1,650 ($1,523)	$3,641 ($3,611)
Average Racing Index (RI)	1.16	2.36

Courtesy of the Thoroughbred Times

foals will race, and around 46 percent will win. For the time covered by the survey of results published in the Times, the breed produced three percent stakes winners, as well as .8 percent graded winners and .2 percent Grade 1 or Group 1 winners.

Therefore, if a stallion is siring six percent stakes winners from his first 200 racers, he is exceeding the breed averages rather nicely, but he is not exceeding the par values for top-quality stallions, who normally sire about 10 percent stakes winners to foals. Statistics from the random samples, as well as select sub-groups, do not prove much by themselves, but they help to keep expectations and results in perspective as a breeder develops a program and follows through with it.

The par values for the breed help breeders in two ways. They show which horses to upgrade with better mates and those to cull. But always in making these decisions, breeders should attempt to assess the opportunity their horses have had.

The number and the quality of mares brought to a stallion will influence his success. A bad stallion can stop almost any mare, but a few good mares can really help most sires get off the ground. Overall, if the quality of a stallion's mates is low, the resulting foals should have fairly low expectations, and vice-versa. The most widely used indexed averages, such as the average earnings index and standard starts index, help breeders to put this into consideration as they appraise their stock.

As a means of selecting the best prospects, the baseline numbers for the breed help to identify horses, such as Mr. Prospector, that are outperforming their opportunity significantly, and indicate that these are very serious breeding stock that ought to be patronized. As an example, Mr. Prospector, although a very talented racehorse, was not a champion or a major winner at the top level of competition. He won stakes and ran very fast times, but he had physical problems that almost certainly prevented him from showing how much he could have accomplished.

Not surprisingly, there wasn't much clamor for his services when he went to stud. He wasn't a bum, either, and breeders in Florida sent him some reasonably good mares, as well as some pretty moderate ones. He sired a bushel of stakes winners out of them, regardless.

To the breeders who were studying the returns carefully, Mr. Prospector was outperforming his opportunities in terms of siring athletes with ability and with sufficient class to be good stakes winners. Not surprisingly, a group of serious and wealthy breeders bought up the shares in his syndicate and sent him to Kentucky.

At Claiborne Farm, Mr. Prospector proceeded to reshape the breed in his own way, tending toward a medium-sized, balanced, athletic, and quick individual. Through his sons and daughters, his influence has spread around the globe, and he is one of the most respected sources of racing ability and breeding success.

On the other side of the equation for opportunity and results, the numbers that a stallion or mare generates in comparison to the baseline population study also help determine which horses need to be culled out of a program.

The Uncertainties of Genetic Transmission

Moving from the bigger picture of breed averages to the specifics of individual matings, a breeder must also have a solid understanding of how randomly genes are transmitted. Even in matings that produce full siblings, the results will not be uniform.

Consider the case of the Nashua mare Gold Digger when mated to Raise a Native. This mare became an above-average producer, with three stakes winners to her credit. From seven live foals sired by Raise a Native, however, four didn't race. That is too high a ratio of wastage, and a fifth offspring was an ordinary winner. The first and second foals from this pairing were the reason for persevering, as the first was the stakes-placed Search for Gold, and the second was Mr. Prospector.

A handsome yearling, Mr. Prospector brought the highest price at the Keeneland July select yearling sale in 1971, and he went on to become a very good racehorse. He possessed immense speed and a very light, efficient action that helped him to be more effective as a racer.

And when he went to stud, he was a revelation, indeed. Mr. Prospector led every sire list available, and he has become the most commercially successful sire in the breed. Although he died in 1999 at age 29, Mr. Prospector also left a number of distinguished sons who are breeding on with success, and his daughters are prized producers who have lifted him to the top of the list of leading broodmare sires.

The same, however, cannot be said for any of his siblings. Why?

Courtesy of the Thoroughbred Times

Mr. Prospector, a son of Raise a Native, led every sire list available. He's also an excellent example of the unpredictability of genetics.

The most obvious conclusion, and the right one, is that they did not inherit the same genetic material in the same combination from Raise a Native and Gold Digger. That is the truth in a nutshell.

But most people will say, "But how can that be? They were full brothers and sisters."

Unfortunately, our common terms for inheritance are not very accurate. Well at least, they do not describe, simply and clearly, the way that genetics works.

From our classes in biology, we all know that parents pass on half of their genes to each offspring, but each offspring does not receive the same 50 percent. In gauging how this affects the resulting progeny, here's a thought that will throw a wrench into many works. Full siblings have the same probability of possessing exactly the same genes as they do of having NONE of the same genes.

Either possibility is a longshot, but whether it's 100,000 to 1 or 100 million to 1, it is the same probability. For every other combination, siblings will share some genes and not others. Furthermore, all brothers and sisters will have genes in different combinations, and although we are approaching a completed gene map of the horse, we do not know how the combinations affect one another.

On average, full brothers and sisters will share half of the genetics passed on from their mother and father. Clearly, some will share more and some less. When considering half-brothers and -sisters, our terminology is even less accurate. They won't be half-related. On average, they will tend to share about a quarter of the same genes.

When we consider that these averages are from the first-generation crosses, estimating the influence of animals farther back in a pedigree is obviously a much trickier matter.

In some instances, a few horses in the third or fourth generation will have significantly more influence than expected, and some will have little or no influence at all. And for those farther back in the pedigree, we can only assume that they ever existed. We certainly couldn't prove it from the mangled genetic evidence of only a few generations later.

The lessons to be drawn from the probabilities of inheritance are (1) that genetics is a much more complex and variable process than most summaries suggest and (2) that the best horses — those who produce top racers to any mating — are passing on good genetic material no matter which arrangements of genetic factors are involved.

This is probably the reason that breeders who insist on having "depth of family" in stallions and mares get consistent results. They are concentrating on the gene pool rather than the individual, and if the pool is good enough and close enough to the foal, the results obviously can be outstanding.

Continuing a Male Line

Probability, opportunity, and genetic quality are the primary factors in determining why a male line does or does not breed on. The sire lines that last need to be bushy, with many useful to good avenues of production going at the same time. They need access to good mares and to mares with compatible physiques and genes. These considerations tend to play on both probability and opportunity. And the unknown factor of genetic quality — the right stuff — can make masters or monkeys of us all.

Looking at the main lines that descend from Eclipse, most come through Bend Or. As such, this stallion is worth investigating as a type of successful sire.

Bend Or was a son of the English Derby winner Doncaster, and both were top-class racehorses. Doncaster, described as such an immense horse that he was difficult to keep sound, also won the Goodwood Cup and Ascot Gold Cup.

A foal of 1877, Bend Or was a high-class two-year-old and won the Derby at three. He, too, was a massive beast that had trouble with his legs. In training for the Derby, Bend Or was so frequently sore that he was only just coming right in time for the classic.

To further hinder the colt's chances, his jockey, Fred Archer, had an injured arm at race time; so the pair of them were the walking wounded. Not surprisingly, Bend Or's tender shins kept him from coming down Tattenham Corner very fluently, but when the ground started rising for the run-in to the finish, Archer was able to get him balanced and galloping strongly. Game as they come, Bend Or won by a head.

After a successful season at four, Bend Or went to stud at the Duke of Westminster's Eaton Stud, where he became an immense success. Foaled in the final quarter of the 19th century, Bend Or came along at the proper time to influence the 20th century's bloodlines. Long-term influence comes from results of the first and second-generation offspring of stallions and mares, and timing made Bend Or and St. Simon the international leaders coming into the 20th century.

With enough good sons in particular, a stallion has a chance to become a breed-shaping influence. Due to numerical influence, sires are the shapers of the breed, in fact as well as in the metaphorical sense of moving the breed toward or away from certain aptitudes of performance.

From his first crop, Bend Or got the great racer Ormonde and sired Radium in his next-to-last crop, when a 25-year-old. In between came many good horses, and from his seventh crop came a good colt named Bona Vista, who won the 2,000 Guineas. Although neither Ormonde nor Bona Vista had extensive stud careers in England, they sired offspring that have conspired to become the dominating forces in bloodlines across the world.

Ormonde sired Orme and Goldfinch before he was sold abroad. From Orme came many fine specimens, and in the male line, he is still prominent through Teddy, with his descendants including Sir Gallahad III, Bull Dog, Bull Lea,

Sword Dancer, and Damascus. Goldfinch sired Chelandry, an immensely important broodmare.

Bona Vista had three crops before his sale to Prince Louis Esterhazy for the Hungarian government, but from his English foals, Bona Vista sired the great stallion Cyllene, as well as the dams of The Tetrarch and Roamer. A winner of nine races from 11 starts, Cyllene was a splendid racer. He was not entered for the classics in England because he was such a little beggar as a foal. But Cyllene did well with his opportunities and was well-known as a high-class colt, winning the Jockey Club Stakes and Ascot Gold Cup. While at stud in England, Cyllene sired four winners of the English Derby: Cicero, Minoru, Lemberg, and Tagalie. In early 1908, he was sold to the Ojo de Agua Stud and sent to the Argentine, where he remained until his death in 1925.

His sale didn't appear quite such a terrible idea at the time, as three of his Derby winners won after the sale. Among the others he left behind was the good horse Polymelus, who was at his best over the straight course at Newmarket, winning the Champion Stakes. A useful horse, he was not a champion or classic winner.

Yet upon his retirement to stud, Polymelus left his racing form well behind and led the English sire list five times. Among his best winners were English Triple Crown winner Pommern, English Derby winner Humorist (who died without going to stud), 2,000 Guineas winner Corcyra, Derby and Oaks winner Fifinella, 1,000 Guineas winner Dinna, and a pretty quick horse named Phalaris.

There is no question who was Polymelus's best son at stud. Phalaris created a revolution in breeding and set Lord Derby's already eminent stud upon a pinnacle of excellence that took decades to diminish.

Such is the stuff of history.

The questions for contemporary breeders to ask themselves include: "Was this sequence of circumstances predictable? Was this outcome probable?" After only a bit of cogitation, most of us will come to the same conclusions. No, Polymelus wasn't supposed to be a major stallion, and no, not Lord Derby, George Lambton, or myself would have expected Phalaris to carry on best for his sire and expand his dominions across the globe.

Then how are we to explain the expansion of Bend Or as the dominant strain of Eclipse, particularly through his descendant Phalaris?

With hindsight we can discern the historical trends as racing became more internationally competitive. The promotion of dash racing (a single dash around the course, typically at a mile or less) placed an emphasis on horses with quick, fluent action, and the sires who passed on those traits most effectively were instantly rewarded at the end of the 19th century and early in the 20th.

In addition to Bend Or, other sires to gain ground in this sphere were St. Simon, Domino, and to a lesser extent, The Tetrarch. All these sires had first-class speed, and they were able to sire horses with light, quick action who could carry their speed over the distances of the classic races.

With this quality in hand, the next hurdle for these stallions to overcome was sufficient representation in the breed. Did they have enough sons of quality to give them a chance to carry on and pass along their superior traits?

In the cases of Domino and The Tetrarch, the answer was no. Although Domino has remained alive in the male line, almost all of his influence (and the influence is there, just as if he were on the top line) comes through the internal lines of the pedigree. Domino died young, and despite the success of his son Commando, his male line was tenuous from the start. The Tetrarch descended into the innards of pedigrees with even greater speed, largely due to his very uncertain fertility.

That left the Teddy and Phalaris lines of Bend Or and the St. Simon stock to thrash out the competition as leading sires. Early in the century, St. Simon appeared to have them all over a barrel. Then Teddy took control during the 1940s and 1950s through the work of Bull Dog, Bull Lea, and others. But for the last 40 years or so, the story has been all about Phalaris.

Now, in fact, the question of dominance is not so much a question of which male line, as it is of which Phalaris male line. With greater and greater frequency, pedigrees show horses with both parents sired by a Phalaris-line stallion, and with both parents' dams by a Phalaris-line sire, as well. Pedigrees of this type offer a fascinating amount of linebreeding, but they also raise the specter that the breed is becoming too inbred and therefore weakened.

Both are legitimate thoughts. The benefits of inbreeding or linebreeding have been seen with considerable degree in other species, and I will have something more to say about this under the heading of biomechanics, which offers some thoughts about creating similarities through type. But in addition to benefits, inbreeding can have some harmful effects, and only the most objective breeders, willing to cull and go on, should experiment too greatly with an extensive program using this tool.

In Conclusion

The genetics of the Thoroughbred offer a vast and almost endlessly intriguing field for investigation and innovation for breeding and raising a better horse. Some of the things we will find out as the gene mapping continues will not be of use for breeding, but some are likely to help or at least to raise questions that can be fruitful subjects for study among practical breeders.

The variations that are the natural result of any breeding can be beneficial or harmful. They may produce a top horse from modest parents, but they are more likely to produce a modest horse from top-class parents. Such a regression to the mean is one of the standard concepts of genetic study, and horsemen can attest to its truth with personal experience.

As a result of natural variation, keeping a balanced and well-planned program of breeding is the way for a practical horseman to overcome some of the hurdles in getting good stock with consistency. The pragmatic breeder will realize that a program, because it offers a yardstick to measure what works and what does not, will provide more success in the long term than simply shooting in the dark.

As part of a program approach, put probabilities on the breeders' side by having good stock, good land, and experienced advisers. All these contribute toward making the whole process of breeding horses as rewarding as possible and help to emphasize good relationships and ties to both horses and people. With all these things in place, breeding horses can be one of the most enriching and pleasant and utterly fascinating ways of life we human beings have yet invented.

CHAPTER 3

The BLUP Trotting Index

The BLUP Index is an approach to using statistical analysis for assessing livestock production developed in the U.S. by Dr. C.R. Henderson in 1948. BLUP means best linear unbiased prediction, and this method allows breeders of horses and other breeds of livestock to predict the breeding value of their herd animals, as well as adjust for environmental effects. Therefore as a static index and system of evaluation, the BLUP works to measure genetic differences between herds and generations.

As a tool of statistical analysis, the BLUP ratings are best-suited to evaluate studies for the mass production of similar, good-quality livestock. Not surprisingly, the BLUP indices have been used to assess the herd quality and potential of sheep, cattle, chickens, and various types of horses.

In the large scheme of economic, technological, and social change, the BLUP index has been a tool over the past decades as a means of transferring agricultural pursuits from a family-oriented way of life into mechanized and statistically predictable corporate farming.

As the best linear unbiased prediction, the BLUP rating is called "linear" because of the constant updating of the numbers over time and "unbiased" because there is relatively little subjectivity in the method. The resulting indices offer breeders the opportunity to make informed estimations of success and quality when choosing their breeding stock.

For instance in Sweden, breeders have been using the BLUP for nearly two decades to establish the initial breeding values of their stallions, and the breeders of Sweden were the first in the world to apply the BLUP methodology to the complex set of problems encountered in breeding horses.

To make this practical and successful, Dr. Jan Philipsson, who is a professor of animal breeding and a former president of the Swedish Warmblood Association, worked to adapt the BLUP Index for Swedish stallions. The index is updated annually and is a valuable tool for breeders, as well as for the riders and fanciers shopping for a performance horse.

Warmbloods are not the only group of horses categorized and evaluated using the BLUP index. In addition to the members of various Warmblood registries and jumping horse associations, the French trotting horse breeders use a BLUP index in their breeding and racing program.

Even though it is touted as an objective measure of the horse, not all BLUP indices are the same. BLUP indices are calculated by various warmblood registries in quite different ways; each registry in Europe has its own formula and database.

The Swedish Warmblood Association noted that, "BLUP-indexes are not 'holy numbers,' and it is necessary to understand what traits are included and how those traits were obtained" in evaluating the index and making an assessment of the horse for an individual's purpose.

For instance, the Swedish Warmblood Association computes an index that includes only stallions located in Sweden. For inclusion in the index, a stallion must have at least 15 inspected offspring out of inspected mares in order to have enough data to be included. And as with any statistical assessment, the smaller the pool of offspring evaluated, the less certain are the results. And in the case of the Swedish Warmblood Association, a stallion's results from offspring outside the country are not included in the index.

Despite the popularity of the index in Europe, it has not caught on in the U.S. The Swedish Warmblood Association noted that "Due to cultural differences, as well as the horse industry diversity and vast land mass of North America, it is currently not possible to collect the data necessary to create a BLUP Index for North American stallions. The Swedes have been testing young horses for over 30 years, and have accumulated the results in their database containing over 20,000 horses . . . It's a matter of national pride. The North American culture has not wholeheartedly embraced the performance testing and mare inspections" which are mandatory for gaining inclusion to most registries and to the statistics upon which the BLUP index is based.

The French Trotter

As with many other European breeds of performance horses, French breeders and analysts of the trotting horse, correspondent to the Standardbred in the U.S., use the BLUP to gauge their horses' success and potential as gaited athletes and breeding stock. In short, the BLUP is an estimation of a horse's genetic value for the ability to trot.

The ratings and records of French trotting form a core of information that help to provide a stable basis of comparison for making up the BLUP ratings. The factors that go into rating the trotter are the best distance as derived from the racing record of the horse and its average earnings per start. These factors help to summarize the horse's strongest athletic qualities and emphasize its soundness and competitive success.

Outside factors are taken into account with these ratings, and these are age, sex, the year of performance, type of track, type of start, configuration of course, driver, and mode of breeding. However, experiments show that only age, sex, and year of performance impact the rating.

The distribution of trotters according to this rating shows that half of the winning trotters are ranked above 100, and an individual that has a rating of more than 120 is in the top 15 percent of its generation and sex. A horse who rates more than 140 is in the top 2.5 percent of its generation and sex for that year. Knowing these individual annual ratings allows breeders to compare horses that do not have the same age, sex, or performance year.

The BLUP index for trotting

The BLUP estimates the genetic value of a horse for its ability to trot and the genetic value of all the horse's relatives.

To arrive at this estimation, you must take account of as much information as possible that allows evaluation of the horse's genetic quality and eliminate as much information as possible that is not genetically related.

BLUP takes account of the performances of the horse in question, its parents, its offspring, its siblings, as well as the siblings of its sire and dam. As a result, almost all trotters and their descendants have a BLUP rating, of which the precision is variable.

To construct the BLUP, breeders use the relationship coefficient (RC) between the various groups of relatives and the horse in question. For instance, the relationship coefficient between a horse and its sire, dam, or siblings is one-half. The RC between the sample horse and its maternal half-sibling is one-quarter and between the sample horse and its half-siblings' offspring is one-eighth.

Thus the performances of the sample horse will count four times more in the BLUP rating of a sibling than that of a half-sibling's offspring.

The BLUP integrates influences on the horse that are not genetic. For instance, the maternal environment during gestation and lactation cannot be dissociated from breeding, as only two out of every three offspring race. This factor is given four percent in the total variability in harness racing performance.

The same environment and the same driver factor in as six percent of performance variability. And the value of the mate is factored in so that when a stallion is bred to a mare of high quality, this is added to his genetic value and also to that of the offspring.

In all, genetic value is allowed to be worth 26 percent in the BLUP rating. The rating is expressed in positive and negative points of individual ratings that the horse is likely to pass to its descendants. A positive BLUP animal is an improvement, while a horse with a negative BLUP is deterioration.

The BLUP of a foal can be estimated by adding the BLUP ratings of the sire and the dam and dividing by two.

Determination Coefficient

This measure is indispensable to assessing the BLUP. The coefficient de determination (CD) or determination coefficient is a sort of boundary or limit for the interpretation of the BLUP. The CD varies between zero and one, and it is a function of the quantity of information available. To arrive at a foal's CD, the CDs of the sire and dam are added together and divided by four. A very weak CD, for instance, of .10 signifies that the estimation of genetic value was based on only a few pieces of information concerning a rather distant relative.

The CD is greatly increased by taking into account the individual horse's performances and also those of its descendants; therefore the CD and the BLUP are dynamic ratings, prone to change through an individual horse's life.

A BLUP of zero is the average of the founding individuals in the archives, and it corresponds more or less to the level of the population in 1970.

Conclusion

The BLUP is a very complete and precise rating in the view of those who use it. It offers, among other things, one value for genetic worth; a universal scale that can be used for stallions, mares, and their progeny; and allows the measurement of genetic improvement in a population or sub-population.

Trot ratings are available through SIRE, the Institut du Cheval, or through the French National Studs.

As the BLUP index has risen in popularity and has begun to loom as the dominating consideration in breeding performance horses in many countries, critics have surfaced and begun to voice their reservations about the index.

In critiquing the BLUP's negative influence by shifting emphasis from the horse and horsemanship, Bernard le Courtois, a breeder of French sport horses, noted that, "It turns out that the equine BLUP index is nothing more than an adaptation of the American milk BLUP index."

This fact in itself is no reason to discard the BLUP as a tool of some use, but at its root, the BLUP was designed - and seems to function most effectively - as a means of assessing populations, not individuals. This is a fine state of affairs when breeders are testing thousands of chickens for volume of egg production from six to 12 months of age. Chickens, for instance, reproduce quickly, allowing relatively small improvements in selection to offer significant dividends over a short time.

However, applying a tool for population assessments to individuals can have some definite shortcomings.

In addition, horses are not cows, pigs, sheep, or corn. They are not bred for a single trait or pair of traits, and the expression of speed is not a purely genetic result. So many different systems go into the making and maintenance of an equine athlete that anyone wishing to use the BLUP index should take it as a tool, a starting point, or a means of gaining a broad view - not as an end in itself.

CHAPTER 4

How Joe Estes Transformed Breeding and Pedigrees

No figure in the study of Thoroughbred pedigrees is of more singular importance than Joe Estes. A slight, quiet, scholarly man, Estes was also editor of *The Blood-Horse* from the time it came out of Tom Cromwell's desk drawer and became a serious national journal on Thoroughbred racing and breeding until the early 1960s. In that period, Estes helped to shape many writers on the sport, and he helped to reorder the priorities of breeders as they culled their stock and chose which mares to send to the best stallions and vice-versa.

He relied on sound scientific principles as he approached the questions that interest all breeders: "How can I breed better horses? How can I judge which stock is most likely to succeed at breeding and at racing? Which mares do I sell and which do I keep for breeding?"

In undertaking these larger issues, Estes began searching for ways to assess the racing ability of a horse, and he eventually found it through statistical analysis of earnings. He called the new indicator of racing class the average earnings index (AEI), and he used it extensively as he continued his studies on bloodlines and performance. Estes found that it was an immensely useful tool and that it helped to point out the most likely good producers with high accuracy. Among the racers he studied, Estes discovered that mares with an AEI of 4.0 or more were a very elite class, judging from the racing performances of their offspring.

His understanding of racing class and its value as a predictor of breeding success led him to promote the publication of information that helped breeders make informed choices about their breeding stock. Chief among these were lists and charts of stallions with AEI indices and the publication of the series, American Broodmare Records, which recorded the race records and earnings of each year's starters under their dams. Such information proved invaluable to breeders in those days long before computers and internet links.

Spending many of his days working through mounds of statistics, Estes made the search for truth and fair judgment a cornerstone of his life. As anyone can understand from his writing, Estes was a man of great sincerity in the interests of the Thoroughbred and its people, and he possessed an intense sense of integrity and honesty. When he thought breeders were being led astray by accepted opinion or by a misunderstanding of the practical questions of breeding, he couldn't help but speak his mind.

He was one of the first writers to bring attention to the study of genetics and its potential for Thoroughbred breeders. Estes did this not in a single story but in article after article through his decades of writing. A thorough reading of his work provides the breeder with a condensation of the learning and explorations of many years.

In many instances, due to a thorough use of mathematics, horsemanship, and solid logic and good sense, he was able to expand our understanding of the Thoroughbred and how to breed better horses.

That he found practical answers to these questions is a tribute to his determination and industry, as Estes researched and wrote before computers came into use and reduced the trouble of statistical analysis to the click of a few buttons.

But Estes did the work and, with imagination and insight, found ways to assess the breed that we use effectively today. Estes also harassed forms of what he thought of as superstition applied to breeding horses.

Those who heeded his advice became a little wiser and in some cases wealthier due to the success of their programs, and some of the most successful breeders of the mid-century and later (Rex Ellsworth and Bunker Hunt, for example) used the principles and plans that Estes advocated.

Coming to *The Blood-Horse*

In the beginning, Joe Estes worked for the *Morning Telegraph* in New York, but when Tom Cromwell decided to take his publication, called *The Blood-Horse*, out of its spot in his desk drawer and turn it into a national venue for news and commentary about racing and breeding, he hired Estes to return to Kentucky and run the magazine.

They persuaded Joe Palmer to join the team as business manager and writer for the publication. Together, Palmer and Estes did anything that was necessary for the magazine. Estes, for instance, was writer, editor and photographer, and their work was a major success. In 1935, *The Blood-Horse* was sold to the American Thoroughbred Breeders' Association (now the Thoroughbred Owners and Breeders Association).

In covering all of racing and breeding, Estes created a column called "Pedigree Points" that he used as a forum to address the business and sport of breeding horses.

He took his position seriously, although he had a lot of fun being serious. As an example, in the April 24, 1937, issue of the magazine, Estes roasted the believers of the same-age theory in a rich basting of their own turkey juices. On the topic, Estes wrote that, "As propounded by several well-known experts, this theory holds that the best results are obtained by making matings between parents of the same age or nearly the same age."

Believers in such romantic notions should have smelled something burning, but as Estes proceeded with quiet irony, most were taken in and doubtless thought, "Well now, this Estes chap is finally beginning to get the picture."

In his article, Estes recounted how an English-bred mare named Fatima II had been bred to some very good stallions in England over the years with no success, before finally being culled and selling for 710 guineas to Lucas Combs while in foal to Hurry On in the fall of 1925. Combs had immediate financial success with the mare, as he sold the colt that Fatima II produced at the Saratoga yearling sales for $70,000 in 1927, "though the mare had not produced a winner" at that time.

After three more foals intermingled with four barren years, Combs leased the mare to John Hay Whitney. The latter was interested in Fatima II because he wanted to reproduce the cross that resulted in the American Derby winner Toro, who was by The Porter out of a Radium mare, and Fatima II was also a daughter of Bend Or's fine son Radium.

In quick succession, Whitney bred two foals out of the mare, and both were stakes winners, the Jerome winner Pasha and Demoiselle winner Inhale.

Estes noted that "Until she was bred to The Porter, Fatima II had never been mated with a stallion of her own age. The knowledge must have inhibited her hereditary faculties." If the adherents to the same-age theory weren't getting wise to the playful twists of humor in Estes, he was getting ready for the richest fun of all. Early in his career, Estes had been intrigued by the concept of nicks and nicking, and he knew that was the reason Whitney had leased the mare in the first place. So, keeping up the role of a fan of same-age matings, he concluded that Whitney "thought the nick was the thing, and unwittingly stumbled upon success."

A reader who didn't know his man could mistake the situation and come away believing that the same-age theory held some water, but Estes finished this pedigree point with a paragraph in italics: "Aside to pedigree experts: That's the way to make theories. Don't say anything about them until a good example comes along, then jump up and wave your arms and raise Cain generally. Pretty soon people will begin to notice how many times the theory works out, and then they will start following you around asking for more theories, of which you should always keep a large stock on hand. In a surprisingly short time you can have them believing almost any kind of tommyrot."[1]

The level of his weekly work in *The Blood-Horse*, accompanied by that of Joe Palmer, excelled for clarity and interest. Together, they made the magazine the most important publication in the sport. Estes's and Palmer's enthusiasm and commitment to racing and breeding made them look for topics, subjects and modes of presentation that were interesting to people. Breeders read the publication, whether they liked the writers' views or not, and they profited from it. So did breeding and the sport at large.

Tackling Statistics

Clearly, Estes was a rationalist, a believer in logic and clear thinking, and a fellow who preferred facts, no doubt of the cold and hard variety. Naturally this led him to investigate the use of statistics as a means to help breeders find out which of their stock was best or was most likely to do well.

This is no small undertaking, as there were no computers to quickly tabulate results, no bloodstock information services to quickly download pedigrees, and none of the averages and lists that breeders today can consult in a moment. All the data, spun out by thousands of horses at dozens of racetracks, had to be worked up by hand, and nobody really knew how to do it.

In the same issue of *The Blood-Horse*, Estes discussed the initial results from the early crops by Triple Crown winner Gallant Fox. A very handsome son of Sir Gallahad III, Gallant Fox had made a fabulous start to his stud career, with Triple Crown winner Omaha in his first crop and Belmont Stakes winner Granville in his second. The third included Perifox, who started as joint-favorite for the English Derby. The colt finished fourth to Mid-Day Sun.

Those are pretty fancy results from a young stallion, but even at this early date, Estes was evaluating the results from sires such as Gallant Fox using statistics. He noted the results of the crops age three and older, along with their number of starters, winners, and stakes winners. In doing this, trying to place the stallion in a context with his overall stud performance, Estes was striking out in a different direction from his contemporaries.

Typically they would take a result and then use that anecdotal information to suggest that the stallion was top class. This may or may not have been the case, but Estes was trying to find ways to gain perspective on breeding. He didn't want to provide simply a boosting comment for a young horse's stud career; he wanted to find out what was happening with the sire's performance.

At this point, there was little to complain about with Gallant Fox. Instead, the opposite is true, as he appeared to be the best young sire on the horizon, but among the statistics and comments that Estes provided, one suggests that all might not be well with the sire's long-term chances. He noted that "he comes as near being a sire of stayers as any horse in America."[2]

Then as now, if a sire typically gets stayers, his offspring's opportunities in America are almost entirely limited to performances in the most elite stakes in the country. If they cannot compete there, they have to run at distances that don't really suit their needs. The races for maidens and allowance horses, as well as almost all the claiming stock, are run at six to eight furlongs. And if a stallion cannot get a strong complement of second- and third-tier stock, breeders desert them, taking their best mares elsewhere and leaving the stallion to fend for himself.

Whether that was exactly the case with Gallant Fox is hard to say, but he continued to produce a small body of good runners during his stud career without ever menacing the glories from his early years.

In addition to studying the records of stallions and trying to assess which were the best sires, Estes also turned a great deal of attention to broodmares. Without the tools for research that we possess today, if someone said that his mare had done this or that, the only way to check it was to purchase a set of chart manuals from the *Daily Racing Form* and check through the charts by hand. Not surprisingly, most people accepted the recollection of breeders they trusted, but after a few seasons as a broodmare or a couple of sales, much of the racing class of mares was obscure.

Estes concluded that was a shame because the research into racing class suggested that it was the best single indicator of producing class. So Estes himself went into the library and tested the results themselves. Time after time, the conclusion was that the best producers were — over the entire population — the best runners as well.

Since he had studied statistical applications, he knew that a researcher couldn't just take a sample and say that the results of the test were true. Instead, he had to establish a baseline on what the breed was doing as a whole and then find a way to rank the success or failure of the individuals themselves.

In time, he was able to compile what we would now call a database that showed how a large number of horses performed on the racecourse and at stud. The results showed the performances of good and bad horses, as well as the wide variety in between. And his conclusion was that "the racing class of the parents is the only dependable index I have ever found to indicate the probable racing class of the offspring. That index is, of course, reliable only to a limited degree. But it is far more reliable than any other index."[3]

The long-term developments from the research were many, but they included the average-earnings index, the publication of volumes of Thoroughbred Broodmare Records to make researching more feasible, and eventually the addition of black type to sales catalogs, a formal recognition that racing class should be highlighted for buyers' attention in the public market.

But to reach these conclusions and develop these valuable tools for breeders and researchers, Estes had to sift all the knowledge available about bloodstock and breeding. He then had to judge what made sense and what did not hold together. It was a marvelous journey for him and his readers as his understanding evolved and his views on the matter hardened and took a sharper edge.

Defining the Basics

As Estes approached his material in writing a breeders' magazine, his natural curiosity and seeking after truth led him to study all the work then available about bloodstock breeding. And by the mid- to late-1930s, he had developed an impressive grasp of his subject and a light and interesting way of telling the tale.

In a speech to the Thoroughbred Club of America in 1937, Estes elaborated on his views about breeding horses and about inheritance, with some particulars as they concern that year's Triple Crown winner, War Admiral. A significant portion of that public address is set down in the following:

"A pedigree is divisible into an infinite number of units, limited by nothing except the durability of vocal chords or the world's supply of typewriter ribbon. One might begin the discussion of War Admiral with Matchem, or the Godolphin Arabian. But it seems to me that it should be the main business of anyone discussing the breeding of a Thoroughbred to eliminate as much of the background of a pedigree as possible . . .

"On this basis, I see no necessity for going beyond Man o' War in considering the top side of War Admiral's pedigree. In the future of American Thoroughbred breeding, whenever a breeder's eye goes back in a pedigree and finds the name of Man o' War, he can stop there, for he will know he has reached solid ground."

But in saying solid ground, Estes wasn't speaking with hyperbole or with an ad man's interest in selling a horse. He meant that, in terms of breeding horses in the 1930s and the approaching 1940s, there was no guessing or gainsaying the value of using Man o' War and his offspring in any rational breeding program. For Estes, the proof was obvious in the stallion's results from his breeding history, and breeders could only cloud the issue by trying to introduce other theories into the practical business of mating broodmares to quality stallions.

Estes summarized the statistics of Man o' War's stud record to that point, noting that the stallion had sired an average of 18 live foals annually and also noting that they had earned more than $2.1 million cumulatively, with average earnings of more than $9,000. These were the highest sums for any stallion in history to that time. Estes also assessed the quality of Man o' War's produce, with the great horse having sired 46 stakes winners, which was more than 19 percent of his foals. The great technical analyst concluded that "There is no horse of recent years that can rival this record, unless it is Fair Play himself."

As a result of Man o' War's proven excellence, "a horse like War Admiral comes in the natural course of events.

"It was to be expected, as I say, that Man o' War would sire a War Admiral, because the record of the sire was in the books. I have no higher opinion of Man o' War now than I had before the Derby" because the stallion had proven himself not only a great sire but also the preeminent classic sire in America over the preceding 10 to 12 years.

But in judging the quality of pedigree and the likelihood of producing a top horse, the situation was much different with War Admiral's dam, Brushup, Estes said.

In deciding how well a mare will produce, Estes said, "It is a much more difficult matter to appraise the breeding possibilities of a mare than of a stallion. It is natural that there should be a wide variation in the racing quality of different foals of the same parentage. The average good stallion can number his offspring by the scores or hundreds, and thus a fairly definite expectation may be calculated. But the average mare produces only about six foals, and our calculations as to her probable worth as a broodmare are never very dependable. I know, for instance, that the good race mare is a better prospect for a broodmare than is a poor race mare. But that is a matter of averages, and the breeder cannot be guided by averages alone when he must work with individuals. To a great extent he remains always in the dark concerning the mares he must use. He must come up on the good ones largely by accident.

"Brushup was a mare that none of us could have picked out as likely to be the dam of a Derby winner — that is, no more likely than a thousand other mares. She was by Sweep, a grand sire of winners and a grand sire of broodmares. Her dam was Annette K., which had produced the good stakes winner War Glory, by Man o' War . . . Brushup had about the average racing class, as far as broodmares are concerned. She had started three times at two, finished once second, once third, once unplaced."

But the evidence of racing class is slim in the direct female line of War Admiral. Estes said, "We have to go back to the sixth dam, Reprieve, before we find a good race mare."

One reason that it was so hard for breeders of the day to discover which mares might be good broodmares was that the racing evidence was much shakier than it is today. Races devoted solely to fillies and mares were much rarer in the early part of the 20th century. After the juvenile season, they could be extremely hard to find, and the only option was to race them against colts. This made racing them a difficult proposition, as the earning power of fillies was correspondingly lower than colts, just as their likelihood of winning open events was lower. This made keeping them in training more a matter of personal inclination than a reasonable financial decision, and if the filly had an attitude about her job, keeping her in training was more aggravation than many owners would take.

For instance, the important producer Ormonda, a stakes winner during her own racing career, was sold to Joseph E. Widener as a broodmare. For Widener, she produced the top-class sprinter Osmand and the very talented stakes winner Brevity. But Estes's interest was drawn to a pair of Ormonda's daughters, neither of whom ran a race.

The first of the pair was Golden Melody, a daughter of Mont d'Or that Widener sold as a yearling to Dr. Charles E. Hagyard "a few weeks before Osmand broke his maiden," Estes recounted. This certainly gave Golden Melody some cachet, but when put in training, she began to show considerable talent of her own, as she "turned in extraordinary workouts, but she developed osselets, and had to be put aside. When she was a three-year-old, though she apparently was sound enough to stand racing, Dr. Hagyard decided to breed her . . . Golden Melody was a rather willful mare, hard to get along with when crossed, a fact which largely influenced Dr. Hagyard's decision to take her out of training."[4]

Golden Melody's best foal was King Cole, a really useful colt by Pharamond who won five stakes, including the Withers, Junior Champion, and Paumonok, but King Cole was even better known for finishing second in both the Futurity at two and the Preakness at three.

Golden Melody's year-younger half-sister was the Sweep mare Dustwhirl. As a racing proposition, Estes wrote that "Dustwhirl was broken at Elmendorf Farm, and I understand she also showed exceptional speed. She went into the training stable, but never got to the races. She was, like Golden Melody, marked by a distinct willfulness which may have been the cause for her failure to race and for her retirement to the stud as a three-year-old. She has been owned by three of America's most noted breeders, and for each of them she produced a stakes winner, Feudal Lord for Mr. Widener, Reaping Reward for A.B. Hancock, and Whirlaway for Warren Wright."[5]

In this article, Estes was writing just before the 1940 Futurity Stakes, in which King Cole was second and Whirlaway third. And his point was that "It is the high-strung and willful disposition of these two daughters of Ormonda which interests me as much as anything about them. One of the best horsemen in Kentucky once told me that he didn't like a broodmare that wasn't nervous. I don't know much about the personalities of good broodmares, but I suspect that he has something there. For in the race horse the nervous constitution is as important as the muscular and osseous constitution, and the superlative horse is frequently the one of imperious will (e.g., St. Simon, Barcaldine, Fair Play, Man o' War, Display).

"In mares the possession of an extraordinary store of nervous energy is frequently associated with an inconclusive racing career. Some of them will show high speed in workouts and then 'go to pieces' in the paddock. Many of them never get to the races at all. It is perhaps significant that the only sample of mares I have ever taken in which racing class showed no correlation with production was among the daughters of Fair Play, that grand old scoundrel which had no tolerance for anything except his own will. Alice Carneal, the dam of Lexington, was a classic example of the fast and nervous mare."[6]

Estes went on to log many other mares of an excitable nature who raced in the previous century and who had both successful racing and breeding careers. His conclusion was that the previous scheme of racing, heat racing over distances up to four miles, was more reliable as a predictor of producing success. The present system, which gives preeminence to precocity and sprinting ability, puts mares at a greater disadvantage than colts, he believed. Estes wrote that the "early training and the extreme tightening that is necessary for sprint racing — has an extremely adverse effect upon the nervous system of fillies." As a result, "these immature fillies are likely to be neurotic cases throughout their entire racing career, and by the time they might be settling down for a real demonstration of their ability, they are snatched out of the racing stable and sent to the breeding paddock. In short, when we seek to find out their racing class, we ask the question too early and too insistently — and get an inadequate answer or no answer at all."[7]

Estes knew that we could not return to the earlier pattern of racing because the economics of that sport were appropriate only in an aristocratic society whose approach to racing accepted huge losses of time and cash in return for the sporting pleasure of the most demanding tests of the racehorse.

He did believe, however, that much could be done to improve racing, including more opportunities for fillies to race against only their own sex. In time, not only did this prove popular with bettors, but it also recommended itself to breeders by giving them a truer indication of the racing merit of the stock they were using and to track owners by giving them larger fields and larger profits.

As these examples indicate, Estes's use of statistics was lively and inquisitive. He was looking for answers, and the numbers helped him to decide which option was better or more correct. They weren't an end in themselves. But the answers he got from his inquiries touched all areas of sport, and over the decades, his influence had a positive and generally creative influence on racing and more especially on breeding.

Estes and Breeding Theory

Among some sectors of the breeding world, however, Estes was not immensely popular. Scholarly and reserved in person, he was well-respected and even sought out by breeders and owners wanting practical advice. But those in love with particular theories of breeding did not count him as their hero. Estes wanted fact; he wanted evidence that he could chop and dice, not opinion. And for those who chose to cross swords with him, Estes was the dickens of a sparring partner.

In asserting his opinions about nicks, Estes drew considerable fire, as nicking was the predominant way of planning matings at that time, as it continues to be widely popular today. Estes's thoughts on this subject were sometimes categorized as "blasphemous," his attitude as "heretical," and his mental state as "unbalanced." Clearly, breeders who had fixed themselves on a particular method of arranging matings were prepared to hold their ground under fire.

Not that Estes worried about that. In an address to the Thoroughbred Club of America in May of 1937, he assessed nicks in this way. "Lexington got many of his best horses from mares of Glencoe blood. (If he hadn't it would have been amazing, for the Glencoe mares were the best in America at the time Lexington was the best stallion in America.) The amazing success of James R. Keene's Castleton and later of the Whitney stud was built upon a combination of Domino and Ben Brush blood.

"At the old Nursery Stud the nick was between Fair Play and Rock Sand mares, and I must say it worked to a fare you well. But one does not need the doctrine of affinities to explain the success of the Nursery Stud. The best mares owned by Major Belmont were Rock Sand mares. The best stallion he owned — or anyone owned, for that matter — was Fair Play. It was as natural as water running downhill for the Fair Play-Rock Sand combination to show up in the pedigrees of some of America's best horses. The same situation prevails at the Idle Hour Stock Farm of Col. E.R. Bradley, where Black Toney and North Star III held forth together for many years. Since both were good horses it was inevitable that they should combine well. Both Major Belmont and Colonel Bradley maintained relatively independent establishments, clung mainly to their own bloodlines, had a splendid appreciation of horses as individuals, made good selections, and prospered, not because they knew the secret of nicking bloodlines, but because they had good horses to breed from. By and large, the success of any great breeding establishment must be based upon the concurrent presence of at least two great bloodstrains, and no bloodstrain can be considered great which must depend entirely upon another strain for its successes. The principal concern of the breeder is to discover good breeding material, and whatever measures he can employ to find and possess such material should be employed. If you give a man a multiplicity of good sires and mares he can throw all the history of nicks and combinations into the ashcan."

Estes picked up on the larger picture that each of these great breeders was part of. The availability of top stock, particularly in the days when only a small minority of horses were really "top stock," put those breeders in the position of consistently breeding the best horses, year after year. And who, looking at their successes, would not try to emulate them, and as a first step in doing that, the contemporary breeders picked up on the pattern of their matings as the primary ingredient to their success.

However, as Estes argues the point, the pattern was a by-product of using their best and most compatible stock. That is, the pattern came after and not before in considering matings for Castleton, Brookdale, Nursery Stud and Idle Hour.

In his discussion of nicking and other theories, Estes had no personal animosity against the concepts, but he was a careful researcher and a man who was very honest with himself. After all his research into nicks, he said, "Personally I can find no more pattern in them than in fishing worm tracks on a rainy morning."

He used the results from Fair Play's daughters as an example of the variety found in good results from matings. Also as part of his address to the Thoroughbred Club, Estes said, "Take Fair Play's daughters as an example. The best of their produce have been Sun Beau, Jamestown, High Quest and Time Supply. Sun Beau is by Sun Briar, Jamestown by St. James, High Quest by Sir Gallahad III and Time Supply by Time Maker. But Time Maker is by The Porter, son of Sweep, so here we have the Fair Play-Sweep nick again. Well, there it is, if you want it. But as far as I am concerned, it seems to me that the repeated combinations of the same bloodlines in the pedigrees of good horses fall out in accordance with the mathematical expectancy based on the general prevalence of the said bloodlines in the pedigrees of good horses.

"Let us go a little further, and consider Fair Play's half-brother Friar Rock. I suppose the four best horses out of daughters of Friar Rock are High Strung, Spinach, Tintagel, and Pompoon, three of them Futurity winners. High Strung is by High Time, Spinach by Sir Martin, Tintagel by Sir Gallahad III, Pompoon by Pompey — another Joseph's coat.

"You can take the list and go all the way down the line, and I challenge anyone to find a pattern definite enough to give any sort of a clue as to how to breed the successful horses of tomorrow on the basis of affinities. And yet you will see almost any day some wealthy breeder going far out of his way to purchase a mare or a stallion which will permit him to repeat a combination of bloodlines which has been successful in the past."

The fault that Estes found with nicking and its greatest difficulty in practice is that it is essentially a historical way of making and evaluating matings. As many practitioners of nicking will candidly state, all nicks are not created equal. To evaluate them requires a reasonable amount of data that should be applied with a broad understanding of the horses involved, not used as a shortcut or simple formula. So Estes's arguments with nicking can be complex and finely drawn, and an oversimplification of its use was sure to draw fire.

Estes's arguments are a finely spun web, and when a great fancier of nicking went in too deep and declared that the Teddy-Commando cross (or whatever) was the truth and the way, Estes would just as quickly say, "Prove it." When the statistics for the overall performance of the nick was trotted out, it never held up, and Estes never believed in something that could not be proven and proven again in study after study.

The same historical fault could be noted in all the most prominent theories, especially Dosage, inbreeding patterns, and of course the Bruce Lowe family numbers, because the historical element is such an important part of the construction of each.

In *The Blood-Horse's* Silver anniversary publication from 1941, *A Quarter Century of American Racing*, Estes speared both Lowe and Dosage in his overview of breeding. He wrote that Lowe's contribution had all the elements of a good story, as well as "enough simplicity that there was no one so foolish but that he could grasp the main plot."[8] He went on to say that Vuillier "had one that was even better for mathematics, profundity, suspense, and intricacy, but it wasn't simple enough for popular consumption."[9] Such was the case more than 60 years ago, but oh, how things change. Estes said that both theories would have their followers in the future, but he had no inkling of the "dumbing down" of American education and the nearly parallel reworking of Vuillier's concepts to make them more palatable to the mass market. Now, almost everyone knows a little about Dosage, but only a relative few can say anything about Lowe's family numbers.

But then, as now, the real workhorse of breeding theory was nicking. It was pragmatic because anyone who read the racing charts could see that matings along particular lines worked. It was sophisticated enough that breeders had to take a little thought in using it but didn't get the sense that they needed a degree just to discuss it in public. And clearly in the hands of a skilled breeder, there was more to it than just fitting together names to match the accepted pattern. Conformation, temperament, racing type and character all played into the equation for the practical horseman.

Practical Horsemanship and Breeding

The daily considerations of what good horses look like and how to match up the animals so that breeders get the best possible foals constitute an art many people only understand in bits and pieces. But it was this approach that most attracted Estes, where intuition and experience worked hand in hand with practical considerations of racing class and conformation.

So he never missed an opportunity to tell his audience that they ought to use their experience to best advantage. He said that "Whenever a horse of the class of War Admiral is produced by a mare of the class of Brushup (which started three times, was once second, once third, once unplaced) the average breeder wonders again whether there is any advantage in breeding from a mare of good racing ability . . . and possibly comes to the conclusion that the mare with little or no racing class is as likely to throw a good horse as is a mare which won stakes races.

"I have made several investigations of this question, and have always come out with the same answer. Namely, that the mare of good racing class is a far better producer, on the average, than the average mare."[10]

He then goes on to conclusively demonstrate that good racemares have a better producing record overall and that mares with little or low-class racing ability make very shaky propositions as investments for producers. They are low-percentage propositions, but breeders will still find them, Estes noted in his Thoroughbred Club speech, because "It is, of course, much easier for a mare to conceal excellent hereditary qualities under a poor racing record than for a stallion to do so. Hence the owner of any sort of mare may live in hope of having her produce a high-class racer. But he may as well know the odds in the game." The odds of the poor racemare producing a champion are very long, indeed.

Estes said that "there is no more sense in laying down rules for breeding race horses than in laying down rules for throwing dice. What you need to know in both instances is odds and percentages, not rules and exceptions. The six comes up once in six casts, 16 2/3 percent of the time, and the odds against the six showing on any cast are 5-1.

"I am not suggesting that any breeder confine his breeding stock to high-class race mares and stallions. There are other ways of discovering prepotence for racing class. There is one method which is far superior, and that is the progeny test. If a mare produces a Jacola [leading filly of 1937 and 1938], she is far more likely to produce a Johnstown [Kentucky Derby and Belmont winner] than if she had not had Jacola. The dam of Black Helen is more likely to be the dam of Bimelech than if she had not had Black Helen. The sire of Black Servant, Captain Hal, Black Gold, and Brokers Tip had already demonstrated that he might get a Bimelech. That is the sort of gold which can be recognized after you find it. By all means let breeders continue to search for such metal, but let us not try to delude them as to the odds against their finding it. Even with the best of credentials as to racing and pedigree, the odds against exceptional breeding success are high. Without such credentials, the odds are well nigh incalculable."[11]

The odds of producing a good horse are long enough that many breeders must have wondered if it's worth the trouble and expense. But on they go, and Estes was one to encourage them to take their best chance with the opportunities at hand. Whether he was advocating a stallion whose merits were overlooked, or skewering a theory that might be leading someone astray, or investigating ways for breeders to judge more likely prospects, Estes was always focused on the goal of breeding the best horse possible.

To his commonsense approach, breeding a horse that can just get around the track is pointless. Those horses all lose money. Only by breeding for the best can an owner have a realistic chance of coming out ahead in the long run.

He and Palmer wrote stories about the history of the breed, with Palmer producing a book called *Names in Pedigrees* about the animals that dot the pedigrees of the mid-20th century. In covering the sales, Estes discusses pedigree and conformation, noting which sires are getting sound and athletic stock and which young animals are siblings to champions or top racers of the day.

For him, the process of breeding good horses was a practical affair without much need for theory of a purely academic sort. The statistics and mathematics and research needed to address the animal itself was what made the game go round.

In context with the progression of Estes's thoughts on breeding horses, he was obviously well aware of the best research going on related to equine inheritance, as shown by this quotation about the work of Dr. Harry Laughlin in *The Blood-Horse* of May 21, 1938. Estes said, "The best clue to the future success for the Thoroughbred breeder is in this year's racing charts, and the whole subject is still mysterious enough. The practical horseman is quite right when he says, 'To the deuce with that stuff.' [Referring to genetics, and so forth] . . . Walter J. Salmon has spent a great deal of money employing a very reputable scientist, Dr. H.H. Laughlin, and a staff of workers to establish a scientific basis for breeding Thoroughbreds. Dr. Laughlin's published comments on his findings have nothing to say about genes. He has applied himself almost exclusively to creating probability formulae based on racing charts — and it is no reflection on him that he has not improved the output of Mereworth Stud, which was good enough in the first place."[12]

Mereworth bred some good horses and stood some good stallions, including Display, the sire of Discovery, and Sunglow, the sire of Sword Dancer, who won the 1959 Belmont Stakes.

Despite his appreciation for the work of Laughlin, Estes had no inclination to set up a monolithic approach to breeding horses. He recognized that it is a fluid process, governed by chance, but he also demanded that as much sense and reason be applied to it as was possible. He said, "There are no rules to breeding race horses. There are only odds and percentages. I am still waiting for someone to reveal a better way of calculating odds and percentages than by the use of racing class. But I do not expect to see any such calculation." [13]

Some breeders thought he was out in left field, but Estes was so sincere in his address and so candid in his writing that he won over most of his detractors. In one memorable exchange that he recorded in his column, he spoke with one of the great nicking breeders of the mid-century, Tom Piatt.

Thomas Piatt had bred the winner of the 1940 Wood Memorial, a good colt named Dit who later finished a close third in the Kentucky Derby, and Estes inquired about the reasons for Piatt acquiring the colt's dam, the stakes-winning mare Ingrid. Piatt said that he had owned another mare from the family and this was a strong female family but that especially he wanted her because Ingrid had Hamburg on her female side. Estes asked him if he wanted Ingrid also because she was a good racemare, and Piatt said no, but "I had a good race mare out here once, and she had one bad one after another until she finally produced a horse that ran third in the Kentucky Derby."[14] So, from this pair of good-class racemares, Piatt bred a pair of runners who managed to show in the country's richest and most prestigious event for three-year-old colts.

Piatt was well-known as a breeder of racehorses and also for his intense appreciation of the American lines of Hamburg, Broomstick, Fair Play and Domino. But Estes included his discussion of Piatt's rationale for purchasing Ingrid because he wanted to show how firmly horsemen clung to mating by pattern and pedigree rather than by racing quality.

He wrote that "Mr. Piatt has been breeding Thoroughbreds virtually all his adult life, knows his horses thoroughly, is a superb judge of what is good and what is bad in horseflesh. He has no patience with academic arguments, but draws his wisdom from his own rich experience.

"For years Mr. Piatt has patterned his pedigrees after those of the Whitney successes (even his farm is named Brookdale). So I knew without his telling me that he must have had Whitney horses in mind when he bought Ingrid. He paid $450 to get her, out of the consignment of Lee Rosenberg to the Fasig-Tipton Company sale at Lexington May 2, 1935."[15]

Estes noted that Ingrid had been a very useful racemare, winning 15 races. After retirement, she had produced three foals, and "When Mr. Piatt bought her she was carrying a sister to Robber Baron later named Dinah Desmond, a winner of four races last year at three. Mr. Piatt bred her to Transmute, and Dit was the result. Dit is by long odds the best horse Transmute ever got, and he is possibly the best horse Mr. Piatt ever bred. To him it seems perfectly reasonable to account for Dit's success on the grounds that he made a proper nick of bloodlines, and it seems altogether unreasonable to account for it on the grounds that Ingrid was a good race mare."[16]

Although Dit was a very useful racer, the best horse Piatt ever bred was a yearling in 1940. His name was Alsab.

This bay colt was one of two dozen yearlings that Piatt sent to the Saratoga yearling sale in 1940 and was one of four yearlings in the group sired by the young sire Good Goods. He was a typical Piatt yearling in his lines of descent, being sired by a Domino-line stallion (through Colin) and out of a mare from the Ben Brush line whose own dam was by Fair Play.

Lost in the bustle and fanfare over more popular pedigrees, Alsab sold for only $700, less than half the average for the Saratoga sale that year. But Piatt took yearlings to Saratoga to sell, not get them appraised; so the colt went home with Albert Sabath and proved an outstanding champion.

This most typical Piatt horse had an appeal to Estes also, as Alsab was by a much-neglected sire in Good Goods. Disregarded by the majority of breeders, Good Goods was an excellent example for Estes's dictum to breeders to take quality where they found it. Good Goods had been an above-average racehorse and was a pretty good sire.

Good Goods passed the racing test and the breeding test, and Alsab's dam, the Wildair mare Winds Chant, passed only the latter. But once proven, both were much above-average stock to use. Neither ever produced anything to compare with Alsab, but then Estes wouldn't have expected them to. Only the best and most consistent sires and dams produce several top-class offspring, but the ones who have already done so have a much greater likelihood than those who never have.

Focus on the Family

This intense scrutiny of the parentage — especially the parents and grandparents — of a foal was a major facet of Estes's approach to mating horses and estimating what breeders should expect from them. From his own experience in watching the successful and unsuccessful products of matings and from his own researches into the statistics of the overall racing and breeding populations, he concluded that racing class was the first bar of accomplishment to give breeders a hint of the animals' likely success at stud. The second and final hurdle was actual success in the production of good athletes.

In reviewing the prospects of the top colt Bimelech, Estes said: "In view of my contention that the racing class of the parents is the most important item in connection with the pedigree of a race horse, I had anticipated that I would be reproached with Bimelech, and I have. His sire was not a top-class horse, and his dam had very little class of any kind, as far as the records show. I refuse to be made uncomfortable by this. In the first place, it seems altogether unreasonable to suppose that both Black Toney and La Troienne possessed more class than those eloquent volumes of racing charts reveal. But I shall soft-pedal that part of the matter, on the grounds that it is better to accept the racing charts as they are than to encourage improvisation upon the themes they may suggest.

"I have stated repeatedly that there is one test — and only one — more efficient than racing class for the selection of breeding material, and that is the progeny test. After the produce of a stallion or a mare have raced, you have before you the best evidence it is possible to obtain. Bimelech is a case in point if ever there was one.

"Black Toney went into the stud at a fee of $50. There was no concerted rush of prescient breeders to whom his coming greatness was apparent. Colonel Bradley himself had only a few mares he could spare to breed to the son of Peter Pan. In his first three crops were a total of 13 foals. But in the first crop, of four foals, was a high-class stakes-winning filly, Miss Jemima, winner of $42,057. In the second crop, of three foals, was Black Servant. After that it was obvious that Black Toney had something. In later years he got such cracks as Black Gold, Captain Hal, Beau Butler, Broadway Jones, Black Maria, Black Panther, Blackwood, Brokers Tip, Black Helen, and Balladier. Bimelech, got when his sire was 25 years old, is obviously the best of all the get of Black Toney."[17]

Few realized Black Toney's immense value until he began siring high-class racehorses.

Later in this same column, Estes assessed La Troienne's qualifications. He noted that "La Troienne, the dam of Bimelech, bred in France, raced four times unplaced in that country at two and three. She must have been rather highly tried, as she raced against good-class company. In 1930 the noted French breeder Marcel Boussac consigned her to the Newmarket December Sales in England. She was then a four-year-old and carrying her first foal, by Gainsborough. The late H.J. (Dick) Thompson was in England buying a few mares for Colonel Bradley, and at his instructions the British Bloodstock Agency bought La Troienne for Colonel Bradley, paying 1,250 guineas.

"In the spring of 1931 La Troienne had her foal by Gainsborough. It was a bay filly, a misshapen, worthless-looking thing which died as a yearling.

"Consider La Troienne at that stage of her career. She was not a good race mare, or at least the charts did not reveal her as such, so the application of the racing class test would not have indicated that she was a potentially great producer. But neither would any other test that might have been applied. It was to her credit that she was a sister to a fairly high-class race horse called Leonidas. She was by Teddy, a very successful sire, but on the basis of

Photo Courtesy of the Grayson/Sutcliffe Collection

Legendary broodmare La Troienne failed as a racehorse but became one of the important broodmares of the 20th century.

pedigrees there were many, many daughters of Teddy that would have rated higher, and many, many daughters of other sires as well . . ."[18]

Estes then recounts the following offspring from La Troienne: Black Helen, winner of the Florida Derby, American Derby, and Coaching Club American Oaks; stakes winner Biologist; the winner Baby League; and Big Hurry, winner of the Selima Stakes. Of her three best offspring to that time, all of them — Black Helen, Big Hurry, and Bimelech — were by Black Toney.

As Bimelech came from Black Toney's last crop, no further matings with him were possible, but with his purchase of La Troienne, "Colonel Bradley has happened upon one of the great broodmares of the century. As is usually the case, her extreme greatness cannot be explained from her pedigree, that is, her pedigree cannot be used to set her apart from and higher than a thousand of her contemporaries. I suspect that in her days on the race track she might have gained prominence but for her none-too-robust constitution, a characteristic which she has passed on to several of her offspring, not excluding Bimelech."[19]

The evidence of the day made La Troienne a great broodmare. The results of the past 60 years have made her a legend. Probably the most important broodmare of the 20th century in America, La Troienne was, in Estes's opinion, an unknowable quantity until her produce came onto the racetrack.

But that candid conclusion did not stop him from trying to find ways to help breeders to decipher form and probability. His first major conclusion from his researches into breeding was that the racing class of mares was of immense importance.

In study after study, conducted by Estes or under his observation, the results confirmed his initial efforts into this inquiry. The best racemares became the best producers overall. Individually, they faced as many challenges as any other mare, and more than a few good racemares had trouble getting in foal, or had poor-quality foals, or had pure bad luck with the foals they produced. Yet even with these individual losses and disappointments, as a group, the best racemares consistently produced a greater proportion of high-quality racing stock for the next generation than any other group of mares.

The consistency and repeatability of these results confirmed Estes in believing that the test of racing was the best initial method for choosing good broodmares. As corollaries to this conclusion, he observed that the effort of racing did not have bad effects on the breeding class of mares, that "so-called good pedigrees are not primarily important in judging the potential breeding class of a broodmare"[20], and that the soundness required for a solid racing career was a necessary component for becoming a good broodmare.

The Breeding Test

Those horses who passed the racing test in some fashion then had their second hurdle to clear in the progeny test. Could they produce foals that were athletic and raceable? Were the foals consistent enough to make breeders persevere with them and have a reasonable chance of reward?

One of the great success stories in the writings of Estes comes from the convoluted career of High Time, an extremely inbred stallion from the Domino line. He managed to flunk the racing test, found himself a home at stud anyway, and passed the progeny test like a champion, getting the top racer Sarazen.

Estes wrote, "When High Time entered the stud at Haylands under the management of Miss Elizabeth Daingerfield in 1920 at an advertised fee of $200, no one took him seriously except Miss Daingerfield. It was she who had planned the mating which was responsible for him. Her father, Major Foxhall Daingerfield, had demonstrated what could be done with Domino inbreeding, and she went a step further, and piled it up until Domino was 50 percent of High Time's pedigree. But High Time had been unsound and a bleeder, to boot, and his pedigree was too unorthodox. Miss Daingerfield managed to talk a few breeders into sending mares to High Time. Among them was Dr. Marius E. Johnston, to whom Thoroughbreds were very much a sideline. In 1921 High Time was represented by a crop of eight registered foals. They all turned out to be winners, and the two stakes winners in the lot, Sarazen and Time Exposure, were from two mares sent to High Time's court by Dr. Johnston."[21]

Estes quizzed Col. Phil T. Chinn, a noted trainer and talker about racehorses, on his connection with Sarazen, and he replied, "'I bought Sarazen and Time Exposure from Dr. Johnston as yearlings. Paid $2,500 for both of them.

"'Hiram Steele had been after me to buy two yearlings out at Dr. Johnston's place. Steele was the greatest judge of a horse I ever knew. He worked for John E. Madden for years. He was a blacksmith, a carpenter, a concrete man, a horseman — and tops in everything he did. Once I had him changing some doors on a barn for me, and when the job was finished he said to me, "Chinn, you've got 20 yearlings in that barn, but there's only one race horse in the whole lot." I said, "Really? Which one is that?" and he said, "That little Sweep filly in the end stall." That filly was Pen Rose.

"'I didn't pay much attention to him about these two yearlings, but one day in July I ran smack into him, and he said, "When you going to look at those two yearlings I told you about?" I said, "Well, there's no time like now. "When we got to the gate I said, "By the way, Hiram, what are these yearlings by?" He said they were by High Time, and I said, "Well, Hiram, if they're by High Time I wouldn't have 'em if you could give 'em to me. But since I don't want to offend you, I'll go ahead and look at 'em. What does the doctor want for 'em?"

"'Well,' Hiram said, 'he wants $2,500 for two of them, but I guess you could get them for less, because he has already offered them to John E. Madden and Kay Spence for that price and they both turned them down.'

"You see, I had trained High Time when he was a three-year-old, and I knew he was a bleeder and the stoppingest horse I had ever seen. I wasn't a public trainer, but I had a few horses for friends, and among them was this colt that belonged to Admiral Grayson. The first time I started him [this was High Time's only race as a three-year-old] he came out 10 lengths in front of the field and wound up far back at the finish. I said to the Admiral, 'Admiral, I don't usually send bills to my friends, but I've got a colt yours over there in my barn, and if he's still there tonight, I may have to take up the practice.' He said, 'Do you mean it?' And I said, 'Yes.'

"I never had another favorable thought about High Time until I saw those two yearlings. They both looked like race horses. I went up to see Dr. Johnston. He said he had been pricing them at $2,500 but that he would take something off for me. I said, 'Don't take anything off, I'll take them for $2,500.'

"The next year I started racing them. I sold Sarazen to Mrs. Vanderbilt for $35,000 and later in the year sold Time Exposure to Frank J. Farrell, owner of the Yankees and big Tammany man, for $10,000 I think it was.

"After Sarazen had shown top class, John E. Madden said to me one day, 'When a man can breed a quarter-horse to a plow-mare and get a horse that can beat everything in America, it's time for me to be selling out.' And he did start selling out.

"'After I saw what kind of colts these were I told Admiral Grayson I would like to have a share in High Time, and, after he conferred with Samuel Ross, his partner, they gave me a half-interest in him. I was talking to Senator Joe Bailey about him, and the Senator said, 'You know, Colonel, I've been studying that horse, and I've come to the conclusion that he'll be great sire or the greatest flop there ever was.' I gave him a half of my half-interest; he had a lot of mares and could help make the horse a reputation. Afterwards I bought Admiral Grayson's half-interest for $50,000 and Senator Bailey's half-interest for $25,000. Once John J. Raskob offered me $300,000 for him." (At the Himyar Stud dispersal in mid-depression 1931, Dixiana bought High Time for $50,000.)"[22]

That must count not only as one of the best stories ever about racing and breeding but also as one of the most unusual accounts of buying a top horse in the history of the breed. And the dam of Sarazen didn't have any credits on the score of racing form. Estes wrote that "I don't know anyone from whom I could get such a colorful account of Rush Box. She was foaled in 1915, at George Carley's farm in Scott County, Kentucky, near the present great trotting horse nursery known as Walnut Hall. I remember Miss Daingerfield telling me that when she went over to look at Rush Box the mare had never had a halter on and when they tried to catch her she lit out across country and jumped two or three fences. That was just before Dr. Johnston bought her. So it is apparently not true that she was used to pull a plow, since Dr. Johnston bred her to High Time when she was a five-year-old.

"But apparently Sallie Ward, Rush Box's dam, was used as a plow-horse. She was bred and owned by Mr. Carley, who was a farmer first and a Thoroughbred breeder only incidentally. Belle Nutter, the dam of Sallie Ward, had been bred in Scott County by Robert H. Nutter, [whose] . . . farm adjoined that of Mr. Carley.

None of Sarazen's first four dams was a winner. Rush Box was never broken. Sallie Ward ran four times unplaced. Belle Nutter placed at three, the only year she raced. Each of them produced winners, but nothing of distinction except Sarazen. The sires in Rush Box's pedigree had little to recommend them except some of their ancestors. Box, foaled in 1894, was a good stakes winner, but was "insane," to use Colonel Chinn's description."[23]

To even the most casual observer, not to mention those steeped in the traditional approaches to making matings, Estes's advocacy of class in the dam and the importance of racing class as the first and most useful gauge of producing class for sire and dam was full of holes. These were not holes from faulty logic or muddled reasoning, however. Estes understood that these were the effects of genetics and probability. The many good horses produced by mares without racing success are the result of the uncertain probabilities of breeding. Nobody understood this better than Estes himself, as he admitted in another of his columns published in *The Blood-Horse*.

He said, "The main reason nobody much will believe The Estes when he insists that good race mares are the best prospects for good broodmares is Man o' War. Another reason is Alsab. Another is Gallant Fox and his brethren. And there are hundreds of others. There are, at any rate, enough to make most breeders and most experts think they can do better by selecting broodmares according to bloodlines than according to racing class."[24]

Nor was Estes a knocker of pedigree. To the contrary, he was as well-informed about pedigrees and what was good and bad in them as anyone in the country. But he did not believe that part of the puzzle should rule all the decisions about matings, and it really galled him that some thorough horsemen could walk away from mares that he saw, through his work with statistics, as the best prospects for breeding the next generation of top racehorses.

When there wasn't a racing record to consult, then he was as liable as the next man to choose the daughters of top sires and good producers.

And yet when it came to assessing his statistics, Estes wasn't swayed by the anecdotal successes of good broodmares who did nothing or next to it on the racetrack. He still counted them as racing unknowns. For instance, in the case of Man o' War, Estes found interesting testimony about the great horse's dam, Mahubah, from racing official Andy Ferguson, who rode Mahubah when he was a jockey under contract with owner-breeder August Belmont.

Ferguson claimed that Mahubah was outstandingly talented but was given little opportunity to show racing class in Belmont's stable. In truth, the mare ran only five times in two seasons, with a victory and a second to show for the effort. In a private sweepstakes at Piping Rock during her juvenile season, Mahubah finished fifth to Pankhurst (later the dam of Upset, winner of the Sanford over Man o' War and second in the Kentucky Derby, Preakness, and Travers), Hester Prynne (the dam of Pillory, winner of the Preakness and Belmont), and Verdure (dam of Wildair).

Judging from that juvenile effort, Mahubah did have some ability and class, but for some reason or another, she did not show it clearly on the racetrack. Considering that both Man o' War and his full sister Masda showed more than a touch of spirit in their preparation for the track, it is quite possible that their dam was highly strung, and that could have been the reason for her limited racing.

Breeder August Belmont, who owned and bred Mahubah, also preferred lightly raced broodmares. In the hands of a savvy and perceptive breeder like Belmont, Mahubah was not culled. Instead she was bred to the best stallion he had, Fair Play,

Photo Courtesy of the Grayson/Sutcliffe Collection

Mahubah, dam of Man o' War, is another example of a quality broodmare with a poor racing record.

who also was the best stallion in the country or very nearly so.

So clearly Belmont realized that there was something of value in Mahubah, but did he visualize her as the dam of Man o' War? No, of course not. He wouldn't have sold the colt — war or not — had he realized what caliber of colt he had just bred.

But questions of that magnitude are regularly asked in racing and breeding, and we as breeders and owners do not know the answers until the horses have performed on the racetrack and we see the evidence in front of us. So the haunting puzzle that Estes addressed was just how to unravel this mystery. To do that, he had to find indicators that, in a bland statistical landscape, would tend to mark the mares and stallions who were going to outperform their opportunity.

Developing a Scale: The Average Earnings Index

The questions that plagued Estes were vast and seemingly unanswerable. He was certain from his research that racing ability was the key to assessing the initial chances of broodmares and stallions. But how could he assess the best prospects from thousands of fillies coming off the track each year? How could breeders, who had farms and businesses to run, sift out the gems from among the many who weren't obviously qualified? Without the intimate knowledge of a breeder who had followed a mare's career and knew her weaknesses and strengths, how was a breeder to know a horse's worth at a glance?

Since personal investigation of each mare was impossible, Estes turned to statistics.

The use of statistics was just coming into use in other sports, particularly baseball, and Estes was able to use his understanding of popular culture to come up with a measure of success for racing horses. Up to this point, rankings of winners, sires, and their "worth" had come from raw earnings totals. These were rough measures of quality, but it was possible to use raw earnings to estimate a horse's success. But the stallions with the most runners typically led the list, unless they were complete disasters.

Statisticians could solve that inequity by the use of averaging. They could take a stallion's number of runners, divide that number into their total earnings, and arrive at a figure that was proportional to the group. Using average earnings per runner was more effective in leveling the field for comparison. Still today, using average earnings by runner and by start is a very useful application of statistics.

But even using averaging, the immense rise of purse values, in the 1940s in particular, made the comparison of horses separated by even five or 10 years seem like a joke because the difference was so large. So Estes began to use indexing of average earnings to evaluate individuals and also sires.

To produce this index was an enormous undertaking. Estes had to know the number of horses that raced, as well as the total earnings by all the horses racing. Using these figures, he could then derive the average earnings, by dividing the gross earnings by the total racers. Each year, the result of this equation was the par figure for the indexing, which Estes set at 1.00. If the average earnings for a year happened to be $3,000, and a horse earned $3,000, its AEI was 1.00. Likewise, if it earned $1,500, its AEI was 0.50; if it earned $1,000, its AEI was 0.33, and so forth.

Estes and his team of researchers at *The Blood-Horse* managed this without the help of our modern computing equipment and numerous aids to computation and statistical management. They performed miracles.

But the results were worth it. Using the figures for average earnings and the results from any horse's racing career, a breeder could figure an individual AEI by hand in seconds. This could get monotonous in attempting to figure the indices for a whole sale of broodmares, but the index was a handy means of sifting through a few dozen similar choices after the preliminary weeding out had been done.

Estes was succeeding in his unending effort to separate good from bad and the very best prospects from useful performers. One shortcoming in the AEI is that it did not standardize earnings by start; in the 1940s and 1950s, the computation time and other expenses to manage such a task were more than a magazine could bear. For this and other reasons, Estes eventually left *The Blood-Horse* and joined the Jockey Club's office in Lexington, where, as director of research for the Jockey Club's statistical bureau, he worked to develop a database of information for use by breeders and owners.

With the AEI, Estes realized that it was not perfect, but he said "in this hazardous game of selecting breeding stock, we must take whatever clues are available."[25]

In addition to helping to select the best mares, AEI also showed its application for stallions. The selection stakes for stallions is stiff competition in the first place, and only those with serious racing records get any reasonable kind of chance from the general population of breeders.

Although judging the stallion's worth was easier, it wasn't absolute. Those stallions with a true chance to become top sires came off the track with big reputations. So for researchers, there wasn't the problem of working through thousands of them to find the ones who mattered. But Estes did find a couple of uses for the AEI in relation to stallions. First, breeders could use the index as a means of judging which of the many unproven mares should receive seasons to the horse, and they could also use it to estimate how competently the stallion was performing his job of getting winners and good earners on the racetrack.

With regard to the first application, in Estes's opinion, the "way to make a reputation for a sire is to breed him to good mares."[26] This seems a common-sense approach to making a stallion as successful as possible, but in another day and with a somewhat different approach to breeding, Estes's comments were fairly revolutionary.

Not everyone was opposed to this way of selecting mares for matings, and the results from the early books of Hyperion bore out Estes's conclusions in America. Estes noted that, from his first three crops to race, the dynamic little chestnut had sired 18 major winners and that two-thirds of them were out of stakes-winning mares.

Stakes mares, however, were already obvious choices as good breeding prospects due to their racing ability, and frankly, not many breeders, then or now, have a barn full of stakes mares. But AEI did open some doors to understanding quality through earnings and did help breeders pick up some useful mares that might otherwise have been overlooked.

Having proven through repeated tests that the best racemares, as a group, were the best producers, Estes used AEI to define the most successful racing stock. Then he could estimate stakes ability in a broodmare, whether the mare actually had earned black type or not. The somewhat arbitrary breakthrough figure for "stakes class" was an AEI of 4.0 or greater. With three-quarters of the breed earning less than 20 percent more than the average earnings (an AEI of 1.20), this was a hefty multiple on average performance or general expectations from the norm of the breed. But these mares, those that exceeded the 4.0 threshold, were premium stock in Estes's opinion.

Only about three percent of the breed meet this standard, and this percentage also approximately corresponds to the proportion of stakes winners to foals annually. Examples of mares that correspond to this figure are lengthy. Consider Attica, a daughter of Mr. Trouble and the Pharamond II mare Athenia. One of the foundation

mares for Alice Chandler's Mill Ridge Farm, Attica was twice placed in stakes and earned a very respectable AEI and a standard starts index of 4.51. At stud, the mare produced one of the greatest and most important Kentucky-breds of the 1960s in Sir Ivor. Purchased for $42,000 at the Keeneland July yearling sale in 1966, the colt was trained by Vincent O'Brien for Raymond Guest. Sir Ivor won the Grand Criterium as a juvenile, then returned at three to win the 2,000

Sir Ivor was the first horse to create international demand for Kentucky Thoroughbreds. His dam Attica's standard starts index of 4.51 labeled her as premium breeding stock.

Guineas at Newmarket and the Derby at Epsom in excellent style. Later in the year, Sir Ivor won the Champion Stakes and the Washington D.C. International. He was such a successful, courageous and versatile horse that European demand immediately grew for more of the same high-quality stock being raised in Kentucky. As a result, Attica's son effectively began the bull market for the international Thoroughbred that continues to the present.

In another example of how the earnings index underlines racing ability and the likely success of a broodmare at stud, *The Blood-Horse's* editor wrote, "It is the best-available one-figure evaluation of racing ability, as measured by earnings in relation to opportunity. It is calculated by dividing each year's earnings by the average distribution per runner in that year, summing the quotients, and dividing the sum by the number of years raced. The result of this calculation shows the ratio between actual earnings and average expectancy.

"For instance, Miss Disco, the dam of Bold Ruler, raced five years, when the average per runner varied as follows: 1946, $2,800; 1947, $2,829; 1948, $2,688; 1949, $2,420; 1950, $2,221."[27] Her earnings in each year was divided by the year's average, and those quotients were then added together for a sum of 29.743. Dividing that number by five, the number of years that Miss Disco raced, yields 5.95, nearly six times the average earnings expectation for the duration of her racing career.

Photo Courtesy of Keeneland Library, Meadors Collection

Miss Disco scored an average earnings index of 5.95 — nearly six times the average — after five years on the racetrack. As a broodmare, she foaled the legendary Bold Ruler.

In addition to the function of AEI as a gauge of quality in the dam, it also had a role in discerning which stallions were succeeding overall with their offspring. Using AEI to help judge a stallion's success at stud requires mathematics that are a bit more complex. Researchers had to work up the stallion's results using all his starters each year in relation to their total earnings.

The method of computing the lifetime progeny index for a stallion was similar to the calculations for Miss Disco above. However, the gross earnings for a stallion's progeny were divided by the year's average earnings figure. This quotient, sometimes called the adjustment figure, was divided by the stallion's total number of starters that year, and the result is the AEI for the stallion during the year in question. To calculate a cumulative earnings index for a stallion, add the adjustment figures for each year and divide by the total number of year-starters (a horse is counted each year that it starts).

The results from these cumulative tabulations of AEI are a ruthless assessment of a stallion's success or lack of it. Really good stallions, the sires of champions and such, could break 2.0 on this scale of evaluation, but only the very best, such as Bull Lea, Nasrullah, Bold Ruler, and other sires of the best horses crop after crop, ranked as high as 4.0 or 5.0.

One of the strengths of this method of evaluation is that the information is available at little expense, and it applies to any region, country, or breed of horse that has an earnings component in competition. It is food for thought and interpretation, but the numbers are there in black and white. Breeders ignore them at the peril of their pocketbooks.

In Conclusion

Such was Estes's prestige as a commentator on breeding and bloodstock that his assessments became a byword for evaluating breeding stock. For instance, in advertising the dispersal of the Almahurst Farm breeding stock owned by Henry H. Knight in 1955, a splendid photograph in *The Blood-Horse* showed four mares in a pasture. They were Elpis, Miss Kimo, Say Blue and Earshot. Part of the caption read, "All together they have won 24 stakes and a grand total of $618,940 . . . and there is no substitute for top-class racing quality."[28] When Estes's research had permeated ad copy, his work was reaching a depth and breadth of acceptance that offered great opportunities to breeders and owners of racehorses.

Then as now, there are no caveats to using Estes's methods. His ability to crush superstition and hearsay under the weight of logic and thoughtful consideration was immense. He used common sense and pragmatism to search for the best evidence of breeding ability available to breeders and did all of us an immense service. Yet he never let scientific rigor cloud his understanding of probability. In one of his published speeches, Estes noted that "In actual experience, good broodmares frequently develop from mares which were not raced at all or which raced without distinction. And of course some of the best racemares fail as producers, for one reason or another. In Thoroughbred breeding, as I have remarked elsewhere, gold is where you find it, but the best place to look is right on the surface — in the individual itself, in the phenotype."

In the estimation of Estes and many other top horsemen, combining the best stock, the best land, management, and veterinary advice along with a reasonable bit of luck gives any breeder a license to beat the probabilities in breeding good racehorses.

The Average Earnings Index Today

The creation of the average earnings index in 1948 by Joe Estes became a benchmark for the Thoroughbred industry to compare stallions' progeny performance from generation to generation. It is a testament to Estes that, more than 50 years later, the AEI still represents the industry standard.

While calculating the AEI remains the same, the applications of this index have increased significantly. The first variation to the AEI was developed in 1951 when Estes calculated the index for broodmare sires. This type of AEI was compiled by getting the average earnings of all the foals of a sire's daughters, then getting the index relative to overall average earnings. *The Blood-Horse*, however, was limited in pursuing further enhancements to the index without the help of computers. For three decades there was no way of comparing the average earnings of a sire's foals to the average earnings of their half-siblings. Thus, one could only guess at which stallions were being bred to the best mares.

By the late 1970s and early 1980s, computers were becoming more commonplace. With the technological advances of computer processing, *The Blood-Horse* finally had the computer output capacity that was necessary to calculate an index for the mares bred to a stallion. So, during the tenure of editor Kent Hollingsworth, *The Blood-Horse* created an index called the comparable index (CI) in 1982 that finds the average earnings index for all the other foals of the mares bred to a stallion. So, when the sire Cozzene has an AEI of 2.89 and CI of 1.75, this means his foals have a higher average earnings index than their dams' foals by other sires.

The Blood-Horse also applied the concept of the CI to broodmare sires. The CI for a broodmare sire represents the cumulative AEI for all the foals sired by the stallions bred to a sire's daughters. While the broodmare sire's AEI measures the racing class of the foals of a sire's daughters, the CI shows the AEI for the other foals by different broodmare sires. One of the great broodmare sires, Buckpasser, has an AEI of 3.20 and CI of 1.83. This means that his daughters' foals have higher average earnings than other mares' progeny that was sired by the same stallions.

Further applications to Estes's index didn't come until the Jockey Club went to a client-server platform for its computer system in 1997. This allowed programmers from *The Blood-Horse* direct access to the Jockey Club's database of more than three million horses using Structured Query Language (SQL). The same year also was the inception of *The Blood-Horse's MarketWatch* newsletter, a publication that provided detailed statistical analysis on Thoroughbred breeding and racing.

One of the questions raised with the new publication was what innovations could be done with the AEI and CI. *MarketWatch* came up with the idea of separating the indexes by each crop year of a sire's foals, instead of having one cumulative AEI and CI for all of a sire's progeny record. For example, Storm Cat's cumulative AEI and CI for his 11 foal crops to race is 3.93 and 3.85, respectively. These figures, however, count not only his most recent foals, but also his offspring that raced 10 years ago. In order to get a more up-to-date record, *MarketWatch* can break down Storm Cat's record for his three most recent crops to race. His foals of 1997 have an AEI of 7.61 and CI of 3.87. His 1998 crop shows an AEI of 2.74 and CI of 7.28 and his 1999 crop, an AEI of 2.12 and 7.15 CI. By separating Storm Cat's AEI and CI year to year, one can gather that his two most recent crops to race have under-performed compared to Storm Cat's earlier foals to race and compared to other foals out of those mares.

Even though *MarketWatch* could study a sire's record by each crop to race with this annual AEI, there still weren't any calculations being done on the foals that were in-utero, weanlings or yearlings. *MarketWatch* soon found that it could get the comparable indexes for the half-siblings to the sires' crops of foals that were yearlings or younger. Going back to the top-class sire, Storm Cat, the foals from his three most recent breeding seasons (2000-2002) have CIs of 8.06, 7.13 and 6.51. Remember, it doesn't matter that the mares' foals by Storm Cat are unraced, since the CI is the AEI for the mares' other foals. Consequently, breeders can judge — in the case of Storm Cat — that he has some very well-bred foals coming up to the races in the next three years. If a commercial breeder sends a mare to Storm Cat this year, he knows that when he sells the resulting foal at public auction as a weanling, yearling or two-year-old that Storm Cat's runners will be advertising themselves by competing successfully.

Some further improvements to these indexes came through the pedigree information products sold by the Jockey Club Information Systems. One product, the statistical sire summary, shows the AEI for a sire's current year runners, his two-year-olds, his male, female, dirt, and turf runners. Information is even presented showing the AEI and CI for certain nicks or a mating of a sire to daughters by certain sires. In the case of Storm Cat, daughters of Alydar have been bred to him the most often, with 31 named foals having an AEI of 9.22 and CI of 4.71.

Even with all these different applications for Estes's index, there is no denying that the AEI is based on an average. This means that a sire's six- and seven-figure earners can inflate his AEI to make a stallion look like a 3.00 sire when he really is a 2.00 sire. With this drawback in mind, *MarketWatch* calculated the AEI for every runner of a sire, then grouped these runners by certain levels of AEI and found out their percentage from named foals that fell into each category. By looking at the high AEI runners on a percentage basis, there would be no inflation of the AEI. Again, using Storm Cat as an example, he had 446 foals from his 1992 to 1998 crops, with 97 (or 21 percent) unraced. Of his foals to race, 31 percent had an AEI less than the average of 1.00, 18 percent had an AEI from 1.00 to 1.99, 17 percent showed an AEI from 2.00 to 3.99, and 13 percent accounted for an AEI of 4.00 or higher. From this distribution, one can see how difficult it is for even the best stallions to get runners that perform significantly better than the average of 1.00.

These are just a few of the ways that the uses of AEI and CI have been enlarged upon since Estes's years at *The Blood-Horse*. As for the future prospects of the AEI, maybe one day the industry will see a median earnings index or an adjusted AEI that limits the influence of a sire's highest earners.

Catesby Clay, Jr. was Managing Editor of MarketWatch, *a division of* The Blood-Horse, *from 1997 to 2002. His interest now in the horse business is with his family's farm, Runnymede, in Paris, Ky.*

All-Time Leading Sires by AEI

Sires	Foals	SWS		AEI
Bold Ruler	356	82	23%	7.73
Alydar	689	77	11%	5.21
Nasrullah	425	98	23%	5.16
Northern Dancer	635	146	23%	5.14
Nijinsky II	850	155	18%	4.74
Danzig	886	165	19%	4.53
Tom Fool	276	36	13%	4.51
Hail To Reason	308	43	14%	4.47
Fappiano	410	48	12%	4.46
Bull Lea	377	58	15%	4.37
Mr. Prospector	1157	176	15%	4.25
Seattle Slew	933	100	11%	4.12
Ribot	423	67	16%	4.09
Round Table	401	83	21%	4.01
Nureyev	750	130	17%	3.99
Blushing Groom	512	92	18%	3.97
Buckpasser	313	35	11%	3.94
Storm Cat	694	93	13%	3.93
Hoist The Flag	246	51	21%	3.88
Equipoise	74	9	12%	3.86
Bold Reasoning	61	10	16%	3.75
A.P. Indy	348	33	9%	3.74
Pleasant Colony	556	67	12%	3.70
Sea-Bird	172	33	19%	3.70
Never Bend	362	61	17%	3.67
Exclusive Native	507	66	13%	3.65
Intentionally	187	20	11%	3.58
Alibhai	395	54	14%	3.51
Heliopolis	346	53	15%	3.41
Roberto	500	86	17%	3.38
Princequillo	482	65	13%	3.31
Herbager	428	64	15%	3.30
Private Account	588	60	10%	3.30
Caro	598	78	13%	3.27
Deputy Minister	779	69	9%	3.27
Kalamoun	122	21	17%	3.26
Lyphard	829	115	14%	3.25
Olympia	324	40	12%	3.25
Vaguely Noble	727	70	10%	3.25
Seeking The Gold	443	47	11%	3.23
In Reality	555	81	15%	3.18
Native Dancer	304	44	14%	3.15
Royal Charger	369	58	16%	3.15
Forty Niner	413	43	10%	3.09
Kingmambo	286	32	11%	3.03
Habitat	694	90	13%	3.00
Mahmoud	408	68	17%	2.95
Dr. Fager	255	35	14%	2.94
War Admiral	371	40	11%	2.40

Bibliography Notes

[1] J.A. Estes, *The Blood-Horse*, April 24, 1937, p. 633.

[2] Ibid.

[3] J.A. Estes, *The Blood-Horse*, April 27, 1940, p. 644.

[4] J.A. Estes, *The Blood-Horse*, October 12, 1940, p. 503.

[5] Ibid.

[6] Ibid.

[7] Ibid, p. 504.

[8] J.A. Estes, *A Quarter Century of American Racing (The Blood-Horse)*, 1941, p. 26.

[9] Ibid.

[10] J.A. Estes, Thoroughbred Club of America, March 3, 1934, speech.

[11] Ibid.

[12] J.A. Estes, *The Blood-Horse*, May 21, 1938, p. 755.

[13] Ibid.

[14] Ibid.

[15] J.A. Estes, *The Blood-Horse*, May 4, 1940, p. 670.

[16] Ibid.

[17] J.A. Estes, *The Blood-Horse*, May 18, 1940, p. 727.

[18] Ibid, p. 727-728.

[19] Ibid.

[20] J.A. Estes, *The Blood-Horse*, December 1, 1940, p. 884.

[21] J.A. Estes, *The Blood-Horse*, December 21, 1940, p. 884-885.

[22] Ibid.

[23] Ibid.

[24] J.A. Estes, *The Blood-Horse*, December 27, 1941, p. 874.

[25] J.A. Estes, *The Blood-Horse*, October 7, 1950, p. 690.

26 J.A. Estes, *The Blood-Horse*, July 5, 1941, p. 8.

27 J.A. Estes, *The Blood-Horse*, March 30, 1957, p. 838.

28 J.A. Estes, *The Blood-Horse*, October 8, 1955, p. 821.

CHAPTER 5

The Humanist as a Thoroughbred breeder: Federico Tesio's work as a breeder and trainer

Attempting to assess in detail the principles of Federico Tesio as an owner, breeder and trainer is beyond the scope of this chapter, but an overview and critical assessment of Tesio's vision of the Thoroughbred and his approaches to the breeding of his stock are worthy of trial. Moreover, such an attempt is virtually required, because as John Hislop notes in the foreword to Tesio's book, *Breeding the Racehorse*, "When those of my generation come to be asked by their grandchildren: 'Who was the greatest breeder, the outstanding sire, the best racehorse of your time?' the answer will probably be: 'Tesio, Nearco, Ribot.'"

Clearly, Tesio is hard to pass over.

In looking at the work of Tesio, it is clear that he was neither a theorist working sums without a thought for the horses themselves nor a horseman who bred and trained horses without regard for ideas about what made some animals better than others. Rather, Tesio unified theoretical principles with practical horsemanship to an extent that is very rare in Thoroughbred breeding.

This is not to say, however, that there is a Tesio formula. There is not. For Tesio, as for all great breeders, there is a synthesis of thought with the practical matters of breeding.

Tesio brought many talents to bear on his approach to breeding. Partly he used his insight into the strengths and weaknesses of individuals and families, partly his observations on the most powerful lines and families in the stud book, partly his intuition about the matings and the training that would produce the most successful animals, and partly his luck.

Given the oddities of chance and the purely fortuitous outcome of some events, there is no question that Tesio is one of the luckiest men in history.

Even so, Tesio put a lot of the right chips on the table, so that, when the roll of the dice came his way, he succeeded at the highest level of international racing.

Making His Own Luck

Tesio's successes were not carved out with limitless wealth. He was, in comparison to the standards of most international Thoroughbred breeders, a relative pauper. Nor were the purses in Italy nearly rich enough to make a man rich as Croesus. His homeland, however, was where Tesio practiced the art and science of breeding and racing horses.

In his final book of essays, *I Have Landed*, the noted scientist and writer Stephen Jay Gould discussed the connection of art and science. He noted that a characteristic trait of men and women with great understanding and excellence was "the almost obsessive attention to meticulous and accurate detail" and declared that the arts and sciences "gain their union on the most palpable territory of concrete things."[1]

This assessment has a clear application to understanding Tesio. He was a man who was obsessed with the Thoroughbred, in the best and most enjoyable sense of an obsession. He was involved with his horses at every stage of their lives, from planning their conceptions, to rearing, racing, breeding, and buying – for generation after generation. They were his joy and his work and his reason for being.

From his Dormello stud in Italy, Tesio bred some of the greatest horses of the 20th century and most of the great horses of the Italian turf. And in addition to breeding his own stock, he trained them. Edward Spinola, in his introduction to Tesio's book, *Breeding the Racehorse*, recounted how Tesio assessed his racing stock as he prepared to venture abroad for international competition.

With regard to Nearco, Spinola wrote: "Tesio himself considered him the best horse he ever trained and gives us the following account of his trial before running in the Grand Prix de Paris, a trial which should be classed with those of The Tetrarch and of St. Simon among the famous trials of Thoroughbred history."[2] Tesio wanted to ascertain whether his unbeaten colt stayed well enough to win the Grand Prix de Paris at nearly two miles and tried the colt over the distance at San Siro.

"To run against Nearco, Tesio selected two other three-year-olds, Ursone and Bistolfi, both top horses. Ursone had run nine races over the distance, with seven wins and two seconds to his credit. Bistolfi instead was a sprinter – the best horse in Italy over 1500 metres – and accordingly it was arranged that he should tie in with Nearco and Ursone after the first 1400 metres. Nearco and Bistolfi were given 119 lbs. while Ursone was to carry 108 lbs."[3]

Nearco crushed them, with Bistolfi second and Ursone left far in arrears for lack of pace. Tesio then fearlessly ran Nearco in the Gran Premio di Milano and Grand Prix de Paris. After beating an extraordinary field in the latter race, Tesio sold Nearco to Martin Benson for 60,000 pounds, and the dark brown son of Pharos went to stud in England, where he altered the shape of international Thoroughbred breeding through the success of his sons and daughters.

Franco Varola, an internationally-recognized thinker and writer about the Thoroughbred, was quite familiar with Tesio and his way of doing things with his stock. And Varola relates a fascinating assessment of Tesio's attention to detail and minute care for his horses. In selecting matings, Tesio believed "in choosing the right sire for the right mare by practically applying his own impressions regarding the size, conformation, the temperament and the individuality, as a whole, of each animal."[4]

As a corollary to this approach, Tesio rarely kept a stallion at Dormello because having a home stallion tends to bias any breeder in favor of using that animal with his mares. Varola wrote in his 1969 article for *The British Racehorse* that the Second World War altered this policy for Tesio: ". . . the war period was bad for Dormello because it interrupted the normal business of sending broodmares to a foreign covering, and consequently it forced Tesio to do what he had never done before, that is, to resort to the use of domestic stallions.

"Niccolo dell'Arca, Bellini and Torbido stood in fact at Dormello for a few seasons until different circumstances made it possible to dispose of them elsewhere."[5] Varola also noted that the results of this unintended episode of homebreeding was quite profitable for Tesio, as the top-class horses Tenerani (later the sire of Ribot), Trevisana, and Antonio Canale resulted from Tesio's home use of his stallions.

Not surprisingly, however, both from this view of mating his stock and from the pressure of finances, Tesio sold his horses when it made sense, especially the colts. In fact, Varola declared that "To win the main classic races in Italy and to be able to sell his horses well at the end of the season, were always his [Tesio's] principal concerns." [6]

Despite the requirements of business and the practical management required to keep his operation working year to year, Tesio never lost his enjoyment of the horse. Rather, this combination of necessity and obsessive pleasure in the Thoroughbred allowed Tesio insights into the nature and composition of his stock that would have been denied anyone further removed from them. But the horses repaid his devotion, and they made him a leading trainer, owner and breeder in Italy with consistency.

This status and reward was not the result of one or two world-beating champions like Ribot or Nearco. They were the international-caliber best of the best. But year after year, Tesio bred and raced some of the best stock in his homeland.

For instance, in 1947, he trained the leading juvenile colt and filly in Italy, Naucide and Trevisana. The former was a half-brother to the unbeaten Nearco and the latter was by Nearco's and Naucide's half-brother, Niccolo dell'Arca. Tesio, as this evidence and much other suggests, built a large part of his breeding and training success on the quality of this family of racehorses.

Yet he acquired the family for almost nothing.

Tesio acquired Nogara's dam, the Spearmint mare Catnip, for only 75 guineas at the 1917 Newmarket December auction. Even though 1917 was a tough year for the bloodstock sales (World War I was not quite over), Tesio paid something less than the equivalent of $400 for the mare.

Moreover, Catnip was young, having been foaled in 1910 in England, was in foal to the high-class stallion Tracery, and her pedigree was quite good. Her sire had won the English Derby, and her dam had won the 1,000 Guineas at Newmarket. So how did Tesio get the mare so cheaply?

In addition to the political and economic uncertainties of the time, the mare's pedigree almost certainly was a factor in wilting English enthusiasm for retaining her. Catnip represented one of the best American female families, tracing back to Maiden, winner of the 1865 Travers and a daughter of Lexington.

This last consideration was not a point in favor for Catnip, as the Jersey Act had dropped a hammer on the registration of the descendants of Lexington or any other horses who couldn't prove themselves purely descended from stock tracing back to the *General Stud Book* of England. Lexington could not so prove his descent, and his stock were barred from the GSB, except in the case of those already registered.

If that sounds silly, just go with it. The Jersey Act never made any sense. It was political and economic at its base, and astute breeders such as Tesio and Marcel Boussac regularly ignored it to their immense credit.

Since Catnip had been registered prior to the Jersey Act, she was "pure," but to all purity-conscious breeders, she still had the taint of those American lines. And that, in all likelihood, is what kept more market-conscious English breeders sitting on their hands when she was in the ring and allowed Tesio to purchase one of the cornerstones of his international success for a pittance.

For Tesio, Catnip produced not only Nogara, who was a high-class racer and a major international success at stud, but also Nera di Bicci, whom Tesio considered the greatest racemare he ever bred. Nera di Bicci, by Tracery, was the foal Catnip was carrying when Tesio purchased her at Newmarket.

The man was lucky.

All in all, over a career that lasted more than 50 years, Tesio bred more good horses for less money than any breeder elsewhere. Without paying top prices, he sent his mares to classic-winning stallions, sold his best stallion prospects abroad, did not improve his balance sheet by keeping a home stallion, and raced only the produce of his own studs. So how did he succeed with this kind of program?

Putting the Pieces Together

The answer is as many-faceted as a glittering gem. From Tesio's own comments in *Breeding the Racehorse* and to other writers, several principles shine forth. These include breeding the best to the best, choosing horses for their athletic qualities, applying his training insights to the matings of his stock, keeping horses in as natural conditions as possible, and matching animals of complementary physical and mental qualities.

He came to these and other general conclusions over the span of his career, and he wrote that "I myself have rummaged through our libraries, experimented and studied."[7] In his own writings about breeding Thoroughbreds, as well as in his comments to others, Tesio was rather inclined to pose matters in paradox.

For instance, when discussing the importance of mares and stallions at stud, he wrote that "It would not be paradoxical to say that the dam of a popular stallion is a female who, through him, can produce many offspring in 11 months. In the same way the sire of a broodmare is a male who, in 11 months, produces one offspring only."[8]

So there is no question that Tesio looked at things, breeding and training the Thoroughbred especially, differently than other people tend to do. As part of his criteria in selecting breeding stock from his own racing stable, he was utterly determined to know which horses were the best. Varola remarks on Tesio's "willingness to sacrifice, if necessary, a half-dozen colts of national standing in order to select the top horse of the generation."[9] This is a practice that would not be accepted in many stables today, but since Tesio raced his own horses, his decisions resulted from a focus on goals for gaining clarity about the larger issues of quality and absolute ability in his horses.

There is not, I believe, much evidence to suggest that Tesio was merciless with his stock. But his aim was to select the best and toughest and most energetic and sound animals possible for his breeding program as a by-product of racing them. Clearly, Tesio did not think of his Thoroughbreds as delicate creations to be pampered. Their purpose was to race and to breed if selected, and his goal was to test them to the maximum.

For instance, the high-class filly Tofanella was not nominated to the Italian classics, and as a result, Varola wrote that "she had the task of pacemaker for Navarro in the Gran Premio di Milano and then won the Brown Ribbon at Munich."[10] Navarro turned out to be the best horse in Dormello's 1931 crop, winning the Premio d'Italia and the Gran Premio di Milano, and Tofanella played an effective role in the colt's victory in the latter race.

Varola wrote: "The fact, however, that Tesio was prepared to risk a horse of the caliber of Tofanella in order to secure a favourable pace in a great race which was to be won by another horse of the stable proves that Tesio had a genius also as a trainer, which is an aspect of his overall performance that should be thoroughly reconsidered in a general judgment of his horsemanship."[11]

If we accept Varola's assessments, then Tesio was a great breeder because he was a great trainer, and he was a trainer of importance because he was a thoughtful sociologist. He was a sociologist because he was a deeply learned historian of the Thoroughbred, and he was a historian who understood the breed because he was a sensitive and imaginative humanist. Tesio was successful and made a lasting mark on the international Thoroughbred not because he was one thing or did one thing. Instead, in a variety of roles, he showed a fluency in many endeavors that, taken together, aided him in understanding some significant elements of the breed and allowed him to synthesize this understanding into a marvelous life with the Thoroughbred.

Bibliography Notes

[1] Stephen Jay Gould, *I Have Landed*, Crown Publishing Group, 2002, p. 46-47.

[2] Edward Spinola, *Breeding the Racehorse*, J.A. Allen & Co., 1958, p. xii-xiii.

[3] Ibid, p. xiii.

[4] Federico Tesio, *Breeding the Racehorse*, J.A. Allen & Co.,1958, p. xi.

[5] Franco Varola, *The British Racehorse*, J.A. Allen & Co.,1969, p. 402.

[6] Ibid.

[7] Ibid, p. 6.

[8] Ibid, p. 10.

[9] Ibid, p. 403.

[10] Ibid.

[11] Ibid.

CHAPTER 6

Biomechanics and Mating

Horses have been central to the development of human civilization, and whether in war, work, or sport, the horse's contributions have made an enormous impact on how different cultures have succeeded and flourished.

Just consider how important horses have been in warfare. Without them, there are no chariots, no mounted knights in Western Europe, no battalions of cavalry for Napoleon or Wellington. Horses have also been necessary for the sport and entertainment of human beings over the centuries, and as modern warfare has kindly removed the horse from modern combat, the animals have become even more important for recreation and leisure sports this century. We have invented sports and games for ourselves and our horses, just as the Greeks, Assyrians and Romans and numerous other cultures.

Human beings take their horses very seriously, and the concept of measuring horses for one purpose or another, usually in an attempt to compare individuals of different times or regions, is really very old. At least by the time of the Greeks, men were trying to assess which horses were best by measurements. As for the proportions of architecture and the human shape in sculpture, the ancient Greeks determined what they regarded as the ideal proportions of the horse. Such concepts changed little over the next 2,000 years, so that ratios and proportions — the mathematics of the ancient Greeks — remained the basis for evaluating measurements of the horse through the late 19th and early 20th century.

America made little contribution to such studies prior to 1950, but in the past 30 years, computers and other scientific developments have become aids in this process of trying to find a measure of the champion.

Thoroughbred breeders and owners have long been trying to catch the elusive lightning in a bottle that determines a champion, and they have been among the leaders in measuring racehorses. Before the more entrepreneurial approaches to biomechanics came to the fore, the most prominent modern use of measurements on racehorses in the U.S. may have been in the annual measurements of leading horses done by Dr. Manuel Gilman in New York.

Gilman's interest in measuring stemmed from both an interest in racehorses and a background in veterinary science, and he hoped that the application of science to

Thoroughbreds would lead to more systematic ways of breeding or evaluating top individuals.

The later developments with measuring that have led to the application of biomechanics to breeding and assessment originated in the Quarter Horse business. The Trimble family of Oklahoma was one of the first to attempt a serious measurement approach to racing stock, and they were the first to use mare and stallion measurements and the computer to predict the potential success of a mating. They established Computer Horse Breeders Inc., which originally concentrated on Quarter Horses but later extended this work to Thoroughbreds. Cecil Seaman was probably the first among the Trimble offshoots to concentrate on the Thoroughbred.

A variety of people attempted to use measuring as a tool to grade horses or mate them, but not until researchers began developing a database of measurements that could be tested on control groups and then used to assess individuals in training or breeding prospects did the measuring of horses reach a solid scientific footing.

Other people also have worked with the horse's physique to produce models or approaches to assessing the animals' likelihood of success. Among these is Jeff Seder, who developed Equine Biomechanics and Exercise Physiology, Inc. (EQB) and took equine measuring in a somewhat different direction to assess the heart and stride motion of the Thoroughbred racehorse.

Of these entrepreneurs, EQB is responsible for a considerable body of published scientific research on equine biomechanics and exercise physiology. Seder noted that "our work is the result of a team of professors, veterinarians, trainers, biomechanists, and engineers [working together] over 20 years."

Equix Biomechanics, whose technology was developed by Paul Mostert after leaving the Trimbles, became possibly the largest bloodstock advisory service in the late 1990s, prior to the dissolution of the partnership that owned the company. The photo accompanying the measurement tables was provided by Data Track International LLC, which has taken biomechanical analysis to the next level by utilizing digital video technology to improve the accuracy of measurements by eliminating variables which can exist with hand measurements that can vary from human to human. The technology is used for measuring horses at rest, as in the photo, as well as at the two-year-old in training sales and at the races. The company is headed by Robert Fierro, former president of Equix Biomechanics, and Jay Kilgore, formerly director of racing at the same company.

As a result of publications and repeated successes from these researchers, biomechanics has become a well-accepted and highly promising method for breeders and buyers to use with their stock. Biomechanics, heart scans, and gait analysis don't guarantee that a horse will be a success on the track or at stud, but these guides help to trim the probabilities so that owners can put resources to work with the more likely candidates for success.

Purpose

The goals of biomechanical analysis are relatively straightforward. It seeks to quantify what good horsemen see and understand intuitively and then to unify their intuition with sound principles of mechanics.

Some of the great horsemen in history seem to have had an intuitive sense of biomechanics, or at least of some of the larger principles behind it, and they succeeded out of all proportion to their opportunity. Much has been made, for instance, of the number of photographs that Federico Tesio had of the great horses of history and the great value he placed in understanding form and function in the racehorse.

This, in my estimation, is an example of an intuitive understanding of biomechanical principles. Tesio understood many things about what the racehorse did and how its legs and shape functioned to make it faster, even if he wasn't using intense mathematical models and formulae.

Tesio, in looking at the horse, was apparently looking for certain traits, even if the horse was faulty in other ways. In his book *Breeding the Racehorse*, Tesio hints about understanding various elements of the Thoroughbred, although he never gives away too much that his competitors could use, unless you count nervous energy.

But even then, I suspect that, had Tesio given away a tip or three, others' results would not likely have matched his own. From my perception of his writing and understanding, Tesio was looking at the Thoroughbred as the result of several systems working in harmony, and the presence of one or two is not enough to make the whole.

Perhaps biomechanics, by systemizing the understanding of these systems, can render a benefit to breeding and the Thoroughbred in general by passing along insights that later horsemen can capitalize on.

The benefit of biomechanics to the horse industry, however, is not only in the preservation of data about which horses are best-suited for racing or breeding. It helps to point out some outstanding breeding stock so that earlier and better use can be made of them. And probably the greatest advantage to using biomechanics is that it offers owners and breeders a way to understand their horses' conformation and likely racing and breeding aptitudes without spending 20 years on the farm learning what makes a good horse run.

Allowing owners to have these insights into their horses is a positive thing for the industry because most owners do not have the time or the training to look at horses with the eye of a trainer or farm owner or long-time breeder. And anything that makes an owner more comfortable in his decisions and helps to make his operation more profitable is good for the horse business in the long run.

How it works

As methods of measuring horses have developed, three distinct areas have received the most attention for analysis. First, there is the static analysis of the various measurements of the horse's body. This is what most people think of when biomechanics is mentioned, and it involves measurement of various parts of the horse while standing and then the analysis of those measurements to assess the athletic potential of the horse or to simulate a mating.

The second type of measuring is dynamic measurement of the horse's motion. The measurements of stride length and gait or motion analysis permit investigation into how the parts of the horse work together when it is running at speed.

And finally, the analysis of cardiac function and capacity by means of ultrasound scans allows for predictions about how this important system will function to aid the racer in its intended job on the racetrack.

Biomechanics is literally the field of applied mathematics concerned with the motion of living things, and this niche in the vast world of mathematics has found its greatest object of interest in the mechanics of biological entities (humans and animals). Understanding the laws of mechanics especially has helped golf and tennis enthusiasts, as well as those in some other professional sports, including baseball and football.

As applied to horses, biomechanics uses mathematical formulae to calculate the weight and stride of horses and to gauge a horse's power, or ability to move itself, over a distance of ground.

To this highly complex mathematical field have come numerous researchers, bringing experience in complex math and its theory, as well as an interest in horses, to bear on the endlessly fascinating puzzle of how one horse is able to run faster than his contemporaries.

To resolve these questions, one process widely in use begins with three dozen measurements of the horse, along with conformation assessments, to begin to compute the biomechanical qualities of a racehorse. The program assesses three principal components of the racehorse: stride, weight, and power or leverage. Measurements of the legs, shoulders, back, and hip are primarily responsible for determining the horse's stride. Girth and body length are the primary components of weight, and the length, muscularity, and angulation of the hind limbs are responsible for generating the power necessary to make a horse run fast.

Stride is a primary characteristic to assess because, as every horseman knows, stride length is important to a racehorse's potential for success. For instance, if horses of otherwise equal ability and biomechanics run even a moderate distance, the horse with the longer stride will be at a significant advantage over one with a shorter stride.

So stride is very important. But stride alone is not an absolute. The quicker-striding horse, for example, can overcome the stride-length disadvantage for relatively short distances. The racehorse (or any other performance horse, for that matter) achieves success because a variety of different systems work together effectively.

The efficiency of the stride has an enormous impact on an animal's success or lack of success. The mechanics of stride are complicated, but their effect is relatively obvious. The horse with the smooth, flowing stride tends to be efficient. The efficient horse, if versatile enough, may be able to do many things with ease. The statement, "He won easy," frequently heard from trainers or jockeys of top horses, is not a simplification. The top horse does everything easily because of the length and efficiency of his stride.

The versatile horse is typically capable of changing gears smoothly, moving through traffic, handling different surfaces and conditions, and adapting to different strategies and circumstances in a race.

SAMPLE MEASUREMENT DIAGRAM

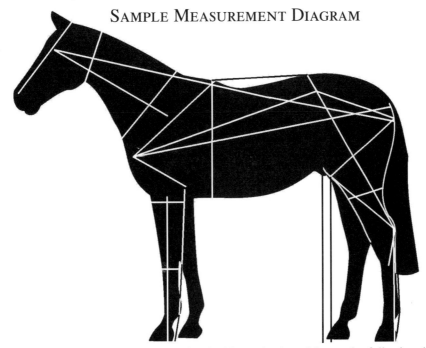

Lines indicate the measurement points for the biomechanics tables on the following three pages.

FULL MEASUREMENTS - STALLIONS

	MR. PROSPECTOR	SEATTLE SLEW	SECRETARIAT	SMILE	FAPPIANO
Flank	41.75	43	44	43.25	43.75
Height	67	68.25	69.5	65.625	70.5
Heart Girth	75.5	78	78.5	73.5	79
Length	91.5	92.75	92.25	88	93
Body Length	67	67.75	67.5	65	68.5
Front Legs	34	33.5	35.25	33	35
Back Pastern	6	6	6	6	6
Front Pastern	6.5	5.75	6	6.125	6.25
Hip to Hock	51.25	52.5	53.75	52.5	53.75
Back Cannon	18	18.5	18.25	18.5	19
Ilium	26.75	26.125	26.5	26.25	27.25
Tuber Calcis	6	6.5	6.25	6.25	6.5
Gaskin	19	19	19.5	18.25	19.5
Tibia	26.75	26.125	26.5	25.75	27.25
Femur	26.75	26.125	26.5	26	27.25
Between Eyes	8	8	8	8	8
Head Length	21.75	22	22	22.125	22
Neck Circ	54	53	56	49.5	50
Neck Length	31.5	31	32	29.5	31.25
Throat Latch	31.5	32	33	33.5	31.5
Shoulders	26	25.5	26	26.375	27
Shld to Hip	44.5	48	44.5	45	47.25
Shld to Withers	29.5	30	30	27.25	31.25
Stifle	38.25	39.75	40	39.5	40
Forearm	26	25.75	27.5	25.875	26
Back	27.5	27.5	27.5	26.5	28
Back to Hip	27.25	27.75	27.5	26.5	28.5
Front Cannon	13.25	12.75	13.5	13.625	13.5
Hind Cannon to Ground	24	24.25	24.5	24.5	25
Humerus	18	18	17.75	19	20.5
Humerus Radius	17.5	18	18	17.25	17.5
Front Cannon Circ	8.5	8.75	8.5	8	8.5
Elbow to Ground	36.75	36.75	38	37	38
Elbow to Ankle	31.25	30.125	32	31	32
Elbow to Withers	30.25	31.5	31	28.625	32.5

	HALO	IN REALITY	RAISE A NATIVE	ROBERTO
Flank	41	41	42	42.5
Height	66.5	66	68	68
Heart Girth	76.5	75	77.25	79.25
Length	88	87.75	91.25	90
Body Length	65.5	65.75	68.5	67.5
Front Legs	33	32.75	34	34
Back Pastern	6	6	6	6
Front Pastern	6	5.75	6	6.125
Hip to Hock	51.5	51.25	52.5	53
Back Cannon	18.5	18	19	19
Ilium	26.25	26.5	26.5	27.25
Tuber Calcis	6.5	6.25	6.5	6.5
Gaskin	19	18.25	20	19.75
Tibia	26.25	26.5	27	27.25
Femur	26.25	26.5	26.5	27.25
Between Eyes	8	8	8	8
Head Length	0	22	22	22
Neck Circ	51.5	50	53	56.5
Neck Length	31.25	30.75	30.75	32
Throat Latch	32	30.5	32	32
Shoulders	26.25	26	26.75	28.5
Shld to Hip	44.5	45	45.5	44.5
Shld to Withers	29.5	28	30.5	31
Stifle	37.5	37.5	39.75	39.25
Forearm	26.25	25.25	27.5	26.75
Back	26.75	26.5	27.5	27
Back to Hip	27	27	27.25	26.75
Front Cannon	12.75	12.5	13.5	13.25
Hind Cannon to Ground	24.125	24	25	24.75
Humerus	17.5	17	17.5	18
Humerus Radius	17.25	18	17.5	17.75
Front Cannon Circ	0	8.25	9	8.75
Elbow to Ground	36.5	36.5	37	37.5
Elbow to Ankle	30.5	30.75	31	31.375
Elbow to Withers	30.75	29.5	30.75	30.75

Full Measurements - Mares

	LADY'S SECRET	DAVONA DALE	FLAWLESSLY	HEAVENLY CAUSE	GLORIOUS SONG
Flank	42.625	42	42.5	43.375	39.75
Height	65.375	69	69.25	70.75	65.25
Heart Girth	73	80.75	79.25	81	77.125
Length	86.5	92.75	94	94	88
Body Length	63.5	68.5	68	68.375	65.375
Front Legs	33.875	34.25	34.5	34.75	32
Back Pastern	6	6	6	6.75	6
Front Pastern	6	6	6.25	6.875	6
Hip to Hock	52.375	54	53.75	55.875	53
Back Cannon	17.75	19.375	19.25	19.25	18.5
Ilium	25.25	26	27.5	26	25.75
Tuber Calcis	6.5	7.25	7	6.75	6
Gaskin	18.5	18.25	19	19	18.5
Tibia	25.25	26	27.75	26	25.75
Femur	25	26	27.5	26	25.75
Between Eyes	7.75	8.25	8.25	9	7.5
Head Length	22	22	22	24	21.5
Neck Circ	49	50	49	55.75	52.5
Neck Length	30	33	32.75	31.5	30.5
Throat Latch	31.5	33	32	35.5	31.75
Shoulders	25.375	27	27	25.5	27
Shld to Hip	44	46	46	46	44
Shld to Withers	28	30	30.75	30.125	28
Stifle	38.625	40	40.5	41	37.25
Forearm	25	27	27	26.625	26.75
Back	26.25	27.875	28	28.5	26.25
Back to Hip	26	27.875	28	28.5	26.625
Front Cannon	12.625	13.75	14	13.25	12.625
Hind Cannon to Ground	23.75	25.375	25.25	26	24
Humerus	17.375	18.625	18.75	18.25	18.875
Humerus Radius	17.25	17.75	18	18.25	17.5
Front Cannon Circ	7.75	8.75	8.25	8.75	8.25
Elbow to Ground	35.25	37	38.25	38.5	35.75
Elbow to Ankle	29.25	31	32	31.625	29.75
Elbow to Withers	29.875	32.25	32.5	32.125	30

There is value to distinguishing between versatility and efficiency. The efficient horse uses less energy than most horses when running at its most effective speed. But the ability to adapt to different conditions and still remain relatively efficient illustrates versatility.

Therefore, even within the elite subset of horses who have efficient action, some are better racers than others. Horses such as Foolish Pleasure or more recently, Fusaichi Pegasus, have shown the ability to cope with differing conditions and distances and succeed because they are versatile.

In addition to versatility and efficiency, other characteristics have an influence on the level of success that a racehorse attains. Oftentimes, this has to do with weight. A horse who is relatively light in weight has some advantages on the racecourse, while the horse who is too heavy has none.

If a horse is very efficient but underweight somewhat, it has the advantage of less weight to lug around the track. If a trainer flinches when his horse has two or three pounds added after a victory in a handicap, what would he say if he could drop 30 or 50 pounds in body weight and still have as good a horse.

The disadvantage for underweight horses is that they don't have as much fuel to keep their bodies running. A racehorse runs on the fuel he carries in his muscles, and a big, strong horse such as Secretariat packs a mighty load of energy along with him. By contrast, a horse like Prairie Bayou, winner of 1993 Preakness, or Horse of the Year John Henry carries a lighter load.

The latter pair were pretty good horses; so being relatively light weight in terms of biomechanics isn't a bad thing. If a horse is too light in weight relative to its natural stride and power, however, it never has enough energy to carry through with the full potential of its mechanics. This is one of the most common problems with racing stock. But the relatively light horse who has an efficient stride doesn't need as much energy or power to carry him around the course as do most horses.

These horses are the sort who frequently take some time to get into their best stride and rarely burst out of the gate like a sprinter. Instead these horses keep up a steady pace, and once they are in motion, they can keep on going in similar fashion and at a similar pace for a long time. Efficiency and a smooth stride rhythm make these horses successful. Horses of this type tend to do well at distance racing, as well as racing on turf.

When in a hard race with a horse of equal efficiency and stride but a better balance of weight (and therefore more fuel), however, these lighter horses typically come up short. The horse with the better balance of weight is able to reach down and expend a little more energy. As a result, the truly balanced horse has more finishing pace, and it will normally prevail over the equal horse who has lighter weight relative to power and stride.

By contrast, the horse with extra weight — weight that is out of proportion to its stride length and power — has few prospects as a racehorse. The heavy horse has the most common fault in racing, a bad case of the slows, and the more extreme examples are simply too heavy to go fast enough for anything.

As with the lighter horse, however, a horse who is only a little overweight has some compensations. He has extra fuel, if his weight comes from muscle rather than bone. Naturally, the horses of this type that succeed do so at sprint distances. And they are the opposite of the lightweight horses in type and racing style. They come out of the gate blazing and keep after it until their weight overcomes their extra energy. With most heavy horses, they are unable to keep up the exertions necessary for success in racing even at six furlongs, which is the shortest distance frequently raced in the U.S.

Some horses who are too heavy, as well as many who are too light, are relatively obvious to the eyes of experienced horsemen. But in both cases, it is not the exact poundage that is the problem with the horse's chances of success at the track; it is the proportion of weight to its stride length and power.

When horses get out of balance, their ability to run fast may be seriously compromised, and having power that is out of proportion to a horse's stride or weight is as much a problem as the other factors getting out of synch. But if the horse with more stride length, more power, or less weight has several factors in the right proportions, it can be very effective. For instance, as a running machine, horses with more power or stride or less weight can be superior. Secretariat, for instance, was phenotyped as an S1 (a larger stride factor). Riva Ridge was an S3 (an extreme length of stride in proportion to weight and power), and plenty of champions and classic winners have been light of weight or very powerful (again in proportion to their other factors).

The ability of a horse in motion to accelerate comes from the muscle and leverage in its hindquarters. The forelegs function almost exclusively as spokes in a wheel that keep the animal in motion but add very little to the forward force. The angulation of the bones in the hindquarters, as well as their relative lengths, provides the lever, and the muscles behind provide the spring that puts the horse in motion and allows him to accelerate.

A runner without much of a hindquarter isn't likely to have much early speed. Most of the horses who are light behind are underpowered, but some are very well-balanced, except for having little muscle. These horses can succeed due to the rhythm of their stride, rather than the force of propulsion. As this suggests, some horses with light quarters can run well over long distances if their other factors are all in good order. These are the types of horses that tend to make pure stayers, and one of the reasons, I believe, that stayers have such a bad reputation as sires is this circumstance of having a relatively light hindquarter. It works for them, but trying to reproduce it with some consistency is very hard to do.

From the standpoint of a practical horse breeder, the problem is that power is relatively easy to reproduce but efficiency of motion is very difficult. The effective stayer is virtually always the horse that has great efficiency of motion if he runs primarily on rhythm. That type of horse seldom is able to pass on his ability (exact biomechanical shape and proportions) to his progeny.

On the other hand, the racehorse with a heavy quarter will tend to be overpowered. Such a horse would have more than enough early speed, but it will not have much staying power. And particularly as it ages, the overpowered horse can be hard on itself. If the animal has any faults in stride or conformation, it will literally pound itself into the track, and this causes injury and soreness.

Photo Courtesy of Del Hancock
Although beautifully balanced in physique, Secretariat had greater biomechanical advantage in stride and power.

These three factors then — stride length, body weight, and power — are the basis for analyzing the biomechanics of any racehorse. Their balance produces the greatest chance for the horse's success at its level of ability, and moderate shifts of proportion can sometimes benefit a horse for performing in a particular aptitude.

For instance, Secretariat was a beautifully balanced animal. Although he was big all over, his stride and power were even bigger (in proportion) than his weight. As a result, and in direct conflict with the way that most people interpreted his pedigree, Secretariat performed at his best when he was allowed to use his stride to greatest benefit.

In the Kentucky Derby of 1973, he broke very well but did not waste energy trying to burn up the track against Shecky Greene and the other speed types in the class at Churchill Downs. By the time he had rounded onto the backstretch, however, the great chestnut son of Bold Ruler was getting into his best stride under the quiet handling of Ron Turcotte, and Secretariat began picking up his rivals one and two at a time.

From tape replays of the race, Secretariat is clearly moving much faster than many of his competition. They already had burned up their energy load and were looking for the gap. Others, however, were not in such difficult circumstances, and as Secretariat moved around the final turn, he came near some really good horses from this exceptional crop. He passed future Horse of the Year Forego, Bluegrass Stakes winner Our Native, and finally Sham.

Through the stretch, only Sham was able to make a race of it with the champion, but Secretariat's greater stride and energy enabled him to keep up his momentum all the way as he broke the track and stakes record that had been set nine years earlier by Northern Dancer.

That exceptional effort showed one dimension of Secretariat's ability. He could drop far off a strong pace and then overwhelm his opponents with a powerful, sustained move. This was the racing style of his juvenile season, when most of his opponents were actually sprinters, and it was far wiser for him to conserve his energy and make a single strong effort.

In the Preakness and Belmont, as he had shown in the Gotham Stakes earlier in the year, Secretariat was at his most supreme when he was able to take the game to his opposition early and simply gallop them to death. The enormous leap that Secretariat made in the Preakness as they were coming onto the backstretch shows what power the horse had. When he put that big hindquarter into top gear, Secretariat had devastating power. And he could keep the powerful stroke of his stride going for furlong after furlong because he had the energy available in his massive muscles and the cardiovascular size and quality to keep his muscles as well supplied with oxygen as possible.

All these factors were interconnected in making Secretariat the racehorse that he was. And all these factors were necessary to make Secretariat the great racehorse that he was.

What would Secretariat have been like without all these different elements all working in harmony? Just look at his offspring, and there we find the answer.

Secretariat was so specialized that any significant change caused the foal to be less than its sire. In effect, Secretariat was nearly perfect. And we can reproduce perfection by cloning it (presumably) but not by changing it.

The most reasonable and consistent explanation of why Secretariat as a stallion didn't succeed to the degree he did as a racehorse is that he was a highly specialized horse, and in the highly complex process of finding mates for him, very few mares that were available to him in the upper ranks of the broodmare population of the time suited him.

There were plenty who suited him on racing ability, as top-tier racemares themselves, or on their proven ability as superior producers. But with so few mares similar to him in type and aptitude, most of his mates were not type to type in terms of their biomechanics, and mating across types is a less predictable way of breeding horses. The probabilities for change or variance are significantly greater in mating different phenotypes, and the chances for actually producing the animal that is the goal of the mating is much less.

Looking backward biomechanically, Secretariat broke the records, and the best chance of reproducing him would have required breaking the mold by using extreme inbreeding. Few serious breeders in Kentucky or anywhere else (excepting Marcel Boussac) would have sent the mares to Secretariat that might have given him the greatest chance of reproducing himself biomechanically. The daughters of Bold Ruler who won at a mile or more, the daughters of Secretariat's grandsire Nasrullah, and Secretariat's own daughters might have been the most likely candidates to have fit the great chestnut biomechanically. In addition, the daughters of Bold Lad, also a son of Bold Ruler out of top Princequillo mare, might have carried enough of Secretariat's own special qualities to have produced some outstanding foals.

Alternatively, since there was more than a trace of offset knees in the Bold Ruler clan, mating Secretariat back to some of the family members might have been total disaster.

Without the benefit of hindsight or of biomechanical studies, Secretariat did pretty well as a sire. He came very close to reproducing himself in Risen Star, who had biomechanical traits almost identical to his sire. Secretariat's daughters have been outstanding broodmares, with Weekend Surprise producing Horse of the Year A.P. Indy and Preakness winner Summer Squall and Terlingua producing the world's current leading commercial sire in Storm Cat.

Horses with Secretariat's highly individual mechanics frequently need this extra generation to "come back" to the general population of the breed in biomechanical traits. Frequently their first-generation offspring (usually fillies in Thoroughbreds due to the intense pressure for

Photo Courtesy of Photos by Z

Secretariat's daughter Weekend Surprise is the dam of A.P. Indy and Summer Squall.

success among colts) aren't as successful on the racetrack as expected, but are retained for breeding. Then the stallion's second-generation descendants through his daughters do better than expected and earn their grandsire a reputation as a broodmare sire.

One of Secretariat's contemporaries who did not need to breed back toward the norm of the breed was Mr. Prospector. Compared to Secretariat, Mr. Prospector wasn't a great racehorse. Compared to the breed averages and expectations, however, he was an outstanding animal. He had immense speed, he could carry it a fair distance, and he was a very willing and competitive racer.

Photo Courtesy of Photos by Z

Mr. Prospector's balance of stride, weight and power made him compatible with a wide variety of broodmares, even though his performance on the racetrack emphasized only speed. His sons continue to be influential in Thoroughbred breeding.

Mr. Prospector had a better balance of stride, weight, and power than most horses, and as a result, he was more compatible with a wider variety of mares than more specialized stallions. He possessed the biomechanically balanced phenotype which is the phenotype of most of the superior stallions in the breed. The biomechanically balanced type allows for more range of variation that still falls within the bounds of a generally good mechanical structure for racing. This circumstance is a great help to any stallion, no matter what level of success he has at passing on desirable traits. For Mr. Prospector, fitting well with such a wide variety of mares helped him to become one of the great stallions of the end of the 20th century, and his sons are setting themselves up as the next great wave of influence in breeding for the present century.

Motion analysis

Obviously, the balance and efficiency of a horse's mechanics have a great deal to do with how it moves, but conformation, training, and some health issues also are major contributors to a horse's way of going. Many of the best selectors of two-year-olds in training have trained their eyes to such an extent that they can evaluate horses, see faults, and estimate how a horse will cope with the added stresses of running longer distances against competition.

The best selectors of juveniles have refined the inquiry to such a degree that they are dictating not only which horses and types of horses bring big money at the sales of two-year-olds in training but also are the driving force in the yearling markets where many of the eventual two-year-olds in training are purchased.

For buyers of two-year-olds who are looking for an additional measure of success in picking good prospects, researchers have developed motion analysis for horses. In selecting two-year-olds and other racing prospects for its clients, EQB, for instance "works from slow-motion films digitized for analysis based on the biomechanics of quadruped locomotion." EQB uses the slow-motion analysis to help predict above-average performance in the racehorse and to cull those that appear too inefficient or too likely to have soundness problems. To make their analysis, EQB's team of specialists look at "stride length, way of going, energy expended, angles of legs, shoulder, neck and joint positions, hoof flight patterns" and other criteria that can affect how a horse succeeds or fails on the track.

They then apply their results to a very large database using a multivariant discriminate analysis that allows EQB to put the data into a context with other racehorses and select those with the greatest probability to succeed.

One way that EQB puts its data to work is in analyzing fatigue under racing conditions. Over the past 15 years, EQB has "studied the first few races of many thousands of two-year-old Thoroughbred racehorses" and has developed logarithmic fatigue curves as a "significant predictor of subsequent stakes performance."

The company's founder and president, Jeff Seder, noted that "our starting theory was that by observing two-year-old Thoroughbreds in their first few races (almost always a short distance), we could establish a signature decay rate function for each horse, and then extrapolate that to predict their race times at classic distances later in life, i.e., develop a technique to more reliably predict major stakes capacity before it could otherwise be generally known using any traditional evaluation criteria, for example, pedigree."

The fatigue curve analysis has proven very successful for EQB. They do not use it as a stand-alone tool, however. In their assessments, they use fatigue, a value for energy expended in the race, maximum velocity, and the actual or estimated time for various distances.

Fatigue is a very important factor to evaluate in motion analysis, as EQB has shown with its studies and its success in advising clients. One reason for this is that fatigue is the end result of such things as biomechanical inefficiency, poor conformation, and ineffective action.

When done with care and precision, the research into motion analysis can identify the same factors that the best sales agents are looking for. These elements of motion include the way the horse reaches out with its legs, how it pushes off, and how it lands. Analysis also shows wasted motion and even negative motion, actions that actually hinder a horse from going fast.

Obviously, if a horse has a really stumpy, choppy action, it isn't going to make much of a racehorse. It will probably break itself down before it gets to the gate if its action is that rough. But slow-motion analysis — and especially frame-by-frame tracking of the horse's motion — allows researchers to see some unexpected faults in more subtle aspects of a horse's stride. These can come at many points in the stride, and a number of them involve the front legs, which don't otherwise have much of a role in the horse's momentum.

In fact, the front legs can even work against a horse's forward motion. If the hoof isn't striking at the proper time, it causes problems with the stride. For instance, if the foot is hitting the ground early, it is actually functioning as a brake — jamming into the track, slowing the horse, and putting extraordinary stress on the foreleg joints. If this is happening as the horse tires, as would usually be the case, the damage potential for the horse is immense, as this braking action is compounded by muscle fatigue and roughened action.

This is just one of the many "little things" that go into making a racehorse a winner or a loser, and motion analysis has been an important breakthrough in helping owners to choose which prospects are the brightest for their stables.

The cardiovascular component

The third element in biomechanical evaluations of the past 20 years or so is cardiovascular analysis. Once again, EQB has done extensive research into hearts over the past couple of decades, and the results have shown some interesting correlations.

EQB has done quite literally thousands of echocardiographs on horses' hearts in the past decade and a half. This has resulted in a database of more than 15,000 horses that the firm has carefully maintained with race records and earnings through at least the three-year-old season.

To assess this mountain of data, Seder and his associates used multivariant discriminate analysis of the multiple factors involved to predict the racing success of horses. If this sounds rather more complicated than brushing your teeth while standing on your head, rest assured that it is.

Multivariant analysis takes a number of variables and uses high-powered computing programs to process these multivariant databases into complex polynomial functions. The outcome is that the EQB team can compare their horses with other horses of the same age and size to get a comparison and prediction of future racing success using their technical information.

In 2003, EQB came out with a heavily scrutinized study of heart size and its correlation to function in the Thoroughbred. Dr. Frederick Fregin, director of the Marion duPont Scott Equine Medical Center, complimented the strictly controlled nature of the study and its size, as well.

The study, conducted over a six-year period from 1995 through 2000, included more than 7,000 horses. Seder said that, "Our study controlled variables by sex, age, and weight – no study has ever done that with such a large sample size. Past models were poor at best. The data was just not there, and the database sample sizes were just too small to make any real claims." EQB gathered data for its study at race tracks, as well as farms and auctions. They took two-dimensional echocardiograms as part of pre-purchase evaluations of Thoroughbreds offered for sale as potential racehorses at U.S. and European auctions and on private farms. The data was collected and correlated to pedigree, conformation, and subsequent racing performance results.

TABLE 1 - MEAN STANDARDIZED SCORES
LOW VS. HIGH EARNERS

Variables	Earnings Per Start ≤ $2,000	Earnings Per Start ≥ $10,000
	($n \geq 1061$)	($n \geq 418$)
LVD	45.93	53.12
LVS	46.45	52.72
SW	46.22	53.29

Means of High vs. Low Earners. Three of the heart measurements EQB made with ultrasound were the size of the left ventricle in diastole (LVD - when the heart expands to fill with blood), the size of the left ventricle in systole (LVS - when the heart contracts), and the thickness of the interventricular septal wall (SW). All of the measurements were taken before horses ever raced. A standardized score was calculated for each measurement, answering the question: This heart measurement was bigger than what percentage of other measurements among horses of the same age, sex, and physical size? Thus, the measurements were standardized for age, sex, and physical size. The average standardized scores of high and low earners are summarized in Table 1. All of the differences were statistically significant ($P \leq 0.0001$).

"We learned that larger horses generally had larger hearts regardless of their racetrack results. And we learned that the definition of what were good heart measurements was especially sensitive to the sex and to the chronological age in the number of days," said Charles Vickery, who assisted Seder in the statistical analysis. "So we put a tight grip on those variables and only compared horses that were on the same playing field in every way, so to speak. In the end, the normalized data showed a strong and simple relationship between the two things we were left with – heart measurements and subsequent racing performance." The study also came to some other interesting and potentially significant findings for breeders and owners.

Other statistically significant conclusions were that heart size was a significant indicator of ability at any distance, that horses at the Keeneland select yearling sales (July and the first two days of September) had consistently larger hearts than horses at other American sales year after year, that the average heart size showed a correlation to the average sale price at each auction, and that certain sires and dams consistently produced offspring with a specific type of heart.

These conclusions should be of great interest to breeders, as they indicate that pedigree does play a role, not only in determining heart size and therefore its contribution to the racing athlete but also that selectively determined "better bred" stock also yield better hearts than less select stock.

Applications of biomechanics to matings

Type to type

These are the three primary components of biomechanical study, and their first use is to select racing prospects who have the greatest probability of success on the track. But it takes no great leap of imagination to see how the conclusions drawn from these biomechanical studies can be applied to mating horses more successfully.

The specific study of biomechanics is the animal itself, and that is the soundest starting point in beginning a mating. Then considerations of pedigree, racing character, constitution, and so forth naturally follow and can provide a rounded view of the prospects of any mating.

Regardless of whether a breeder is using biomechanical analysis as a primary tool, the mating with the highest likelihood of reproducing the individual's characteristics is a type-to-type mating. When a breeder is able to use a type-to-type mating, this is the path of least resistance because there is really very little or no change necessary to produce a good horse, providing the breeder starts with good individuals. Type to type is the simplest and surest way to success.

The reason that mating like types is more successful is that these matings reduce genetic variation. They work to produce a homogenous physical type, and some breeders with a very sensitive eye for type and physique have managed to produce a particular type of horse in the course of their breeding programs.

For instance, Col. E.R. Bradley owned Idle Hour Farm outside of Lexington, Ky., on Old Frankfort Pike, and at this nursery he bred some of the best racehorses in America during the early to middle part of the 20th century. Furthermore, Bradley liked a certain type of horse. He wanted a neat, medium-sized, very well-balanced, sturdy animal who showed speed and did not show faults of temperament in its training and racing. As a gambler, he had a close personal understanding of probability, and this type of racehorse recommended itself to him as the most reliable animal to carry his money.

The Bradley type can be seen in photos of Black Toney, Bimelech, Blue Larkspur, and numerous other top racers and producers at stud. Bradley used these concepts of type and bred many of the most exciting horses of his time. Among his best stock, he bred and raced four winners of the Kentucky Derby, as well as a pair of even better colts who did not win the classic in Blue Larkspur and Bimelech.

The latter was about the last top colt that Bradley bred. Coming from the tiny last crop of his sire, Black Toney, Bimelech is also the best son of the great broodmare La Troienne. As an individual, Bimelech was exceptional. A strong and precocious two-year-old, Bimelech was unbeaten as a juvenile, and at the end of the season, Bradley's confidence in the colt was so high that he offered to match him against the top older horses, Kayak or Challedon, at weight for age. Considering the amount of weight that a two-year-old would have received from his elders, the other horses' connections declined the challenge.

Photo Courtesy of Keeneland Library, Meadors Collection

Bimelech, a son of Black Toney and La Troienne, was E.R. Bradley's "type." Well balanced and fast, he was one of the best classic colts of the 1940's.

Bimelech grew from his juvenile height of 15.2 to 16.1 as a three-year-old, when he swept the Preakness and Belmont Stakes but lost the Kentucky Derby and the possible Triple Crown which could have sealed his breeder's record of success. An outstanding colt, Bimelech had scope and quality. He was very well-balanced, with a deep, well-sloped shoulder and good length in his neck. He had good length through the body and a good hindquarter. Although on the top end of middle-sized, Bimelech was handy enough to make a very effective two-year-old and grew up to be one of the best classic colts of the 1940s, when a supreme colt came along nearly every year as seen with Triple Crown winners Whirlaway, Assault, Count Fleet, and Citation.

When Bradley died in 1946, his Thoroughbreds were sold by his executors to a group that split up the stock among themselves. The members of this syndicate were Ogden Phipps, Greentree Stable, and King Ranch. A two-year-old at that time was a Blue Larkspur filly named But Why Not, who went to King Ranch. A smallish filly like her dam and second dam, Bimelech's full sister Black Helen, But Why Not won the Acorn, Alabama, and Beldame, as well as the Arlington Classic, in which she defeated colts.

It's tough to find a flaw in But Why Not's conformation. She won the Arlington Classic and other races for King Ranch,

She was Bradley's type of filly, and the *Daily Racing Form* described her as "the beau-ideal of a race mare. The remarkable family that Colonel Bradley bred up from Black Toney has been noted for its individual elegance, while Sickle, sire of her dam, was an exquisite little horse. A whole-colored, rich dark bay, it is difficult to pick a flaw in her conformation. She has a very fine head and neck, which she carries with great animation, her bodily length is exceptional, but her coupling smooth and firm, her middle piece is excellent, shoulders and quarter admirably modeled, limbs slim and deerlike but of the best."

This level of consistency is one that discerning breeders can develop over decades of trial and error, rigorously culling those individuals who don't possess the desired traits and using only the best examples to breed on for the next generation. With Bradley's program at Idle Hour, he had immense capital resources, and he enjoyed his sport enough to spend decades working on the American classic type of horse who could run well early, show speed, and still develop at three into classic material.

Northern Dancer is a Type I horse. His overall physique makes him a dominant example of biomechanical balance.

Using biomechanical analysis, breeders today can further narrow the probabilities as they try to define type in their breeding stock. They can use modern studies of phenotype, or the physical expression of a horse's genetic makeup, to define type and then mate those most similar to each other in an effort to maintain those excellent qualities.

In assessing these physical qualities, biomechanical analysis can refine concepts of phenotype. As mentioned with regard to Mr. Prospector, the dominant or most central type of good horse has the biomechanical balance named Type I. This is Bradley's type, and most of the transcendent sires of the breed fit into this category. Northern Dancer, most of his successful sons, and many others are all Type I horses.

Horses who deviate from this central core of the breed may fall into Type II, which has general balance but is somewhat stronger in one respect than another. Again, balance in biomechanical terms is not simply a balanced look but also the balance of the stride, weight, and power that allows an animal to have the finesse and variability to handle many different situations and do many different things.

The animals who are strongly defined by one element of the three are designated by those types, either weight (Type E for light and Type W for heavy), stride (Type S), or power (Type P).

TYPE I - BEST BALANCED BIOMECHANICALLY

Blushing Groom	Key to the Mint	Round Table
Bold Bidder	Little Current	Seattle Slew
Bold Forbes	Lyphard	Sham
Chief's Crown	Mr. Prospector	Sharpen Up
Easy Goer	Nijinsky	Snow Knight
El Gran Senor	Northern Dancer	Spend a Buck
Fappiano	Private Account	Stage Door Johnny
Foolish Pleasure	Raise a Native	The Minstrel
Grey Dawn	Riverman	
In Reality	Roberto	

TYPE W - MORE WEIGHT THAN OTHER FACTORS

Blade (IIW)	Irish Castle	Rollicking (IIW)

TYPE E - LESS WEIGHT THAN OTHER FACTORS

Bates Motel	Hawaii	Sagace
Cigar	Irish River	Silent Screen
Cougar	Lord Avie	Shahrastani
Cox's Ridge	Manila	Storm Bird
Cure the Blues	Olden Times	Sunshine Forever
Ferdinand	Pass Catcher	Val de l'Orne
Forli	Precisionist	What Luck
Gate Dancer	Rubiano	Youth

TYPE S - STRONGER IN STRIDE

Alydar	His Majesty (IIS)	Risen Star
Arts and Letters	Honest Pleasure	Riva Ridge
Avatar	J.O. Tobin	Sassafras
Big Spruce	Key to the Kingdom	Secretariat
Cannonade (IIS)	King Pellinore	Sir Ivor (IIS)
Caro (IIS)	Kris S.	Slew o' Gold
Caveat (IIS)	Le Fabuleux	Sovereign Dancer
Coastal	L'Emigrant	Sword Dancer
Copelan (IIS)	Lemhi Gold	Time for a Change
Crow	Lord at War	Top Command
Dust Commander	Lure	Topsider (IIS)
Exceller	Naskra (IIS)	Unbridled
Exclusive Native	Nodouble (IIS)	Vaguely Noble
Gato del Sol	Pleasant Colony	Wajima
Graustark (IIS)	Pretense	

TYPE P - STRONGER IN POWER

Ack Ack (IIP)	Known Fact	Secreto
Best Turn (IIP)	Mr. Leader (IIP)	Spectacular Bid
Buckpasser (IIP)	Ogygian	Tom Rolfe (IIP)
Clever Trick	Pentelicus	Tri Jet (IIP)
Damascus (IIP)	Raja Baba (IIP)	Valid Appeal
Groovy	Saint Ballado	

The various types designated above are a shorthand for different phenotypes, or the physical expression of the genes that a horse has inherited. Assessing horses by type is what Federico Tesio did, as his memory retained an immense amount of material about the traits and characteristics of his horses. Some of the best trainers and breeders do this too, but today many more people are removed from the horses, making matings from offices using statistics, so that these labels for phenotype are very useful for keeping in mind what the physical animal is really like.

Tesio, who was the leading trainer in Italy for decades with his homebred stock, is best known internationally for breeding and racing Nearco and Ribot, both of whom became very important international sires, with Nearco virtually taking over the male-line descent of Phalaris in some countries.

So phenotype has a very useful role to play in breeding and in gauging the racing qualities of a horse, and it gives breeders some hints about what types of mates might work best with their stock. Yet humility is never misplaced in breeding horses. And if we do not possess the quality when we enter the horse business, our experience will soon teach us.

For whenever a new foal is produced, it receives half of its genetic information from each parent, as every biology student will tell you. But that combination is never exactly the same twice. Just look at Mr. Prospector and his many siblings.

Technically, by pedigree, they are the same horses, but by genotype and certainly by the phenotypes that are expressed, the animals are very different.

These are the everyday facts that breeders live with in the uncertainty of genetic transmission. Evaluating horses by their biomechanical phenotype is one way of categorizing this endlessly changing pattern of genes and types. By taking those types and mating animals of similar phenotype and good performance and conformation, breeders can begin to make the probabilities work in their favor by decreasing the likelihood of needless variation.

There is always variation, however. Nature is constantly experimenting, and even type to type matings need to be compatible, with the weaknesses of one individual balanced by strengths in the other for weakness or faults. That correction process introduces additional variations.

Another way of reducing variation and generally fixing a type is inbreeding. Although this subject is addressed in a chapter all its own, there is some application of inbreeding to a study of biomechanics. Both approaches, at least in some of the applications for biomechanics, seek to maintain or fix a type of successful racehorse.

Inbreeding has a function in this goal, although it is used very sparingly and conservatively by almost all Thoroughbred breeders. Livestock breeders in other spheres, particularly cattle, have used inbreeding very intensively and have produced strains of stock that are immensely uniform. But the reticence of Thoroughbred breeders with regard to inbreeding doubtless stems from their concern that it could cause deformities or reproductive problems or even manifest faults of character that have lain dormant in the parents.

There may be reason for these concerns, particularly in some strains of the breed, and for better or worse, very few serious breeders inbreed more closely than the third generation, and most are more comfortable with inbreeding out in the fourth and fifth generations.

Mating by phenotype, however, provides the benefits of inbreeding without the risks.

The breeder can take the type he prefers or that fits his program and use that as the basis of his endeavor. Mating type to type allows a breeder to produce an animal that is essentially inbred for phenotype. When you "fix" a character, as Bradley tried to do in his breeding program, it is a homogenous genotype that is fixed and is expressed as a phenotypic character. When you breed like to like, you are breeding genotype to genotype, so far as appearances indicate. But whereas inbreeding has some risk of fixing undesirable recessive characters, there is much less risk with type-to-type matings. With such matings, there is usually some inbreeding, but it is incidental and not as close as conscious inbreeding. This plan of mating is a very sound and practical application of phenotype because it allows breeders with very high-class stock to mate for a consistent phenotype without the risks of close inbreeding.

Mating different types

Actually, however, being able to mate horses of the same type is almost a privilege. Far too often, a breeder is limited by concerns of pedigree, conformation, or racing aptitude and believes that the only way to produce a successful foal is to correct some inadequacies of his broodmares and mate them to different types of stallions.

Fortunately, biomechanics can often untangle the problem of which stallion is the best match for a mare and give the breeder confidence that he is taking the right path for producing a better line of racing stock.

Mating different types is generally more subject to variation than mating type to type, and therefore matings across type are less likely to be generally successful. The reason for this can be visualized by thinking of one successful combination of traits (your mare) on one hill and another successful combination on another hill (your stallion). Sometimes matings of this sort are successful and produce an animal on a hill of its own; oftentimes, however, the resulting foals end up in a very deep ravine.

But biomechanical analysis offers hope to the breeder trying to bridge this chasm. Biomechanical mating programs can put the probabilities in the breeder's favor by discovering which phenotypes are too removed for a high-probability mating and which may be favorably similar in enough ways to give the match a decent chance of success.

Photo Courtesy of The Thoroughbred Times

European champion Blushing Groom was an exceptional racehorse and an exceptional sire.

Photo Courtesy of The Thoroughbred Times

Height of Fashion passed her powerful stature on to her progeny.

Photo Courtesy of Fiona Vigors and The Thoroughbred Times

Nashwan's success came from the combination of his dissimilar sire and dam.

One hurdle to consider in mating different types is size. In the case of European champion Nashwan, he is by the European champion Blushing Groom, an exceptional two-year-old who went on to race with distinction at three. Retired to stud at Gainesway Farm in Kentucky, Blushing Groom became one of the most successful sires of the great era of international bloodstock trading. His offspring won classics, became champions in Europe and America, and his sons and daughters became top-quality producers for the next generation. One of his best offspring was Nashwan.

The determining factor in Nashwan's makeup, however, was not his sire but his dam, Height of Fashion. A top-class racemare, Height of Fashion was a very large and powerful mare. She had the length, depth, and scope to race well over any distance. The lack of size and scope was the most common complaint about the progeny of Blushing Groom. So the mating of these two dissimilar types — although both of the highest athletic ability — produced a happy medium of their best traits.

Nashwan was a very big animal like his dam, but he also showed some of the speed and facility for strong finishes that won his sire so many races. Had Height of Fashion been bred to Blushing Groom 20 times, however, there would not have been 20 Nashwans. Each would have been different, and some would surely have been of much less use than the others.

In addition to showing the providential benefits of a mixed mating, the instance of Nashwan also illustrates another facet of the considerations to bring into matings of different types because the dam tends to contribute more to size than the sire.

It is fairly well agreed among geneticists that this is proven and consistently true. Other examples of offspring resembling their dams in size include Northern Dancer, a small to medium-sized horse out of a small to medium-sized mare; Nijinsky, a son of Northern Dancer and a big and powerful horse out of a big and powerful mare; Vice Regent, another son of Northern Dancer who was very similar to his sire in his shape and expression but of very large proportions.

Even though this is a general rule, with mares contributing more to size, there are mares and stallions which tend to stamp their stock more and less heavily. Breeders will want to use their own judgment and experience with the animals as they plan individual matings, as different horses pass on their traits in different measures, and the experienced horseman will want to consider all these factors as he is making his mating decisions.

Conclusion

If biomechanics were a solution to all the questions about what makes a horse run or what makes a mare produce top stock, the game would be over pretty quickly. There is no danger of this, however. Biomechanics is a tool, and a useful one, in the search for ways to understand the Thoroughbred. But it is not the end of the quest.

The measuring systems provide information about the mechanical efficiency and about the probability of success in either racing or breeding. That information is only as good as the accuracy of the measurement data and the vision and ability of the people who perform the analysis of it.

Used carefully and thoughtfully in conjunction with an analysis of pedigree, an insightful appreciation of conformation and physique, and a sound training regimen, biomechanics can be a solid component of a racing or breeding program.

CHAPTER 7

Inbreeding

The basic purpose of all livestock breeding is to fix, or ingrain, the most desirable traits of a breed while improving or eliminating the least desirable ones. History shows us this is usually achieved through a combination of inbreeding and outcrossing – returning the best blood present in a stallion or mare's pedigree, while adding the best bloodlines missing. By inbreeding and linebreeding, we can ingrain the best traits. By outcrossing we can add new blood to improve the weaker traits.

It is essential to realize that inbreeding, on the whole, neither improves nor diminishes the quality of the offspring but rather intensifies what is already present – for better or worse. By the luck of the draw, a few fortunate individuals will inherit the best of the duplicated ancestor, but just as often they will inherit the worst. Most often they will inherit a combination of the two. The dangers of inbreeding are well known, but the potential rewards sometimes make this gamble worthwhile.

The early years of a breed's development typically show pronounced inbreeding, as desirable traits are ingrained by inbreeding to exceptional ancestors. The developmental years of the Thoroughbred were marked by frequent inbreeding of 3x3 (two strains in the third generation) to the foundation sires Eclipse and Herod, and this practice continued in America when the founding fathers of our country were also fashioning the leading lines of the American Thoroughbred.

Although it was a much different time, with access to good stallions restricted much more than today, the breeders of the Revolutionary period through the early 1800s were advocates of intense inbreeding. Abram Hewitt noted that it was even "fashionable to breed the great Sir Archy to his own daughters." It is hard to estimate how successful such a practice was, but some of those lines provided the foundation stock of the American stud book.

In more modern times, the most intriguing use of inbreeding in America surrounded the Castleton Farm of J.R. Keene in the early part of the 20th century. Before Keene or his manager Foxhall Daingerfield had any idea how important a stallion Domino was, the dark brown son of Himyar was dead. With only two viable sons of Domino to use at stud, Keene and Daingerfield tried a radical experiment: they bred Domino's sons to some of his daughters in an effort to retain that fabulous horse's genetic excellence.

Ultimus, for instance, was produced by mating Domino's classic-winning son Commando with Domino's classy daughter Running Stream. And in Hewitt's estimation, the most highly inbred horse of the 20th century was a son of Ultimus named High Time. High Time added a third cross of Domino, as he was out of the stallion's daughter Noonday. Bred on the recommendation of Elizabeth Daingerfield, the daughter of Major Daingerfield, High Time was remarkably fast, but his racing use was limited by a problem with bleeding and possibly a wind affliction.

Yet as a sire, he was a major factor in the early-century prevalence of Domino in pedigrees, and High Time sired a truly first-class racer in the gelding Sarazen. The stallion sired numerous other good racers, and his daughters bred on well.

But overall, the use of inbreeding with Domino was the result of desperation. The stallion died very young, and his best son Commando did likewise. And those close to the Castleton operation and the best Domino stock were motivated to breed high-quality individuals in their quest to retain the genetic factors for speed.

In most cases, however, a breeder's desperation is inspired by somewhat different circumstances. Most typically, intense inbreeding has been used when the individuals at hand were, shall we say, disappointing their ancestors. Back in the 1970s, a fellow possessed a full brother to Triple Crown winner Citation named St. Crispin. The latter distinguished his parentage by never racing and was retired to stud.

To make matters worse, as St. Crispin's stud career moved along, he was bred to one of his own daughters, Belle W. This was repeated thrice, and the resulting foals made 32 starts all together, with not a placing among them.

Clearly, the success of this or any other approach to mating Thoroughbreds is highly dependent upon the quality of the stock used. But when the individuals are properly chosen and the practice used cautiously, close inbreeding can fix traits and simplify matings within a population, as shown in the early American Thoroughbred and the Domino strains of the early 20th century.

Likewise, the early harness horse showed similar inbreeding of 3x3 to its foundation stud, Hambletonian. Hambletonian himself was inbred 3x4x4 to Messenger, giving him a relatively pure and uniform genetic make-up with which to stamp his descendants. The Quarter Horse is more of a hybrid, growing out of a mixture of Spanish, Thoroughbred, and western ranch horse bloodlines, but even there we find some noteworthy inbreeding patterns in the development of the breed.

The goal of inbreeding essentially is to recreate the quality of the ancestor being duplicated. Repeated generations of inbreeding usually ingrain a few negative traits as well, and certainly there can be too much of a good thing where inbreeding is concerned. Many of today's show dogs have developed chronic hip dysplasia from generations of breeding for superficial looks with little attention to health or soundness. The Great Potato Famine in Ireland in the 1840s also resulted from too many generations of a closed gene pool.

Today's Thoroughbred racehorse may also be showing signs of growing unsoundness – at the expense of speed, more speed, and commercial appeal. Ironically, today's major stakes races are run no faster than they were in the 1960s and 1970s, suggesting the Thoroughbred's restricted gene pool may have reached a genetic plateau that will be hard to escape.

In 1991, the *Thoroughbred Times* published an eight-part series by David Dink analyzing the results of Thoroughbred inbreeding in North America for the foal crop of 1983. This crop numbered 45,643 foals, who by 1991 had essentially completed their racing careers. The study found that 27.6 percent showed duplicated ancestors within four generations – but this includes horses with a parent inbred 3x3, who do not otherwise show inbreeding themselves. For instance, Spectacular Bid was inbred 3x3 and all his offspring would therefore show duplications of 4x4. Such foals are termed "incidental inbreds" in this study, and the breed average would be closer to 20 percent inbreds (4x4), excluding this group.

The overall results for inbreeding are very close to average for a total foal crop that produced 44.52 percent winners and 3.03 percent stakes winners from foals. Some very close patterns (3x3 or closer) were well below average – only 1.85 percent stakes winners – while inbreeding 4x4, 4x5, and 5x5 was very slightly above average:

Inbreeding	Runners	Winners	SWs
3x3 or closer	66.99%	40.27%	1.85%
4x3 or closer	71.10%	45.60%	2.33%
4x4	71.54%	46.31%	3.76%
5x5	70.09%	45.19%	3.14%
Outcrossed	66.31%	40.65%	2.50%
Crop average	69.70%	44.52%	3.03%

While this study debunks any simplistic formulas for inbreeding success, it does not consider that within any particular pattern of inbreeding, some strains may do well below average and others well above average. Great stallions like Nasrullah and Northern Dancer were such important sires that even their mediocre sons and daughters went to stud, whereas most stallions have only their best offspring go into production. Inbreeding to Nasrullah and Northern Dancer, et al., will therefore be limited statistically by those mediocre strains of their blood, and in this respect they are the victims of their own success.

While all inbreeding to Northern Dancer produces only average results, certain strains of Northern Dancer blood have been remarkably successful through inbreeding, particularly through his sons Nijinsky II and Lyphard. While overall inbreeding to Northern Dancer has produced slightly more than 3 percent stakes winners from foals (almost exactly the national average), when one strain includes Nijinsky II, this resulting figure jumps to more than 10 percent, and when the other strain comes through Lyphard combined with Nijinsky II, it has produced more than 25 percent stakes winners from foals, (according to Roger Lyons's studies in *Owner-Breeder*, 1995-'98).

Historically and statistically, certain strains of a great progenitor's blood have often lent themselves to inbreeding more than others, and it can be inferred that these strains offer the very best of the genetic pool, since inbreeding to the prominent ancestor through weaker strains would only ingrain these weaknesses. Studies by both Dink and Lyons, however, indicate that "sex-balanced inbreeding" (through a son and daughter of the duplicated ancestor) hold no value in general.

Positions in Pedigrees

The concept of inbreeding to particular positions in a pedigree, referred to in some permutations as balanced-sex breeding, derives from a logical observation of success. One sees that a stallion or mare is highly successful in one generation of the pedigree and concludes that some more of that would be a benefit to any prospective mating.

In a recent telephone conversation, David Dink noted that "as far as inbreeding goes, the most obvious case for this sort of logic is Northern Dancer. He is extremely popular in the third generation of the male line and as sire of the broodmare sire, which results in a 3x3 inbreeding." Both of those positions are male-line positions, and Northern Dancer was exceptionally successful as a sire of stallions, and many of his grandsons and granddaughters have been mated to produce the 3x3 cross.

While this may be a sound proposition with Northern Dancer, as a general rule, Dink noted the "problem with inbreeding in this manner is the assumption that Name A in the sire line and Name A in the dam is a good thing. Individually, that might be so, but the belief that putting them together is better doesn't usually hold up" over the whole population.

In his multi-part series on inbreeding published in the *Thoroughbred Times*, Dink evaluated the different types of positional inbreeding and their relative success across the breed as a whole.

One of the most popular forms of this is the one mentioned above with regard to Northern Dancer: inbreeding to a stallion in the direct male line and in the broodmare sire line. Likewise, inbreeding can be done with broodmares in the direct female line (or tail-female line) and the female line of the sire.

In between the direct lines of descent are numerous positions in a pedigree's third and fourth generations, and in these generations, as well as more distant ones, the concepts of using balanced-sex inbreeding (matching lines of descent through both a mare and a stallion) come into play.

The rationale for balanced-sex inbreeding is that by tracing the inheritance through both a mare and stallion, all the genetic possibilities of the ancestor are captured. This is not how genetic transmission works, since each offspring gets only half the genetic code of each parent, but there is enough possibility in the concept to attract a number of breeders to it.

Outside of sire-line inbreeding, the most popular pattern of inbreeding is pedigree repetitions of dams through different individuals, which is covered in a separate chapter.

All these different approaches of inbreeding to specific horses in particular positions in pedigrees had some success in Dink's study, but overall there was a significant regression to the mean, which indicates that the quality of the horses used for inbreeding was more important than the method itself.

For instance, Dink said that "inbreeding to Secretariat is probably not a good idea in male line, but he has become a major force as a broodmare sire and as the broodmare sire of the sire."

Understanding where a horse contributes the most in a pedigree is valuable, even if we don't understand why. In Dink's survey of 45,643 foals from the 1983 crop, one of the most productive patterns for inbreeding by position was the presence of a stallion in the male line and in its recurrence as sire of a broodmare in the tail-female line.

Most successful in the study at 4x4, this pattern may also be an indicator of pedigree quality, as the stallions repeated in this type of inbreeding tended to be some of the best influences in the breed, including Nasrullah, Princequillo, Hyperion, and Nearco.

Dink said that "in terms of a long-term project, it would make sense to arrive at each horse's value at each position, taking into account the influence of opportunity, so that we'd be able to say which horses are likely to contribute the most in each position, and with the technology out there now, that is probably just about feasible."

Patterns in Inbreeding

While inbreeding may be average overall, this overlooks patterns that are average in general but occasionally sensational – the kind of patterns that produce champions. In his book *Bloodstock Breeding*, English author Charles Leicester reported that among English Derby winners from 1900 to 1956, 57.1 percent were inbred 4x4 or closer. This figure tailed off slightly to 46.8 percent for the years between 1957 and 1976, but both figures are far above average for the breed as a whole.

Breeding advisor Jack Werk in the *Owner-Breeder* newsletter of June 1992 studied the pedigrees of the 118 Eclipse Award winners from 1977 through 1991. While about 21 percent of the breed was inbred 4x4 or closer during that time, the group of Eclipse Award winners showed 35.6 percent inbred 4x4 or closer. If we add the six champions whose dams were inbred 3x3 and the three whose sires were 3x3, we find 43.2 percent of the Eclipse winners showed duplications within four generations. So perhaps it is fair to say that while inbreeding in general succeeds no more often than normal, when it does succeed it can be sensational.

The Standardbred breed of the harness racing industry is a newer breed than the Thoroughbred and stems from a more diverse genetic background. Consequently race times are still improving and close inbreeding is still common. While studies of today's Thoroughbreds show crosses of 4x4 and 4x5 are most common and most effective, crosses of 3x3 and 3x4 are still very common and successful among Standardbreds.

Federico Tesio and J.J. Vuillier were two of the most celebrated Thoroughbred breeders or theorizers of the 20th century. Tesio was an eccentric Italian genius who bred and raced 20 Italian Derby winners, and the undefeated champions Nearco and Ribot – arguably the best European racehorses of the 20th century. Vuillier was the pedigree advisor to the Aga Khan and creator of the original dosage theory. Their primary principles of mating, carefully studied from history, hold significant similarities.

In his book *Breeding The Racehorse*, Tesio writes, "From the atom to the star, the life of the universe is based on speed extended in time. Among living beings, speed extended in time means staying power. Theoretical scientists have come up with a variety of theories on the subject of speed and staying power. What is more, they keep coming up with new ones, which means that they have not yet found one that is entirely satisfactory. Practical horsemen, among them myself, have bred both speed horses and stayers, without having yet found a sure formula for producing one or the other at will . . .

"Besides the material contribution of rational feed, fresh air, freedom and exercise which all make up the best possible conditions for raising a good athlete, I can see three factors which contribute to his development:

    1) Inbreeding

    2) "Nicks," or the almost constantly successful matching of certain bloodlines

    3) Selection of the best quality stock . . .

"If we wish the successive patterns [or types within the Thoroughbred breed] to have a better chance of resembling each other . . . our only course is to diminish the variety of their shapes and colours. In the same manner, although we cannot reduce the number of a horse's ancestors, we can select his parents in such a way that one particular ancestor will occupy more than one place in his pedigree, thus insuring a greater probability that certain desired characteristics will be inherited. Inbreeding is the surest way of obtaining this result, by reducing the number of different ancestors and thereby making it easier to fix or establish their characters."

Vuillier echoed the very same factors but developed his dosage theory to quantify the ideal proportions of 16 great ancestors, or "chefs-de-race," that should be blended in a pedigree like a recipe. Evidently this idea had some merit, as great horses like Bahram, Mahmoud, and Nasrullah were bred and raced by the Aga Khan with Vuillier's advice. Bahram (5x5x5x4 to St. Simon) won the English Triple Crown in 1935 and Mahmoud the English Derby in 1936, while Nasrullah was sold off for stud duty largely because of the uncertain political climate in Europe during World War II. Nasrullah and Mahmoud were both grandsons of the "Flying Filly," Mumtaz Mahal, who was also owned by the Aga Khan.

In his Memoirs, the Aga Khan wrote:

> "My own view is that you must try to secure the best and most suitable breeding through both the sire and dam, bring it both inbreeding and outcrossing as near and perfect in the abstract as you can. Success will depend on whether any particular foal takes after his dam and the majority of his maternal ascendants or after his sire and the majority of his paternal ascendants."

It should be pointed out that distant outcrossing has produced many of the greatest Thoroughbreds like Man o' War (5x5), Secretariat (6x5), and Native Dancer (6x6), while harness racing greats Bret Hanover, Nevele Pride, and Niatross show nothing closer than 4x5.

Perhaps one of the factors that might explain this is the concept of hybrid vigor. The value of hybrid vigor is well known throughout the livestock kingdom, especially through its role in helping farmers to breed stronger, larger, and more efficient production animals like cattle and hogs. While no Thoroughbreds or any other horse breeds are hybrids in the strictest sense, (crossing horses with other species like zebras), such outcrossing between horse breeds or strains within breeds, as implied in hybrid vigor, is about the closest thing possible. However, it should be noted that random outcrossing of unrelated bloodlines generally produces a mishmash of unwanted traits – but when it does work, it can be sensational.

Bull Hancock presided over Claiborne Farm in Kentucky in an era when the famed Kentucky nursery imported or stood European-bred stallions such as Sir Gallahad III, Blenheim II, Nasrullah, and Princequillo. And the results of this breeding venture and the exceptional successes obtained at Claiborne and other important farms has been so revolutionary for the breed that it became known as the international outcross.

The crossing of the Nasrullah and Princequillo lines proved particularly successful, producing the likes of Secretariat, Mill Reef, the American Bold Lad, Shuvee, and Riverman, among many others. But just as repeated generations of inbreeding eventually may cause problems, repeated generations of outcrossing eventually un-fix the very qualities we seek to ingrain. Evidently a happy medium is needed.

Photos courtesy of The Keeneland Library

The crossing of the Nasrullah (top) and Princequillo (bottom) lines proved particularly successful, producing the likes of Secretariat, Mill Reef, the American Bold Lad, Shuvee, and Riverman.

The Quarter Horse is an unusual case, since its registry did not begin until 1940, and many of the foundation bloodstock had questionable bloodlines. It is certain that registered Thoroughbreds soon came to play a large role, especially among the racing branch of the Quarter Horse family, and this created something closer to hybrid vigor.

A favorite breeding strategy throughout the horse and livestock kingdom has been to cross a sire inbred to one bloodline with a mare inbred to another bloodline. Since each line has a relatively pure and uniform genetic make-up, its offspring will tend to show consistent results, and when two bloodlines show an affinity, or nick, for each other, consistently good results may follow.

R.J. Kleberg, Jr. of King Ranch in Texas rose to prominence first as a cattle breeder who later brought these principles to the breeding of Thoroughbred racehorses. In this manner he bred Stymie (1941), who rose to become the sport's all-time leading earner despite his very modest parents. His sire Equestrian, however, was inbred 4x4 to the great sire Ben Brush, while his dam Stop Watch was inbred 2x4 to Colin (a grandson of Domino). Stymie himself was inbred 3x3 to the great Man o' War; so Kleberg essentially concentrated the three greatest American bloodlines of the early 20th century in this mating.

Now, technically, Stymie was not bred by King Ranch. His breeder of record was Max Hirsch, the trainer for King Ranch, but Kleberg was the mind behind the mating. For the effort, however, Kleberg got nothing but glory. Hirsch Jacobs claimed Stymie when it seemed certifiable that the chestnut was nothing more than a mane and a tail and then proceeded to win something more than $900,000 with him.

Across an ocean and in a very different racing environment, Marcel Boussac was the owner-breeder of 12 French Derby winners in the first half of the 20th century. In an effort to fix a type and maintain the high quality of his stud, Boussac specialized in close inbreeding, concentrating on the stallion Ksar (inbred 2x3) and his son Tourbillon. Two of Boussac's best were the fillies Coronation V (2x2) and Apollonia (2x3), both closely inbred to Tourbillon. Several decades of intense inbreeding eventually undermined Boussac's breeding operation, however, as his failure to import fresh blood ultimately left him bankrupt and heartbroken. Boussac built his operation on a foundation combining bloodlines from England, America, and France, but in later years concentrated almost solely on his own bloodlines, and perhaps this led to his downfall.

Pedigree analyst and author Ken McLean writes of Boussac:

> "Genetic influence from superior ancestors becomes diluted after one or two outcrossed generations, yet when the same superior ancestors are reinforced in a single pedigree it allows for the recapture of the original source for classic speed. You must first duplicate the source, then go away from it, and then make sure it is reinforced again."

Olin Gentry saw the greatest American racehorses of the 20th century as breeding advisor to Colonel E.R. Bradley's Idle Hour Farm in Kentucky and later John

Galbraith's Darby Dan Farm – where the latter stood Ribot, Graustark, His Majesty, and Roberto. Gentry felt that when inbreeding, it was important to inbreed in the same generation, and Roberto was certainly a classic example – being inbred 4x4 to both Nearco and Blue Larkspur.

It should be noted there are just as many exceptions to this rule, however, and Tesio was very fond of the 3x4 cross. It should also be noted that a 3x4 cross in modern times involves far more homogeneity than a 3x4 cross at the dawn of the breed when many unrelated bloodlines were still in effect. A closed stud book over centuries greatly reduces the genetic variation of a breed, and the Thoroughbred now has less genetic variation than any breed of horse. (*Horse Genetics*, Ann T. Bowling, 1996)

Close inbreeding has produced modern-day Thoroughbred greats like Spectacular Bid, Turn-to, Broad Brush, and Rock of Gibraltar, all inbred 3x3. The great Dr. Fager was 3x4, Hyperion was 4x3, while Buckpasser and Seattle Slew were both inbred 4x4, among many others.

We also find that Northern Dancer and Mr. Prospector, the two dominant bloodlines in the world today, were both grandsons of Native Dancer, so that crosses between their sons and daughters have produced inbreeding of 4x4 to Native Dancer. (Northern Dancer himself was 4x5 to Gainsborough, while Mr. Prospector was 4x7x5 to Teddy, reading from the top down in their pedigrees.)

Northern Dancer inbred descendants include the likes of:

Skimming (2x3-Northern Dancer), winner of the 2000 Pacific Classic
Lammtarra (2x4), winner of the 1995 English Derby
Spinning World (2x4), winner of the 1997 Breeders' Cup Mile
Touch Gold (3x3), winner of the 1997 Belmont Stakes
Desert King (3x3), winner of the 1997 Irish Derby
Rock of Gibraltar (3x3), winner of the 2002 Two Thousand Guineas
Gentlemen (3x4), winner of the 1997 Hollywood Gold Cup
Sakhee (4x3), winner of the 2001 Prix de l'Arc de Triomphe
Tiznow (4x4), winner of the 2000 and 2001 Breeders' Cup Classics

Perhaps the surest and safest way to fix desirable traits, however, is to use multiple linebreeding patterns beyond the fourth generation. This incorporates the strengths of inbreeding, with fewer dangers of physical and mental problems. It can also be inferred that the more distantly removed the crosses are, the more it is that selective breeding has filtered out the weaker traits of the ancestor in question.

Great racehorses like Damascus, Affirmed, Sea-Bird II, and Brigadier Gerard were produced by less-talented parents and showed no close inbreeding in their pedigrees. But Damascus was deeply linebred 5x6x4 to Phalaris – the dominant genetic influence of the 20th century.

Photo courtesy of Monica Thors
Pacer Jenna's Beach Boy is inbred 3x4x4 to Meadow Skipper.

Brigadier Gerard (6x7x6x6x4 to Phalaris) and Sea-Bird II (6x4x6 to Phalaris) were two of the greatest European Thoroughbreds of the 20th century, while American Triple Crown winners Affirmed (5x5x6x7x6 to Teddy), Count Fleet (5x5x6x6 to St. Simon), and Citation (5x6x5x4 to St. Simon) were likewise deeply linebred to great genetic influences. Undefeated European champion, Nearco, was linebred 5x4x4x5 to St. Simon and was said by veteran horsemen to resemble the great stallion.

Among the Standardbreds of harness racing, we find that the legendary pacer Dan Patch, a foal of 1896, was inbred 3x4 to George Wilkes – a top son of Hambletonian. More recently, Triple Crown-winning trotter Super Bowl was inbred 3x3 to Volomite, while the great pacing stallions Most Happy Fella and his son Cam Fella were each inbred 3x3, as were the pacing rivals Nihilator and Dragons Lair in the 1980s. Royal Troubador (2x3 to Stars Pride) and Wesgate Crown (2x3 to Speedy Crown) were champion trotters in the 1990s, and the 2001

Photo courtesy of Monica Thors
Trotter Valley Victory is inbred 4x5x4x5 to Stars Pride.

Harness Horse of the Year was the 3-year-old filly pacer Bunny Lake, inbred 4x5x3 to Meadow Skipper. Such close inbreeding tends to be the hallmark of top breeding stock across the livestock kingdom as well.

The fastest harness mile ever was recorded by Cambest, who time-trialed 1:46 1/5 in 1993. Cambest is inbred 4x4 to Adios. In the harness world and other fields of livestock, crosses more distant than 3x3 are often called linebreeding rather than inbreeding. Cambest's son Blissful Hall won the pacing Triple

Crown in 1999. He is 4x3 to Meadow Skipper and 4x4 to Bret Hanover. The fastest harness horse ever in a race has been pacer Jenna's Beach Boy, with a mile in 1:47 4/5, who is 3x4x4 to Meadow Skipper and is currently off to an outstanding start at stud.

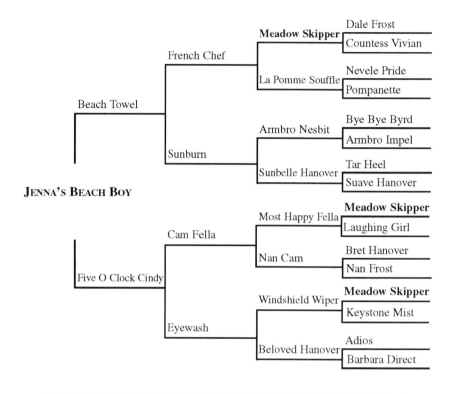

JENNA'S BEACH BOY

- Beach Towel
  - French Chef
    - **Meadow Skipper**
      - Dale Frost
      - Countess Vivian
    - La Pomme Souffle
      - Nevele Pride
      - Pompanette
  - Sunburn
    - Armbro Nesbit
      - Bye Bye Byrd
      - Armbro Impel
    - Sunbelle Hanover
      - Tar Heel
      - Suave Hanover
- Five O Clock Cindy
  - Cam Fella
    - Most Happy Fella
      - **Meadow Skipper**
      - Laughing Girl
    - Nan Cam
      - Bret Hanover
      - Nan Frost
  - Eyewash
    - Windshield Wiper
      - **Meadow Skipper**
      - Keystone Mist
    - Beloved Hanover
      - Adios
      - Barbara Direct

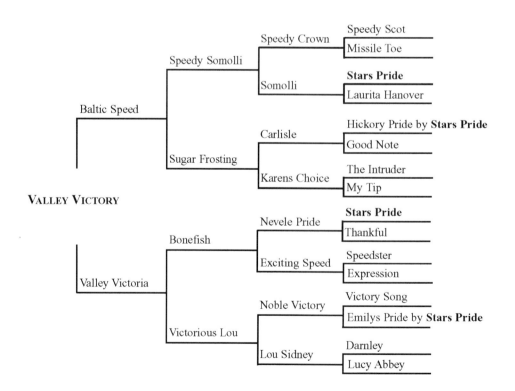

VALLEY VICTORY

- Baltic Speed
  - Speedy Somolli
    - Speedy Crown
      - Speedy Scot
      - Missile Toe
    - Somolli
      - **Stars Pride**
      - Laurita Hanover
  - Sugar Frosting
    - Carlisle
      - Hickory Pride by **Stars Pride**
      - Good Note
    - Karens Choice
      - The Intruder
      - My Tip
- Valley Victoria
  - Bonefish
    - Nevele Pride
      - **Stars Pride**
      - Thankful
    - Exciting Speed
      - Speedster
      - Expression
  - Victorious Lou
    - Noble Victory
      - Victory Song
      - Emilys Pride by **Stars Pride**
    - Lou Sidney
      - Darnley
      - Lucy Abbey

Deeply linebred Standardbred greats include pacers like Niatross (4x5x5 to Hal Dale), No Nukes (5x5x5x4x5 to Hal Dale), On The Road Again (5x5x5x6x5 to Hal Dale), and Matt's Scooter (4x5x7x5 to Volomite), while trotting greats include Speedy Crown (5x4x4 to Scotland), Nevele Pride (5x5x5x5 to Peter The Great), Peace Corps (4x5x3x5 to Stars Pride), and Valley Victory (4x5x4x5 to Stars Pride).

GREAT PACERS

Dan Patch (3x4)

Bret Hanover (4x5)

Adios Butler (4x4)

Meadow Skipper (4x4)

Handle With Care (m) (354)

Most Happy Fella (3x3)

Silk Stockings (m) (444)

Cam Fella (3x3)

Cambest (4x4)

Blissful Hall (4x3)

Albatross (3x4)

Fan Hanover (m) (4x3)

Niatross (455)

Nihilator (3x3)

Dragons Lair (3x3)

No Nukes (4x4)

Jate Lobell (5x5x3)

On The Road Again (5x5x5x6x5)

Matt's Scooter (4x5x7x5)

Jenna's Beach Boy (3x4x4)

Bunny Lake (m) (4x5x3)

GREAT TROTTERS

Greyhound (4x4)

Rodney (4x4x4)

Stars Pride (4x4x6x4)

Nevele Pride (5x5x5x5)

Super Bowl (3x3)

Speedy Crown (5x4x4)

Moni Maker (m) (3x4x4)

Peace Corps (m) (4x5x3x5)

Valley Victory (4x5x4x5)

Muscles Yankee (4x2)

Royal Troubador (2x3)

Wesgate Crown (2x3)

Self-Possessed (5x3x4)

Standardbred greats (m) = mare

Among the Quarter Horse racing greats who were inbred, we find names like Dash for Cash and his son First Down Dash, along with Go Man Go, Easy Jet, and Special Effort. All showed major crosses with Thoroughbred blood close-up in their pedigrees.

Dash for Cash (foal of 1973) became perhaps the greatest racing sire in the breed's history. His sire, Rocket Wrangler, was a Quarter Horse, but his dam, Find a Buyer, was a Thoroughbred. His fourth dam was Imperatrice, who was also the second dam of the great Thoroughbred Secretariat. In fact, 13 of the 16 ancestors in Dash for Cash's fourth generation appear to be Thoroughbreds.

His best son, First Down Dash, shows linebreeding to Top Deck (5x5x6), and Three Bars (4x6x7), both of whom were Thoroughbred stallions. Top Quarter Horse stud Easy Jet, a foal of 1967, was inbred 4x2 to Three Bars.

The great Special Effort (1979) was sired by the Thoroughbred stallion Raise Your Glass, a son of Raise a Native, who was an important influence upon both the Quarter Horse and Thoroughbred. In addition, Raise a Glass was inbred 3x3 to Polynesian – the sire of the great Native Dancer. Special Effort's dam, Go Effortlessly, was a Quarter Horse mare who was inbred 3x2 to Spotted Bull – a son of Thoroughbred stud Bull Dog. Three-time Horse of the Year Go Man Go (1955-56-57), was by the Thoroughbred sire Top Deck out of a mare who was half-Thoroughbred.

Let breeders try as they might, but there will always be a high degree of chance involved when you shuffle together 35,000 genes from a stallion with 35,000 more from a mare. (*The latest estimate of the equine gene pool based on the human genome of 37,000 genes and mouse genome of 30,000.) But the thoughtful breeder can certainly improve those odds by observing the breeding patterns that have proved themselves over the course of history.

About the Author

Jay Leimbach is a freelance writer, pedigree analyst, and Thoroughbred owner. He has written regularly for Thoroughbred Times, Owner-Breeder, Mid-Atlantic Thoroughbred, *and* Horseman and Fair World. *He is now at work on a book entitled,* Kelso and the Golden Age of Racing.

INBREEDING IN THE TOP THOROUGHBREDS
OF THE 20TH CENTURY

Ack Ack (5x4 to Sickle)
Affirmed (5x5x6x7x6 to Teddy)
Alydar (4x6x7x6 to Teddy)
Alysheba (4x4 to Nasrullah)
Armed (4x5 to Trenton)
Assault (4x5 to Commando)
Best Pal (5x4 to Princequillo)
Bold Ruler (5x5 to Sundridge)
Buckpasser (4x4 to Teddy)
Cigar (4x6 to Turn-to & Princequillo)
Citation (5x6x5x4 to St. Simon)
Colin (6x4 to Stockwell, 6x6x5x6 to Touchstone)
Count Fleet (5x5x6x6 to St. Simon)
Damascus (5x6x4 to Phalaris)
Dr. Fager (3x4 to Bull Dog, 4x5x5 to Teddy)
Equipoise (4x5 to Hampton)
Exterminator (5x5 to Blair Athol, 6x6x6 to Stockwell)
Foolish Pleasure (5x4x4 to Blenheim II)
Forego (6x5x5 to Teddy)
Graustark (5x4 to Tracery)
Holy Bull (5x5 to Questionnaire)
John Henry (7x6x4 to Black Toney)
Kelso (5x6x5 to Rock Sand)
Man o' War (5x5 to Galopin & Hermit, 5x6x6x6 to Stockwell)
Nashua (5x6 to Rabelais)
Native Dancer (6x6 to Isinglass)
Northern Dancer (4x5 to Gainsborough, 4x6 to Phalaris & Selene)
Point Given (4x4 to Raise a Native)
Precisionist (3x4 to Olympia)
Riva Ridge (6x4 to Swynford & Gainsborough, 6x6x5 to Phalaris)
Seabiscuit (6x5x4 to St. Simon)
Seattle Slew (4x4 to Nasrullah)
Secretariat (6x5 to Polymelus, 6x6x6 to Sundridge)
Silver Charm (4x5 to War Admiral)
Skip Away (5x5 to Mahmoud, 6x5x6 to Blenheim II)
Slew o' Gold (5x4 to Princequillo, 6x6x4 to War Admiral)
Spectacular Bid (3x3 to To Market)
Stymie (3x3 to Man o' War, 4x4 to Commando)
Sunday Silence (4x5 to Mahmoud)

Swaps (5x4 to Polymelus)
Sysonby (4x5x6 to Stockwell)
Tom Fool (4x6 to Polymelus, 6x5x5 to St. Simon)
War Admiral (5x6 to Australian, 6x6x6 to Hermit)
Whirlaway (5x5 to Cyllene, 6x6x5x6 to St. Simon, 6x6x6x6 to Hermit)

MARES
All Along (4x4 to Prince Rose)
Allez France (6x5 to Sir Gallahad III & Fair Play)
Bayakoa (4x4x4 to Nasrullah)
Dahlia (4x5x4 to Hyperion)
Lady's Secret (3x5 to Nasrullah)
Paseana (4x4 to Nasrullah)
Ruffian (4x5x4 to Discovery)
Serena's Song (4x6 to Nasrullah, 5x4 to Tudor Minstrel)
Winning Colors (4x4x5 to Nasrullah)

EUROPEANS
Brigadier Gerard (6x7x6x6x4 to Phalaris)
Dancing Brave (4x6 to Nearco, 5x5 to Mahmoud)
Dubai Millenium (4x5 to Native Dancer & Tom Fool)
Galileo (4x5 to Native Dancer)
Mill Reef (5x6 to The Tetrarch, Gay Crusader)
Nashwan (3x6 to Wild Risk)
Nearco (5x4x4x5 to St. Simon)
Nijinsky II (5x7x5 to Phalaris & Selene)
Ribot (6x5x6x6 to Cyllene, 6x6x6x6x6 to St. Simon)
Rock of Gibraltar (3x3 to Northern Dancer)
Sakhee (4x3 to Northern Dancer)
Sea-Bird II (6x4x6 to Phalaris)
Sir Ivor (6x6x4 to Phalaris, 5x5 to Plucky Liege)

CHAPTER 8

Nicking

Every so often, we encounter certain mixtures that go particularly well together.

In the breeding of Thoroughbred racehorses, nicking theory suggests that specific combinations of bloodlines facilitate conditions in which a greater than expected share of superior individuals are produced. In other words, certain lines appear to have an affinity for, and produce exceptional results when mated to, other specific lines. This phenomenon has long been referred to as a nick.

The rationale of applying nicking principles in one's breeding decisions is quite analogous with much of the logic and strategy we see in professional baseball. When a manager replaces his right-handed pitcher with a southpaw to face the left-handed hitter, he is attempting to create a situation in which his team is more likely to succeed. In other words, he is playing the averages. These averages and their resulting implications are obtained through the appropriate collection and processing of data to create accurate and relevant comparisons. Fundamentally, all of these ratios measure the same thing: success divided by opportunity, or the rate of success. In baseball, once a sufficient amount of data becomes available, any particular batting average can be calculated by dividing the number of hits by the number of times at bat. In the world of racing and breeding, similar ratios compare the number of superior individuals under review with the total number of individuals under review.

All of this requires the proper use of statistical analysis. While the science of statistics has been developing since the beginning of the 20th century, its greatest impact has come in the past three decades. This is largely the result of personal computers, making it possible now to deal with a much larger amount of data rapidly and efficiently.

Numerous interactive web sites, as well as commercial software, are now available to conduct detailed research on many aspects of a Thoroughbred's ancestry. Pedigrees extending to the fifth generation and beyond can now be instantly constructed, affording study and perspective not previously possible without extensive work.

So what, then, are we looking, if not yearning, for? What defines success in this exciting and expensive game we play? Different horsemen have different goals.

Nevertheless, the industry's gold standard, the stakes race, provides the most valuable international measuring stick to compare different sets of Thoroughbred populations. The percentage of stakes winners (SWs) within a given group under review is the most widely accepted measure of success. It is also a most discriminating parameter, as only three percent of the total North American Thoroughbred population will reach this level. Other ratios that are commonly quoted include the percentage of starters and the percentage of winners (about 70 percent and 45 percent of the total population). Earnings indices can be another useful benchmark. Usually, but not always, when an affinity exists, all measures of relative success will be higher than the breed norms.

In the study of nicking patterns, we seek to establish whether a specific sub-group within a general population significantly outperforms its opportunities. The stallion Chief's Crown, for example, appears to have had a solid affinity with the daughters of Habitat. The relevant statistics are as follows: When Chief's Crown was bred to Habitat mares, he sired 13 foals, 12 of which were starters (92 percent), eight of which were winners (62 percent), and five of which became stakes winners (38 percent). Looking at his progeny as a whole (a total of 516 individuals), Chief's Crown sired 83 percent starters, 57 percent winners and nine percent stakes winners. The comparisons suggest a very productive combination.

For nicking patterns to be considered truly worthy in their predictive value, they must meet a number of statistical standards. Statistical reliability is the extent to which a measuring procedure yields the same result on repeated trials. The overwhelming majority of bloodline combinations never manifest any semblance of a definable nick. This is either due to a lack of samples (opportunities) or simply because the statistics are unremarkable from the population at large. Regarding the former, a cross that has been tried only a couple of times has very limited statistical reliability in regard to the future, regardless of whether the initial attempts were successful or not.

While reliability is concerned with the notion of accuracy, statistical validity is involved with the assurance that we have, in fact, measured and then compared only what we have intended to. It is, of course, not at all difficult to make faulty comparisons leading to unsound reasoning, not to mention propaganda.

> "There are three kinds of lies . . . lies, damned lies and statistics."
> Benjamin Disraeli (1804-81)
> English prime minister & author

The following is an excerpt from a frequently run advertisement in an international breeding journal:

"Nick Ratings Explained"

"In response to the increasingly popular use of sire line nicking patterns by breeders and yearling buyers, [we] have developed a proprietary method of evaluating nicks and presenting them through [our] unique grading system.

"The ratings measure the success a particular sire line has had with a specific broodmare sire line. The unique method compares that success with the success that particular sire line has had with the broodmare population as a whole.

> *"Example 1: Northern Dancer line stallions have sired 6.9 percent of the SWs produced by Noholme II line mares. Sounds great, right? WRONG! Northern Dancer line stallions have sired 8.04 percent of all SWs over the past 14 years, so Northern Dancer line stallions sire 14 percent fewer SWs when bred to Noholme II line mares than they do with the population as a whole. This is barely a 'C' nick.*

> *"Example 2: Northern Dancer line stallions have sired 44 percent of the SWs produced by Mill Reef line mares. Sounds good, right? RIGHT! Northern Dancer line stallions have sired 8.04 percent of all SWs over the past 14 years, so Northern Dancer line stallions have sired 448 percent more SWs when bred to Mill Reef line mares than they do with the population as a whole. This would be an 'A' nick and very close to an 'A+.'"*

This is a case of arriving at a series of conclusions which lack statistical validity. In Example 1 it is stated that 6.9 percent of the SWs produced by Noholme II-line mares were sired by Northern Dancer line stallions. This figure is then compared to the percentage of total SWs sired by the Northern Dancer sire line. This is a classic case of mixing apples with oranges. The comparative figure needed is the percentage of total foals produced by Noholme II-line mares that were sired by Northern Dancer line stallions. If this percentage is significantly lower than 6.9 percent, you have isolated a favorable relationship that has outperformed its opportunities.

The same scenario presents itself in Example 2. What we need to know is the percentage of total foals produced by Mill Reef line mares sired by Northern Dancer line stallions. If this figure is significantly below 44 percent, then there is good reason to believe that an affinity worth further examination exists.

In short, nicking pattern analysis requires comparing success to opportunity ratios between a select subset (individuals that carry the potential nick under review) and the total population from which it derives.

Establishing the population frequency of a potential nick can often become a difficult statistic to calculate as it requires looking at a large population as a whole rather than just the stakes-winning subset. To derive population frequencies, one would need to consider every individual produced out of a particular sire's daughters and then establish how many (and what percent) of them were sired by stallions of particular lines, whether Northern Dancer, Raise a Native, or Seattle Slew, not at all an easy assignment, even with today's cutting-edge computer software. But this is all the more reason to steer toward affinity patterns that can be properly tested.

Are there really any rational explanations why nicks even exist? The great Italian horseman, Federico Tesio, took an eloquent, albeit ethereal, approach to explaining the question in his 1958 text, *Breeding the Racehorse*:

"The energetic makeup [of a nick] is perhaps the result of harmonic combinations of electromagnetic waves, just as certain harmonic combinations of planes and volumes will determine physical beauty and other harmonies will produce pleasant musical effects, color schemes and sensations in taste."

While electromagnetic waves do help to explain the phenomena of sight and sound, they add little to the understanding of Thoroughbred affinities. Moreover, there has been essentially nothing, so far, to be gleaned from the world of physical or biological science to suggest a basis for nicks.

How then can we explain these statistical clusters of success? The most feasible approach to understanding is ardent pedigree analysis. What ultimately follows is the recognition that an extraordinary proportion of favorable nicks demonstrate distinct inbreeding patterns. Over the course of time, one of the patterns most closely associated with successful runners and producers are those of female family inbreeding. This involves the crossing of family strains, creating inbreeding patterns to influential matriarchs.

Another series of distinct patterns commonly observed in the pedigrees of productive nicks is the crossing of close relatives. In these situations, both the sire and dam carry ancestors who are remarkably similar in concentrations of common blood.

The previously noted Chief's Crown/Habitat mare nick demonstrates the following pedigree:

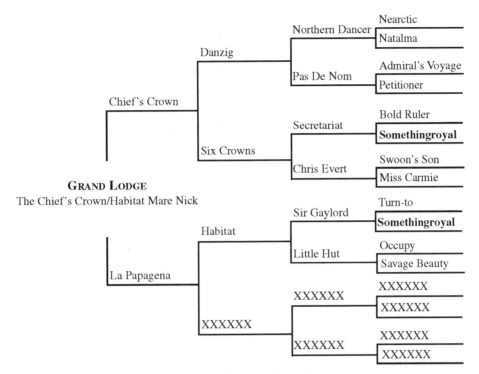

	Danzig	Northern Dancer	Nearctic
			Natalma
		Pas De Nom	Admiral's Voyage
Chief's Crown			Petitioner
	Six Crowns	Secretariat	Bold Ruler
			Somethingroyal
		Chris Evert	Swoon's Son
			Miss Carmie

GRAND LODGE
The Chief's Crown/Habitat Mare Nick

	Habitat	Sir Gaylord	Turn-to
			Somethingroyal
		Little Hut	Occupy
La Papagena			Savage Beauty
	XXXXXX	XXXXXX	XXXXXX
			XXXXXX
		XXXXXX	XXXXXX
			XXXXXX

*The XXXs indicate the quadrant of the pedigree that would change when using the Chief's Crown with any Habitat mare.

This cross exhibits inbreeding 4x4 to the great matriarch Somethingroyal. She is dam of both Secretariat (the broodmare sire of Chief's Crown) and Sir Gaylord (the sire of Habitat). The most distinguished member of this specific nick was the English juvenile champion and successful international sire Grand Lodge.

Throughout much of Thoroughbred history, the development of superior male and female lines has followed pathways in which female family inbreeding has taken place. All of this has been comprehensively detailed in the book, *Inbreeding to Superior Females* (by Rommy Faversham and Leon Rasmussen, 1999).

Nicks, then, can be divided into two major categories. Explainable nicks can be supported by specific reasons why the affinity manifests itself. This usually involves these key inbreeding patterns but may also rely on other Thoroughbred-related issues, including salient relationships of conformation or temperament that might be expressed. Unexplainable nicks, on the contrary, are those that "just work" without any observable reason.

This distinction becomes useful in that explainable nicks are more likely to be 1) predictable, 2) reversible, and 3) transmissible.

Explainable nicks are much more likely to be predictable. For example, since Chief's Crown would generate progeny inbred to Somethingroyal whenever bred to Habitat mares, a fortuitous combination might have been forecast. Inbreeding to this key matriarch had already become an established method for success internationally. Anticipating favorable patterns of female family inbreeding is a valuable method in mating decisions, particularly among untested or unproven sires and dams.

Explainable nicks are also more likely to be reversible, in that they work favorably in either direction. While it is early to evaluate Chief's Crown as a broodmare sire, there is anecdotal evidence (first returns) that his daughters cross well with stallions who carry Habitat blood.

It is also more likely that explainable nicks will be transmissible. This means that the same successful affinities and inbreeding patterns will continue from one generation to the next. In the case of Chief's Crown as a sire-of-sires, the early yield shows good anecdotal evidence that a number of his sons at stud cross particularly well with mares who contribute additional complementary strains of Somethingroyal.

More than anything else, a successful nick is the result of providing enough opportunities to manifest the potential synergy. Some of the most powerful nicks have been cultivated by breeders who stood a pair of stallions with a strong blood affinity for each other on the same farm, thus facilitating the cross.

A classic illustration of this was the potent combination of the great stallion Fair Play with the blood of Rock Sand. In the early 20th century, August Belmont II developed a Thoroughbred dynasty at his Nursery Stud in Kentucky. This reshaping of the American racehorse was in large part associated with marked accumulation of foundation matriarch Pocahontas.

Fair Play, bred by Belmont in 1905, was a multiple major stakes winner (Jerome H., etc.) at age three when ranked third-best of his generation. His pedigree demonstrated 5x5 inbreeding to Pocahontas. By the time Fair Play returned to Nursery Stud to commence stallion duty in 1910, Rock Sand was already in his fourth season there.

Rock Sand (1900), an English Triple Crown winner, was purchased by August Belmont in 1906 and transferred to his Nursery Stud. There, he would stand for the next six seasons. Rock Sand's pedigree was a cornucopia of Pocahontas strains, a total of five through her three best sons.

Fair Play became one of the most dominant stallions of his era, leading the U.S. sires list three times (1920, 1924, and 1927). It was, however, his remarkable affinity with Rock Sand that represented the overwhelming majority of his influence.

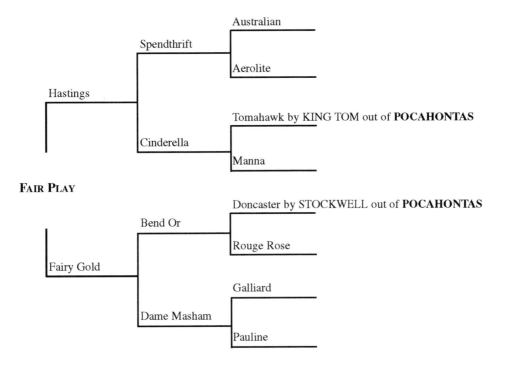

FAIR PLAY

Hastings
- Spendthrift
  - Australian
  - Aerolite
- Cinderella
  - Tomahawk by KING TOM out of **POCAHONTAS**
  - Manna

Fairy Gold
- Bend Or
  - Doncaster by STOCKWELL out of **POCAHONTAS**
  - Rouge Rose
- Dame Masham
  - Galliard
  - Pauline

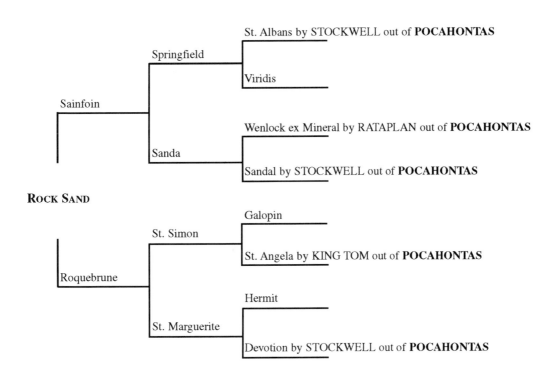

ROCK SAND

Sainfoin
- Springfield
  - St. Albans by STOCKWELL out of **POCAHONTAS**
  - Viridis
- Sanda
  - Wenlock ex Mineral by RATAPLAN out of **POCAHONTAS**
  - Sandal by STOCKWELL out of **POCAHONTAS**

Roquebrune
- St. Simon
  - Galopin
  - St. Angela by KING TOM out of **POCAHONTAS**
- St. Marguerite
  - Hermit
  - Devotion by STOCKWELL out of **POCAHONTAS**

	Total	Stakes Winners(% SWs)
All Fair Play offspring	260	47 (18%)
Fair Play offspring with Rock Sand blood	81 (31%)	24 (30%)
Fair Play offspring without Rock Sand blood	179 (69%)	23 (13%)

Fair Play sired a total of 260 offspring; 47 (or 18 percent) were stakes winners. Comprehensive review of the pedigrees of Fair Play's entire produce record reveals he sired 81 offspring carrying Rock Sand blood (appearing as broodmare sire, sire of the broodmare sire, or sire of the second dam). In other words, 81 divided by 260 equals 31 percent, the proportion of Fair Play's total foals that had the cross. This is the nick's population frequency. From this select subset of 81 individuals, a very healthy figure of 24 (30 percent) became stakes winners.

When the population frequency of a nick under review is relatively high, as it is here (31 percent), it is also useful to compare rates of success between the nick subset and the remainder of the population. In this case, Fair Play's offspring with Rock Sand blood were almost two and one-half times (31 percent to 13 percent) more likely to become stakes winners than those without it.

Actually, further scrutiny of the Nursery Stud shows this famous cross was probably even more intense.

	Total	Stakes Winners (% SWs)
Fair Play offspring with Rock Sand blood	81	24 (30%)
Males	30	19 (63%)
Females	51	5 (10%)

Of the 81 offspring, 30 were colts and geldings; 19 of these became stakes winners (an incredible 63 percent). The other 51 were fillies, only five of which became stakes winners (10 percent). What appears to be a most powerful sex bias was really a renowned breeder's aversion to the racing of fillies, as Belmont had the rooted idea that the racing of females was likely to have an adverse effect on their career as broodmares. Indeed, the large majority of Fair Play fillies out of Rock Sand mares show no record of ever having been raced. (A good number of them did go on to become important broodmares including Etoile Filante, Mlle. Dazie, and Oval.)

Fair Play was the first stallion in U.S. history to sire six winners of $100,000 or more. Five of these had first or second dams by Rock Sand.

Top Representatives Of The Fair Play/Rock Sand Nick

MAD HATTER	c. 1916	Jockey Club Gold Cup, $194,525, sire (22 SWs)
MAN o' WAR	c. 1917	Won 20 of 21 at 2 & 3, $249,465, leading sire 1926 (64 SWs)
SPORTING BLOOD	c. 1918	Travers S., Latonia Championship S., sire (4 SWs)
CHATTERTON	c. 1919	Falls City H., leading sire 1932 (11 SWs)
MY PLAY	c. 1919	Jockey Club Gold Cup, Aqueduct H., sire (8 SWs)
DUNLIN	c. 1920	Hopeful S., Dwyer S., Knickerbocker S., sire (8 SWs)
MAD PLAY	c. 1921	Belmont S., Brooklyn H., Saratoga Cup, $136,432
FAIRMOUNT	g. 1921	American Steeplechase Hall of Fame
CHANCE PLAY	c. 1923	Jockey Club Gold Cup, Saratoga Cup, $137,946, leading sire twice 1935 & 1944 (23 SWs)
CHANCE SHOT	c. 1924	Belmont S., Saratoga Special, Withers S., $142,946, sire (22 SWs)

Types of Nicking Patterns

Nicks can be classified according to their relative positions within a pedigree.

> 1) The Sire-Dam Nick
> 2) The Sire-Broodmare Sire Nick
> 3) The Sire-Broodmare Sire Line Nick
> 4) The Sire-Key Ancestor Nick
> 5) The Sire Line-Broodmare Sire Nick
> 6) The Sire Line-Broodmare Sire Line Nick
> 7) Common Key Ancestors
> 8) The Sire (Line)-Family Nick

The Sire-Dam Nick occurs when a series of breedings between a particular sire and dam produce progeny that are collectively better than the offspring from the couple's other matings.

Analysis of a potential sire-dam nick requires examination of the dam's produce record, as well as the cumulative sire record of the stallion.

The affinity between Danzig and Razyana serves as a good example. Razyana's produce record has been as follows:

1986	**DANEHILL**	c. by Danzig	Champion 3 y/o sprinter in Europe; Ladbroke Sprint Cup G1}, Cork and Orrey S.{G3}, 3rd English 2000 Guineas, etc.: champion sire
1987	Emerald	f. by El Gran Senor	Unraced; dam of winners
1989	**EUPHONIC**	f. by The Minstrel	Prix Amandine (L), 3rd Prix d'Astarte {G2}; dam of a winner
1991	**EAGLE EYED**	c. by Danzig	Arlington Classic {G2}, Sausalito H. L}, Pirate Cove H.{L}, 2nd Prix d'Arenberg{G3}, etc.: sire
1993	**Anziyan**	c. by Danzig	Winner at 2 & 4, 3rd Prix Daphnis {G3}, Prix de Cabourg {G3}: sire
1994	**HARPIA**	f. by Danzig	Shirley Jones H. {G3}, 2nd First Flight H.{G2}, Molly Pitcher Breeders' Cup H.{G2}, Top Flight (G2), Genuine Risk S.{G2}, etc.
1995	Gombeen	f. by Private Account	Placed twice
1996	NUCLEAR FREEZE	c. by Danzig	Winner
1997	**SHIBBOLETH**	c. by Danzig	Criterion S. {G3}, Jaipur H. (G3), King Charles II S.{L}
1998	**Quick to Please**	f. by Danzig	Winner at 2, 3rd EBF Conqueror S.{L}
1999	Family	f. by Danzig	Unraced
2001	Far Shores	f. by Distant View	Unraced
2002	Razzle	f. by Danzig	Unraced

	Foals	Winners (%)	Stakes Winners (%)	Graded/Group SWs (%)	Grade/Group One SWs (%)
The matings of Danzig and Razyana	9	7 (78%)	4 (44%)	4 (44%)	1 (11%)
Danzig's cumulative sire record	1,025	580 (60%)	178 (18%)	100 (10%)	42 (4%)
Razyana's produce with other stallions	4	1 (25%)	1 (25%)	0 (0%)	0 (0%)

Initiated in the early 1970s, the pattern system of sorting top international stakes races into groups (or in America, grades) 1, 2, and 3 is particularly useful in evaluating elite contemporary populations, such as the total progeny of a highly successful stallion. Only about 0.7 percent of the total North American Thoroughbred population will ever win a group or graded stakes race. Only 0.2 percent will win a Group 1 or Grade 1 race.

Danzig, with an extraordinary rate of 10 percent graded or group stakes winners from foals, has done exceedingly well with Razyana, siring four graded or group winners from eight foals, including Danehill, a European champion who has become one of the most influential international sires of our time.

The sire-dam nick considers the entire pedigree of the resulting progeny. In the case of Danehill and his full siblings, the cross is well supported by potent inbreeding 3x3 to Natalma, the dam of the great Northern Dancer. Inbreeding to Natalma and her dam, Almahmoud, has, in fact, become the predominant pattern of female family inbreeding in the world today.

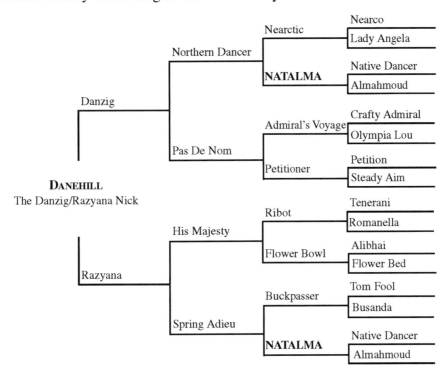

The Sire-Broodmare Sire Nick occurs when a sufficient number of matings between a specific sire and broodmare sire get progeny that are significantly better, collectively, than the offspring from that sire's other matings.

Analysis of a potential Sire-Broodmare Sire Nick requires examination of the sire's total progeny to determine the subset of individuals out of mares by the particular broodmare sire.

In the previously noted affinity between Chief's Crown and the daughters of Habitat:

	Foals	Starters (%)	Winners (%)	SWs (%)
Chief's Crown Progeny out of Habitat mares	13 (2.5%)	12 (92%)	8 (62%)	5 (38%)
Chief's Crown Progeny out of other mares	503 (97.5%)	417 (83%)	287 (57%)	43 (8%)

Thirteen of the 516 foals by Chief's Crown were out of a Habitat mare for a population frequency of 2.5 percent. In this limited, but statistically significant, number of opportunities, the offspring of Chief's Crown out of Habitat mares became stakes winners almost five times more frequently than the balance of his progeny.

The Sire-Broodmare Sire nick considers 75 percent of the pedigree: All of the sire's pedigree and the broodmare sire's half of the dam. Not included is all information pertaining to the second dam.

The contrasting relationships of influential stallion, Buckpasser, serve as another interesting example of Sire-Broodmare Sire analysis.

	Foals	Starters(%)	Winners(%)	SWs(%)
Buckpasser's total progeny $56,837 Ave Earnings per Starter	320	215 (69%)	169 (54%)	36 (12%)
Out of Bold Ruler mares $23,403 Ave Earnings per Starter	33	25 (76%)	18 (55%)	2 (6%)
Out of Northern Dancer mares $182,732 Ave Earnings per Starter	10	8 (80%)	8 (80%)	6 (60%)

Buckpasser (1963) and Bold Ruler (1954) both stood at the legendary Claiborne Farm in Kentucky. This, in combination with the stallions' ownership by members of the Phipps family, allowed a good number of daughters of the great Bold Ruler to be mated to Buckpasser. In all, 33 (just over 10 percent) of Buckpasser's total progeny were out of Bold Ruler mares. Unfortunately, the results were less than good. Collectively, these individuals were able to become winners at a comparable rate as the progeny total but could not stay in training long enough to make even half the average career earnings of the total population. Subsequent theorization has included observations that Buckpasser often got horses with knee and foreleg problems, while Bold Ruler had a tendency to pass on arthritis, thus the formation of a "negative nick."

No such bad fortune occurred between the daughters of Northern Dancer (1961) and Buckpasser. From only 10 foals, six were stakes winners including L'Enjoleur and Norcliffe, who between them were honored as Canadian Horse of the Year three consecutive years (1974-76).

The Sire-Broodmare Sire Line Nick occurs when a sufficient number of matings between a specific sire and broodmare sire line get progeny that are significantly better, collectively, than the offspring from that sire's other matings.

Analysis of a potential Sire-Broodmare Sire line nick requires examination of the sire's total progeny to determine the subset of individuals out of mares by the particular broodmare sire line.

During his years at Claiborne Farm, Round Table (1954) developed a number of strong affinities with particular lines of mares. By far, the most potent of these was his cross with the daughters of fellow Claiborne stallion, Nasrullah (1940), and his male line. The following table demonstrates that the stallion, when bred in this fashion (36 percent of the time), was more than twice (31 to 15 percent) as effective in producing stakes winners as compared with all of other broodmare sire lines combined.

	Foals (% of Total)	SWs (% of Total)
Round Table's total progeny	405	83 (20%)
Out of Nasrullah-line mares	144 (36%)	44 (31%)
Out of other mares	261 (64%)	39 (15%)

The Round Table-Nasrullah nick was a six-generation outcross, with little to support it from a pedigree point of view. One theory suggested an ideal blending of temperaments between the fiery nature of Nasrullah stock and the more sobering, subdued character of Round Table.

The Sire-Broodmare Sire Line nick considers a smaller portion of the total pedigree. Nevertheless, examination of the remaining pedigree structure may often provide useful information to help explain the affinity.

This schematic pedigree of Breeders' Cup Turf champion In the Wings demonstrates one of the most successful contemporary nicks in Europe: the cross of champion sire Sadler's Wells with Never Bend-line mares. The pedigree shows inbreeding to the influential matriarch Lalun 4x5 through her sons Bold Reason [the broodmare sire of Sadler's Wells (1981)] and Never Bend (1960).

	Foals	Stakes Winners(%)	Group SWs(%)	Group 1 SWs(%)
Sadler's Wells's total progeny	1,348	213 (16%)	124 (9%)	60 (4%)
Out of Never Bend-line mares	206 (15.3%)	45 (22%)	26 (13%)	15 (7%)
Out of other mares	1,142 (84.7%)	168 (15%)	98 (9%)	45 (4%)

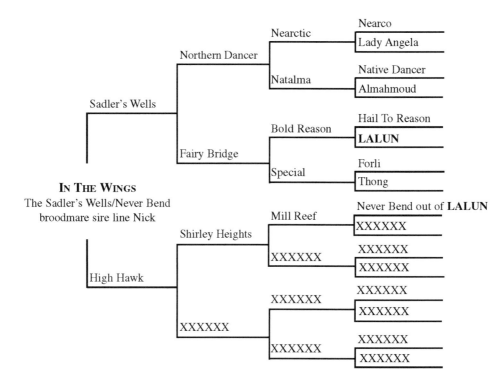

IN THE WINGS
The Sadler's Wells/Never Bend
broodmare sire line Nick

The statistics indicate that 15.3 percent (one-eighth) of Sadler's Wells's offspring have been out of Never Bend-line mares. Individuals with this nick have become black-type winners about 50 percent more frequently than their sire's other foals. This same group has gone on to become Group 1 winners about 80 percent more frequently than the rest.

SADLER'S WELLS' GROUP I WINNERS
OUT OF NEVER BEND-LINE MARES

Out of a Darshaan mare:	EBADIYLA, GREEK DANCE, HIGH CHAPARRAL, MILAN, QUARTER MOON, YESTERDAY, ISLINGTON
Out of a Doyoun mare:	DALIAPOUR
Out of an Irish River mare:	INSIGHT, SAFFRON WALDEN, SEQUOYAH
Out of a Riverman mare:	CARNEGIE
Out of a Shirley Heights mare:	IN THE WINGS, SUBTLE POWER, ALBERTO GIACOMETTI

The Never Bend Line

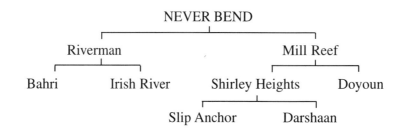

The affinity between Sadler's Wells and Never Bend-line mares is another classic example of an explainable nick that demonstrates predictability, reversibility and transmissibility.

Successful results from inbreeding to Lalun, a Kentucky Oaks winner and member of the already distinguished Bloodroot family, certainly could have been anticipated.

Secondly, the reverse cross of Never Bend-line stallions with Sadler's Wells' mares is already showing to be extremely effective.

	Dams	Foals	Stakes Winners (%)	Group SWs (%)
Sadler's Wells' cumulative broodmare sire totals	341	1,197	78 (7%)	38 (3%)
By Never Bend-line stallions	110	124 (10%)	12 (10%)	7 (6%)
By other stallions	231	1,073 (90%)	66 (6%)	31 (3%)

Through 2003, 10 percent of the foals out of Sadler's Wells mares have been by Never Bend-line sires. This select subset has demonstrated about twice the rate of stakes success than the rest of the produce from broodmares by Sadler's Wells. Among these black-type performers are multiple Group 1 winners Morshdi (Slip Anchor - Reem Albaraari, by Sadler's Wells) and Sakhee (Bahri – Thawakib, by Sadler's Wells).

Finally, there is significant early evidence that the sons of Sadler's Wells at stud continue to manifest this affinity. At least 12 different sons of Sadler's Wells have already sired group winners out of Never Bend-line mares. It's also worth noting that Sadler's Wells's full brother Fairy King did exceptionally well with this same line of broodmares.

The Sire-Key Ancestor Nick occurs when the matings between a specific sire and all of the mares carrying the blood of a particular ancestor (anywhere in the pedigree) are significantly better, collectively, than the offspring from the sire's other progeny.

Analysis of a potential Sire-Key Ancestor nick requires examination of the pedigrees of all of the sire's offspring to determine the subset of individuals involved.

The previously reviewed Fair Play/Rock Sand cross is an example of this nick. As noted, Fair Play's offspring out of mares carrying Rock Sand blood somewhere in their pedigree were almost two and one-half times more likely to become stakes winners than those without his presence.

The Sire Line-Broodmare Sire Nick occurs when a sufficient number of matings between a specific sire line and a key broodmare sire get progeny that are significantly better, collectively, than the offspring from all of that sire line's other matings.

Analysis of this kind of nick requires examination of the sire line's total progeny to determine the subset of individuals out of mares by the particular broodmare sire.

An example of this is the extraordinary affinity that sons of Nasrullah (1940) had with the daughters of Princequillo (1940). It represents a near reversal of the previously noted nick between Princequillo's son, Round Table, and the daughters of Nasrullah.

Nasrullah was himself the sire of only one individual out of a Princequillo mare, a filly who failed to earn a dime in two lifetime starts. So much for first impressions, as the following statistics on his sons at stud indicate.

	Named Foals	Winners (%)	SWs (%)	Earnings Index
The Sons of Nasrullah as sires	17,069	8,062 (47%)	945 (5.5%)	1.31
Out of daughters of Princequillo	142 (0.8%)	75 (53%)	25 (17.6%)	5.20

TOP REPRESENTATIVES BY SONS OF NASRULLAH OUT OF PRINCEQUILLO MARES

		Sire	
BOLD LAD	c. 1962	Bold Ruler	U.S. juvenile champion, $516,465, Champagne S.
DIPLOMAT WAY	c. 1964	Nashua	$493,760, Blue Grass S., Oaklawn H., Arlington-Washington Futurity
SUCCESSOR	c. 1964	Bold Ruler	U.S. juvenile champion, $532,254, Champagne S.
SYRIAN SEA	f. 1965	Bold Ruler	$178,245, Astarita S., Selima S., Colleen S.
MILL REEF	c. 1968	Never Bend	Horse of the Year in Europe at 3, English Derby, Arc de Triomphe
SAN SAN	f. 1969	Bald Eagle	Prix de l'Arc de Triomphe (G1), Prix Vermeille (G1)
SECRETARIAT	c. 1970	Bold Ruler	U.S. Horse of the Year at 2 & 3, Triple Crown
GELINOTTE	f. 1977	Never Bend	Venezuelan Horse of the Year, Cl. Ciudad de Caracas (G1)

The sons of Nasrullah combined to sire 17,069 named foals. Cumulatively, they got 47 percent winners and 5.5 percent stakes winners. One hundred and forty-two, or less than one percent of the total foals, were out of Princequillo mares. This elite group yielded a rate of stakes winners better than three times the average (17.6 percent to 5.5 percent). The group's earnings index was four times that of the average.

The Sire Line-Broodmare Sire Line Nick occurs when the matings between a particular sire line and broodmare sire line are significantly better, collectively, than the offspring from the lines' other progeny.

Nicks of this type that involve sire lines and broodmare sire lines extending well beyond two generations can be very difficult to study, as the collection and processing of all of the data becomes an increasing problem. One would need to look at every individual foaled out of three or four generations of mares and determine which stakes winners (and what percentage of them) were sired by one of the four or five generations of stallions. This level of data processing is still well beyond the scope of most nicking applications and software.

All of this is not to say that compelling anecdotal evidence cannot be used to support the notion that powerful affinities between different sire and broodmare sire lines exist.

One of the most successful practices in early 20th century American breeding was the mating of sires and dams from the sire lines of Domino and Ben Brush (in either direction).

Top Representatives Of The
Domino Line-Ben Brush Line Cross

			Sire	Broodmare Sire	
SWEEP	br.c.	1907	Ben Brush	Domino	Futurity, Belmont S., influential sire
BLACK TONEY	br.c.	1911	Peter Pan	Ben Brush	Independence H., influential sire
PEBBLES	br.c.	1912	Ben Brush	Domino	A leading 2yo, 3yo, 2nd in Ky Derby
DOMINANT	br.c.	1913	Delhi	Domino	Hopeful S.
BONNIE MARY	b.f.	1917	Ultimus	Ben Brush	Fashion S., Great American S., Juvenile S.
DR. CLARK	ch.c.	1917	Broomstick	Peter Pan	Sire's richest off-spring, Mt. Vernon H.
JOHN P. GRIER	ch.c.	1917	Whisk Broom II	Disguise	Aqueduct H., Queens County H.
WILDAIR	b.c.	1917	Broomstick	Peter Pan	Metropolitan H., Delaware H.

STEP LIGHTLY	ch.f.	1918	Ultimus	Delhi	Futurity S.
BUNTING	b.c.	1919	Pennant	Broomstick	Futurity S., Havre de Grace H.
FLUVANNA	ch.f.	1921	Cudgel	Ultimus	Astoria S.
MAUD MULLER	b.f.	1922	Pennant	Broomstick	Astoria S., Demoiselle S.
CROYDEN	b.c.	1923	Peter Pan	Broomstick	Jerome H., Manhattan H.
BOSTONIAN	blk.c.	1924	Broomstick	Peter Pan	Preakness S.
BONNIE PENNANT	ch.f	1924	Pennant	Whisk Broom II	Spinaway S.
OSMAND	ch.c.	1924	Sweeper	Superman	Jerome H., Carter H., Toboggan H.
WHISKERY	br.c	1924	Whisk Broom II	Peter Pan	Kentucky Derby
SORTIE	b.c.	1925	On Watch	Broomstick	Knickerbocker H., Brooklyn H.
VICTORIAN	b.c.	1925	Whisk Broom II	Peter Pan	Preakness S., Withers S., Manhattan H.
DIAVOLO	ch.c.	1925	Whisk Broom II	Peter Pan	Saratoga Cup
HALCYON	b.c.	1928	Broomstick	Peter Pan	Hopeful S., Jamaica H., Bay Shore H.
EQUIPOISE	ch.c.	1928	Pennant	Broomstick	Pimlico Futurity, Metropolitan H., Whitney S., Suburban H.

The Domino Line

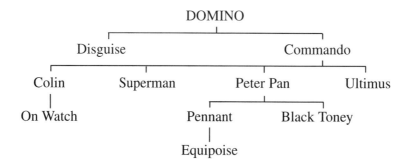

The Ben Brush Line

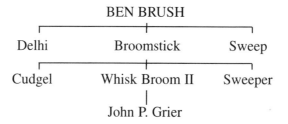

Famed horseman James R. Keene bought Domino (1891) as a yearling for $3,000. The Black Whirlwind, as he would be called, became the fastest horse of his era. Domino died prematurely after only two years at Keene's Castleton Stud, but the line was perpetuated by his son Commando. Keene also acquired Kentucky Derby winner Ben Brush (1893) at the conclusion of his racing career in 1897, the same year as Domino's death. Keene then proceeded to breed many of the best racehorses of his time by crossing these two home lines of his.

After Keene's death in 1913, Harry Payne Whitney purchased much of the former's best stock, including most of the Domino and Ben Brush stallions that would carry on each line. The H.P. Whitney Stud continued utilizing this cross well into the 1930s with unrivaled success.

Common Key Ancestors describes a strong affinity between two influential progenitors that has manifested itself across a wide array of pedigree positions.

Again, it is usually very difficult to collect and process all of the necessary data to calculate the population frequency and statistical effectiveness of this type of nick when it extends through several generations. Nevertheless, evaluation of key pedigrees throughout the course of Thoroughbred evolution has identified strong anecdotal evidence of particular sires and dams that have gone particularly well together, regardless of their place within a pedigree.

A classic example of this was the cross of Galopin (1872) with Hampton (1872). These two sires worked exceedingly well together, producing many top English runners in the late 19th and early 20th centuries. Additionally, the development of the Galopin and Hampton sire lines depended on each other. The cross was supported by inbreeding to full siblings. Galopin's paternal grand-sire, Voltigeur, was a full brother to Volley, the grandam of Hampton's sire.

TOP REPRESENTATIVES OF THE GALOPIN/HAMPTON CROSS WITHIN THREE GENERATIONS

AYRSHIRE	c.1885	Hampton & Galopin 1x2	Derby, influential sire
FLORIZEL II	c.1891	Galopin & Hampton 2x2	Goodwood Cup, Jockey Club Cup, sire
BAY RONALD	c.1893	Hampton & Galopin 1x3	Hardwicke S., Epsom Gold Cup, influential sire
PERSIMMON	c.1893	Galopin & Hampton 2x2	Derby, influential sire
DIAMOND JUBILEE	c.1897	Galopin & Hampton 2x2	English Triple Crown, influential sire
GORGOS	c.1903	Hampton & Galopin 2x3	2,000 Guineas, July S., sire
FLAIR	f.1903	Galopin & Hampton 3x3	1,000 Guineas, Middle Park Plate
COURT DRESS	f.1904	Galopin & Hampton 3x2	Top-class in U.S., influential mare
WITCH ELM	f.1904	Galopin & Hampton 3x3	1,000 Guineas, Cheveley Park S.
BAYARDO	c.1906	Hampton & Galopin 2x2	Middle Park, Dewhurst, Eclipse, St. Leger, Champion, Ascot Gold Cup, influential sire
CHERIMOYA	f.1908	Hampton & Galopin 2x3	English Oaks (in her only race)

This led to another successful pattern several generations later with the combination of foundation stallions Gainsborough (1915) and Teddy (1913). Each carried a cross of Galopin and Hampton, and both originated from the same family. Their common matriarch, May Queen, was the fourth dam of Teddy and the fifth dam of Gainsborough. For good measure, the cross also brought together the potent brother-sister combination of St. Simon and Angelica.

TOP REPRESENTATIVES OF THE GAINSBOROUGH/TEDDY CROSS WITHIN THREE GENERATIONS

CHULMLEIGH	c. 1934	Gainsborough & Teddy 2x2	St. Leger S.
TANT MIEUX	c. 1937	Teddy & Gainsborough 2x3	Highweight 2yo in England, Gimcrack S.
OWEN TUDOR	c. 1938	Gainsborough & Teddy 2x3	English highweight at 3 & 4, Derby S.
CITATION	c. 1945	Teddy & Gainsborough 3x3	U.S. Horse of the Year at 3, juvenile champion
BOREALIS	c. 1941	Teddy & Gainsborough 2x3	Coronation Cup
COHOES	c. 1954	Gainsborough & Teddy 3x3	Saranac H., Brooklyn H., Whitney S.
AURELIUS	c. 1958	Gainsborough & Teddy 3x3	St. Leger S., Craven S.

The Sire (Line)-Family Nick occurs when a sufficient number of matings between a particular sire (or his male line) and the tail-female descendants of a given family get progeny that are significantly better, collectively, than the offspring of other matings to that sire and family.

This type of affinity is usually uncovered by analyzing family tables of racehorses and noting exceptional success with select stallions and their male lines.

The stallion Grey Dawn II (1962) enjoyed a most remarkable nick with the family of Shy Dancer (1955). Figure 1 shows her family tree. The 23 group or graded stakes winners issued by the Shy Dancer line are noted in bold capital letters. Of these, five were by Grey Dawn II (including champion juvenile filly Heavenly Cause). Another four were out of Grey Dawn II mares, and one was sired by a son of Grey Dawn II (Vigors). In all, Grey Dawn II appears in the pedigrees of 15 of the 23 group or graded winners that the Shy Dancer family has produced through 2003.

The statistics are even more impressive from the stallion's point of view.

	Foals	Stakes Winners	Graded SWs
Grey Dawn II total progeny	765	74 (10%)	30 (4%)
$48,585 Avg Earnings per Starter			
With Shy Dancer-line mares	32 (4.2%)	8 (25%)	5 (16%)
$168,427 Avg Earnings per Starter			

FIGURE 1 - GRADED AND GROUP STAKES WINNERS FROM THE FAMILY OF SHY DANCER

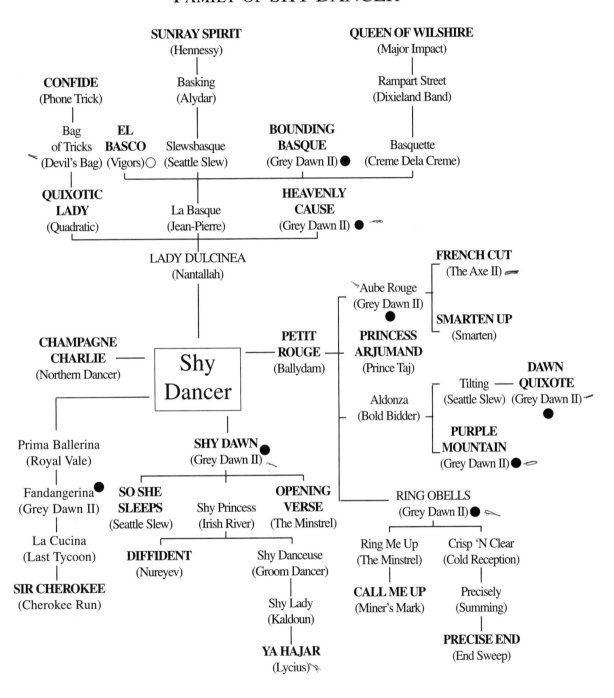

Thirty-two of Grey Dawn's progeny were out of Shy Dancer-line mares, a population frequency of 4.2 percent. This select subset earned, per starter, three and a half times more than their sire's overall total.

Another contemporary American example of a strong Sire (Line)/Family nick is the male line of Northern Dancer (1961) with the family of Thong (1964). So far, 13 of the 23 group and graded stakes winners from the tail-female line of Thong have been sired by a Northern Dancer-line stallion. Five of these were champions or highweights, including Nureyev and Sadler's Wells.

A noteworthy European nick of this kind was the affinity the Tourbillon (1928) sire line shared with the family of Sweet Lavender (1923). It was spearheaded by a trio of closely-related individuals, My Babu, Ambiorix, and Klairon.

The Tourbillon Line

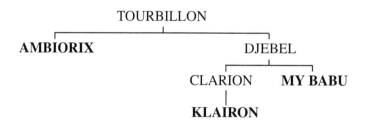

The Sweet Lavender Line

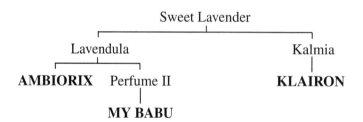

My Babu	(1945)	English highweight, 2,000 Guineas, Sussex S., sire (41 SWs)
Ambiorix	(1946)	French highweight, Prix Lupin, Prix Greffulhe, sire (51 SWs)
Klairon	(1952)	French highweighted miler, 2,000 Guineas, Prix Jacques le Marois, sire (37 SWs)

From relatively few opportunities, the Tourbillon/Sweet Lavender nick yielded these three superior runners and sires. Interestingly, all were French-bred bay colts who became leaders of their age, winning stakes at two and three. All three were brilliant milers, found wanting when tested beyond a middle distance. All of them became influential stallions, siring between 11 and 12 percent stakes winners. Despite the overall regression of the Tourbillon sire line (as well as the original

Herod sire line as a whole), these stallions have become important maternal influences in contemporary pedigrees.

Thoroughbred History's Five Most Famous Nicks

True nicks occur infrequently. But when, in fact, they do manifest themselves, they are capable of everything from an isolated spurt of success to shifting the whole balance of power within the spectrum of Thoroughbred bloodlines.

Figure 2 identifies the key nicks along the dominant male line of the great foundation stallion, Eclipse. This series of providential crosses was pivotal in making the Eclipse line what it has become today: The line responsible for more than 95 percent of the world's viable tail-male lines.

1) The Cross of Eclipse/Herod/Matchem

It is quite fitting that, among the dozens of male lines that vied for survival during the formative years in Thoroughbred development, it would be the same trio of sires whose blood crossed so well together that ultimately became the only ones to perpetuate their tail-male lines all the way into the 21st century.

At first, the different combinations of Eclipse, Herod, and Matchem established an elite collection of racehorses.

English Classic Winners With The Cross Of Eclipse/Herod/Matchem Within Two Generations

MAID OF THE OAKS	1783 OAKS	By Herod out of Rarity, by Matchem
PHENOMENON	1783 ST LEGER	By Herod out of Frenzy, by Eclipse
SERGEANT	1784 DERBY	By Eclipse out of Aspasia, by Herod
NIGHTSHADE	1788 OAKS	By Pot-8-O's, a son of Eclipse out of Cytheria, by Herod
SKYSCRAPER	1789 DERBY	By Highflyer, a son of Herod out of Everlasting, by Eclipse
HIPPOLYTA	1790 OAKS	By Mercury, a son of Eclipse out of Hip, by Herod
PORTIA	1791 OAKS	By Volunteer, a son of Eclipse out of Sister to Sting, by Herod
EAGER	1791 DERBY	By Florizel, a son of Herod out of a Matchem Mare
VOLANTE	1792 OAKS	By Highflyer, a son of Herod out of Fanny, by Eclipse
TARTAR	1792 ST LEGER	By Florizel, a son of Herod out of Ruth, by Eclipse
JOHN BULL	1792 DERBY	By Fortitude, a son of Herod out of Xantippe, by Eclipse
WAXY	1793 DERBY	By Pot-8-O's, a son of Eclipse out of Maria, by Herod

BENINGBROUGH	1794 ST LEGER	By King Fergus, a son of Eclipse out of a daughter of Herod
PLATINA	1795 OAKS	By Mercury, a son of Eclipse out of a daughter of Herod
METEORA	1805 OAKS	By Meteor, a son of Eclipse out of Maid of All Work, by Herod

Between 1783 and 1795, runners with a form of this cross (within two generations) won an amazing 15 of the 39 English classics. The most important individual on this list is 1793 Derby winner Waxy, who (as indicated in Figure 2) became the unique second-generation descendant of Eclipse responsible for carrying on his dominant male line.

By the early 1800s, Eclipse, Herod, and Matchem were appearing in the third and fourth generations of prominent contemporary pedigrees, while accumulating further relationships with one another. In time, these crosses became the backbone of pedigrees throughout the Thoroughbred population.

Is there any explanation why these three crossed so well together as to shape this newly developing breed? It all goes back to an absolutely remarkable series of family links that the triumvirate of Eclipse, Herod, and Matchem shared with one another.

As almost any casual student of bloodlines knows, every recognized Thoroughbred in the world traces in direct male line to one of three foundation sires: The Darley Arabian, the Byerly Turk, and the Godolphin Arabian. Each had a direct male-line descendant, who in turn became solely responsible for carrying on their respective lines. The Darley Arabian (imported to England in 1704) was the great-great grandsire of Eclipse (1764), the Byerly Turk (imported in 1688) was the great-great grandsire of Herod (1758), and the Godolphin Arabian (imported around 1730) became the grandsire of Matchem (1748). This is depicted in Figure 3 with arrows along each male line.

Remarkably, in the case of all three foundation stallions, their direct heirs (underlined in Figure 3) (the first generation of their male-line to be bred in England) descended from the same matriarch, an unnamed daughter of the sire Spanker. As illustrated in Figure 3, she was the dam of Jigg, the third dam of Bartlet's Childers, and the fourth dam of Cade.

This enigmatic broodmare, foaled around 1690, is the fundamental connection among the great original male lines. It is truly extraordinary, then, to note that all three - Eclipse, Herod, and Matchem - demonstrated multiple, complementary strains of this Spanker mare within their pedigrees.

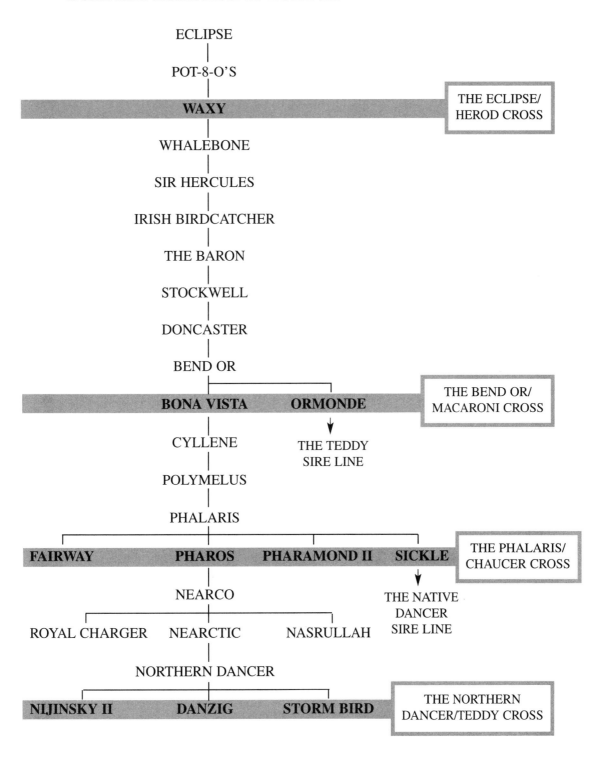

FIGURE 2 - KEY NICKS ALONG THE DOMINANT MALE LINE OF ECLIPSE

ECLIPSE

POT-8-O'S

WAXY — THE ECLIPSE/ HEROD CROSS

WHALEBONE

SIR HERCULES

IRISH BIRDCATCHER

THE BARON

STOCKWELL

DONCASTER

BEND OR

BONA VISTA — **ORMONDE** — THE BEND OR/ MACARONI CROSS

CYLLENE — THE TEDDY SIRE LINE

POLYMELUS

PHALARIS

FAIRWAY — **PHAROS** — **PHARAMOND II** — **SICKLE** — THE PHALARIS/ CHAUCER CROSS

NEARCO — THE NATIVE DANCER SIRE LINE

ROYAL CHARGER — NEARCTIC — NASRULLAH

NORTHERN DANCER

NIJINSKY II — **DANZIG** — **STORM BIRD** — THE NORTHERN DANCER/TEDDY CROSS

All of this should be given further perspective. The Spanker Mare was the only ancestor, male or female, common to the pedigrees of Eclipse, Herod, and Matchem. This makes the multiple strains all three received from her all the more remarkable. The formative course, then, for all three sire lines involved the concentration of this central matriarch's strains. In previous writings, I have referred to her as the "Ancestral Mom." She is the most influential Thoroughbred progenitor of all time.

FIGURE 3

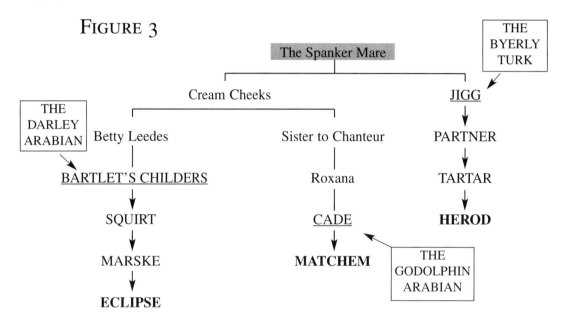

2) Lexington with Glencoe mares

This was, indeed, the union between 19th-century America's greatest sire and broodmare sire. Lexington (1850), the land's dominant stallion throughout the 1860s and 1870s, could rightfully be considered the greatest American sire of all time with an unprecedented 16 sire titles. Previous to this, Glencoe (1831), an imported English classic winner, was America's premier sire from the mid-1840s to the onset of Lexington's even longer reign. Glencoe was a phenomenal sire of fillies, and, if such records had been kept, he would be the most celebrated broodmare sire of all time. Together in one pedigree, Lexington and Glencoe figured to be a major hit.

John Hervey's two-volume masterpiece, *Racing in America* (1944), remains the definitive work in chronicling the development of early American racing and breeding. In it he wrote, "Glencoe mares threw offspring of the highest class to other sires, but so many to Lexington's cover that the cross became the most successful in our breeding history." Hervey emphasized the deliberate nature of Woodburn Farm's R.A. Alexander's work to acquire as many Glencoe mares as possible for the sole purpose of sending them to his star sire.

The cross of Lexington with Glencoe mares was a six-generation outcross without any common ancestors from the 19th century.

All of this begs the question as to whether there really was a genuine nick between these two colossal progenitors or whether the cross was so prodigious because the opportunities were so abundant.

According to Hervey, Lexington sired 543 foals, but the writer noted this probably was not an exact total, given the turbulent times of the Civil War when so many horses were lost and killed. Our thorough review of the first three volumes of the *American Stud Book* identified 506 of the 543 reported progeny by Lexington.

Another subset of Lexington's progeny worthy of examination is his offspring that demonstrated patterns of female family inbreeding. Analysis of all of the pedigrees revealed three patterns:

1) When Lexington was bred to a daughter of the stallion, Vandal, the progeny had inbreeding to the matriarch Lady Grey 4x6. She was the third dam of Lexington and Vandal's fourth dam.

2) When Lexington was bred to a daughter of the important broodmare Levity, the progeny had inbreeding to the Lady Grey 4x6. She was Levity's fourth dam.

3) When Lexington was bred to a daughter of the stallion Albion, the progeny had inbreeding to the full sisters Emily and Diana 5x4.

To compare how Lexington performed with Glencoe mares as compared with his total progeny and with those broodmares that created female family inbreeding patterns, a passage was taken from Hervey's text where he subjectively identified Lexington's best runners. He listed 16 "top flight" colts and nine "top flight" fillies, as well as 19 colts and 13 fillies "a shade below," for a total of 57 he felt were superior to the rest.

LEXINGTON'S BEST RUNNERS

Runner	Out of a Daughter of:	Runner	Out of a Daughter of:
ACROBAT	**Glencoe**	LANCASTER	Hedgford
ALICE WARD*	**Glencoe**	LIGHTNING*	Hedgford
ANNIE BUSH	**Albion**	LILLY WARD	Leviathan
ANSEL	Yorkshire	LOADSTONE*	Hedgford
ARIZONA*	The Cure	MADAM DUDLEY	Flying Dutchman
ASTEROID*	**Glencoe**	MAIDEN	**Glencoe**

BAYFLOWER*	Yorkshire	MERRILL	**Glencoe**
BAYSWATER	Yorkshire	MONARCHIST*	**Glencoe & Levity**
BEACON	Yorkshire	NEVADA	**Glencoe & Levity**
BETTIE WARD*	Whalebone	NIAGARA	Yorkshire
BONITA	**Albion**	NORFOLK*	**Glencoe**
CARRIE ATHERTON	Sovereign	OPTIMIST	**Glencoe**
CROSSLAND	**Albion**	PAT MALOY	American Eclipse
DANIEL BOONE*	**Glencoe**	PREAKNESS*	Yorkshire
DUKE OF MAGENTA*	Yorkshire	R.B. CONNOLLY	Leviathan
ENCHANTRESS	**Glencoe**	RUBICON	Yorkshire
FANNY CHEATHAM*	Leviathan	SALINA*	**Glencoe & Levity**
FOSTER*	Yorkshire	SPARTAN	**Albion**
GENERAL DUKE	Yorkshire	STAMPS	**Glencoe & Levity**
GILROY	**Glencoe**	SULTANA*	**Glencoe & Levity**
HAMBURG	Alex. Churchill	SUSAN ANN	Chesterfield
HARRY BASSETT*	**Albion**	THE BANSHEE	Yorkshire
HARRY OF THE WEST	Leviathan	THUNDER*	Hedgford
HIRA*	Ambassador	TOM BOWLING*	**Albion**
IDLEWILD*	**Glencoe**	TOM OCHILTREE*	Voucher
JACK MALONE	American Eclipse	UNCAS*	**Vandal**
KENTUCKY*	**Glencoe**	VAUXHALL	Yorkshire
KINGFISHER*	Kingston	WANDERER	**Vandal**
LA POLKA	**Glencoe**		

*Hervey's "top flight" individuals

	Total	"Top Flight"	"Second Flight"	Combined Best
Lexington's total progeny	506	25 (4.9%)	32 (6.3%)	57 (11.3%)
With Glencoe mares	168 (33.2%)	9 (5.4%)	9 (5.4%)	18 (10.7%)
With mares creating Female family inbreeding	66 (13.0%)	6 (9.1%)	7 (10.7%)	13 (19.7%)

The numbers, indeed, indicate that a sizable one-third of the matings to Lexington were with daughters of Glencoe. These 168 foals performed just about as expected based on their sire's total progeny averages. Whereas 11.3 percent of Lexington's total foals were on Hervey's elite list, 10.7 percent of those out of Glencoe mares made the roster.

Ironically, it was the collection of Lexington's offspring demonstrating female family inbreeding who outperformed their opportunities, with almost 20 percent of them listed among Lexington's best.

In essence then, the heralded cross of Lexington with Glencoe mares was really not a nick at all, but the union of a phenomenally successful sire and broodmare sire that performed up to its opportunities, based on the quality of Lexington's other foals. Hervey, in fact would note, "The average winnings of Lexington's get out of Glencoe mares were not larger than those by his foals from mares by other sires."

3) Bend Or with Macaroni mares

The strongest connection between a stallion and a broodmare sire in late 19th-century England was the cross of Bend Or with Macaroni mares. It was best exploited by the first Duke of Westminster who bred and owned the Derby-winning Bend Or (1877) and then supplied him at stud with daughters of Macaroni (1860).

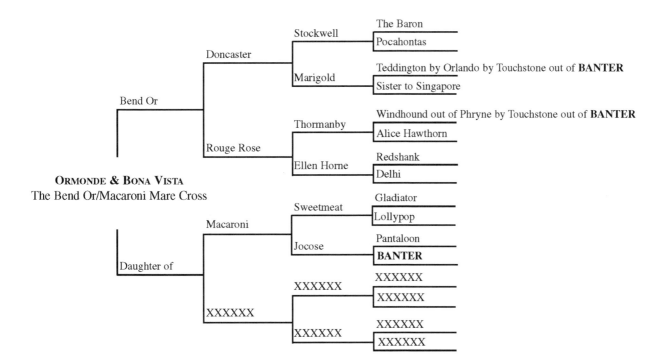

ORMONDE & BONA VISTA
The Bend Or/Macaroni Mare Cross

A review of the resulting pedigree shows Bend Or was inbred 5x5 to the foundation stallion Touchstone, whose dam, Banter, was the grandam of Macaroni. The Bend Or/Macaroni nick, therefore, created inbreeding to the influential matriarch Banter 7x7x4.

Top Representatives With The
Bend Or/Macaroni Mare Cross

ORMONDE	c., 1883	Undefeated in 16 starts, Eng. Triple Crown, Progenitor of the Teddy sire line
KENDAL	c., 1883	July S., Rous Mem. S., influential sire
OSSORY	c., 1885	Criterion S., Prince of Wales S., St. James's Palace S.
MARTAGON	c., 1887	Ascot Gold Vase, Goodwood Cup, influential sire
ORVIETO	c., 1888	Sussex S., Newmarket Derby & St. Leger, influential sire
BONA VISTA	c., 1889	2,000 Guineas, progenitor of the Phalaris line
LAVENO	c., 1892	Jockey Club S., Champion S., influential sire

From incomplete records, Bend Or appears to have sired about one-quarter of his total foals out of Macaroni mares. From this fraction came the majority of his best runners (seven of the top 10). Additionally, Bend Or's get from Macaroni mares accounted for the overwhelming majority of his influence on the breed. This included the undefeated Ormonde, who became the forebear of the Teddy male line that survives to this day through Damascus. Most importantly, it included Bona Vista, who would be responsible for carrying on the dominant male line of Eclipse (Figure 2). If nothing else, Bona Vista got the line to the 20th century and the "Phalaris revolution."

4) Phalaris with Chaucer mares

When Phalaris was foaled in 1913, the Galopin/St. Simon male line had captured 18 of the last 25 English sire titles. By the time Phalaris and his sons had established themselves at stud, his own line had become the mightiest in the land, only to become even stronger with time.

The 16th Earl of Derby generated this shift in the breed and bred both Phalaris and Chaucer (1900). When Lord Derby, in turn, sent the daughters of Chaucer to Phalaris, a stallion he had been unable to sell earlier, the results were providential.

Top Representatives Of The
Phalaris/Chaucer Mare Cross

PHAROS	c. 1920	Champion S., 14 wins in 30 starts., leading sire in England & France, sire of Nearco
WARDENOFTHEMARCHES	c. 1922	Champion S., 9 wins in 21 starts.
COLORADO	c. 1923	English highweight at 4, 2,000 Guineas, Eclipse S., influential sire
SICKLE	c. 1924	Prince of Wales S., leading U.S. sire, progenitor of the Native Dancer sire line
PHARAMOND II	c. 1925	Middle Park S., progenitor of the Buckpasser line

FAIRWAY	c. 1925	English highweight at 2, 3, & 4, St. Leger S., leading English sire four times
FAIR ISLE	f. 1927	English 2yo & 3yo highweight filly, 1,000 Guineas, five wins in 10 starts.
CAERLEON	c. 1927	Eclipse S., Union Jack S.

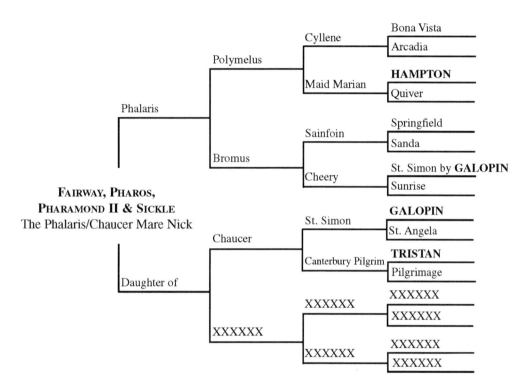

FAIRWAY, PHAROS, PHARAMOND II & SICKLE
The Phalaris/Chaucer Mare Nick

The Phalaris/Chaucer mare nick featured a 4x4 cross of the very close relatives Hampton (1872) and Tristan (1878). Phalaris himself demonstrated the previously noted cross of Hampton and Galopin 3x4. Chaucer was a grandson of both Galopin and Tristan. The latter, like Hampton, was a grandson of Newminster. Their third dam was the taproot mare Queen Mary, and their internal pedigrees contained the full brothers Rataplan and Stockwell, by The Baron out of Pocahontas.

From incomplete sire records, Phalaris appears to have got about 15 percent of his total progeny out of Chaucer mares. From this relatively small share came the majority of his richest winners (six of the top seven), as well as virtually all of his subsequent influence on the breed. Almost all of this came from two sets of full brothers, Pharos and Fairway, as well as Sickle and Pharamond II (Figure 2). Together, they created a series of male-line dynasties that has dominated to the present. Breeding theorist Franco Varola began referring to this pedigree shift as the "Phalaris Revolution." Today, Phalaris accounts for more than 80 percent of the world's male lines. And this dominance was initiated by the Phalaris/Chaucer mare nick.

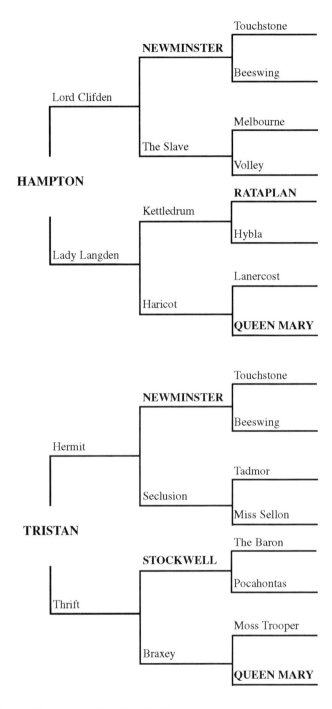

5) Northern Dancer with Teddy-line mares

Northern Dancer has become the breed's most influential stallion for at least the last 25 years. His male line now represents the most prolific and successful branch of Phalaris internationally, with more than a 30 percent share of the world's Thoroughbred population.

As has often been the case, it was Northern Dancer's breeder and owner who benefited most from the stallion's affinity with Teddy-line mares. E.P. Taylor's judicious choices of broodmares for his champion sire yielded many of Northern Dancer's best produce.

The Teddy Line

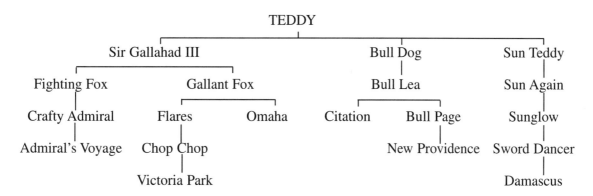

Why did Northern Dancer do particularly well with mares carrying Teddy blood? The connection is this. The closest inbreeding in Northern Dancer's own pedigree was to Gainsborough (4x5), who, as previously noted, had a strong affinity with Teddy (they were both from the same family, each with a cross of Galopin and Hampton).

TOP REPRESENTATIVES OF THE NORTHERN DANCER/TEDDY LINE MARE NICK

		Broodmare Sire	
NIJINSKY II	c. 1967	Bull Page	Eng. Triple Crown, highweight in England, Ireland
FANFRELUCHE	f. 1967	Chop Chop	Horse of the Year in Canada at 3, Alabama S.
MINSKY	c. 1968	Bull Page	Highweight 2yo in Ireland, Railway S.
NORTHERN TASTE	c. 1971	Victoria Park	Prix de la Foret (G1), Prix Djebel, Prix Thomas Bryon, leading sire in Japan
DANCE IN TIME	c. 1974	Chop Chop	Champion 3yo colt in Canada
THE MINSTREL	c. 1974	Victoria Park	Irish & England. Derby, highweight in England
NORTHERNETTE	f. 1974	New Providence	Champion filly in Canada at 2 & 3, Top Flight H. (G1)
GIBOULEE	c. 1974	Victoria Park	Champion older horse in Canada
DANZIG	c. 1977	Admiral's Voyage	Leading sire, undefeated
STORM BIRD	c. 1978	New Providence	Highweight 2yo colt in Ireland, Dewhurst S. (G1)

This would lead one to question whether Northern Dancer performed even better with mares carrying multiple strains of Teddy.

	Foals	Winners	SWs	Champions
Northern Dancer's total progeny	643	367 (57%)	144 (22%)	26 (4%)
Out of Teddy-line mares	70 (11%)	44 (63%)	20 (29%)	8 (11%)
Out of Teddy-line mares carrying at least two strains of Teddy	43 (7%)	29 (67%)	15 (35%)	8 (19%)

The statistics certainly bear out the fact that Northern Dancer's progeny out of Teddy-line mares outperformed their opportunities. The data also indicates that most of the best of these, in fact, carried multiple strains of Teddy.

The influence this lot has achieved at stud is immeasurable. By themselves, Nijinsky II, Danzig, and Storm Bird (Figure 2) have become dominant international sires of sires.

For Northern Dancer, however, the nick with Teddy-rich mares was really just the topper in a list of successful affinities that made him the consummate stallion of his era.

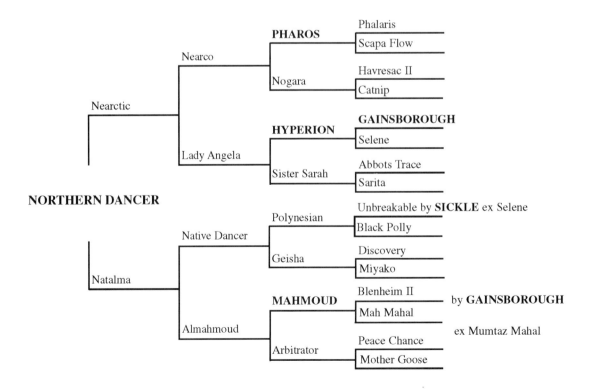

It was, in fact, Northern Dancer's total pedigree that made him such a perfect fit for his breeding environment. It incorporated many of the ingredients necessary to render him particularly compatible with so much of his contemporary broodmare population.

Northern Dancer's pedigree had the Phalaris/Chaucer nick through Pharos and Sickle 3x5. The latter was also the half-brother of Hyperion, Nearctic's broodmare sire. In other words, Northern Dancer carried a duplication of both the Phalaris/Chaucer nick and the foundation matriarch Selene.

The key elements in Northern Dancer's pedigree that made him particularly compatible with the rest of the genetic landscape include:

a) **Sickle and Hyperion**, creating an affinity for mares carrying the blood of their sibling, **Pharamond II**. Six of Northern Dancer's 26 champions had dams with Pharamond II appearing in the fourth generation or closer.

b) **Pharos**, creating an affinity with mares carrying the blood of his full brother, **Fairway**. Five of Northern Dancer's champions had dams with Fairway appearing in the fourth generation or closer.

c) **Mahmoud**, creating an affinity with mares carrying the blood of **Nasrullah** and **Royal Charger**. All three shared the same second or third dam, the great matriarch Mumtaz Mahal. Five of Northern Dancer's 26 champions were out of mares with Nasrullah appearing in the fourth generation or closer. Three of Northern Dancer's champions had dams with Royal Charger appearing within four generations.

d) Inbreeding to **Gainsborough** 4x5 (as previously discussed), creating an affinity with mares carrying the blood of **Teddy**. Thirteen of Northern Dancer's 26 champions had dams with *multiple strains* of Teddy. Eight were from the Teddy broodmare sire line. Five others had non-Teddy broodmare sire lines.

In all, 22 of Northern Dancer's 26 champions were out of broodmares carrying at least one of these key elements in their pedigrees. All of these represent examples of explainable affinities.

Over the past 30 years, Northern Dancer has become "the universal donor and recipient" in the exchange of Thoroughbred blood.

Top Contemporary Nicks

Relatively speaking, there is little variation in the design of the modern racehorse's pedigree. A majority of the world's most prestigious races (group and graded stakes) are won by horses with various combinations of the following dominant sire lines:

1) The **Northern Dancer** line.

2) The **Native Dancer** line, predominately represented by his grandson, **Mr. Prospector**.

3) The **Nasrullah** line, represented mainly by his descendants **Seattle Slew**, **Blushing Groom**, and **Never Bend**.

4) The **Royal Charger** line, primarily occurring through the sires **Roberto** and **Halo**.

These four main lines cross with a number of lesser lines which include:

5) Buckpasser

6) Damascus

7) Ribot

8) In Reality

With few exceptions, this is the look of the contemporary Thoroughbred, particularly in North America. Not since the early 19th century has the spectrum of Thoroughbred sire lines been so compressed.

Over the past 25 years, there have been dramatic shifts in the levels of success among the various sire lines. Figure 4 depicts growth patterns of the four contemporary dominant American male lines. All of the other lines have undergone a severe collective recession. The chart shows that from 1975 to 1999:

1) The **Nasrullah** sire line has been able to maintain its level of influence (roughly 20 percent of the total number of graded stakes winners).

2) The **Royal Charger** sire line has more than tripled in influence (from three percent to 10 percent) but may now be leveling off.

3) The **Northern Dancer** sire line has shown the most dramatic growth (from two percent to 30 percent).

4) The **Native Dancer** sire line has also shown a dramatic growth pattern (from eight percent to 21 percent).

FIGURE 4 - GROWTH PATTERNS IN THE DOMINANT MALE LINES OF NORTH AMERICA

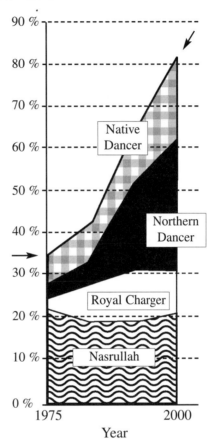

Percentage of Total North American Graded Stakes Winners

Year

The first arrow shows that in 1975 the sire lines of Nasrullah, Royal Charger, Northern Dancer and Native Dancer made up 35 percent of the total North American Graded Stakes winners. The second arrow shows the cumulative total of these four sire lines has risen to 82 percent during the last quarter of the 20th century. The majority of this rise has occurred through the advancement of the male lines of Northern Dancer and Native Dancer.

In recent years, these lines have been crossed, with the majority of combinations yielding results that have been generally commensurate with their opportunities. There are, however, several key exceptions that represent ongoing examples of broad-based affinities certainly worth being aware of. These include:

1) In Europe, the **Sadler's Wells**-line/**Never Bend**-line cross

2) The **Northern Dancer**-line/**Blushing Groom**-line cross

3) The **Mr. Prospector**-line/**Seattle Slew**-line cross

For more than a decade, Northern Dancer-line stallions have crossed particularly well with Blushing Groom-line mares. Likewise, the mating of Blushing Groom-line stallions with Northern Dancer-line mares appears to have significantly outperformed its collective opportunities.

With Northern Dancer appearing mainly in the fourth and fifth generations of current pedigrees, it is not possible to evaluate each of these reversible crosses in total. The statistics through 2003 do, however, demonstrate a significant positive trend throughout each combination.

STATISTICS ON THE
NORTHERN DANCER-LINE/BLUSHING GROOM-LINE CROSS

	Named Foals	Winners(%)	SWs(%)	Earnings Index
Blushing Groom as a sire:	512	293 (57%)	92 (18%)	4.13
With Northern Dancer mares	20	12 (60%)	5 (25%)	5.96
Blushing Groom as a broodmare sire:	1,506	811 (54%)	137 (9.1%)	2.73
With sons of Northern Dancer as sire	172	96 (56%)	24 (14%)	2.85
The sons of Northern Dancer as sires	46,276	23,647 (51%)	3,347 (7.2%)	1.71
Out of daughters of Blushing Groom	175	102 (58%)	24 (13.7%)	2.85
The sons of Blushing Groom as sires	11,860	5,143 (43%)	699 (5.9%)	1.80
Out of daughters of Northern Dancer	113	66 (58%)	15 (13.3%)	3.31
Out of daughters of Be My Guest	67	27 (40%)	2 (3%)	4.29
Out of daughters of Caerleon	47	22 (47%)	3 (6.4%)	9.15
Out of daughters of Danzig	51	25 (49%)	9 (17.6%)	6.82
Out of daughters of Fabulous Dancer	36	21 (58%)	2 (5.5%)	1.83
Out of daughters of Green Dancer	151	92 (61%)	19 (12.6%)	5.06
Out of daughters of Lyphard	97	47 (48%)	6 (6.2%)	3.94
Out of daughters of Nijinsky II	150	81 (54%)	21 (14%)	6.43
Out of daughters of Northfields	32	21 (66%)	8 (25%)	9.23
Out of daughters of Nureyev	102	60 (59%)	6 (5.9%)	4.29
Out of daughters of Pharly	32	13 (41%)	1 (3.1%)	2.06

Out of daughters of Sadler's Wells	85	39 (46%)	9 (10.6%)	19.82
Out of daughters of Storm Bird	43	19 (44%)	2 (4.7%)	2.84
Out of daughters of The Minstrel	61	30 (49%)	7 (11.5%)	3.41
Out of daughters of Topsider	35	15 (43%)	2 (5.7%)	0.78
Out of daughters of Vice Regent	30	13 (43%)	3 (10%)	1.27

The statistics indicate Blushing Groom sired a higher rate of stakes winners when bred to daughters of Northern Dancer (25 percent to 18 percent). Blushing Groom mares were never bred to Northern Dancer. Collectively, they did significantly better when bred to the sons of Northern Dancer (14 percent stakes winners to 9.1 percent). From the reversed perspective, the sons of Northern Dancer have sired a higher rate of stakes winners when bred to Blushing Groom mares, 13.7 percent to 7.2 percent. The data also shows that the sons of Blushing Groom improved when mated with daughters of Northern Dancer (13.3 percent stakes winners to 6.1 percent). Figures for Blushing Groom's sons with Northern Dancer-line mares are shown for all combinations having produced 25 or more foals. They continue to demonstrate a general pattern of good performance in getting superior runners.

TOP REPRESENTATIVES OF THE
NORTHERN DANCER-LINE/BLUSHING GROOM-LINE CROSS

		Sire	Broodmare Sire	
GROOM DANCER	c. 1984	Blushing Groom	Lyphard	Highweight 3yo in France, Prix Lupin
KAHYASI	c. 1985	Ile De Bourbon	Blushing Groom	Highweight 3yo in England, Eng. Derby, Irish Derby
QUEST FOR FAME	c. 1987	Rainbow Quest	Green Dancer	$1,824,642, Eng. Derby, Hol. Turf H. (G1)
ARAZI	c. 1989	Blushing Groom	Northern Dancer	Top 2yo in Europe & U.S.
PURSUIT OF LOVE	c. 1989	Groom Dancer	Green Dancer	Highweight 3yo Sprinter
MISSED THE STORM	f. 1990	Storm Cat	Blushing Groom	Test S. (G1), Astarita S. (G2)
SKY BEAUTY	f. 1990	Blushing Groom	Nijinsky II	Champion older mare in U.S.
GOLD SPLASH	f. 1990	Blushing Groom	Lyphard	Coronation S. (G1), Pr. M. Boussac (G1)
SERENA'S SONG	f. 1992	Rahy	Northfields	$3,283,388, U.S. Champion 3yo filly
WANDESTA	f. 1992	Nashwan	Nijinsky II	Champion U.S. turf mare
EXOTIC WOOD	f. 1992	Rahy	Dixieland Band	$890,695, Santa Monica H. (G1)

LAMMTARA	c. 1992	Nijinsky II	Blushing Groom	Undefeated, Horse of the Year in Europe
PEAKS AND VALLEYS	c. 1992	Mt. Livermore	Green Dancer	Horse of the Year in Canada at 3, $1,589,270
AWESOME AGAIN	c. 1994	Deputy Minister	Blushing Groom	$4,374,590, Breeders' Cup Classic (G1)
TRANQUILITY LAKE	f. 1995	Rahy	Danzig	$1,662,390, Yellow Ribbon H. (G1)
SILIC	c. 1995	Sillery	Sadler's Wells	Breeders' Cup Mile, Shoemaker Mile (G1)
SPANISH FERN	f. 1995	El Gran Senor	Blushing Groom	$748,370, Yellow Ribbon S. (G1)
FANTASTIC LIGHT	c. 1996	Rahy	Nijinsky II	$7,486,957, Horse of the Year in Europe
STRAVINSKY	c. 1996	Nureyev	Blushing Groom	Highweight Eng. sprinter, July Cup
WHITE HEART	c. 1996	Green Desert	Blushing Groom	Woodford Reserve Turf Classic (G1)
GIANT'S CAUSEWAY	c. 1997	Storm Cat	Rahy	Highweight England. 3yo, Eclipse S.
NOVERRE	c. 1998	Rahy	Northern Dancer	Sussex S. (G1)

One particular manifestation of this cross worthy of note is the sire, Rahy, with Northern Dancer-line mares. Blushing Groom's son Rahy has become especially effective in this role, particularly since Northern Dancer also demonstrates an affinity with Rahy's broodmare sire Halo. Both share the same grandam, the great matriarch Almahmoud.

	Foals	SWs(%)	Graded SWs(%)	Grade 1 SWs(%)
Rahy's total progeny	675	57 (8.4%)	23 (3.4%)	7 (1%)
Out of Northern Dancer-line mares	274 (41%)	26 (9.5%)	11 (4%)	5 (1.8%)
Out of other mares	401 (59%)	31 (7.7%)	12 (3%)	2 (0.5%)

While 41 percent of Rahy's progeny have been out of Northern Dancer-line mares, they have so far accounted for five of his seven most accomplished runners. They are listed among the top representatives of the Northern Dancer-Blushing Groom cross.

Another ongoing North American "mega-nick" is the combination of Mr. Prospector (1970) and Seattle Slew (1974). Both descend from the family of Myrtlewood, a top-class sprinter from the 1930s. She is the fourth dam of Mr. Prospector and the fifth dam of Seattle Slew.

Statistics On The
Mr. Prospector-Line/Seattle Slew-Line Cross

	Named Foals	Winners (%)	SWs(%)	Earnings Index
Seattle Slew as a sire:	1,018	493 (48%)	108 (10.6%)	5.10
With Mr. Prospector mares	40	20 (50%)	5 (12.5%)	5.31
Seattle Slew as a broodmare sire:	1,650	861 (52%)	119 (7.2%)	2.30
With Mr. Prospector as sire	32	17 (53%)	5 (15.6%)	5.51
The sons of Mr. Prospector as sires	45,566	22,839 (50%)	2,454 (5.4%)	1.27
Out of daughters of Seattle Slew	304	151 (50%)	21 (6.9%)	2.22
The sons of Seattle Slew as sires	19,460	8,360 (43%)	806 (4.1%)	0.98
Out of daughters of Mr. Prospector	170	98 (58%)	18 (10.6%)	5.02
Out of daughters of Fappiano	82	45 (55%)	11 (13.4%)	2.55
Out of daughters of Miswaki	74	41 (55%)	8 (10.8%)	1.49
Out of daughters of Conquistador Cielo	54	26 (48%)	6 (11.1%)	1.76

While Seattle Slew has not performed much better as a sire when bred to Mr. Prospector mares, all the other interactions have shown to be quite favorable. The daughters of Seattle Slew have produced better offspring, collectively, when bred to Mr. Prospector (15.6 percent stakes winners to 7.2 percent stakes winners). Alternatively, the sons of Mr. Prospector have done significantly better when bred to Seattle Slew mares (6.9 percent stakes winners compared with 5.4 percent). Likewise, the sons of Seattle Slew have done much better when mated with daughters of Mr. Prospector (10.6 percent stakes winners to 4.1 percent). So far (through the end of 2003), three sons of Mr. Prospector have been the broodmare sires of at least 50 foals sired by a son of Seattle Slew. As shown, all three crosses have outperformed their opportunities.

TOP REPRESENTATIVES OF THE
MR. PROSPECTOR-LINE/SEATTLE SLEW-LINE CROSS

		Sire	Broodmare Sire	
GOLDEN OPINION	f. 1986	Slew o' Gold	Mr. Prospector	Highweight 3yo filly in England/France
AGINCOURT	c. 1989	Capote	Conquistador Cielo	$338,483, Futurity S. {G1}, etc.
HISHI AKEBONO	c. 1992	Woodman	Seattle Slew	Champion Japanese Sprinter & Miler
CAPOTE BELLE	f. 1993	Capote	Fappiano	$603,315, Test S. {G1}
GOLDEN ATTRACTION	f. 1993	Mr. Prospector	Seattle Slew	U.S. juvenile filly champion
SEEKING THE PEARL	f. 1994	Seeking The Gold	Seattle Slew	Highweight in France., G1 winner in France, Japan
TOMISUE'S DELIGHT	f. 1994	A.P. Indy	Mr. Prospector	$1,207,537, Ruffian H. {G1}
PULPIT	c. 1994	A.P. Indy	Mr. Prospector	$728,200, Blue Grass S.{G2}
LU RAVI	f. 1995	A.P. Indy	Seeking the Gold	$1,589,781, Cotillion H. {G2}
CAPE TOWN	c. 1995	Seeking the Gold	Seattle Slew	$795,817, Florida Derby {G1}
EVENT OF THE YEAR	c. 1995	Seattle Slew	Mr. Prospector	$1,095,200, Jim Beam S.{G2}
LEMON DROP KID	c. 1996	Kingmambo	Seattle Slew	$3,243,770, Belmont, Travers S.
SURFSIDE	f. 1997	Seattle Slew	Seeking the Gold	$1,548,715, Frizette S. {G1}, champion
TEMPERA	f. 1999	A.P. Indy	Mr. Prospector	BC Juvenile Fillies, champ.
MINESHAFT	c. 1999	A.P. Indy	Mr. Prospector	Pimlico Special {G1}, Woodward S. {G1}, etc.

Another series of contemporary affinities appear to exist between broodmares from the **Royal Charger** line and several well-known stallions, including **Carson City**, **Danzig**, and **Waquoit**. The Royal Charger line has accounted for less than 10 percent of the total population but has been the leading contributor, in this role, to the success of these three sires.

In the case of Carson City (1987, by Mr. Prospector), 13 of his 63 SWs (21 percent) have been out of Royal Charger-line mares, including five of his 21 graded stakes winners [Lord Carson {G2}, Five Star Day {G2}, Paved in Gold {G3}, Leelanu {G3}, and Dublin {G3}]. Carson City is inbred 4x4 to Nasrullah, a three-quarter brother to Royal Charger.

For the great stallion Danzig (1977, by Northern Dancer), 10 of his 42 Grade 1 or Group 1 winners (24 percent) [Blue Duster, Contredance, Dance Smartly, Danzig Connection, Furiously, Green Desert, Pine Bluff, War Chant, Yashmak, and Zieten] and 22 of his 100 Grade 1 or Group 1 stakes winners have been out of Royal Charger-line mares.

Waquoit (1983, by Relaunch) has sired all five of his richest stakes winners from Royal Charger-line mares (including Halo America (G1) and Wicapi (G2)]. Waquoit is inbred to Mahmoud, a three-quarter brother to Mumtaz Begum, Royal Charger's grandam.

A number of other accomplished contemporary stallions have demonstrated affinities (both explainable and unexplainable) with specific broodmare sires or their lines.

Deputy Minister (1979, by Northern Dancer) has shown an affinity with **Prince John** (1953) line mares. Five of his 39 graded or group winners (13 percent) have been from mares of this otherwise declining line [Open Mind (G1), Eloquent Minister (G1), Star Minister (G2), Forest Camp (G2), and French Deputy (G2).

Gone West (1984, by Mr. Prospector) has done extremely well with the daughters of **The Minstrel** (1974). Six of his 41 graded or group winners have been out of The Minstrel mares [Zafonic (G1), Muqtarib (G2), Dazzle (G2), Performing Magic (G2), Tamayaz (G3), and Zamindar (G3)]. This is from only 38 foals (less than six percent of Gone West's total progeny).

Holy Bull (1991, by Great Above) has shown an early affinity with **Green Dancer** (1972) line mares. Two of his three richest stakes winners have been out of mares from this line. [Confessional (G1) and Turnofthecentury (G2)]. This is from only nine such foals, so far. This affinity can be explained, as Holy Bull's grandam is by Grey Dawn II, a member of the same family as Green Dancer.

Jade Hunter (1984, by Mr. Prospector) has done particularly well with **Nijinsky II** (1967) line mares. Four of his 14 graded or group winners and two of his four Grade 1 winners [Yagli (G1) and Stuka (G1)] have been from Nijinsky II line mares.

Lear Fan (1981, by Roberto) has been especially effective with daughters of **Nureyev** (1977). Five of his 62 SWs and four of his 25 graded or group winners [Loup Solitaire (G1), Verveine (G2), Fantastic Fellow (G3), and Far Lane (G3)] have been out of Nureyev mares. This is from only 33 such individuals (four percent of Lear Fan's total progeny). Mating Lear Fan to Nureyev mares creates inbreeding to Lt. Stevens and his full sister Thong 3x4.

Mt. Livermore (1981, by Blushing Groom) demonstrates an affinity with the daughters of **Great Above** (1972). Three of his 22 graded or group winners have been with Great Above mares [Housebuster (G1), Frisco View (G3), and Parlay (G2)]. This comes from only 21 individuals with this cross (three percent of Mt. Livermore's total progeny).

Leading U.S. sire **Storm Cat** (1983) appears to nick well with mares from the **Ribot** (1952) line. Seven of his 72 graded or group winners and four of his 27 Grade 1 or Group 1 winners [Tabasco Cat, Mistle Cat, Sardula, and Forestry] have been out of Ribot-line mares.

Nick Hunting

In recent years, we have seen an incredible rise in the amount of information the world acquires, processes, and then transmits. These advances have helped to make the art and science of creative and intelligent breeding of racehorses a great deal easier.

Basic information on the nicking patterns of contemporary stallions is provided in the annual guide to sire and broodmare sire crosses published by *The Blood-Horse*. There, the reader can find up-to-date nicking statistics on the leading 300 North American sires, as well as a considerable number of broodmare sires.

Caution is advised against putting too much confidence in the results of crosses that currently have small sample numbers. Since small numbers represent a large majority of the book's compilations, it should be re-emphasized that the true indicators of future success are relatively few and far between. Some of the most valuable information in these guides can be found in the sections where totals for sires of sires and sires of broodmare sires are provided and the sizes of the sample populations become more statistically reliable.

To acquire additional data on nicking patterns not furnished in this guide, a number of internet systems have commercial information banks available on a pay-per-report basis. Among these are the Jockey Club and Bloodstock Research Information Services. Various combinations of crosses can be researched and analyzed, even in rather customized form. Most of the numerical data in this chapter was supplied by *The Blood-Horse's Nicks 2004* and Bloodstock Research Information Services.

There are also several excellent websites where a surprising amount of free interactive pedigree research can be conducted. Perhaps the best of these is the Thoroughbred Pedigree Query (http://www.pedigreequery.com).

To determine if any affinities exist for an established stallion, one should start by studying the pedigrees of his best offspring. The purpose is to detect any recurrent patterns among his top offspring. The next step is to compare each of these patterns (sub-groups) statistically to the sire's total progeny to determine if the yield has, indeed, outperformed its opportunities, and if so, by how much? Also determine if this cross has been attempted enough to be statistically reliable. Finally, try to establish if this nick is explainable.

To establish whether any affinities might exist for a relatively new stallion, one should start by determining what key families and key ancestors are carried in his pedigree. This should then help to ascertain which lines this stallion would be most likely to do well with, based on the concept of explainable nicks.

It should also be determined if the stallion's sire expressed any affinities that could be transmissible. For example, a good case could be made that a new son of Seattle Slew at stud would figure to do well with Mr. Prospector-line mares.

Duplicating a Successful Nick: "Crossing the Cross"

The final, if not ultimate, way in which to utilize successful nicks is to duplicate them in subsequent generations. Over the course of Thoroughbred evolution, a remarkable number of the world's most important individuals have had pedigrees that demonstrated the crossing of different members of the same successful affinity.

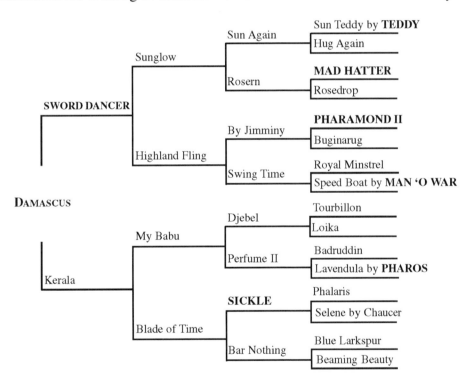

For example, the pedigree of 1967 Horse of the Year Damascus shows a 4x3 cross of the brothers Pharamond II and Sickle, both distinguished representatives of the Phalaris/Chaucer nick. The sire of Damascus, 1959 Horse of the Year Sword Dancer, has a 3x4 cross of Mad Hatter and Man o' War. They, of course, are bred on the Fair Play/Rock Sand nick. Damascus's male line traces back to the great foundation stallion Teddy, whose own pedigree showed a 4x2 cross of Ormonde and Doremi, both by Bend Or out of Macaroni mares.

Previously, I have written about the extraordinary results from crossing the strains of My Babu, Ambiorix and Klairon, the three primary representatives of the Tourbillon/Sweet Lavender nick ("A Relative Matter," *Thoroughbred Times*, Dec. 7, 1996). The article demonstrated both quantitative and qualitative evidence of a remarkable level of success with the crossing of these lines. Representative stallions were shown to have performed twice as well in the production of group/graded stakes winners when their mates carried complementary strains of this cross.

Given the near ubiquity of Northern Dancer blood throughout the breed, it would be valuable to consider, theoretically at least, the best ways to inbreed to this all-important predecessor. What are his optimal strains to duplicate?

If we return to the Northern Dancer/Teddy line cross and the most potent sources of its success, we are left with three specific broodmares: Flaming Page, her daughter Fleur, and her very close relative South Ocean.

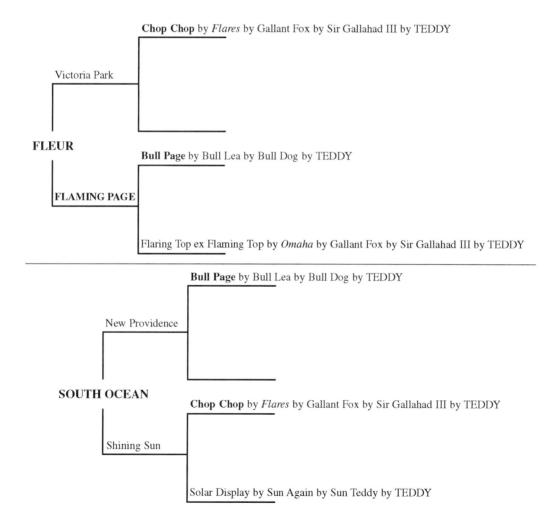

All three featured multiple strains of Teddy, particularly Bull Page, as well as the brothers Flares and Omaha. To the cover of Northern Dancer, Flaming Page produced the great Nijinsky II, while her daughter Fleur got The Minstrel and Far North. The key offspring from the union of Northern Dancer and South Ocean was Storm Bird.

This, then, would be the short list of premier representatives of the Northern Dancer/Teddy line nick most worthy of crossing (Nijinsky II, Storm Bird, The Minstrel, and Far North).

As previously discussed, patterns such as these (beyond two or three generations) are extremely difficult to investigate statistically. Nevertheless, early anecdotal evidence from the crossing of these four sons of Northern Dancer has shown great favor.

The cross of Nijinsky II with Storm Bird has already produced Grade 1 or Group 1 winners High Yield, Spain, Golden Ballet, and Black Minnaloushe. The cross of Storm Bird with The Minstrel has already produced 1996 juvenile filly champion Storm Song, while the cross of Nijinsky II and his three-quarters brother Far North has already delivered Australian racing sensation, Northerly. None of these horses had begun their racing careers when I first presented this material ("Shaping the Breed for the 21st Century," *Thoroughbred Times*, February 3, 1996). I think it's still safe to say the best from this cross is yet to come.

The affinity between Northern Dancer and the Thong family is also worthy of duplicating. This can be achieved by crossing the strains of 1) Sadler's Wells (or his brother, Fairy King), 2) Nureyev, and 3) Number (dam of Numerous and Jade Robbery). From relatively few opportunities, this duplication has already produced Canadian champion Numerous Times (G1), undefeated at three and four, as well as top international performer El Condor Pasa.

Familiarization with the top nicks of recent decades can inevitably lead to sharper breeding decisions in the near future.

Nicking theory, when applied in a statistically reliable and valid fashion, can be a powerful adjunct in the planning of Thoroughbred matings. True nicks occur infrequently, but their identification can provide valuable caveats in a realm where the past bears so much influence on the future.

It has been said that statistics, like dreams, are nothing but a form of wish fulfillment. Just the same, it's nice to have both the dreams and numbers on your side.

About the Author

Rommy Faversham is a pedigree analyst living in Los Angeles. He is co-author of the book Inbreeding to Superior Females *in collaboration with Leon Rasmussen, who popularized this well-known concept in his weekly "Bloodlines" column for* Daily Racing Form. *Faversham's articles on bloodline topics have appeared in many of the leading Thoroughbred journals. He is a formerly practicing board-certified physician. His training included the co-authoring of research articles in the field of medical genetics. His website is located at http://www.equicross.com.*

CHAPTER 9

Pedigrees and Statistics

Two subjects near the heart of any bloodstock researcher are pedigrees and statistics. Depending upon their individual bent, most tend to worship one or the other. Few researchers, if any at all, have applied the use of statistics to analyzing pedigrees in the way that Dave Dink has done. An irrepressible researcher, Dink has combed thousands of pedigrees in his work and pleasure in assessing the names in pedigrees.

In doing this for more than a decade, Dink has written about statistical approaches to analyzing pedigree theories, with most of his work appearing in the *Thoroughbred Times* and earlier in *The Thoroughbred Record*. Many readers of those publications will be familiar with his studies of inbreeding and Dosage, for example, which scrutinized the success of those methods of interpreting pedigree through the fine screen of population analysis.

In this use, population analysis is the development of breed norms across the spectrum of the Thoroughbred population and then the use of those norms to judge the impact of sires, breeding methods, and whatnot against the standards developed from this database of information. The use of a large database of pedigrees, both good and bad, has led Dink to some very firm benchmark figures about what it means to be successful in breeding Thoroughbreds.

It has also led him to a fascination with the influence of particular horses in pedigrees. Not only as they succeed or fail as sires and dams, but also as these horses age back through pedigrees, Dink has followed the statistical fortunes of some of the great racehorses and sires of the past 40 years or so. And one of things that he has found is that the "success" of a horse can vary greatly depending on where it is in a pedigree.

The use of position analysis is not an unusual approach to pedigrees, although most of us think of Bold Ruler as the same thing, without regard to where he appears in the pedigrees of his descendants. The researches of Dink, however, have shown that position does matter. There are simply some avenues of descent through which a stallion is much stronger than others.

These researches raise some collateral issues about the influence of horses and how it dissipates with time and also in showing some trends about how the breed is changing over time. Dink's work, innovative as ever, offers a challenging look at this great statistical puzzle we call horse breeding.

By David L. Dink

"Beware of Boojum"

Names in pedigrees. Ever wonder what they are really worth? If you read almost anything written about pedigrees these days, you get the impression that certain names are sacrosanct (automatically assumed to be "good" or "positive" no matter what). How valid is that assumption?

Actually, the value of individual names in pedigrees can be effectively and objectively measured.

Let us begin by determining which sires appear most often in the third and fourth generations of three recent crops of North American-bred foals (1995-97). I decided to examine the top 20 sires in each generation. Those sires were determined by a random sample of the foal books for each of those three crops (five foals per page for each book, or about 2,800 plus foals from each crop). The results were then extrapolated in Table 1 for the third generation and in Table 2 for the fourth generation.

Additionally, the results were sorted by the position at which the sires appear within each generation. See accompanying pedigree for the naming of those positions. Basically, they start at the top with P1 (male line) and continue to the bottom (female line, P4 for the third generation, P8 for the fourth generation) for each pedigree.

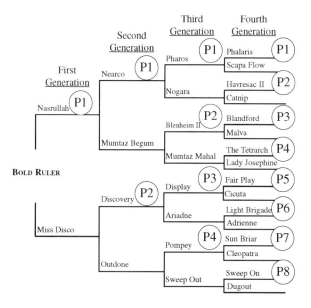

The next step was to ascertain the best horses (stakes winners) from all three of these crops. The three crops combined contain 103,334 foals, of which 3,172 (3.07 percent) were stakes winners through December 31, 2001. Of those 3,172 stakes winners, 696 (0.67 percent) were graded winners (the best of the best, including group winners from around the globe).

In order to emphasize the greater importance of graded winners versus mere stakes winners, the former group was counted twice in Tables 1 and 2. So 3.07 percent plus 0.67 percent (graded winners counted twice) equals 3.74 percent, and that is the benchmark for this entire study. Anything above 3.74 percent is good. Anything below 3.74 percent is not so good. For purposes of concision, the word "percent" and the percent sign (%) will be dropped from the rest of this discussion.

Turning our attention to Table 1, it lists the number of times each sire appears at each position on the top line. The next line down lists the number of times each sire appears at each position among stakes winners (graded winners counted twice). The third line lists the percentage of the latter from the former (the result, good or bad). Totals for all four positions are also shown.

For example, Northern Dancer appears most often (20,400 times) among these three crops. He is followed by Raise a Native (17,722), Mr. Prospector (12,190), etc. The sires are listed in descending order by total number of appearances (or presences, if you prefer). Northern Dancer's results are 4.83 at P1, 3.96 at P2, 5.66 at P3, and 9.83 at P4 for an overall result of 5.19.

Keeping in mind that the benchmark is 3.74, those results are really good. They are above 3.74 at all four positions. Raise a Native and Mr. Prospector are similarly above 3.74 at all four positions. So are His Majesty and Vice Regent (down toward the bottom of Table 1). The other 15 sires all have at least one position at which they are below 3.74, at which their results are not so good, in other words.

That was one of the reasons why these results were apportioned among positions, to show how widely the results vary within the same sire. Raise a Native is the most consistent of these 20 sires (best 4.39, worst 4.02). Hoist the Flag is the most inconsistent (best 13.27, worst 1.95). The average variance from best to worst for these 20 sires is 5.13 (average of the best is 7.89; average of the worst is 2.76). That is a large variance and illustrates how widely results fluctuate for the same sire among the possible positions.

Fifteen of these 20 sires have good results (better than 3.74) overall. Five do not (Bold Ruler, Never Bend, Prince John, Intentionally and Round Table). The year of birth of each sire was also included on Tables 1 and 2 (immediately after each name). Seven of the 20 sires in Table 1 were born in 1960 or earlier. Among sires born prior to 1960, Nearctic and Hail to Reason are still hanging on very well in the third generation, but the other five are the aforementioned quintet whose numbers are suffering as they age out of the population. Five of the seven oldest sires have overall results below 3.74. The 13 youngest sires all have positive results (above 3.74). Chronology evidently has something to do with these results, and older definitely is not better.

It is also interesting to note that the four individual positions were won by four different sires. Hail to Reason was best at P1 at 5.84 (thanks mainly to his son

TABLE I
NORTH AMERICAN-BRED FOALS OF 1995-97

Third Generation Sire	P1	P2	P3	P4	Totals
Northern Dancer (1961)	**11,459**	**1,542**	**6,799**	**600**	**20,400**
Stakes Winners	553	61	385	59	1,058
Results (%)	4.83	3.96	5.66	9.83	5.19
Raise a Native (1961)	**11,970**	**1,305**	**3,700**	**747**	**17,722**
Stakes Winners	496	55	162	30	743
Results (%)	4.14	4.21	4.38	4.02	4.19
Mr. Prospector (1970)	**6,822**	**1,255**	**3,734**	**379**	**12,190**
Stakes Winners	286	77	207	39	609
Results (%)	4.19	6.14	5.54	10.29	5.00
Bold Ruler (1954)	**3,450**	**753**	**3,124**	**196**	**7,523**
Stakes Winners	74	14	94	12	194
Results (%)	2.14	1.86	3.01	6.12	2.58
Buckpasser (1963)	**1,335**	**3,429**	**1,568**	**539**	**6,871**
Stakes Winners	31	163	52	38	284
Results (%)	2.32	4.75	3.32	7.05	4.13
Damascus (1964)	**3,016**	**1,071**	**2,157**	**600**	**6,844**
Stakes Winners	105	60	100	30	295
Results (%)	3.48	5.60	4.64	5.00	4.31
Hail to Reason (1958)	**4,245**	**733**	**1,372**	**282**	**6,632**
Stakes Winners	248	24	77	18	367
Results (%)	5.84	3.27	5.61	6.38	5.53
Nijinsky II (1967)	**1,070**	**1,677**	**2,290**	**551**	**5,588**
Stakes Winners	44	41	99	38	222
Results (%)	4.11	2.44	4.32	6.90	3.97
Nearctic (1954)	**4,103**	**66**	**1,053**	**258**	**5,480**
Stakes Winners	237	1	42	12	292
Results (%)	5.78	1.52	3.99	4.65	5.33
Bold Reasoning (1968)	**4,199**	**37**	**564**	**37**	**4,837**
Stakes Winners	191	1	47	5	244
Results (%)	4.55	2.70	8.33	13.51	5.04
Never Bend (1960)	**1,470**	**1,227**	**1,641**	**416**	**4,754**
Stakes Winners	42	20	60	43	165
Results (%)	2.86	1.63	3.66	10.34	3.47

TABLE I CONTINUED
NORTH AMERICAN-BRED FOALS OF 1995-97

Third Generation Sire	P1	P2	P3	P4	Totals
In Reality (1964)	**1,735**	**1,079**	**1,531**	**380**	**4,725**
Stakes Winners	41	54	103	27	225
Results (%)	2.36	5.00	6.73	7.11	4.76
Secretariat (1970)	**354**	**2,231**	**980**	**539**	**4,104**
Stakes Winners	10	167	39	31	247
Results (%)	2.82	7.49	3.98	5.75	6.02
Hoist the Flag (1968)	**565**	**1,150**	**1,445**	**294**	**3,454**
Stakes Winners	11	74	55	39	179
Results (%)	1.95	6.43	3.81	13.27	5.18
Prince John (1953)	**424**	**1,250**	**870**	**442**	**2,986**
Stakes Winners	10	52	26	20	108
Results (%)	2.36	4.16	2.99	4.52	3.62
Tom Rolfe (1962)	**923**	**1,045**	**552**	**331**	**2,851**
Stakes Winners	27	64	12	26	129
Results (%)	2.93	6.12	2.17	7.85	4.52
His Majesty (1968)	**1,445**	**577**	**551**	**234**	**2,807**
Stakes Winners	59	49	32	19	159
Results (%)	4.08	8.49	5.81	8.12	5.66
Vice Regent (1967)	**1,450**	**495**	**491**	**319**	**2,755**
Stakes Winners	80	21	44	24	169
Results (%)	5.52	4.24	8.96	7.52	6.13
Intentionally (1956)	**2,052**	**291**	**295**	**87**	**2,725**
Stakes Winners	57	4	23	3	87
Results (%)	2.78	1.37	7.80	3.45	3.19
Round Table (1954)	**531**	**741**	**1,005**	**404**	**2,681**
Stakes Winners	14	18	43	25	100
Results (%)	2.64	2.43	4.28	6.19	3.73

Roberto), nosing out Nearctic at 5.78. Not as ballyhooed as other "sires of sires," Hail to Reason remains very effective in the male line, at least through three generations.

His Majesty is best at P2 at 8.49, thanks mainly to Dynaformer, a son of Roberto. Secretariat at 7.49 was a lot more obvious candidate for honors at this position, being the broodmare sire of Storm Cat, A.P. Indy, Gone West, Summer Squall, et al.

Vice Regent at 8.96 tallies over Bold Reasoning at 8.33 as best at P3. The former owes most of his success to his son Deputy Minister; the latter to his son Seattle Slew. Bold Reasoning also emerges as best at P4 at 13.51, but those results should be taken with a grain of salt, based as they are on a very limited number of foals. Hoist the Flag, at 13.27 with a more reasonable number of foals, is more deserving of the title here. Of his 26 stakes winners at P4, half (13) were graded, which is really impressive.

The overall title went to Vice Regent (6.13) over Secretariat (6.02). Vice Regent's worst result, 4.24 at P2, was better than the worst result of any other sire in Table 1. He was consistently good across the board, in other words.

Table 2 is the same as Table 1 except that it covers twice as much territory (eight positions instead of four). Not one of the 20 sires in Table 2 has positive results (3.74 or better) at all eight positions.

TABLE 2
NORTH AMERICAN-BRED FOALS OF 1995-97

Fourth Generation Sire	P1	P2	P3	P4	P5	P6	P7	P8	Totals
Bold Ruler (1954)	**5,421**	**1,136**	**8,557**	**1,594**	**7,388**	**1,569**	**7,178**	**796**	**33,639**
Stakes Winners	144	34	341	90	228	38	296	36	1,207
Results (%)	2.66	2.99	3.99	5.65	3.09	2.42	4.12	4.52	3.59
Native Dancer (1950)	**12,475**	**4,612**	**2,114**	**1,612**	**4,618**	**1,751**	**2,241**	**441**	**29,864**
Stakes Winners	537	248	72	75	182	64	86	26	1,290
Results (%)	4.30	5.38	3.41	4.65	3.94	3.66	3.84	5.90	4.32
Nearctic (1954)	**12,576**	**35**	**2,166**	**1,349**	**7,839**	**283**	**1,471**	**624**	**26,343**
Stakes Winners	598	1	75	71	433	14	98	27	1,317
Results (%)	4.76	2.86	3.46	5.26	5.52	4.95	6.66	4.33	5.00
Northern Dancer (1961)	**5,781**	**1,028**	**6,302**	**951**	**5,757**	**1,078**	**3,247**	**404**	**24,548**
Stakes Winners	232	22	247	36	290	43	186	33	1,089
Results (%)	4.01	2.14	3.92	3.79	5.04	3.99	5.73	8.17	4.44
Raise a Native (1961)	**8,101**	**835**	**3,469**	**387**	**7,018**	**808**	**2,915**	**453**	**23,986**
Stakes Winners	328	37	168	14	334	29	155	23	1,088
Results (%)	4.05	4.43	4.84	3.62	4.76	3.59	5.32	5.08	4.54
***Nasrullah (1940)**	**7,488**	**338**	**4,065**	**627**	**7,193**	**796**	**2,464**	**588**	**23,559**
Stakes Winners	231	2	95	16	214	10	96	19	683
Results (%)	3.08	0.59	2.34	2.55	2.98	1.26	3.90	3.23	2.90
Nashua (1952)	**178**	**10,182**	**1,508**	**831**	**209**	**1,912**	**1,139**	**649**	**16,608**
Stakes Winners	9	546	38	22	6	106	41	22	790
Results (%)	5.06	5.36	2.52	2.65	2.87	5.54	3.60	3.39	4.76

TABLE 2 CONTINUED
NORTH AMERICAN-BRED FOALS OF 1995-97

Fourth Generation Sire	P1	P2	P3	P4	P5	P6	P7	P8	Totals
*Turn-to (1951)	6,160	535	2,746	893	3,112	771	1,862	490	16,569
Stakes Winners	303	42	90	71	163	25	93	25	812
Results (%)	4.92	7.85	3.28	7.95	5.24	3.24	4.99	5.10	4.90
*Princequillo (1940)	989	2,377	2,503	1,803	2,132	3,027	1,801	1,054	15,686
Stakes Winners	17	46	76	53	74	104	81	31	482
Results (%)	1.72	1.94	3.04	2.94	3.47	3.44	4.50	2.94	3.07
Tom Fool (1949)	1,583	1,381	4,181	1,645	2,082	1,495	1,274	466	14,107
Stakes Winners	38	55	175	73	61	66	60	29	557
Results (%)	2.40	3.98	4.19	4.44	2.93	4.41	4.71	6.22	3.95
*Ribot (1952)	3,057	746	3,181	244	2,389	894	1,814	330	12,655
Stakes Winners	105	26	167	6	79	28	101	18	530
Results (%)	3.43	3.49	5.25	2.46	3.31	3.13	5.57	5.45	4.19
Hail to Reason (1958)	2,259	363	1,842	1,622	2,499	563	1,702	576	11,426
Stakes Winners	75	23	110	89	81	21	69	49	517
Results (%)	3.32	6.34	5.97	5.49	3.24	3.73	4.05	8.51	4.52
Prince John (1953)	699	1,309	1,812	1,293	1,005	1,838	1,224	797	9,977
Stakes Winners	19	40	72	22	34	65	65	54	371
Results (%)	2.72	3.06	3.97	1.70	3.38	3.54	5.31	6.78	3.72
Buckpasser (1963)	142	2,843	498	1,557	440	2,020	625	367	8,492
Stakes Winners	11	76	23	101	26	143	22	44	446
Results (%)	7.75	2.67	4.62	6.49	5.91	7.08	3.52	11.99	5.25
Round Table (1954)	95	1,142	1,083	744	686	1,592	1,874	674	7,890
Stakes Winners	1	18	45	32	18	67	62	40	283
Results (%)	1.05	1.58	4.16	4.30	2.62	4.21	3.31	5.93	3.59
Never Bend (1960)	527	234	1,322	1,052	1,520	711	1,776	454	7,596
Stakes Winners	16	2	27	45	41	26	89	32	278
Results (%)	3.04	0.85	2.04	4.28	2.70	3.66	5.01	7.05	3.66
Sword Dancer (1956)	3,017	30	1,238	44	2,169	86	637	196	7,417
Stakes Winners	105	0	60	0	100	5	30	8	308
Results (%)	3.48	0.00	4.85	0.00	4.61	5.81	4.71	4.08	4.15
Intentionally (1956)	1,764	230	1,460	415	1,984	478	821	171	7,323
Stakes Winners	44	14	77	0	111	17	46	16	325
Results (%)	2.49	6.09	5.27	0.00	5.59	3.56	5.60	9.36	4.44

TABLE 2 CONTINUED
NORTH AMERICAN-BRED FOALS OF 1995-97

Fourth Generation Sire	P1	P2	P3	P4	P5	P6	P7	P8	Totals
Nearco (1935)	**4,437**	**201**	**412**	**69**	**1,163**	**172**	**405**	**37**	**6,896**
Stakes Winners	254	2	19	1	49	4	24	2	355
Results (%)	5.72	1.00	4.61	1.45	4.21	2.33	5.93	5.41	5.15
Sir Gaylord (1959)	**529**	**99**	**2,297**	**476**	**931**	**820**	**1,237**	**490**	**6,879**
Stakes Winners	5	0	80	18	25	25	55	30	238
Results (%)	0.95	0.00	3.48	3.78	2.69	3.05	4.45	6.12	3.46

By far the oldest sires in Table 2 are Nearco (1935) and *Nasrullah and *Princequillo (both 1940). The next oldest is Tom Fool (1949). Nearco still holds up very well in the fourth generation (thanks mainly to his son Nearctic in the third generation). *Nasrullah and *Princequillo do not hold up well at all, which lends some more credence to the chronology factor. *Nasrullah's poor showing is somewhat attributable to his son Bold Ruler in the third generation.

Let us use this as an example. *Nasrullah shows up 23,559 times among all foals in the fourth generation, 683 times among stakes winners there. Bold Ruler shows up 7,523 times among all foals in the third generation, 194 times among stakes winners there. Subtracting the latter from the former leaves 16,036 presences of *Nasrullah in the fourth generation NOT through Bold Ruler in the third generation, 489 presences among stakes winners. The latter (489) divided by the former (16,036) still leaves *Nasrullah at 3.05 (better than 2.90 but still not good at all).

Five other sires in Table 2 have overall results below 3.74: Bold Ruler, Prince John, Round Table, Never Bend and Sir Gaylord. Bold Ruler is helped enormously by Secretariat in the third generation. Removing the latter from the former (as detailed in the example of *Nasrullah and Bold Ruler above), Bold Ruler's results in the fourth generation fall even further, from 3.59 to 3.25.

At 3.59, Bold Ruler actually fared better in the fourth generation than in the third generation overall (2.58). That is not quite as unusual as it appears. Ten sires appear in both Tables 1 and 2 (because they qualified in both the third and fourth generations). Six of them fared better overall in the fourth generation than in the third generation. Aside from Bold Ruler, they were Raise a Native (4.19 to 4.54), Prince John (3.62 to 3.72), Buckpasser (4.13 to 5.25), Never Bend (3.47 to 3.66), and Intentionally (3.19 to 4.44). Explanation? Reality does not always adhere to theoretical strictures. The four who did the opposite from the expected (fared better in the third than the fourth) were Nearctic (5.33 to 5.00), Northern Dancer (5.19 to 4.44), Hail to Reason (5.53 to 4.52) and Round Table (3.73 to 3.59).

As for the individual leaders in Table 2, honors were a bit more concentrated. *Turn-to was best at P2 (7.85) and P4 (7.95). Those two positions correspond with anything sired by Broad Brush, who deserves a good deal of the credit.

Hail to Reason was best at P3 at 5.97. That corresponds to sires out of mares by sons of Hail to Reason such as Roberto, Halo, et al. Hail to Reason is pretty good across the board at all eight positions. His worst two are 3.32 at P1 and 3.24 at P5 (the two positions in the fourth generation at which most people probably think that Hail to Reason does best). Notice also that Hail to Reason drops from 5.84 at P1 in the third generation to 3.32 at P1 in the fourth generation. That means that his male line is struggling to make a successful transition from the third to the fourth generation. Sons of Roberto, Halo, et al. are doing fine. Paternal grandsons are not, so far.

Nearctic leads at 6.66 at P7. That is largely due to Northern Dancer's 9.83 at P4 in the third. Removing the latter from the former leaves Nearctic at 4.48 at P7 in the fourth, which is still quite respectable.

Ranking first at P1 (7.75), P5 (5.91), P6 (7.08) P8 (11.99), and overall (5.25) is Buckpasser. Take that P1 ranking with some grains of salt. It is based on very low numbers, and 10 (seven stakes winners overall, three graded) of his 11 stakes winners there were sired by one horse, Lil E. Tee. So give that P1 title to Nearco at 5.72, thanks mainly to Nearctic in the third (5.78). That P5 ranking might also be taken with some grains of salt. Intentionally (5.59, thanks mainly to In Reality's 6.73 in the third generation) and Nearctic (5.52, thanks mainly to Northern Dancer's 5.66 in the third generation) achieved their results with much higher numbers of foals.

That Buckpasser ranks best at P6 and P8 is no surprise at all. He is well known as a great broodmare sire and was leading broodmare sire four times. As a sire of males in the fourth generation, his overall results are a respectable 4.81. As a sire of females in the fourth generation, his overall results are 5.36 from a much larger number of foals (6,787 to 1,705). The latter results are depressed by his surprisingly poor showing at P2 (2.67, by far the worst of his eight; sons of Miswaki and Woodman, for instance, are not cutting the mustard so far (Wavering Monarch-Maria's Mon-Monarchos notwithstanding). Buckpasser's combined overall results at P4, P6, and P8 (the other three positions as the sire of a female) are 7.30.

Learning from the Numbers

It should be emphasized that the results detailed herein are past performances, and as sellers of mutual funds are fond of saying, past performances are no guarantees of future results. These results are for foals of 1995-97. By the time you can compile these statistics, they are already nearly a generation out of date.

But be not disheartened. These statistics were never intended to be predictors of future performance. Rather, they are a means of promoting a better understanding of pedigrees themselves. Here is one example. Secretariat's fine performance at P2 in the third generation has been duly noted. By foals of 2003, however, he will have moved back numerically to P2 in the fourth generation. How well will he fare there?

And the answer is . . . wait and see, because we do not know yet. Certainly, Secretariat is receiving plenty of opportunity at P2 in the fourth generation. Among Keeneland September yearlings, the perennial leader at that position has been Nashua (since overtaking Native Dancer in 1992). But look at the change from 2000 to 2001 among Keeneland September yearlings. Nashua had a commanding lead over Secretariat at P2 in the fourth generation (726 to 418) in 2000. Only one year later, however, that lead had been trimmed to 570 to 533. Keeneland September yearlings are an indication of the overall population (and they are indeed a pretty good indication), and Secretariat has blown right by Nashua as the leader at P2 in the fourth generation.

As the leader among the population, that is. Quality of results could be another story. The sires who place Secretariat at P2 in the fourth generation are sons of Storm Cat, A.P. Indy, Gone West, Summer Squall, and others. Storm Cat is almost universally regarded (or at least advertised) as the next "great sire of sires." On what evidence? Very little, it seems to me.

Who is the best son of Storm Cat with foals of racing age now at stud? With due credit to Forest Wildcat and Tale of the Cat, the consensus answer would probably be Hennessy, especially after his son Johannesburg won the Breeders' Cup Juvenile (G1). Largely on the strength of that victory, the stud fee for Hennessy was just about doubled to $45,000 for 2002. Through foals of 2001, Hennessy has sired 26 stakes winners from 716 foals current to December 31, 2003. That works out to 3.63. The breed norm for stakes winners among the foals of 1995-97 is 3.07 (not counting graded winners twice). It is true that Hennessy is eligible to improve on that 3.63 figure in the future, but he will never be a high-percentage (10 percent stakes winners from foals or better) sire. So if you still think that Hennessy is worth a $45,000 stud fee, it is your money.

For the sake of argument, I will concede that Johannesburg constitutes one home run for sons of Storm Cat at stud. Can anyone name another one? Lion Heart could be one for Tale of the Cat, but one home run does not a baseball season make, and it seems to me that sons of Storm Cat need 60 or 70 more home runs such as Johannesburg before crowning Storm Cat as a "great sire of sires."

It is true that Storm Cat has several very high-class sons in the pipeline (most notably Giant's Causeway, whose first foals race in 2004). But because of their sire's overblown reputation, jillions of lower-class sons of Storm Cat are going to stud as well, which will definitely hurt his statistics eventually (as well as those of Secretariat at P2 in the fourth generation).

Anyway, wait and see about Storm Cat. Compile the numbers on foals of 2003 around 2010 and see what they say. Patience is a virtue, or so we are told. And in a historical and statistical approach, it is better to compile numbers patiently and retroactively than to predict success for scores of first-year sires and then jump up to claim credit as soon as one of them actually does some good.

Getting back to Secretariat at P2 in the fourth generation, his fate there of course does not depend exclusively on Storm Cat. Sons of A.P. Indy are still too young to have had much impact yet. They could have a positive impact in the future. Gone West holds promise with Grand Slam, Elusive Quality, and Mr. Greeley. It all remains to be seen whether Secretariat will be anywhere near as good at P2 in the fourth generation as he was at P2 in the third generation. He might become as good as Nashua (broodmare sire of Mr. Prospector, Roberto, et al.) at P2 in the fourth generation. Or he might fail the test there, just as Buckpasser has done already. ("Only time will tell who has fell and who's been left behind/When you go your way and I'll go mine.")

At any rate, I hope the preceding discussion has illustrated the usefulness of these numbers, not in predicting future results, but in understanding the overall behavior (you could even call it demographics, or maybe equinographics, to be more specific) of names in pedigrees. Tables 3 and 4 will attempt to summarize the overall patterns of that behavior.

Table 3 shows the composite results for all 20 sires in the third and fourth generations. For example, of these 103,334 foals, 62,618 (more than 60 percent) had one of these 20 sires at P1 in the third generation. Of these 103,334 foals, 77,278 (almost 75 percent) had one of these 20 sires at P1 in the fourth generation. Little wonder that P1 is the worst of the four positions in the third generation and among the worst in the fourth generation. Quantity and quality do not go hand in hand. There is nothing particularly unique or advantageous about having one of these 20 sires at P1 in the third or fourth generation in a population-wide sense because their descendants (good and especially bad) are too numerous.

In contrast, only 7,635 of these 103,334 foals (a little more than 7 percent) had one of these 20 sires as the sire of the second dam. Only 10,057 of these 103,334 foals (less than 10 percent) had one of these 20 sires as the sire of the third dam. Look at those results: 7.05 for the former, 5.61 for the latter, by far the best for each generation.

TABLE 3
COMPOSITES OF SIRES IN THIRD AND FOURTH GENERATIONS

Third Generation

Position	Presences	Stakes Winners	%
P1	62,618	2,616	4.18
P2	21,954	1,020	4.65
P3	35,722	1,702	4.76
P4	7,635	538	7.05
P1-P2	84,572	3,636	4.30
P3-P4	43,357	2,240	5.17
P1-P3	98,340	4,318	4.39
P2-P4	29,589	1,558	5.27
TOTALS	127,929	5,876	4.59

Fourth Generation

Position	Presences	Stakes Winners	%
P1	77,278	3,072	3.98
P2	29,656	1,234	4.17
P3	52,756	2,057	3.90
P4	19,208	835	4.35
P5	62,134	2,549	4.10
P6	22,664	900	3.97
P7	37,707	1,755	4.65
P8	10,057	564	5.61
P1234	178,898	7,198	4.02
P5678	132,562	5,768	4.35
P1357	229,875	9,433	4.10
P2468	81,585	3,533	4.33
TOTALS	311,460	12,966	4.16

In fact, the results align perfectly in the third generation: 4.18 for P1, 4.65 for P2, 4.76 for P3, and 7.05 for P4. The results for the fourth generation do not align perfectly, but the overall pattern is clear. In the third generation, these 20 sires appear almost twice as often in the top of the pedigree (84,572 times, with a result of 4.30 at P1-P2) as in the bottom of the pedigree (43,357 times, with a result of 5.17 at P3-P4). Similarly, these 20 sires appear more than three times as often as a sire of a male (98,340 times, with a result of 4.39 at P1-P3) than as a sire of a female (29,589 times, with a result of 5.27 at P2-P4).

Tom Fool is the one individual sire who exemplifies this pattern most clearly. His results are 2.40-3.98-4.19-4.44 at P1-P2-P3-P4 (steady improvement from P1 to P4). His results are 2.93-4.41-4.71-6.22 at P5-P6-P7-P8 (steady improvement from P5 to P8, with P5 better than P1, P6 better than P2, P7 better than P3, and P8 better than P4).

The fourth generation follows the same overall pattern and will not be belabored. To summarize, as Shakespeare said, "Familiarity breeds contempt," and the more often that sires appear in the overall population, the less significant the appearance really is and the lower the results. The less often the sires appear in the overall population, the more significant it is when they do appear and hence the better results.

This is just plain common sense. Since 92+ percent of the population does not have one of these sires as the sire of its second dam, the 7+ percent that do have one of these sires as the sire of its second dam have significantly better results. These names actually mean something in the female line, more so than anywhere else in the pedigree anyway. Bruce Lowe is probably dancing a jig in his grave.

The purpose of this study, however, is not to lend credibility to Bruce Lowe or to any other theories. As stated earlier, reality does not always adhere to theoretical strictures. If you really want to study pedigrees, study their reality. Do so objectively. Use the scientific method (as opposed to examining good horses and good horses only to "prove" whatever your pet theory may be). Recognize and take into account the fact that good horses and bad horses share many of the same pedigree characteristics. If you espouse any specific pedigree theory and fail to recognize the fundamental realities detailed herein, chances are that you need to reexamine your sense of reality.

One final recommendation. Keep in mind that each foal inherits half of its genes from it sire and half from its dam. Stop right there. Your 100 percent of "influence" has been totally accounted for right there. Anything beyond that is mere speculation, mystification, or at worst, sheer fantasy.

Perhaps the following verse will serve as a summary.

"Beware of Boojum"

Names in pedigrees are a worthy avocation
Study 'em all you like with quiet dedication
But don't mistake paradise for any permutation
Factor opportunity into each and every equation
Data before theory, the horse before the cart
Hold no opinion at ALL whenever you start
Examine facts first and foremost of all
An open mind MIGHT just keep you from a fall
Names in pedigrees are just so many pence
Mr. P in the first is a great one indeed
Mr. P in the second follows no certain creed
Mr. P in the third is worth about two cents
Mr. P in the fourth . . . do you have ANY sense?
Names in pedigrees are like alphabet soup
There's a reason for calling this "genetic goop"
If you insist on hunting that elusive SNARK
Beware of BOOJUM before you even embark.

David L. Dink
9-12-01

About the Author

A graduate of Kenyon College, David L. Dink is a native to Ohio who became a racing enthusiast at the ripe age of nine years and 11 months because of the 1965 Kentucky Derby. His choice that year was the hard-charging closer Dapper Dan, "beaten a filthy neck" in the main event. Dink's lifetime allegiance to the cherry and black colors of the Phipps family was cemented the following year with the Horse of the Year campaign of champion Buckpasser.

His love of Buckpasser, rivaled only by his affection for Bob Dylan, continues to this day, and it inspired some of Dink's statistical researches, as the great son of Tom Fool receded farther into pedigrees. Writing primarily for The Thoroughbred Record and the Thoroughbred Times, from 1982 to 1993, Dink weighed in on most of the topics of breeding interest, especially those with a statistical application. Dink works for the Jockey Club, having edited their Daily Dispatch for eight years and also working as a catalog editor. This chapter is Dink's first published work in a decade, but he continues to indulge his fascination with statistical assessments of pedigrees.

CHAPTER 10

Birth Rank and Success

The influence of the dam, in study after study, has been shown to be of immense importance to the development and success of the foal. And various researchers have shown that the early foals out of broodmares are more successful overall than those produced at more advanced ages. This is called birth rank, and it is not so much a theory of breeding as a management and selection tool for horsemen and breeders.

Dr. E.J. Finocchio, an equine practitioner in Rhode Island, began research on this aspect of horse husbandry a couple of decades ago. In addition, two writers who have contributed chapters to this book, David Dink and Frank Mitchell, also have researched birth rank, although with slightly different emphases, and found that the results held up well in different situations.

In general, both Finocchio's work and other studies show that the first five foals that a mare produces have a better probability of success than those born later in her producing career. Finocchio came to this conclusion by gathering information on 689 selected winners, which either had won a Breeders' Cup event, a Triple Crown race, an Eclipse Award, or earned more than $1 million. These horses were out of 680 dams, who produced a total of 5,901 foals. Finocchio grouped the select winners according to birth rank and assessed the percentage of winners that came from each grouping.

BIRTH RANK STUDY - 1995

Birthrank	Number of Foals	Number of Selected Winners	% Selected Winners
1	689	112	16.2
2	686	148	21.5
3	660	123	18.6
4	643	99	15.3
5	615	66	10.7
6	563	46	8.1
7	498	32	6.4
8	418	27	6.4
9	343	16	4.6
10	274	8	2.9
11	216	8	3.7
12	166	2	1.2
13	130	2	1.5

Birth Rank Study - 1985

Birthrank	Number of Foals	Number of Stakes Winners	% of Stakes Winners
1	1641	276	16.9
2	1641	319	19.4
3	1641	336	20.5
4	1641	316	19.3
5	1641	320	19.5
6	1641	254	15.5
7	1641	233	14.2
8	1641	210	12.8
9	1641	180	11.0
10	1641	138	8.4
11	1095	85	7.8
12	680	46	6.8
13	409	19	4.6
14	192	7	3.7
15	101	4	3.9
16	27	1	3.7

In working on his study, Finocchio chose to investigate whether the age of the mare or the birth rank itself was of primary importance, since many breeders give preference to younger mares. He found that the number and birth ranking of the foals a mare produced, rather than her age, correlates with the success of her offspring. Using mares who were more than 10, Finocchio found that the first foals were more successful than those born later, and he concluded that the amount of stress that has been put on a mare's uterus has more influence on the foal's success than the chronological age of the mare.

The conclusion of Finocchio's study was that mares should be bred to quality stallions from the beginning of their stud careers, giving the resulting foals the best opportunity for success. And since age of the mare was less important than the numerical birth rank of the foal, the racing careers of mares need not be cut short in order to breed earlier.

In his studies on birth rank, David Dink chose a larger and much less select group to study. In work published in the *Thoroughbred Times*, Dink found that Finocchio's general conclusions from a sample of elite horses was, in this case, borne out in the results from a broad spectrum of animals. The earlier foals were more successful than the later foals. In particular, the first four or five foals showed notably higher levels of success at the races.

The best broodmares, however, did not show an inclination to discontinue producing good foals as they aged. Rather, some of the most renowned racers, Secretariat for instance, were produced out of sync with these conclusions on birth rank.

Broodmare Age - 1995 Study

Age of Dam	Number of Foals	Number of Selected Winners	% Selected Winners
4	128	15	11.7
5	342	49	14.3
6	703	88	12.5
7	670	87	13.0
8	630	76	12.0
9	779	92	11.8
10	515	63	12.2
11	411	47	11.4
12	484	46	9.5
13	296	32	10.8
14	242	24	9.9
15	184	17	9.2
16	210	23	10.4
17	168	17	10.1
18	79	7	8.8
19	25	3	12.0
20	0	0	0.0
21	10	1	10.0
22	25	2	8.0

Broodmare Age - 1985 Study

Age of Dam	Number of Foals	Number of Stakes Winners	% Stakes Winners
3	19	3	15.8
4	429	79	18.4
5	890	150	16.8
6	1093	220	20.1
7	1229	259	21.0
8	1267	255	20.0
9	1247	229	18.3
10	1247	248	19.8
11	1234	220	17.6
12	1194	208	17.4
13	1176	179	15.2
14	1166	152	13.9
15	1126	136	12.0
16	1057	137	12.9
17	972	90	9.2
18	871	63	7.2
19	737	32	4.3
20	655	31	4.7
21	506	25	4.9
22	377	15	4.0
23	240	10	4.1
24	127	2	1.5
25	58	1	1.7

But as a general trend, the earlier the better, so far as the birth rank of foals is concerned.

Mitchell, in a study of foals produced after barren years, found that foals produced after a barren season succeeded at a higher rate than their peers. This effect, which was labeled "The Post-Barren Effect" by Jack Werk when published in the breeding newsletter *Owner-Breeder*, occurred at a significant frequency at all times in a mare's producing life, and it showed less of a tendency to follow the pattern of the birth rank statistics of Dink and Finocchio.

Doubtless, the post-barren effect is the result of the mare's natural system getting the benefit of a year's break from the strenuous process of producing foals, and this also would tend to account for its moderating effect on the influence of birth rank.

Conclusions

Studies show that early foals succeed out of proportion to their numbers, compared to later foals. Physiologists will, no doubt, hardly be surprised with these results; nor will many farm managers who have seen the best and least of many a mare's produce. The natural strain of producing foals year after year clearly has an effect on the success of a mare's later foals, with regard to the greater energy and athleticism of earlier foals over all.

Aside from the expected decline of a mare's constitution, there are other factors to consider. For one thing, superior producers — and perhaps this is a physiological advantage that helps to make them superior producers — tend to be able to produce very good foals at an advanced age and frequently have stakes winners, even classic winners, well past mid-life.

Among the other factors that contribute to the decline of a mare's foals, the quality of stallions is also a significant contributing element. Typically, a mare is sent to the best stallions she will visit in the first three or four years of her producing life. If she hasn't produced foals that give her owner encouragement or if she hasn't produced a stakes winner among this early group, a mare is probably going to be traded on, and her opportunities will diminish.

Even accounting for these pragmatic factors, the evidence of birth rank makes it a fascinating component of the selection process for breeders and buyers.

CHAPTER 11

Dosage: A Pedigree Classification Technique

Dosage is a non-traditional method of Thoroughbred pedigree analysis. Originated as a breeding theory, Dosage could be described more accurately as a pedigree classification technique in its latest form. Dosage largely ignores the typical historical interpretation of a pedigree that catalogs ancestral accomplishments. Rather, it differentiates pedigrees by evaluating the qualities of speed and stamina inherited from selected ancestors. The essence of Dosage and its classification of pedigrees is its use as a means to identify aptitudinal type and relate that type to performance on the racetrack.

The Origins of Dosage: Vuillier

Dosage was created in the early part of the 20th century by Lt. Col. J. J. Vuillier, a retired French military officer and pedigree authority who was an active participant in the pedigree debates of his day. One of the more contested issues at the time among racing devotees focused on the relative merits of two of the three stallions from which all of today's Thoroughbreds descend, Eclipse and Herod. Vuillier contributed to a resolution through an in-depth analysis of the pedigrees of major European winners, classic and otherwise. To the delight of one side and to the dismay of the other, he found that Herod was the dominant influence of the two. More importantly, he determined that the proportion of Herod's influence in extended pedigrees through 12 generations was essentially the same in all of the horses analyzed. This was indeed a remarkable discovery, laying the groundwork for further research and development of the Dosage system, eventually published in *Les Croisements Rationnels* (Rational Crossbreeding).

Vuillier noted that very few ancestors among the thousands present in the extended pedigree of the good horses he studied appeared with great frequency. Furthermore, as with Herod, the influence of these special ancestors through 12 generations also became relatively constant, each with a unique contribution (or "dosage"). This critical observation led to Vuillier's identification of three series of key Thoroughbred ancestors separated by discrete time frames. He called these ancestors *chefs-de-race*, a term he used to distinguish those rare individuals he believed had a unique, profound, and long-term effect on the breed.

Vuillier's first series, from the early 19th century, includes the stallions Pantaloon, ch., 1824 (Castrel - Idalia, by Peruvian); Voltaire, br., 1826 (Blacklock - Phantom Mare, by Phantom); Touchstone, br., 1831 (Camel - Banter, by Master Henry); Bay Middleton, b., 1833 (Sultan - Cobweb, by Phantom); Birdcatcher, ch., 1833 (Sir Hercules - Guiccioli, by Bob Booty); Gladiator, ch., 1833 (Partisan - Pauline, by Moses); and Melbourne, br., 1834 (Humphrey Clinker - Cervantes Mare, by Cervantes). The series also includes one mare, Pocahontas, 1837 (Glencoe - Marpessa, by Muley), the only mare Vuillier ever included among his *chefs-de-race*.

The second series, from the middle of the 19th century, includes just two *chefs-de-race*, Newminster, b., 1848 (Touchstone - Beeswing, by Dr. Syntax) and Stockwell, ch., 1849 (The Baron - Pocahontas, by Glencoe).

The third and final series of Vuillier's *chefs-de-race*, now from the late 19th century, includes Hermit, ch., 1864 (Newminster - Seclusion, by Tadmor); Hampton, b., 1872 (Lord Clifden - Lady Langden, by Kettledrum); Galopin, b., 1872 (Vedette - Flying Duchess, by The Flying Dutchman); Isonomy, b., 1875 (Sterling - Isola Bella, by Stockwell); Bend Or, ch., 1877 (Doncaster - Rouge Rose, by Thormanby) and St. Simon, br., 1881 (Galopin - St. Angela, by King Tom).

This process, in which new series of *chefs-de-race* periodically emerge, achieve dominance, and establish a constant influence in pedigrees over time, is a rational model for the evolution of the Thoroughbred. Vuillier's method for measuring the influence of each *chef-de-race* depends on the fact that 4,096 ancestors populate the 12th generation in a pedigree. Using that number as a point total, he allowed that each generation should tally that same figure of 4,096. This leads to the obvious conclusion that every occurrence of a 12th generation ancestor is worth one point since that ancestor occupies one of 4,096 positions. A parent occupies one of two positions, equivalent to 2,048 of 4,096. The respective figures assigned for each occurrence in the 1st through the 12th generations are 2,048; 1,024; 512; 256; 128; 64; 32; 16; 8; 4; 2; and 1. A result of Vuillier's counting technique was the observation that by 1900 the actual percentage of blood of some of the most significant foundation animals in the breed (e.g., Eclipse, Herod, and Highflyer) was close to the same in all pedigrees, generally varying by no more than three-quarters of one percent. The same was true for the *chefs-de-race* assigned to Vuillier's three series, although each *chef-de-race* had a different "Dosage" number that could vary greatly from one *chef-de-race* to another. The well-known pedigree authority Abram S. Hewitt noted in *The Great Breeders and Their Methods* that St. Simon's Dosage figure was more than twice that of Bend Or, even though the latter's sire line was far more prevalent in England in the 1920s.

In matings, Vuillier wanted to reproduce the ideal proportions of the *chefs-de-race* that he had observed in his research, and he believed in designing a mating to align the Dosage figures in the foal with those established for the breed. If, for example, the sire's Dosage figure for St. Simon was too high, then the mare's figure should be lower in order to compensate. Vuillier applied his skills in the employ of H. H. The Aga Khan who, following World War I, decided to expand his interests in racing greatly. Utilizing Lord Derby's trainer, the Hon. George Lambton, to select individuals, and Lt. Col. Vuillier to evaluate pedigrees, the Aga Khan established one of the most successful buying, racing, and breeding operations in history. Among the yearlings purchased were Teresina, by Tracery (dam of Irish Oaks winner Theresina and of the high-class American sire Alibhai); Mumtaz Mahal, by The Tetrarch (tail-female ancestress of Nasrullah and Mahmoud); Friar's Daughter, by Friar Marcus (dam of English Triple Crown winner Bahram and of Irish Derby winner Dastur); Diophon, by Grand Parade (winner of the 2,000 Guineas); Salmon Trout, by The Tetrarch (winner of the St. Leger); Blenheim II, by Blandford (winner of the English Derby and a top-class sire); and Qurrat-al-Ain, by Buchan (dam of 1,000 Guineas winner Majideh, she the dam of Belmont Stakes winner Gallant Man and of English and Irish Oaks winner Masaka). Over a period exceeding 30 years, the Aga Khan also bred an impressive number of superior horses, including a host of champions and classic winners. Some of the more prominent include the aforementioned Bahram, Dastur, Majideh, Gallant Man, Nasrullah and Mahmoud, as well as Firdaussi, Turkhan, Khaled, Migoli, Tulyar, Saint Crespin III, Sheshoon, Charlottesville, and others.

The direct impact of Vuillier on the Aga Khan's success cannot be quantified, nor can the actual role of Dosage methodology be accurately measured. However, we can be certain that Vuillier's creation was instrumental in shaping his pedigree insights and preferences. There is an undeniable link between Vuillier's philosophy and the Aga Khan's achievements.

Vuillier's work leaves many questions unanswered. Will his data and conclusions hold up in the light of today's more sophisticated analytical techniques? Can dosages be shown to differentiate the qualities of a pedigree? Do the principles that he developed still apply to contemporary Thoroughbreds? There are students of pedigree who continue to seek answers to these questions. Regardless of the outcome and regardless of one's acceptance of Vuillier's ideas, it is clear that he made a revolutionary contribution to pedigree evaluation. By creating a methodology that classifies the configuration of an individual pedigree in quantitative terms, he changed forever the philosophical basis of pedigree analysis.

The Origins of Dosage: Varola

The next major step in the evolution of Dosage is attributed to Dr. Franco Varola. An Italian lawyer, Varola introduced his approach to pedigree interpretation in a series of articles published in *The British Racehorse* between 1959 and 1972 and in two books, *Stalloni Capirazza dal 1900 ad oggi* published in 1960, and *Nuovi Dosaggi del Purosangue* published in 1967. These were followed by two more comprehensive volumes, *Typology of the Racehorse* published in 1974, and *The Functional Development of the Thoroughbred* published in 1980.

Varola accepted Vuillier's premise that the evolution of the Thoroughbred takes place through a tiny fraction of the stallions standing at stud in any era. Over time, only a few names will survive in pedigrees, while the rest will pass into obscurity. A consequence of this convergence of thought was that Varola also limited his selection of *chefs-de-race* to a relatively small number, although larger than Vuillier's.

The fundamental difference between Vuillier and Varola is the difference between quantitative analysis and qualitative analysis. Whereas Vuillier concerned himself only with the frequency (a quantity) with which his *chefs-de-race* appeared in a pedigree, Varola shifted the emphasis to the aptitudinal type (a quality) contributed to a pedigree by his *chefs-de-race*. Like Vuillier, Varola applied his technique to extended pedigrees. Unlike Vuillier, Varola did not differentiate the contributions of his *chefs-de-race* by generation. In other words, Varola allowed that an aptitudinal contribution in one generation would have the same significance as an aptitudinal contribution in another. Although his arbitrary dismissal of Galton's Law may disturb purists who believe in a diminishing influence with increasingly remote generations and despite questions about the scientific accuracy of his approach, Varola offered a new perspective on pedigree interpretation. Instead of simply considering the historical exploits of the various ancestors in a pedigree, he emphasized the dynamic interplay of aptitudinal types that defined the character of the horse being analyzed. Concentrating on the aptitudinal influences passed along at stud rather than highlighting accomplishments on the track is a profound and significant change in direction.

Varola explains his resistance to applying Galton's Law to his being a "humanist" and "not a geneticist nor a scientist." By this exercise in logic, Varola rationalizes the position that he "can afford to take an independent view of the influence of early progenitors" and that he "is concerned with typology in a functional sense, and not with percentage of influence in a genetic sense." Choosing to ignore scientific principles simply because one is not a scientist may be construed by some as a peculiar and self-serving thing to do, but it is consistent with Varola's excitement over his "sociological" rather than genetic interpretation of the Thoroughbred. On the other hand, if one chooses to overlook certain rules of logic, then observing pedigrees in terms of the distribution of aptitudinal qualities is refreshing and often quite revealing.

Varola's initial selection of 20 *chefs-de-race* was largely based on his perception of those sires that had the greatest overall impact on the breed in the 20th century. To ensure adequate typological variation among his *chefs-de-race*, he had to lower his standards somewhat in making later assignments, focusing primarily on their functional contribution. The final list included 120 stallions. The *chefs-de-race* were then separated into five aptitudinal groups he called Brilliant, Intermediate, Classic, Stout, and Professional. These groups differ in their "essence or character," not necessarily in their inclination to pass along distance capability. That having been said, Brilliant *chefs-de-race* tend to transmit quickness, speed, and early maturity.

Intermediate *chefs-de-race* are so-called "mixers," necessary for a satisfactory balance of class and finesse. They are a connecting link between the aptitudinal extremes. Classic *chefs-de-race* are most often associated with the three-year-old classic races. Stout *chefs-de-race* produce runners of diminished brilliance, but with soundness, a good constitution, and a steady temperament. The Professional *chefs-de-race* generally get pure plodders.

More broadly, Varola likened the five aptitudinal groups to positions along the political spectrum ranging from Left (Brilliant), Left of Center (Intermediate), Center (Classic), Right of Center (Stout), and Right (Professional). He believed the political analogy would avoid any misconceptions that the range of aptitudinal groups paralleled distance capability.

The mechanics of Varola's analysis are fairly straightforward and involve the creation of a Dosage diagram. *Chefs-de-race* in a pedigree are placed one by one into a table according to their designated aptitudinal group. When all of the *chefs-de-race* are accounted for, the presences in each aptitudinal group are added. The sums of the presences within each group constitute the Dosage diagram. For illustration, we will use the Dosage diagram of English Derby winner St. Paddy, b., 1957 (Aureole - Edie Kelly, by Bois Roussel):

The Dosage diagram of St. Paddy does not necessarily correlate with any specific performance attributes. In fact, Varola insists that Dosage diagrams have no relation to racing ability. Rather, the Dosage diagram of St. Paddy fits within the larger framework of what Varola described in 1980 as "a behavioural perspective of the development of the breed in the course of this century." Each Dosage diagram stands alone, symbolizing the type of horse one may expect by revealing the "proportional representation of the five aptitudinal groups." Varola does remind us that a balance of aptitudinal factors is desirable in a racehorse. The ability to observe that balance was a primary driving force in the development of his methodology.

Brilliant	Intermediate	Classic	Stout	Professional
Hyperion		Aureole	(3)Chaucer	Bayardo
Cicero		Gainsborough	Bois Roussel	Son-In-Law
Phalaris		Blenheim II	Vatout II	Dark Ronald
		Blandford	Spearmint	
		Clarissimus		
		(2)Swynford		
		Tracery		
		Rock Sand		
3	0	9	6	3

The parentheses before a sire's name indicates the total number of presences for that sire found in the pedigree.

Varola distinguishes among several types of Dosage diagrams based on the aforementioned proportional representation. The balanced pattern displays a comparable number of influences in each group. Foals by stallions with a balanced pattern will largely retain the Dosage diagram characteristics of their dam. The classical pattern has the highest representation in the Classic group and allows for a variety of mating possibilities. The wing pattern has its greatest representation in the Brilliant and Professional groups to the detriment of the Intermediate, Classic, and Stout groups. Presumably this pattern is created by breeding at the extremes in the hope of producing an average. Varola notes that this effect is not often achieved, a fact that he offers as evidence of the virtue of a balanced distribution. The brilliant pattern is dominated by presences in the brilliant group. Unlike the wing pattern, which may require several generations to bring back into balance, the brilliant pattern is easily "redeemed" according to Varola. The stout pattern occurs when the number of stout *chefs-de-race* is the highest. This particular pattern was noted as typical of French- and Italian-bred horses. Finally, the void pattern describes a situation in which multiple or contiguous groups have no representation at all. Here again, Varola suggests that the existence of top-class sires and runners that display this pattern is further evidence that Dosage diagrams have no relation to racing ability. They simply establish "type," thereby reinforcing Varola's main point that "Dosages are the study of the differentiation of functions within the Thoroughbred, and not magic formulae."

Varola's complete works are far more intricate than can be fully covered here. His introduction of split aptitudinal groups, half-point sires, and split-personality sires – intended to enhance "differentiation" – either enrich his theories or make them over-ly complex, depending on one's point of view. Nevertheless, students of pedigree would be well-served by reading Varola's publications on their own because, despite any reservations one may have about the specifics of his methodology, the approach offers a novel perspective on the meaning of a Thoroughbred pedigree.

Modern Dosage Methodology

Vuillier and Varola established the foundations of Dosage using distinct quantitative and qualitative approaches. In some ways their philosophies overlapped. In other ways they were quite different. Both employed extended pedigrees, and both believed that evolutionary or developmental influences within the Thoroughbred could be defined by a relatively small number of key ancestors. On the one hand, Vuillier applied Galton's Law, assuming a diminishing influence of *chefs-de-race* as generations became more remote. On the other, Varola rejected Galton's Law and gave every *chef-de-race* the same weight regardless of which generation he populated. Vuillier attempted to identify the actual genetic influence of a *chef-de-race* through a quantitative measurement of its presences in a pedigree. Varola tried to assign an aptitudinal type through the qualitative assessment of characteristics prepotently handed down from generation to generation. Neither method relies entirely on conventional pedigree analysis where the emphasis is on the ancestors' achievements on the track or in the breeding shed.

Despite the new directions offered by Vuillier and Varola, some practical problems remained. Not the least of these is the access to extended pedigrees for the vast majority of horsemen. Thanks to computers and both offline and online databases, such pedigrees now may be conveniently generated. Software can be written to calculate the Vuillier Dosage numbers and create the Varola Dosage diagrams. However, the availability of technology does not guarantee its widespread use, particularly when it is likely to be expensive. Under any circumstances, an analysis technique involving extended pedigrees will always have marginal utility for a general racing audience.

A second limitation of the Vuillier and Varola methodologies is the lack of a statistical framework. Without a statistical base, it is difficult to put one's analytical results in the proper context. In other words, if one fails to define control groups or measurable variables that compare the results of one analysis to another, the significance of the results may not be clear. This is particularly true in the case of Varola who specifically dissociated his Dosage diagrams from any aspect of racing performance. Under those circumstances, it is especially difficult to appreciate the real-world significance of pedigree type. Varola opted for "art" over science, and he succeeded. However, his disregard for scientific method clearly puts the user of his technique at a disadvantage, particularly if he or she is looking for a practical application that generates a set of probabilities applicable to real situations.

With these limitations in mind, we sought a next-generation approach to Dosage that retained the best elements of the earlier versions while significantly expanding its utility. To that end, we abandoned the extended pedigree in favor of the readily accessible four-generation pedigree. We also rejected Varola's dismissal of Galton's Law, preferring instead to use a counting method similar to that employed by Vuillier. Finally, we felt that Varola's dissociation of his aptitudinal groups from distance capability was arbitrary and not supported by evidence. The hypothesis we proposed was that the aptitudinal groups cover the entire spectrum of speed to stamina and that the relationship between speed and stamina in the individual will affect every aspect of his racing character, including distance ability. Rather than being contradictory qualities, speed and stamina are opposite sides of the same coin. They are inextricably linked. One is always sacrificed in favor of the other. Individual horses, because of the unique traits they have inherited, are positioned at discrete points along the speed-stamina continuum. These points determine their type and affect the full range of performance capabilities.

The *chefs-de-race* list used in our original study is displayed in Table 1. The selections are, with minor adjustments, those of Varola as modified by Hewitt in his article on Dosage that appeared in *The Blood-Horse* of May 2, 1977. Hewitt modified the Varola list of largely European *chefs-de-race* in order to make Dosage more applicable to American pedigrees. In several cases the two authors disagreed

TABLE I

Chefs-de-race USED IN THE INITIAL CONTEMPORARY DOSAGE STUDIES

BRILLIANT

Abernant	Heliopolis	Pharis
Black Toney*	Hyperion*	Pompey
Bold Ruler	My Babu	Raise a Native
British Empire	Nasrullah*	Reviewer
Bull Dog	Nearco*	Roman*
Cicero	Never Bend*	Royal Charger
Court Martial	Olympia	Sir Cosmo
Double Jay	Orby	Tudor Minstrel
Fair Trial	Panorama	Turn-to*
Fairway	Peter Pan	Ultimus
Grey Sovereign	Phalaris	What a Pleasure

INTERMEDIATE

Ben Brush	King Salmon	Sir Ivor
Big Game	Mahmoud*	Star Kingdom
Black Toney*	Nashua	Star Shoot
Broomstick	Nasrullah*	Sweep
Colorado	Native Dancer*	T.V. Lark
Congreve	Never Bend*	The Tetrarch
Djebel	Northern Dancer	Ticino
Eight Thirty	Petition	Tom Fool*
Equipoise*	Pharos	Traghetto
Full Sail	Polynesian	Turn-to*
Havresac II	Princequillo*	
Khaled	Roman*	

CLASSIC

Alibhai	Gundomar	Prince Chevalier
Aureole	Hail to Reason	Prince Rose
Bahram	Herbager*	Ribot*
Blandford	Hyperion*	Rock Sand*
Blenheim II*	Mahmoud*	Sicambre
Blue Larkspur	Midstream	Sideral
Brantome	Mossborough	Sir Gallahad III
Buckpasser	Native Dancer*	Swynford
Bull Lea	Navarro	Tom Fool*
Clarissimus	Nearco*	Tom Rolfe*
Count Fleet	Never Say Die	Tourbillon*
Equipoise*	Persian Gulf	Tracery
Gainsborough	Pilate	Vieux Manoir
Graustark*	Prince Bio	War Admiral

SOLID

Asterus	Graustark*	Sunstar
Bachelor's Double	Herbager*	Tantieme
Ballymoss	Man 'o War	Teddy
Blenheim II*	Oleander	Vatout
Bois Roussel	Princequillo*	Worden
Chaucer	Right Royal	
Discovery	Rock Sand*	
Fair Play*	Round Table	
Gallant Man	Sea-Bird	

PROFESSIONAL

Admiral Drake	Foxbridge	Solario
Alcantara II	Hurry On	Son-in-Law
Alizier	La Farina	Spearmint
Alycidon	Le Fabuleux	Sunny Boy
Bayardo	Massine	Tom Rolfe*
Bruleur	Mieuxce	Tourbillon*
Chateau Bouscaut	Ortello	Vaguely Noble
Crepello	Precipitation	Vandale
Dark Ronald	Rabelais	Vatellor
Donatello II	Ribot*	Wild Risk
Fair Play*	Sardanaple	

as to aptitudinal placement. In those instances we accepted the assignments at face value, placing the *chef-de-race* in both categories. These *chefs-de-race* are shown in Table 1 with an asterisk (*) next to their names.

We used a counting system based on 16 points for each of the four generations, analogous to Vuillier's 2,048 points for each of his 12 generations. Like Vuillier, we halved the influence of *chefs-de-race* found in each receding generation. In this way, a first generation *chef-de-race* receives 16 points, each second-generation *chef-de-race* receives eight points, each third-generation *chef-de-race* receives four points and each fourth-generation *chef-de-race* receives two points. We opted for the 16-8-4-2 pattern over the more obvious 8-4-2-1 pattern to accommodate *chefs-de-race* split between two groups. In this manner, a fourth generation split *chef-de-race* receives a full point in each aptitudinal category rather than a more cumbersome half-point.

Finally, for simplicity we stayed with five aptitudinal groups instead of the 10 ultimately proposed by Varola through the splitting of aptitudes. This required combining some categories and repositioning some *chefs-de-race*. We also used the nomenclature adopted by Hewitt for defining the aptitudinal groups; i.e., Brilliant-Intermediate-Classic-Solid-Professional.

With the key elements in place, the analysis proceeds in a manner similar to Varola's creation of a Dosage diagram, the main difference being that the points tallied in each aptitudinal group depend on the generational position of the *chef-de-race*. Finally, the output of the analysis is called a Dosage profile (DP) to differentiate it from Varola's Dosage diagram.

The best way to illustrate the procedure is by example. For this purpose we will use the current *chefs-de-race* list as of November 2002 displayed in Tables 2 and 3. Table 2 is an alphabetical listing, while Table 3 is a listing by aptitudinal group. Again, sires split between two aptitudinal groups are displayed with an asterisk after their name in Table 3.

TABLE 2 - *Chefs-de-Race* (199) As Of November 2002
LISTED ALPHABETICALLY

Abernant (B)	Djebel (I)	My Babu (B)	Sardanapale (P)
Ack Ack (I/C)	Donatello II (P)	Nashua (I/C)	Sea-Bird (S)
Admiral Drake (P)	Double Jay (B)	Nasrullah (B)	Seattle Slew (B/C)
Alcantara II (P)	Dr. Fager (I)	Native Dancer (I/C)	Secretariat (I/C)
Alibhai (C)	Eight Thirty (I)	Navarro (C)	Sharpen Up (B/C)
Alizier (P)	Ela-Mana-Mou (P)	Nearco (B/C)	Shirley Heights (C/P)
Alycidon (P)	Equipoise (I/C)	Never Bend (B/I)	Sicambre (C)
Alydar (C)	Exclusive Native (C)	Never Say Die (C)	Sideral (C)
Apalachee (B)	Fair Play (S/P)	Nijinsky II (C/S)	Sir Cosmo (B)
Asterus (S)	Fair Trial (B)	Niniski (C/P)	Sir Gallahad III (C)
Aureole (C)	Fairway (B)	Noholme II (B/C)	Sir Gaylord (I/C)
Bachelor's Double (S)	Fappiano (I/C)	Northern Dancer (B/C)	Sir Ivor (I/C)
Bahram (C)	Forli (C)	Nureyev (C)	Solario (P)
Baldski (B/I)	Foxbridge (P)	Oleander (S)	Son-in-Law (P)
Ballymoss (S)	Full Sail (I)	Olympia (B)	Speak John (B/I)
Bayardo (P)	Gainsborough (C)	Orby (B)	Spearmint (P)
Ben Brush (I)	Gallant Man (B/I)	Ortello (P)	Spy Song (B)
Best Turn (C)	Graustark (C/S)	Panorama (B)	Stage Door Johnny (S/P)
Big Game (I)	Grey Dawn II (B/I)	Persian Gulf (C)	Star Kingdom (I/C)
Black Toney (B/I)	Grey Sovereign (B)	Peter Pan (B)	Star Shoot (I)
Blandford (C)	Gundomar (C)	Petition (I)	Sunny Boy (P)
Blenheim II (C/S)	Habitat (B)	Phalaris (B)	Sunstar (S)
Blue Larkspur (C)	Hail to Reason (C)	Pharis II (B)	Sweep (I)
Blushing Groom (B/C)	Halo (B/C)	Pharos (I)	Swynford (C)
Bois Roussel (S)	Havresac II (I)	Pia Star (S)	T.V. Lark (I)
Bold Bidder (I/C)	Heliopolis (B)	Pilate (C)	Tantieme (S)
Bold Ruler (B/I)	Herbager (C/S)	Polynesian (I)	Teddy (S)
Brantome (C)	High Top (C)	Pompey (B)	The Tetrarch (I)
British Empire (B)	His Majesty (C)	Precipitation (P)	Ticino (C/S)
Broad Brush (I/C)	Hoist the Flag (B/I)	Pretense (C)	Tom Fool (I/C)
Broomstick (I)	Hurry On (P)	Prince Bio (C)	Tom Rolfe (C/P)
Bruleur (P)	Hyperion (B/C)	Prince Chevalier (C)	Tourbillon (C/P)
Buckpasser (C)	Icecapade (B/C)	Prince John (C)	Tracery (C)
Bull Dog (B)	In Reality (B/C)	Princequillo (I/S)	Traghetto (I)
Bull Lea (C)	Intentionally (B/I)	Prince Rose (C)	Tudor Minstrel (B)
Busted (S)	Key to the Mint (B/C)	Promised Land (C)	Turn-to (B/I)
Caro (I/C)	Khaled (I)	Rabelais (P)	Ultimus (B)
Chateau Bouscaut (P)	King Salmon (I)	Raise a Native (B)	Vaguely Noble (C/P)
Chaucer (S)	King's Bishop (B/I)	Relko (S)	Vandale (P)
Cicero (B)	La Farina (P)	Reviewer (B/C)	Vatellor (P)
Clarissimus (C)	Le Fabuleux (P)	Ribot (C/P)	Vatout (S)
Colorado (I)	Luthier (C)	Right Royal (S)	Vieux Manoir (C)
Congreve (I)	Lyphard (C)	Riverman (I/C)	War Admiral (C)
Count Fleet (C)	Mahmoud (I/C)	Roberto (C)	What a Pleasure (B)
Court Martial (B)	Man o' War (S)	Rock Sand (C/S)	Wild Risk (P)
Creme dela Creme (C/S)	Massine (P)	Roman (B/I)	Worden (S)
Crepello (P)	Midstream (C)	Rough'n Tumble (B/C)	
Damascus (I/C)	Mieuxce (P)	Round Table (S)	
Danzig (I/C)	Mill Reef (C/S)	Royal Charger (B)	
Dark Ronald (P)	Mossborough (C)	Run the Gantlet (P)	
Discovery (S)	Mr. Prospector (B/C)	Sadler's Wells (C/S)	

TABLE 3 - *Chefs-de-Race* (199) AS OF NOVEMBER 2002
LISTED BY APTITUDINAL GROUP

BRILLIANT

Abernant 1946
Apalachee 1971
Baldski* 1974
Black Toney* 1911
Blushing Groom* 1974
Bold Ruler* 1954
British Empire 1937
Bull Dog 1927
Cicero 1902
Court Martial 1942
Double Jay 1944
Fair Trial 1932
Fairway 1925
Gallant Man* 1954
Grey Dawn II* 1962
Grey Sovereign 1948
Habitat 1966
Halo* 1969

Heliopolis 1936
Hoist the Flag* 1968
Hyperion* 1930
Icecapade* 1969
In Reality* 1964
Intentionally* 1956
Key to the Mint* 1969
King's Bishop* 1969
Mr. Prospector* 1970
My Babu 1945
Nasrullah 1940
Nearco* 1935
Never Bend* 1960
Noholme II* 1956
Northern Dancer* 1961
Olympia 1946
Orby 1904
Panorama 1936

Peter Pan 1904
Phalaris 1913
Pharis II 1936
Pompey 1923
Raise a Native 1961
Reviewer* 1966
Roman* 1937
Rough'n Tumble* 1948
Royal Charger 1942
Seattle Slew* 1974
Sharpen Up* 1969
Sir Cosmo 1926
Speak John* 1958
Spy Song 1943
Tudor Minstrel 1944
Turn-to* 1951
Ultimus 1906
What a Pleasure 1965

INTERMEDIATE

Ack Ack* 1966
Baldski* 1974
Ben Brush 1893
Big Game 1939
Black Toney* 1911
Bold Bidder* 1962
Bold Ruler* 1954
Broad Brush* 1983
Broomstick 1901
Caro* 1967
Colorado 1923
Congreve 1924
Damascus* 1964
Danzig* 1977
Djebel 1937
Dr. Fager 1964
Eight Thirty 1936
Equipoise* 1928

Fappiano* 1977
Full Sail 1934
Gallant Man* 1954
Grey Dawn II* 1962
Havresac II 1915
Hoist the Flag* 1968
Intentionally* 1956
Khaled 1943
King Salmon 1930
King's Bishop* 1969
Mahmoud* 1933
Nashua* 1952
Native Dancer* 1950
Never Bend* 1960
Petition 1944
Pharos 1920
Polynesian 1942
Princequillo* 1940

Riverman* 1969
Roman* 1937
Secretariat* 1970
Sir Gaylord* 1959
Sir Ivor* 1965
Speak John* 1958
Star Kingdom* 1946
Star Shoot 1898
Sweep 1907
T.V. Lark 1957
The Tetrarch 1911
Tom Fool* 1949
Traghetto 1942
Turn-to* 1951

CLASSIC

Ack Ack* 1966
Alibhai 1938
Alydar 1975
Aureole 1950
Bahram 1932
Best Turn 1966
Blandford 1919
Blenheim II* 1927
Blue Larkspur 1926
Blushing Groom* 1974
Bold Bidder* 1962
Brantome 1931
Broad Brush* 1983
Buckpasser 1963
Bull Lea 1935
Caro* 1967
Clarissimus 1913
Count Fleet 1940
Creme dela Creme* 1963
Damascus* 1964
Danzig* 1977
Equipoise* 1928
Exclusive Native 1965
Fappiano* 1977
Forli 1963
Gainsborough 1915
Graustark* 1963
Gundomar 1942
Hail to Reason 1958
Halo* 1969

Herbager* 1956
High Top 1969
His Majesty 1968
Hyperion* 1930
Icecapade* 1969
In Reality* 1964
Key To The Mint* 1969
Luthier 1965
Lyphard 1969
Mahmoud* 1933
Midstream 1933
Mill Reef* 1968
Mossborough 1947
Mr. Prospector* 1970
Nashua* 1952
Native Dancer* 1950
Navarro 1931
Nearco* 1935
Never Say Die 1951
Nijinsky II* 1967
Niniski* 1976
Noholme II* 1956
Northern Dancer* 1961
Nureyev 1977
Persian Gulf 1940
Pilate 1928
Pretense 1963
Prince Bio 1941
Prince Chevalier 1943
Prince John 1953

Prince Rose 1928
Promised Land 1954
Reviewer* 1966
Ribot* 1952
Riverman* 1969
Roberto 1969
Rock Sand* 1900
Rough'n Tumble* 1948
Sadler's Wells* 1981
Seattle Slew* 1974
Secretariat* 1970
Sharpen Up* 1969
Shirley Heights* 1975
Sicambre 1948
Sideral 1948
Sir Gallahad III 1920
Sir Gaylord* 1959
Sir Ivor* 1965
Star Kingdom* 1946
Swynford 1907
Ticino* 1939
Tom Fool* 1949
Tom Rolfe* 1962
Tourbillon* 1928
Tracery 1909
Vaguely Noble* 1965
Vieux Manoir 1947
War Admiral 1934

SOLID

Asterus 1923
Bachelor's Double 1906
Ballymoss 1954
Blenheim II* 1927
Bois Roussel 1935
Busted 1963
Chaucer 1900
Creme dela Creme* 1963
Discovery 1931
Fair Play* 1905
Graustark* 1963
Herbager* 1956
Man o' War 1917

Mill Reef* 1968
Nijinsky II* 1967
Oleander 1924
Pia Star 1961
Princequillo* 1940
Relko 1960
Right Royal 1958
Rock Sand* 1900
Round Table 1954
Sadler's Wells* 1981
Sea-Bird 1962
Stage Door Johnny* 1965
Sunstar 1908

Tantieme 1947
Teddy 1913
Ticino* 1939
Vatout 1926
Worden 1949

PROFESSIONAL

Admiral Drake 1931
Alcantara II 1908
Alizier 1947
Alycidon 1945
Bayardo 1906
Bruleur 1910
Chateau Bouscaut 1927
Crepello 1954
Dark Ronald 1905
Donatello II 1934
Ela-Mana-Mou 1976
Fair Play* 1905
Foxbridge 1930
Hurry On 1913
La Farina 1911

Le Fabuleux 1961
Massine 1920
Mieuxce 1933
Niniski* 1976
Ortello 1926
Precipitation 1933
Rabelais 1900
Ribot* 1952
Run the Gantlet 1968
Sardanapale 1911
Shirley Heights* 1975
Solario 1922
Son-In-Law 1911
Spearmint 1903
Stage Door Johnny* 1965

Sunny Boy 1944
Tom Rolfe* 1962
Tourbillon* 1928
Vaguely Noble* 1965
Vandale 1943
Vatellor 1933
Wild Risk 1940

Dosage Calculations

The subject of the analysis is Hero's Honor, b.c., 1980 (Northern Dancer - Glowing Tribute, by Graustark). His four-generation pedigree follows, with *chefs-de-race* highlighted in bold type.

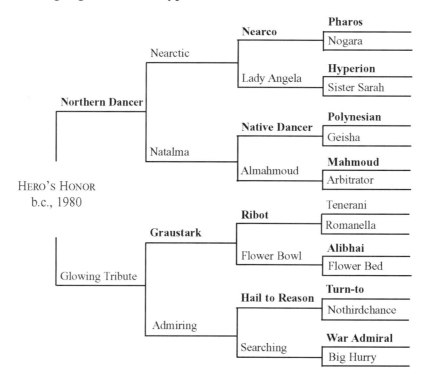

The first-generation sire, Northern Dancer, is a *chef-de-race* split between the Brilliant and Classic categories. With 16 points reserved for a *chef-de-race* in generation one, he is assigned eight points in Brilliant and eight points in Classic.

In the second generation, worth eight points for each *chef-de-race*, Nearctic is not a *chef-de-race*, while Graustark is a *chef-de-race* split between Classic and Solid. No points are added for Nearctic, while Graustark is assigned four points each in Classic and Solid. We use the same procedure for generations three and four, leading to the distribution of points found in Table 4.

Table 4
Calculation of the Dosage Profile (DP) for Hero's Honor

Generation (Pts)	Sires (Aptitudinal Group(s))	B	I	C	S	P
1st Generation (16)	Northern Dancer (Brilliant/Classic)	8		8		
2nd Generation (8)	Nearctic (N/A)					
	Graustark (Classic/Solid)			4	4	
3rd Generation (4)	Nearco (Brilliant/Classic)	2		2		
	Native Dancer (Intermediate/Classic)		2	2		
	Ribot (Classic/Professional)			2		2
	Hail to Reason (Classic)			4		
4th Generation (2)	Pharos (Intermediate)		2			
	Hyperion (Brilliant/Classic)	1		1		
	Polynesian (Intermediate)		2			
	Mahmoud (Intermediate/Classic)		1	1		
	Tenerani (N/A)					
	Alibhai (Classic)			2		
	Turn-to (Brilliant/Intermediate)	1	1			
	War Admiral (Classic)			2		
	Dosage Profile:	12	8	28	4	2

After accounting for all 15 sires within four generations, we add the points in each column. In the example, we are left with a DP having 12 points under Brilliant, eight points under Intermediate, 28 points under Classic, four points under Solid, and two points under Professional. The distribution is normally displayed as DP 12-8-28-4-2.

Hero's Honor's DP has representation in each of the five aptitudinal groups. This is not always the case. Quite often horses will lack representation in one or more categories, and their point totals can vary widely. The 54 points out of a possible 64 assigned to Hero's Honor indicate the presence of numerous *chefs-de-race* among the 15 four-generation sires. Within the Thoroughbred population, we find considerable variation in DP point totals, as well as in the distribution of points in the DP. The many possible configurations lend themselves to other calculations based on the DP that capture the differences in a readily visible form. These are alternative expressions of the aptitudinal characteristics in a pedigree. In combination with the DP, they provide a more complete picture of aptitudinal type.

The first of these expressions is the Dosage index (DI). The DI is a ratio of speed to stamina as portrayed in the DP. It is derived first by dividing the DP into separate speed and stamina components. The speed component is defined as the Brilliant points plus the Intermediate points plus one-half the Classic points found in the DP. Similarly, the stamina component is defined as one-half the Classic points plus the Solid points plus the Professional points. In effect, we've split the DP down the middle. For Hero's Honor, the speed component is 12 plus eight (equals 20) plus one-half of 28 (14), for a total of 34. The stamina component is one-half of 28 (14) plus four (equals 18) plus two, for a total of 20. The DI is simply the ratio of the speed component divided by the stamina component. For Hero's Honor, the proportion is 34 over 20, or 1.70.

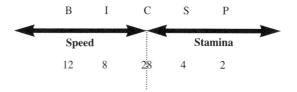

If we imagine the five aptitude groups as points spaced equally along a linear scale where Brilliant is assigned a value of +2.00, Intermediate is assigned a value +1.00, Classic is assigned a value of 0.00, Solid is assigned a value of -1.00, and Professional is assigned a value of -2.00, the DP allows for the calculation of the second expression, the Center of Distribution (CD). Think of the scale as you would a seesaw where the aptitudinal groups are evenly spaced and the assigned values represent distances to the left and right of center. Now consider that the seesaw is pivoted in the middle and that the points in the DP are weights placed on the seesaw at the location corresponding to their aptitudinal group. Depending on the weights, the seesaw will tip to the left or to the right. The CD is that position along the seesaw where the pivot must be moved to bring the system back into balance. In a sense, it is similar to a center of gravity where all of the weighted aptitudes supplied by *chefs-de-race* in the four generations merge into a single point. A graphical representation of the concept is shown below.

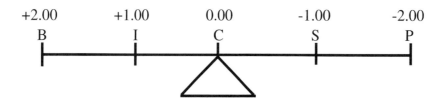

The CD is calculated by adding twice the Brilliant points plus the Intermediate points minus the Solid points minus twice the Professional points and dividing that number by the total points in the DP. For Hero's Honor, the numerator is 24 plus eight minus four minus four, or 24. The denominator is the sum of total points for Hero's Honor, which is 54, as shown above. The CD is then 24 divided by 54, or +0.44. In the following graphic, we can see that the pivot point has moved 0.44 units to the left to rebalance the weights.

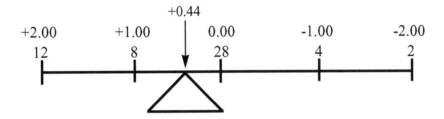

Summarizing the Dosage figures for Hero's Honor, he has DP 12-8-28-4-2, DI 1.70 and CD 0.44. By themselves, these numbers mean very little. As we will see, their significance becomes clear when we compare them to the Dosage figures of other Thoroughbreds. With these calculations now available, we can evaluate runners with similar performance characteristics in an attempt to identify patterns linking aptitudinal type to track performance.

In our original research conducted between 1977 and 1980, we examined several categories of performance by distance, surface, and age, grouping the average Dosage figures of the winners. The results are summarized in Tables 5, 6, and 7.

TABLE 5 - DOSAGE FIGURES BY DISTANCE AND SURFACE, STAKES WINNERS OF 1980

Race Category	Average DI	Average CD
Sprints on dirt (less than 8f)	5.52	0.91
Middle distances on dirt (8-10f)	4.05	0.71
Routes on dirt (greater than 10f)	1.74	0.29
All races on dirt	4.62	0.79
Sprints on grass (less than 8f)	5.90	0.90
Middle distances on grass (8-10f)	4.22	0.70
Routes on grass (greater than 10f)	3.48	0.39
All races on grass	4.23	0.66
ALL RACES	**4.53**	**0.76**

TABLE 6 - DOSAGE INDEX BY AGE, STAKES WINNERS OF 1980 AND GRADED STAKES WINNERS OF 1978-79

Age	Average DI, North American SWs,1980	Average DI, North American Graded SWs,1978-79
Two-year-olds	5.59	5.71
Three-year-olds	4.16	4.06
Older horses	4.41	4.07
ALL HORSES	**4.53**	**4.30**

TABLE 7
DOSAGE FIGURES OF CHAMPIONS BY DECADE

Race Category	Average DI	Average CD
Two-year-old colt champions (1941-1980)	2.20	
Two-year-old colt champions (1941-1950)	1.63	0.15
Two-year-old colt champions (1971-1980)	2.84	0.84
Three-year-old colt champions (1941-1980)	1.98	
Three-year-old colt champions (1941-1950)	1.43	0.24
Three-year-old colt champions (1971-1980)	2.46	0.70
Handicap champions (1942-1980)	1.87	
Handicap champions (1942-1950)	1.52	0.27
Handicap champions (1971-1980)	2.65	0.78
Sprint champions (1971-1980)	3.85	0.72
Grass champions (1971-1980)	2.06	0.32
Kentucky Derby winners (1971-1980)	2.68	0.89
Belmont Stakes winners (1971-1980)	2.37	0.60

Even in this relatively small study, obvious distinctions may be seen between juveniles and older runners, between sprinters and stayers, between dirt horses and turf horses, and even by racing era. The uniformly higher figures observed for the various champions of the 1970s compared to those of the 1940s parallels what many believe is an ever-increasing infusion of speed into the Thoroughbred over time. The ability of Dosage to detect these changes makes it a powerful tool for monitoring the evolutionary trends within the breed.

Contemporary Dosage Data

Table 8 presents a more complete picture based on data accumulated between 1983 and 2001 from almost 19,000 open stakes races. We examined races of all types and arranged the data by racing category, including distance, surface, age, and class of race. The table shows the number of races in each category, the average distance of the races, the average DP of the winners, the average number of points in the DP, the average Dosage index (ADI), the average CD (ACD), the composite Dosage index

Horse 1:	DP 10-7-1-0-0	DI 35.00	CD 1.50
Horse 2:	DP 6-6-12-2-0	DI 2.25	CD 0.62
Horse 3:	DP 2-4-12-4-2	DI 1.00	CD 0.00

Average DP 6.00-5.67-8.33-2.00-0.67   *Composite DI* 2.32
Average DI 12.75   *Composite CD* 0.63
Average CD 0.71

TABLE 8 - DOSAGE DATA FOR NORTH AMERICAN OPEN STAKES RACES BETWEEN 1983 AND 2001

Category	Races	Dist.	DP	PTS	ADI	ACD	CDI	CCD
All races	18617	8.09	7.88 - 4.76 - 9.59 - 1.60 - 0.91	24.73	3.42	0.72	2.39	0.69
Dirt races	13046	7.75	8.15 - 4.91 - 9.11 - 1.39 - 0.78	24.35	3.74	0.77	2.62	0.75
Turf races	5571	8.89	7.24 - 4.39 - 10.71 - 2.07 - 1.21	25.63	2.67	0.59	1.97	0.56
<8 furlongs	5913	6.29	8.55 - 4.90 - 8.29 - 1.18 - 0.57	23.48	4.34	0.86	2.99	0.84
8-10 furlongs	11706	8.69	7.63 - 4.72 - 10.09 - 1.70 - 1.00	25.15	3.07	0.67	2.24	0.65
>10 furlongs	998	11.78	6.81 - 4.29 - 11.46 - 2.83 - 1.82	27.21	2.12	0.44	1.62	0.42
2-year-olds	2474	7.17	8.11 - 4.75 - 8.88 - 1.28 - 0.65	23.67	3.91	0.80	2.72	0.78
3-year-olds	5393	8.16	7.92 - 4.78 - 9.70 - 1.54 - 0.86	24.80	3.41	0.73	2.42	0.70
Older runners	10750	8.27	7.81 - 4.74 - 9.70 - 1.70 - 0.99	24.94	3.32	0.69	2.31	0.67
G1 races	2004	9.22	8.35 - 5.03 - 11.29 - 1.89 - 1.22	27.78	2.93	0.64	2.17	0.63
G2 races	2675	8.61	8.06 - 4.77 - 10.60 - 1.79 - 1.04	26.26	3.16	0.67	2.23	0.65
G3 races	4123	8.28	7.90 - 4.72 - 10.01 - 1.65 - 0.93	25.21	3.27	0.70	2.32	0.67
Listed races	9815	7.64	7.73 - 4.71 - 8.79 - 1.46 - 0.80	23.49	3.66	0.75	2.53	0.73
5.50 furlongs	353	5.50	8.08 - 4.69 - 7.94 - 1.29 - 0.56	22.56	4.56	0.84	2.88	0.82
6.00 furlongs	2903	6.00	8.64 - 4.93 - 7.99 - 1.09 - 0.49	23.14	4.65	0.90	3.15	0.87
6.50 furlongs	782	6.50	8.04 - 4.50 - 7.92 - 1.25 - 0.59	22.30	4.04	0.84	2.85	0.81
7.00 furlongs	1566	7.00	8.91 - 5.21 - 9.07 - 1.28 - 0.69	25.17	4.00	0.83	2.87	0.81
8.00 furlongs	2091	8.00	7.92 - 4.73 - 10.07 - 1.69 - 0.87	25.28	3.21	0.70	2.33	0.68
8.32 furlongs	286	8.32	7.91 - 4.75 - 8.66 - 1.49 - 1.10	23.92	3.44	0.73	2.45	0.71
8.50 furlongs	4491	8.50	7.63 - 4.72 - 9.84 - 1.61 - 0.94	24.75	3.18	0.69	2.31	0.67
9.00 furlongs	3768	9.00	7.46 - 4.70 - 10.20 - 1.73 - 1.01	25.10	2.97	0.65	2.20	0.63
9.50 furlongs	253	9.50	7.28 - 4.54 - 10.52 - 2.30 - 1.28	25.92	2.58	0.56	1.93	0.55
10.00 furlongs	813	10.00	7.72 - 4.85 - 11.37 - 2.00 - 1.54	27.48	2.60	0.57	1.98	0.55
11.00 furlongs	394	11.00	6.96 - 4.30 - 11.89 - 2.83 - 1.70	27.68	2.10	0.45	1.64	0.43
12.00 furlongs	503	12.00	6.68 - 4.25 - 11.24 - 2.87 - 1.84	26.88	2.06	0.42	1.60	0.41

(CDI) and the composite CD (CCD). Composite figures represent the DI and CD as calculated directly from the average DP rather than the average of all the individual DIs and CDs in the sample. In a sense, the average DP describes the complete distribution of aptitudes within the entire population being examined. The composite figures also attenuate the impact of outliers, as illustrated below.

In this example, the dramatic effect on the averages of Horse 1's DI of 35.00 and CD of 1.50 is greatly moderated in the composite numbers.

Table 8 clearly reveals dramatic differences among the figures within the various categories. These data provide the strongest evidence of Dosage's ability to correlate pedigree type with racetrack performance.

Differences by surface: The average numbers for open stakes winners on dirt (DI 3.74, CD 0.77) are significantly higher than those for open stakes winners on grass (DP 2.67, CD 0.59). These results indicate that the pedigrees of the winners on the respective surfaces are configured differently from one another with regard to the specific *chefs-de-race* influencing each performance category. At the same time, note the significant difference in the average distance of the races on the main track and on turf. The dirt races at an average distance of 7.75 furlongs are more than a furlong shorter than the turf races, which are run at an average distance of 8.89 furlongs. Considering that the DI and the CD reflect a ratio of inherited speed over stamina, it is entirely consistent that the higher average Dosage figures are associated with the shorter races, while the lower average Dosage figures are associated with the longer races. Also note the presence of more than twice the number of Dosage points in the Solid and Professional aptitudinal groups for the turf winners compared to the winners on the dirt.

Differences by distance range: We observe a similar pattern here where the races are split between sprints (less than eight furlongs), middle distances (between eight and 10 furlongs) and routes (greater than 10 furlongs). As the average distance of the races in each group increases from 6.29 to 8.69 to 11.78 furlongs, the DI and CD numbers decrease proportionately and as expected. The precision of the analysis is vividly demonstrated by the patterns found within the DP itself. Note that in the transition from sprints to middle distances to routes, the average number of points decreases in the Brilliant and Intermediate groups and increases in the Classic, Solid, and Professional groups. Again, we observe the smooth shift from speed influences to stamina influences as the distances grow longer.

Differences by age: In the age category, we find a significant difference between the figures for juveniles and those for three-year-olds and for older runners. The two-year-olds compete at an average distance that is a furlong or more shorter than the average for their older counterparts. On the other hand, the difference in average distance between three-year-olds and older runners is quite small. It should come as no surprise, then, that the Dosage figures for the juveniles are higher than those for the three-year-olds and older runners, while the figures for the latter two groups are close together. Even here, though, we observe that the differences in the figures are in the right direction with the three-year-old figures being marginally higher than those for the older runners, which compete at slightly longer distances on average.

Differences by class of race: The data indicate a direct correlation between the class of races and their average distance, with the highest-class races being the longest and the lowest-class races being the shortest. In moving from Grade 1 races through Grade 2 and Grade 3 races to listed events, the average distance declines from 9.22 furlongs to 8.61 furlongs to 8.28 furlongs to 7.64 furlongs. Consistent with this progression is the gradual increase in the Dosage figures with declining class. We also find a drop in the average point contributions in the Brilliant, Classic, Solid, and Professional aptitudinal categories, resulting in a modestly lower DP point total with each successive level below Grade 1.

Differences by specific distance: The final set of figures in Table 8 are for races run at specific distances between five and 12 furlongs. The trends are similar to those seen in the other performance categories, with the Dosage figures inversely correlating with the average distance. We can capture the significance of the differences from one distance to another using simple statistical techniques such as a Student's T-Test. This method can determine the likelihood that the figures for winners at one distance are different from those for winners at another distance. For example, we can compare the Dosage numbers for the six-furlong winners with those for the seven-furlong winners, and we can establish a level of confidence that the two groups are not the same. In the analysis, we generate what is known as a P value. If the P value is less than 0.05, we can be confident that the two populations are indeed different from one another. Table 9 displays the P values resulting from a comparison of the average CD of populations at specific distances.

TABLE 9 - STATISTICAL ANALYSIS COMPARING THE AVERAGE CD AT DIFFERENT DISTANCES

Distances Being Compared	P Value
6f and 7f	0.000000009
7f and 8f	0.00000000000000000003
8f and 9f	0.000008
9f and 10f	0.00004
10f and 12f	0.00000002

The results are striking. For the distances analyzed, the probability that the respective populations as reflected in the average CD are the same is essentially zero. Said another way, Dosage analysis is precise enough to differentiate the pedigrees of horses that win at distances as little as one furlong apart in many cases. In particular, the difference observed between the winners at seven furlongs and a mile is exceptional and represents the logical break between one- and two-turn runners.

The Fundamental Relationship Between Dosage Figures and Distance

Plotting the average DIs and average CDs listed in Table 8 against the corresponding average distance for each performance category affords the graphical outputs shown in Charts 1 and 2.

CHART 1 - AVERAGE DI VS. AVERAGE DISTANCE FOR RACING CATEGORIES IN TABLE 8

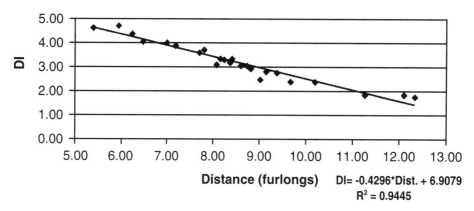

Average DI vs. Distance
North American Open Stakes, 1983-2001

DI= -0.4296*Dist. + 6.9079
$R^2 = 0.9445$

CHART 2 - AVERAGE CD VS. AVERAGE DISTANCE FOR RACING CATEGORIES IN TABLE 8

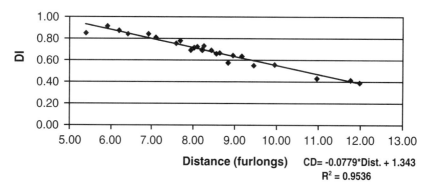

Average CD vs. Distance
North American Open Stakes, 1983-2001

CD= -0.0779*Dist. + 1.343
$R^2 = 0.9536$

Subjecting the data to the statistical technique called linear regression confirms that both the DI and the CD values are inversely related to the distance over the range from five to 12 furlongs. This relationship is easily visible in the trend lines generated from the data and which slope from the upper left to the lower right. In other words, both the DI and the CD decrease as the distances increase. It is also noteworthy that virtually all of the data points fall very close to the straight line created by the regression. This is significant because the closeness of the data points to the line as a measure of the strength of the correlation. The R^2 values on the charts quantify the correlations. If every data point fell directly on the linear regression line, R^2 would be exactly 1.0000. The closer R^2 is to 1.0000, the better the fit. In Chart 1, the R^2 value of 0.9445 indicates that more than 94 percent of the variability in DI (or aptitudinal type) is explained by changes in distance. The result is even better in Chart 2 where more than 95 percent of the variability in CD (an alternative expression of aptitudinal type) is explained by those same distance changes. The remaining variability is attributable to other, undefined factors. It is evident that despite Varola's insistence that no such relationship exists in his methodology, the correlation between modern Dosage methodology and the distance of races is extremely strong. Furthermore, Charts 1 and 2, displaying the effects of distance on aptitudinal type, provide the most definitive graphical expression of the contemporary Dosage model.

Dosage and Two-Year-Olds

A fascinating and validating use of Dosage as a tool for understanding aptitudinal trends is revealed in its application to the analysis of two-year-old racing. Specifically, we can monitor the moving average of the DI for winners of juvenile stakes throughout the year. A moving average is simply a shifting average over a series of successive events. The moving average changes with each additional data point. In our example, we arranged the two-year-old stakes winners in chronological order for each of the years 1983 through 2001. We then determined the average DI for each of the races in sequence through the year. In other words, we calculated the average DI for all of the first juvenile stakes from 1983 through 2001, then did the same for the second, the third and so on. We then plotted the change in the average DI from race one through race 120, encompassing more than 2,200 races in all. The result of the plot is displayed in Chart 3.

Although there is considerable but not unexpected scatter within the data, the computer-generated trend line is unequivocal and exactly as one would expect. The average DI drops continuously throughout the year as the average distance of the races increases. The analysis graphically captures the progression from the 4½ furlong baby races at Keeneland in April through the 8½ to nine furlong races leading up to and beyond the Breeders' Cup, with speed-bred, high-DI horses dominating the early season races and more stamina-bred, lower-DI horses taking over in the fall.

CHART 3 - DOSAGE APPLIED TO TWO-YEAR-OLD RACING

Moving Average of DI for 2YO Races Through the Season (1983-2001)

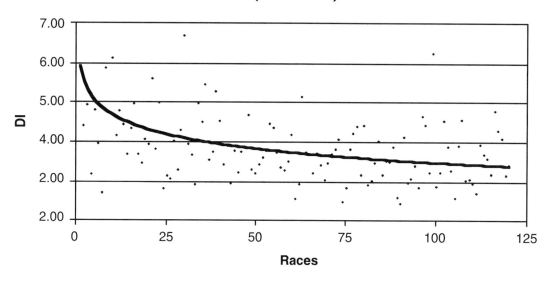

The Relationship Between the DI and the CD

The essence of contemporary Dosage methodology is the Dosage profile, or DP. It is the series of five numbers that summarize the aptitudinal contributions from *chefs-de-race* in the first four generations of a pedigree. Quite often, much information can be derived from the DP alone. For example, regardless of the DI or the CD, a horse with a DP having double-digit representation in the Brilliant group is often a candidate to win sprints. To illustrate the point, among a selected group of horses with a DI of exactly 3.00, those with at least 10 points in the Brilliant category of their DP have won 39 percent of their races in sprints. Those with fewer than 10 points in the Brilliant category have won only 33 percent of their races in sprints. Clearly a large component of inherited speed is an asset in shorter races. Although the average DI is the same for both groups, we do see real differences in the average CD. The first group, with at least 10 Brilliant points in their DP, has an average CD of 0.89. The second group, with fewer than 10 points in their DP, has an average DI of 0.81. The point here is that the relationship between DI and CD is the direct consequence of how the aptitudinal points are distributed within the DP.

There are numerous examples demonstrating the critical nature of point distribution within the DP. As a standard for comparison, we will use our database of open stakes with an added purse of at least $50,000. Of these races, 32 percent are sprints. First we will consider a DP with a "down-the-ladder" pattern. This is a term describing a DP distribution with more Brilliant than

Intermediate points, more Intermediate than Classic points, more Classic than Solid points, and more Solid than Professional points. DP 8-6-4-2-0 fits the definition. Among horses in the stakes database, those with a down-the-ladder pattern won 44 percent of their races at less than a mile, a significantly higher percentage than for the entire population.

Similarly, horses with zero points in either the Solid or the Professional category win 40 percent of their races at sprint distances. This, too, exceeds the percentage found for all stakes winners in the database. Both examples show the importance of DP distribution to an analysis.

We can explore in greater detail how DP distributions can affect overall type by examining several DP configurations for a given DI. The DPs in Table 10 are all equivalent to a DI of 3.00. Note, however, the wide range of possible CD values depending on how the DP is configured.

TABLE 10 - VARIATION IN CD FOR DI 3.00 DEPENDING ON THE DP DISTRIBUTION

DP	CD
0-3-0-0-1	0.25
0-3-0-1-0	0.50
0-2-2-0-0	0.50
2-0-2-0-0	1.00
3-0-0-0-1	1.00
3-0-0-1-0	1.25

The CD range for any DI spans one full CD unit. For DI 3.00, the median CD is 0.75, and the range is from 0.25 to 1.25. It is reasonable to suspect that a horse with DI 3.00 and CD 0.25 may be quite different in type from a horse with DI 3.00 and CD 1.25. In fact, we find real differences between those horses with DI 3.00 and CDs greater than and less than 0.75. In the former case, 36 percent of the races won are sprints and the average distance of their wins is 7.88 furlongs. In the latter case, the percentage falls to 30 percent sprint wins and the average distance rises to 8.24 furlongs. Thus, we confirm that horses with the same DI are not necessarily the same type in terms of performance attributes.

For reference, the general equation to find the median CD for any given DI is:

$$\text{Median CD} = \frac{3 \times (DI - 1)}{2 \times (DI + 1)}$$

The median, maximum, and minimum CDs for some common DI values are displayed in Table 11.

Table 11 - Median, Maximum and Minimum CDs for a Range of DI Values

DI	Median CD	Maximum CD	Minimum CD
0.00	-1.50	-1.00	-2.00
0.50	-0.50	0.00	-1.00
1.00	0.00	0.50	-0.50
2.00	0.50	1.00	0.00
3.00	0.75	1.25	0.25
4.00	0.90	1.40	0.40
5.00	1.00	1.50	0.50
6.00	1.07	1.57	0.57
7.00	1.13	1.63	0.63
8.00	1.17	1.67	0.67
9.00	1.20	1.70	0.70
10.00	1.23	1.73	0.73
20.00	1.36	1.86	0.86
30.00	1.40	1.90	0.90

Some important observations emerge from this analysis. First, differences in DI at the lower end of the DI range are more significant than they are at the higher end. For example, the difference in the median CD for DIs 1.00 and 2.00 is 0.50 CD units. In contrast, the difference in the median CDs for DIs 10.00 and 20.00 is only 0.14 CD units. Doubling the DI at the lower end has a far greater effect on the median CD than it does at the higher end. Second, and most important, neither the DI alone nor the CD alone is sufficient for an adequate aptitudinal evaluation of a pedigree. The critical component remains the DP, and its configuration is responsible for the interplay between the DI and the CD. Consequently, all of the Dosage figure components - the DP, the DI, and the CD - are complementary, and all are necessary for the best and most accurate interpretation.

Dosage and Elite Thoroughbreds

Table 12 includes Dosage figures for selected groups of elite Thoroughbreds since 1983. We define elite Thoroughbreds for this exercise as superior performers either on the racetrack or in the breeding shed. They include winners of the Kentucky Derby, Horses of the Year, annual leading earners, annual leading sires by progeny earnings, annual leading broodmare sires by progeny earnings, and Kentucky broodmares of the year. The individual and combined figures are compared to those for open stakes winners over the same time frame. Abbreviations in the table are ADI for average Dosage index; ACD for average center of distribution; CDI for composite Dosage index; and CCD for composite center of distribution. Recall that we derive composite figures by adding the points in each aptitude category for all members of the group and then calculating the DI and CD in the normal way.

TABLE 12 - DOSAGE FIGURES FOR "ELITE" THOROUGHBREDS

	DP	ADI	ACD	CDI	CCD	PTS
Kentucky Derby Winners, 1983-2002 (20)	8.30 - 4.60 - 11.65 - 1.65 - 1.50	2.87	0.64	2.09	0.60	27.70
Horse of the Year, 1983-2001 (19)	8.53 - 4.16 - 11.21 - 2.11 - 0.00	2.85	0.77	2.37	0.73	26.00
Leading Earners, 1983-2001 (19)	7.53 - 5.95 - 14.42 - 1.74 - 0.05	2.77	0.65	2.30	0.65	29.68
Leading Sires, 1983-2001 (19)	12.16 - 8.05 - 15.32 - 1.68 - 0.68	3.22	0.80	2.78	0.77	37.89
Leading Broodmare Sires, 1983-2001 (19)	10.89 - 9.00 - 16.68 - 5.32 - 2.42	2.24	0.45	1.76	0.47	44.32
Kentucky Broodmares of the Year, 1983-2001 (19)	11.26 - 6.74 - 16.21 - 3.11 - 1.63	3.78	0.61	2.03	0.59	38.95
Total Elite (115)	9.77 - 6.40 - 14.23 - 2.59 - 1.05	2.95	0.65	2.16	0.62	34.03
Open Stakes Winners, 1983-2001 (18,617)	7.88 - 4.76 - 9.59 - 1.60 - 0.91	3.42	0.72	2.39	0.69	24.73

Several differences between the elite horses and typical stakes winners are immediately obvious. Although there is some variation from group to group, all of the elite groups show double-digit representation in the Classic aptitudinal category. The typical stakes winners do not. All of the elite groups have more total Dosage points than the stakes winners, mainly concentrated in the breeding stock (sires, broodmares, and broodmare sires). The elite runners have fewer Dosage points than the elite breeding animals. The elite horses as a group have more representation in the stamina wing of the DP (Solid and Professional aptitudinal categories). The leading sires possess far more Brilliant and Classic points than do the stakes winners, while the broodmares and broodmare sires are most heavily weighted toward stamina, having the largest Solid and Professional representation of any elite group. The Dosage figures are generally lower for the elite horses, again with variation from group to group. Note that the ADI of the Kentucky broodmare of the year group is heavily influenced by one representative with very high numbers. This is not as obvious in the CDI. The conclusion one might draw from this data is that we can differentiate the pedigrees of superior Thoroughbreds from the pedigrees of typical Thoroughbred stakes winners by the magnitude and degree to which they have inherited elements of speed and endurance.

Dosage and the Breeders' Cup

Even though the Breeders' Cup has a relatively short history, a discernable pattern is emerging for the average Dosage figures of the winners in the various divisions. Table 13 displays the average figures, along with the average distance of the races in each division, from the initial Breeders' Cup in 1984 through 2001. Several divisions show unusual average distances because of occasional past changes in distance from year to year.

TABLE 13 - THE HISTORY OF DOSAGE IN THE BREEDERS' CUP

Race	Avg. Dist.	DP					DI	CD	PTS
Classic	10.00	8.89 -	5.74 -	13.37 -	1.68 -	1.47	2.52	0.61	31.16
Distaff	9.21	9.32 -	6.63 -	11.63 -	1.32 -	1.00	3.45	0.77	29.89
Filly & Mare Turf	10.50	4.00 -	6.25 -	17.75 -	2.50 -	0.50	1.78	0.36	31.00
Juvenile	8.45	11.63 -	7.00 -	12.89 -	0.89 -	1.26	3.49	0.82	33.68
Juvenile Fillies	8.45	8.16 -	5.11 -	11.74 -	1.47 -	1.11	3.07	0.68	27.58
Mile	8.00	8.95 -	5.37 -	16.42 -	3.00 -	0.79	2.06	0.55	34.53
Sprint	6.00	11.26 -	5.32 -	10.37 -	1.47 -	0.63	4.66	0.87	29.05
Turf	12.00	6.47 -	4.47 -	14.11 -	4.63 -	2.21	1.49	0.26	31.89

Most striking are the data for the Sprint and the Turf, where the highest and lowest figures correlate with the shortest and longest distances. Also of note are the generally lower figures for the turf races compared to those on dirt. These results parallel those for the stakes population at large. Finally, the average DP point totals in every division are equal to or greater than those for all Grade 1 winners since 1983 as shown in Table 8. To the extent that high DP point totals result from a combination of more or closer up *chefs-de-race* in a pedigree and that the appearance of these *chefs-de-race* may represent superior breeding, it seems as though the winners of the Breeders' Cup races are better bred than even typical Grade 1 winners.

Dosage and Steeplechasing

Table 14 displays the Dosage figures for North American steeplechase champions since 1948.

The relatively low DI and CD numbers resulting from large *chef-de-race* contributions to the Solid and Professional aptitude groups are generally consistent with the longer distances of steeplechase races. However, there are some unusual patterns one may observe.

TABLE 14 - DOSAGE FIGURES FOR STEEPLECHASE CHAMPIONS SINCE 1948

Year	Champion	DP					DI	CD
1948	American Way	0	4	5	3	2	0.87	-0.21
1949	Trough Hill	0	0	4	0	12	0.14	-1.50
1950	Oedipus	12	4	16	6	0	1.71	0.58
1951	Oedipus	12	4	16	6	0	1.71	0.58
1952	Jam	0	0	0	3	3	0.00	-1.50
1953	The Mast	4	0	1	11	2	0.33	-0.39
1954	King Commander	2	2	0	0	0	0.00	1.50
1955	Neji	2	2	0	6	8	0.29	-0.89
1956	Shipboard	2	0	1	16	5	0.12	-0.92
1957	Neji	2	2	0	6	8	0.29	-0.89
1958	Neji	2	2	0	6	8	0.29	-0.89
1959	Ancestor	1	1	16	2	0	1.00	0.05
1960	Benguala	18	0	7	14	3	1.05	0.38
1961	Peal	0	2	2	0	6	0.43	-1.00
1962	Barnaby's Bluff	4	0	8	4	0	1.00	0.25
1963	Amber Diver	2	4	12	2	6	0.86	-0.23
1964	Bon Nouvel	9	3	0	4	0	3.00	1.06
1965	Bon Nouvel	9	3	0	4	0	3.00	1.06
1966	Tuscalee	4	0	6	0	0	2.33	0.80
1967	Quick Pitch	4	4	6	6	0	1.22	0.30
1968	Bon Nouvel	9	3	0	4	0	3.00	1.06
1969	L'Escargot	0	0	2	0	2	0.33	-1.00
1970	Top Bid	28	2	8	2	0	5.67	1.40
1971	Shadow Brook	6	4	4	4	6	1.00	0.00
1972	Soothsayer	1	1	6	6	2	0.45	-0.44
1973	Athenian Idol	9	0	6	1	14	0.67	-0.37
1974	Gran Kan	0	0	1	5	2	0.07	-1.13
1975	Life's Illusion	1	3	4	2	2	1.00	-0.08
1976	Fire Control	8	14	10	6	4	1.80	0.38
1977	Café Prince	20	2	14	10	0	1.71	0.70
1978	Café Prince	20	2	14	10	0	1.71	0.70
1979	Martie's Anger	19	3	5	1	0	7.00	1.43
1980	Zaccio	2	12	2	0	2	5.00	0.67
1981	Zaccio	2	12	2	0	2	5.00	0.67
1982	Zaccio	2	12	2	0	2	5.00	0.67
1983	Flatterer	9	2	3	0	0	8.33	1.43

Year	Champion	DP					DI	CD
1984	Flatterer	9	- 2	- 3	- 0	- 0	8.33	1.43
1985	Flatterer	9	- 2	- 3	- 0	- 0	8.33	1.43
1986	Flatterer	9	- 2	- 3	- 0	- 0	8.33	1.43
1987	Inlander	2	- 0	- 6	- 8	- 2	0.38	-0.44
1988	Jimmy Lorenzo	5	- 2	- 7	- 0	- 6	1.11	0.00
1989	Highland Bud	10	- 3	- 16	- 5	- 2	1.40	0.39
1990	Morley Street	8	- 0	- 8	- 0	- 4	1.50	0.40
1991	Morley Street	8	- 0	- 8	- 0	- 4	1.50	0.40
1992	Lonesome Glory	2	- 3	- 21	- 4	- 0	1.07	0.10
1993	Lonesome Glory	2	- 3	- 21	- 4	- 0	1.07	0.10
1994	Warm Spell	6	- 4	- 7	- 5	- 0	1.59	0.50
1995	Lonesome Glory	2	- 3	- 21	- 4	- 0	1.07	0.10
1996	Correggio	9	- 8	- 26	- 9	- 0	1.36	0.33
1997	Lonesome Glory	2	- 3	- 21	- 4	- 0	1.07	0.10
1998	Flat Top	8	- 5	- 13	- 1	- 5	1.56	0.31
1999	Lonesome Glory	2	- 3	- 21	- 4	- 0	1.07	0.10
2000	All Gong	5	- 1	- 8	- 4	- 2	1.00	0.15
2001	Pompeyo	6	- 2	- 12	- 0	- 0	2.33	0.70
AVERAGE		**6.09 - 2.87 - 7.74 - 3.74 - 2.33**					**2.06**	**0.22**

The DI distribution is somewhat bimodal with the vast majority (76 percent) of the champions having a DI of less than 2.00. Surprisingly, another 17 percent have a DI above 4.00, while only 7 percent have a DI in the typical middle distance range of 2.00 to 4.00. A graphical representation of the bimodal distribution is seen in Chart 4 (solid line) where it is compared to the DI distribution found among open stakes winners (dashed line).

Thus, there appear to be predominantly two types of pedigrees associated with championship performance in North American steeplechasing. The first is the strongly endurance-oriented pedigree in which stamina influences prevail, enabling the horse to be competitive over marathon distances. The second is the sprint-type pedigree in which speed is dominant. Although the latter initially may seem contradictory, many handicappers have observed the successful transition of sprinters on the flat to races over jumps. The rationale is that the typical pace of steeplechase races is not so demanding that sprinters necessarily will falter. In fact, any fatigue characteristics may be compensated by increased agility and quickness over the jumps. The desired interaction between stamina and jumping ability seems to find its best expression when shifted more to one trait or the other. The paucity of middle-distance pedigrees among these champions is certainly

DI Distributions Since 1983

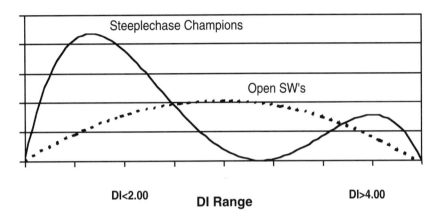

surprising considering that almost 50 percent of open stakes winners on the flat since 1983 have a DI between 2.00 and 4.00. In fact, there hasn't been a steeplechase champion since 1968 through 2000 with a pedigree that has fallen within the DI 2.00 to 4.00 range.

The Universality of Dosage

Contemporary Dosage methodology has its largest following in North America, with the vast majority of data collected in support of Dosage coming from races run in the United States and Canada. The analysis and interpretation of that data built the foundation for most of Dosage's applications. Nevertheless, the general utility of Dosage as a pedigree classification technique requires a broader geographic scope, especially as borders and oceans no longer present barriers to international competition. As it happens, there are Thoroughbred pedigree researchers in other parts of the world who have an intense interest in the subject and whose contributions have increased our understanding of Dosage's universality. Among them is Steve Miller from the United Kingdom, who has been instrumental in identifying modern European-based sires for inclusion on the *chef-de-race* list. John Hutchinson in Australia has gone so far as to create a supplementary *chef-de-race* list specifically for racing in Australia and New Zealand. Similar efforts are under way in other parts of the world as well, including South America.

In order to demonstrate the relevance of Dosage across a range of racing venues, it is necessary to generate data for other locations similar to those generated in North America. This task involves the calculation of Dosage figures for the winners of races over a range of distances in other countries and on other continents, followed by an analysis to determine whether the data fit the model already established for North America. The results of such a study are presented in Chart 5. The chart graphically displays the relationship among the average CDs of major race winners in North America, Europe, Australia, and South Africa with the average distance of the races won.

The North American data (also separated by racing surface) include all Grade 1 stakes since 1990. The European data come from 38 group events in England, Ireland, and France also since 1990. The Australian data were obtained from Hutchinson and include data for five Group 1 races, three since 1960 and two since 1980. In this particular case, the CDs were calculated using Hutchinson's amended *chef-de-race* list. Finally, the South African data include 20 Group 1 races since 1990. The plot shows the relationship between the average CD of the winners and the average distance of the races over the time involved. The straight lines were generated by linear regression performed on each data series.

It is immediately obvious that the Dosage model holds not only for North America but for Europe, Australia, and South Africa as well. The inverse relationship between Dosage figures and distance transcends racing surfaces, nations, continents, and hemispheres. Of particular interest is the closeness of the trend lines for European races and for North American races on the turf.

The Selection of *Chefs-de-race*

All versions of Dosage accept the principle that relatively few individuals account for most of the evolutionary forces within the breed. A consequence of this principle is the belief that a reasonable aptitudinal interpretation of a pedigree can be achieved by limiting the analysis to include only those select individuals. In reality, every ancestor plays a role, although not many will pass along definable traits in a regular manner. For our purposes, we exclude the non-prepotent influences solely because of their unpredictability. Such exclusion can lead to errors if actual prepotence for type hasn't been confirmed. This is something to consider particularly when dealing with newer stallions that haven't yet proven their case for prepotency. For example, young sires like A.P. Indy, Kingmambo, and Thunder Gulch are showing signs they may be consistent sources of classic stamina. If future developments confirm these suspicions, they could eventually emerge as *chef-de-race* candidates. In the meantime, it is a good idea at least to consider the possibility of unacknowledged aptitudinal prepotence in a pedigree and to make mental adjustments to the Dosage figures to account for them. This procedure may affect the analysis for an individual horse, while having virtually no effect on the figures for the general Thoroughbred population.

CHART 5 - DOSAGE RELATIONSHIPS IN NORTH AMERICA, EUROPE, AUSTRALIA, JAPAN AND SOUTH AFRICA

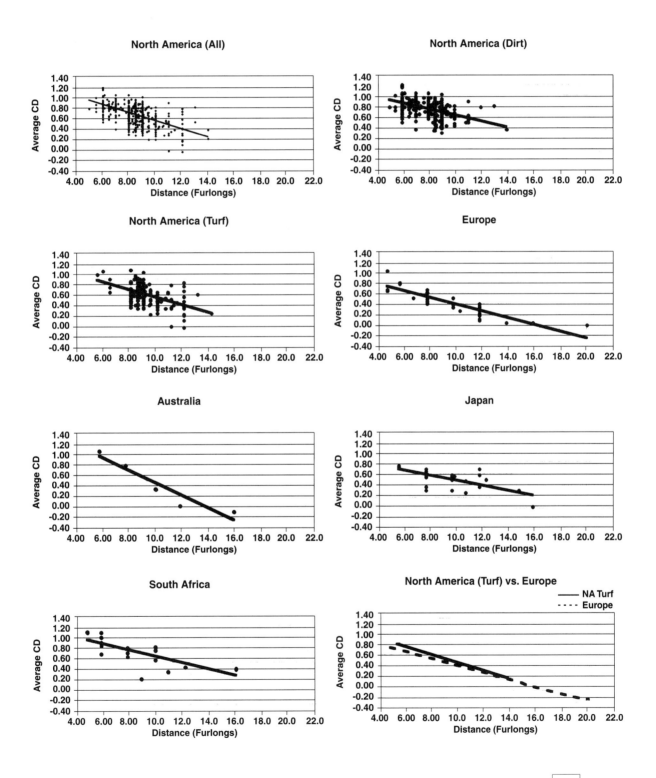

Nevertheless, Dosage reserves the term *chef-de-race* for the aptitudinally prepotent and uniquely influential animal. At the beginning of the 20th century, Vuillier was content to name only 15 *chefs-de-race* in three series covering the early, middle, and late 1800s. Varola created an expanded *chef-de-race* list to include 120 stallions foaled mainly after 1900. The current number of *chefs-de-race* (as of February 2002) stands at 199 and includes Varola's 120, plus additions made by Hewitt in the 1970s. Since the introduction of the latest Dosage version in 1981, we have made further additions and refinements.

The method of identifying new *chefs-de-race* is inextricably linked to the philosophy that drives each variation of Dosage. Vuillier had it relatively easy. He observed that a select group of ancestors in the pedigrees of top-class horses appeared with a frequency far greater than that of the other horses that were present. His task was to confirm this dominance by tallying those appearances. Among more recent sires, names such as Bold Ruler, Raise a Native, Northern Dancer, Ribot, and perhaps Turn-to come to mind as meeting the Vuillier requirement.

Varola focused on only "those sires who had transmitted such prepotent and unmistakable traits that any study of pedigrees would be meaningless without them." That in itself is a reasonable goal. However, Varola then compared the influence of sires to peaks in a mountain range, and he excluded sires that failed to attain a particularly high altitude. As noble as his intentions may have been, his approach denies the existence of prepotence for type in any other than the most highly regarded stallions. Apart from there being no evidence for such a phenomenon, it weakens, through a largely arbitrary exclusion process, any attempt to accurately define a pedigree in terms of inherited aptitudes.

We apply one absolute criterion to *chef-de-race* selection. The *chef-de-race* candidate must be prepotent for aptitudinal type. Furthermore, we must be able to demonstrate his prepotence using statistical analysis. It would be helpful, although not necessary, to the analysis if the *chef-de-race* candidate were a sire of sires or a sire of quality broodmares. In this way we would increase the sample size and show that prepotent influences carry through to successive generations. This obviously wouldn't be relevant to young sires that may have only a small number of sons and daughters at stud even though their aptitudinal prepotence is clearly visible in their racing progeny. Finally, a sire's reputation at stud is of minimal concern. The critical factor is enough racing data generated by his runners to allow for a meaningful statistical study. Keep in mind that we use the data from stakes races to develop our case. Stakes races are the most formful of all races, and stakes horses are the most consistent of all runners. Horses entered in stakes generally belong in those races, and the outcomes are likely to be the result of a suitable genetic expression of type. A decent stakes sire can often generate more than enough progeny data to make a case for his aptitudinal prepotence. Such was the case of Apalachee, who was not among the leading sires when named a Brilliant *chef-de-race* in the late 1980s. However, between 1983 and 1991, Apalachee sired the winners of more major six-furlong stakes races than any North American sire other than Mr. Prospector and Fappiano. He also got a series of blazingly fast sprinting fillies such as Clocks Secret, Pine Tree Lane, and Lazer Show, each capable of going a half-mile in less than 44 seconds. He did this despite being a son of Solid *chef-de-race* Round Table. Undoubtedly the source of his speed is his female family descended from Rough Shod II through the brilliant Moccasin. Nevertheless, excluding the consistently predictable speed influence associated with Apalachee's name in a four-generation pedigree because he wasn't a "good enough" sire misses the entire point of aptitudinal analysis, not to mention resulting in an incorrect interpretation of the pedigree in which he appears.

We can further illustrate the logic behind *chef-de-race* selection using the previously published assignments for Fappiano and Broad Brush.

Fappiano   *Photo Courtesy of John Noye*

FAPPIANO, C., 1977 (MR. PROSPECTOR-KILLALOE, BY DR. FAGER), ASSIGNED AUGUST 1998:

To determine the prepotent aptitudinal influences contributed by Fappiano to his descendants, we examined more than 200 open stakes races since 1983 where Fappiano or one of his sons is the sire, or where Fappiano is the broodmare sire of the winner. In other words, Fappiano is the one constant in the pedigree of all the winners of these races. At an average winning distance of 7.84 furlongs, the Dosage figures for these winners are average DP 10.81-3.62-9.34-1.13-1.14, average DI 3.37, and average CD 0.86. The comparative standards for distance established by almost 15,000 stakes winners since 1983 are as follows. At seven furlongs: average DP 9.11-5.19-8.99-1.37-0.73, average DI 4.06, and average CD 0.84. At eight furlongs: average DP 8.28-4.83-9.97-1.81-0.94, average DI 3.30, and average CD 0.71. The predicted numbers for Fappiano's descendants, based on an extrapolation of these figures, are average DI 3.42 and average CD 0.76. Although there is good agreement with the average DI value, the average CD of Fappiano's runners is more typical of six-and-a-half to seven furlong performers than of the near milers they actually are as a group. The challenge, then, is to identify aptitudinal placements that best bring the figures for Fappiano's descendants in line with the general population having similar performance characteristics.

It quickly became apparent that no placement of Fappiano alone would adequately satisfy the requirements for bringing this sub-population of runners in line with the population at large. A balanced relationship between the DI and CD could not be achieved. However, invoking prepotent aptitudinal influences from Fappiano's broodmare sire, Dr. Fager, and from Dr. Fager's sire, Rough'n Tumble, provided an acceptable solution.

An accommodation was achieved between the Dosage figures of the general population of stakes winners and the sub-population of stakes winners with Fappiano in their pedigree by making the following aptitudinal assignments: Fappiano, Intermediate/Classic; Dr. Fager, Intermediate; Rough'n Tumble, Brilliant/Classic.

Applying these aptitudinal influences, we obtain revised figures for Fappiano's descendants:

Average DP 11.32-12.46-15.67-1.13-1.14, average DI 3.43, and average CD 0.77. The numbers are now essentially identical to those predicted on the basis of average winning distance and suggest an accurate placement of the three sires.

Some have argued that Fappiano in a pedigree represents true classic stamina. This argument is based on his appearance in the pedigree of Derby winners Unbridled, Grindstone, and Real Quiet, and in the pedigree of Belmont Stakes winner Victory Gallop, all in the decade of the 1990s. In fact, the distance capabilities of Unbridled and his son, Grindstone, can be easily explained by the presence of Professional *chef-de-race* Le Fabuleux as the broodmare sire of Unbridled. Their Dosage figures are already well within the classic range without invoking additional stamina from Fappiano. Similarly, Victory Gallop's figures are within classic guidelines, mainly through the influence of Classic-Professional *chef-de-race* Tom Rolfe, sire of Hoist the Flag, he the broodmare sire of Victory Gallop's sire, Cryptoclearance.

Although Fappiano may, in fact, be transmitting some classic strength, his overall effect (which includes the influences of his close up ancestors) is moderately shifted toward speed. This is reflected in his average winning distance of 7.84 furlongs compared to our database average of 8.11 furlongs. Also, an examination of all sires in the database having at least 20 progeny stakes wins shows Fappiano with 60 percent open stakes winners at a mile or less. The average for all of the sires is 42 percent. Fappiano's speed influence is even more apparent as a broodmare sire. Here his daughters have produced 83 percent open stakes winners at a mile or less.

Inevitably there will be questions about Real Quiet. In 1998 he became the second Derby winner since 1929 to exceed the historical Derby guideline of DI 4.00. Prior to the Derby, Real Quiet's Dosage figures were DP 13-2-7-0-0, DI 5.29, and CD 1.27. The additions of Fappiano, Dr. Fager, and Rough'n Tumble changed these figures to DP 14-12-12-0-0, DI 5.33, and CD 1.05, which leave Real Quiet's DI well above the guideline while lowering the CD. How do we rationalize this? Simply by understanding the nature of statistics. The standard deviation of the DI for descendants of Fappiano is 1.08. Statistics tell us that 95 percent of the data points within a normal distribution will fall within two standard deviations. In other words, 19 of 20 descendants of Fappiano should have a DI that falls between 5.59 (or 3.43 + 2.16) and 1.27 (or 3.43 − 2.16). Fifty percent should fall within one standard deviation, or between DI 4.56 and DI 2.35. In fact, Real Quiet's DI is between one and two standard deviations of the average and is part of the general distribution. He is not what could be called an outlier. On the other hand, if one accepts his Derby as meeting the historical standard of classic performance, we should be prepared to look for other sources of stamina. In that regard, I suggest that Real Quiet's sire, Quiet American, should be watched closely. Although he has had only seven crops to race through the end of 2001, and a limited number of open stakes winners, his average winning distance is a relatively long 8.41 furlongs. Additionally, just 38 percent of his progeny's open stakes wins are at a mile or less. For young sires whose early runners initially have greater opportunity in shorter races, these statistics are indicative of early stamina. Only time can be the judge.

Consider also that forecasts based on moving averages over the last 60 years predict that the average DI of Derby winners will reach 4.00 by about the year 2025. Unless we see a reversion to increased stamina in Thoroughbred bloodlines, it is inevitable that more Derby winners will exceed the historical DI guideline between now and then.

For the present, we are satisfied that the new assignments accurately represent the prepotent aptitudinal influences derived from Fappiano, Dr. Fager, and Rough'n Tumble.

BROAD BRUSH, C., 1983 (ACK ACK-HAY PATCHER, BY HOIST THE FLAG), ASSIGNED JULY 2000:

Open stakes winners by Broad Brush have an average winning distance (AWD) of 8.39 furlongs, which is somewhat longer than the general average of 8.10 furlongs. It is worth noting that the standard deviation, which measures how far the numbers in a data set tend to be from the average, is just 11 percent of the AWD. This is the smallest standard deviation, next to Nodouble's 10 percent, of any sire over the last two decades with at least 50 progeny open stakes wins. The significance of this small standard deviation is that Broad Brush's runners tend to perform within a relatively narrow distance range, suggesting that he prepotently dominates the aptitudinal influences of the mares to which he is bred. Aptitudinal prepotence remains the single most important factor in the identification of a *chef-de-race*.

Further evidence of aptitudinal prepotence is the disparity between the Dosage figures

Broad Brush   *Photo Courtesy of the Thoroughbred Times*

(Dosage profile (DP), Dosage index (DI) and center of distribution (CD)) of Broad Brush's open stakes winners and those for the breed at large displaying similar distance capability. The current figures for Broad Brush's runners are average DP 7.18-9.73-8.81-0.38-1.32, average DI 3.71 and average CD 0.77 based on 79 races. The predicted figures at an average distance of 8.39 furlongs are DI 3.33 and CD 0.68. It appears as though Broad Brush is contributing a moderate degree of stamina beyond that which is found close up in his own pedigree.

An Intermediate/Classic (I/C) *chef-de-race* designation for Broad Brush modifies his progeny figures to average DP 7.18-17.73-16.81-0.38-1.32, average DI 3.37 and average CD 0.67. These revisions create an almost perfect alignment between the Broad Brush stakes winners and those in the general population displaying similar distance characteristics. A direct result of the assignment is a change in the contribution Broad Brush makes to the DP of his offspring: from DP 4-8-5-0-1 (equivalent to DI 4.14 and CD 0.78) to DP 4-16-13-0-1 (equivalent to DI 3.53 and CD 0.65). The closeness of the overall fit is powerful evidence for both the justification and accuracy of an I/C *chef-de-race* designation for this exceptional stallion.

Dual Qualifiers

One of the most provocative applications of Dosage is in combination with an assessment of juvenile form. Together, these factors function as a guide to classic potential and have gone a long way toward defining the unique qualities of the American classic horse.

Each spring, many horsemen and handicappers turn their attention to the dual qualifiers, a select group of three-year-old Thoroughbreds with similar characteristics. These are characteristics typically found among American classic horses but not among the general Thoroughbred population. For this reason, dual qualifiers stand apart from the rest of their generation. In the early 1980s we introduced (in Leon Rasmussen's "Bloodlines" column in *Daily Racing Form*) the idea that classic performers generally have distinguishing traits in common. Since then, the concept's ability to isolate legitimate classic contenders has increased its visibility greatly, although as we'll see later, subtle variations in breeding patterns over time suggest that the long-standing characteristics of classic horses may be changing. The ability of Dosage to rapidly highlight these shifts in pedigree and performance relationships is one of its greatest strengths.

The standard definition of a dual qualifier is a three-year-old with a Dosage index (DI) of 4.00 or less and ranked as a two-year-old within 10 pounds of the high-weight on the Experimental Free Handicap (EFH), or designated a champion in another country. The DI is a mathematical expression of the balance between speed and stamina inherited from selected aptitudinally prepotent ancestors. The higher the DI, the greater is the influence of speed in a pedigree. Historically, only three Derby winners since 1929 had a DI greater than 4.00. Among contemporary stakes winners on dirt, between 25 percent and 30 percent have a DI higher than 4.00. The percentage rises to 35 percent for stakes winners under a mile, but drops to 15 percent for stakes winners at a mile and a quarter.

The EFH is a handicap rating the performance of two-year-olds. A panel of experts evaluates the year's stakes-quality juveniles and assigns them weights relative to one another. Normally, the highest weight for a colt is 126 pounds. On rare occasions, a truly exceptional colt will be weighted higher.

Now the question is: Why should a DI of 4.00 or lower, coupled with a prominent ranking on the EFH be important to classic potential? In the case of the Kentucky Derby (and perhaps to some degree the other classics as well) the reasons are intimately linked to the unique demands of the race, which is like no other run in North America. The answer to the question becomes clearer when we recall that the DI is a guide to distance ability, while the EFH ranking is an approximation of early maturity and outstanding two-year-old form. A pedigree suited to the distance, along with demonstrated high class early in a racing career are the historical trademarks of the majority of classic winners over the last quarter-century and beyond. First and foremost, the distance presents a formidable challenge. None of the contenders, at least none that raced exclusively in North America, have previously been asked to negotiate a mile and a quarter. The suitability of their breeding to the distance is paramount, and the DI suggests that suitability. A horse bred excessively for speed is unlikely to stay the course at this level of competition, except when the pace is especially undemanding or the quality of the field is suspect. That would be an unusual circumstance for America's premier classic. Second, there are several attributes of the Derby that are constant from year to year. The overall quality and depth of the field are normally outstanding, with an abundance of regional superstars converging to meet for the first time. The pace is usually fast, pressure-packed, and stressful. The size of the field can often be very large, resulting in a race that is extremely physical as jockeys maneuver for position. The horses are still young and immature; they are a long way from maturity. The atmosphere is electric and filled with a spectacle that the horses have never experienced. It is reasonable that contenders with an edge in class, as well as an edge in emotional and physical maturity, should have an advantage. The dual qualifiers are blessed with staying pedigrees as expressed in their DI and an advanced degree of class and maturity as reflected by their superior performance at two and acknowledged by their position on the EFH.

The correlation between Dual Qualifier status and success in the Derby is very strong. Between 1972 and 2001, there were 469 starters in the Derby, although in 1998, no dual qualifiers started. Of these, 101 starters (21 percent) were dual qualifiers, representing 99 separate wagering interests. That's an average of three and one-half per race in an average-size field of just over 16 starters. Twice there was just one dual qualifier, and both won. The largest number of dual qualifiers in a single Derby is six, which occurred three times. A dual qualifier has captured 20 of the 29 Derbies (69 percent). Thirteen other dual qualifiers (13 percent) finished second, while another nine (9 percent) ran third. Overall, 43 percent of all dual qualifiers finished in the money. In the 29 Derbies, dual qualifiers accounted for nine exactas and five trifectas. A straight two-dollar win bet on each dual qualifier wagering interest, independent of all other handicapping considerations, has yielded a 70 percent profit, not including exotic payoffs. It should be easy to see why the dual qualifier concept has aroused so much interest. These results are strong evidence that a staying pedigree, early maturity, and an early expression of high class are more critical to a Derby victory than some of the more   conventional criteria used to predict the winner. The Derby favorite is often the form horse, a colt or filly coming off a smashing win in his or her last Derby prep race. However, favorites lost the Derby every year following 1979 until 2000. One conclusion that may be drawn from the success of the dual qualifiers is that form at nine furlongs in the preps is not always a good predictor of form at 10 furlongs in the Derby. The unique circumstances of the Derby provide the environment in which the dual qualifier factors, or rather what they represent, become dominant. Other factors are often less significant.

Despite its predictive value, the dual qualifier concept was never initially intended as a handicapping tool. It was originally offered as a study of the defining qualities of American classic runners, the things that differentiate classic winners from their contemporaries. What may have been lost in its popularization is a full appreciation of the underlying principles. Sometimes a strict application of the rules can lead us astray. Part of the problem lies in the subjectivity that goes into EFH rankings and, for that matter, in the limitations of the DI. The EFH is a product of the collective judgment of experts. Sometimes their judgment is imperfect. The DI is based on data derived from, and applied to, large populations. Occasionally there will be aptitudinally prepotent ancestors in an individual pedigree not accounted for by the current state of knowledge. It was in this framework that we developed the notion of a conceptual dual qualifier; i.e., a Derby contender that satisfies the criteria of a distance pedigree and superior juvenile form, yet may have been overlooked by the rules. The idea first surfaced in the late 1980s with the Derby victories of two racehorses, Winning Colors and Sunday Silence, who were not dual qualifiers. Neither was eligible for the EFH ranking because they failed to compete in stakes races at two. However, Winning Colors won at first asking, while defeating eventual juvenile champion filly Epitome by several lengths in a Saratoga maiden special weight event. An injury kept her away until December when she returned to win an allowance race easily. One could argue, based on her performance, that she would have been near the top of her class had she raced through the fall. Similarly, Sunday Silence had won his maiden at Hollywood Park by 10 lengths in 1:09.2 in mid-November and returned three weeks later to lose an allowance race by a head to Houston. Houston became one of the winter-book Derby favorites after winning the Bay Shore Stakes as an early three-year-old. Both Winning Colors and Sunday Silence were clearly among the best of their respective crops. Both conformed to the principles supporting the dual qualifier concept even though neither fit the rules. In recent years we have highlighted other conceptual dual qualifiers at *The Blood-Horse* Interactive Triple Crown Mania web site. They include Grindstone, Captain Bodgit, and Free House. All performed admirably in the Derby, and all were identified prior to the race.

Often the conceptual dual qualifier will not be apparent until he steps forward as a three-year-old. Horses that he defeated at two may emerge as major forces in the division. His juvenile form may have been obscured by a campaign-stopping injury, yet he may resurface in spectacular fashion the following spring. Again, one must use judgment. However, a conceptual dual qualifier is not a horse that simply faced the battles the previous year. There should be convincing evidence that he was among the best. Several potential candidates will likely emerge during the course of a winter and spring pre-Derby campaign.

Legitimate Derby contenders will always be relatively few in number. The success of dual qualifiers for more than 25 years is a testament to that fact. A horse with a pedigree ill-suited to the distance or an inexperienced, late-developing type, even though highly talented, will often falter when confronted by a true stayer that matured quickly and competed successfully at the highest levels in the early stages of his career. These dual qualifier traits contribute to the definition of American classic horses.

Even though Dosage has come under attack in recent years because its Kentucky Derby success in the 1990s did not match its success in the previous decade, the actual accomplishments of dual qualifiers in Triple Crown races suggest that those who believe "Dosage is dead" are taking a rather narrow view.

The following tables display the record of dual qualifiers (Table 15) and non-dual qualifiers (Table 16) since 1973. The data is presented in terms of overall impact value (IV) by decade and by individual Triple Crown race. IV statistics are calculated by dividing the percentage of classic winners that were dual qualifiers by the percentage of dual qualifiers that started in the classic races. For example, if 20 percent of the races were won by dual qualifiers and 20 percent of the starters were dual qualifiers, then the IV is 1.00. However, if 40 percent were won by dual qualifiers with the same 20 percent dual qualifier starters, then the IV is 2.00 or twice the expectation. As the reader will observe in Table 15, the results are better than that for each of the Triple Crown races over the past 29 years. IV is, in effect, a ratio of success associated with a set of characteristics relative to the opportunity available. By contrast, the results for non-dual qualifiers as presented in Table 16 are generally quite poor. Critics may argue the point, but the success of dual qualifiers in defining North American classic type is undeniable. It should be pointed out, however, that the IV for the Derby has declined in each successive decade since the 1970s. This could mean that the characteristics of Derby winners are slowly evolving and that more speed-bred or late-developing types are emerging as stronger Derby candidates. On the other hand, the Preakness and Belmont IV numbers have held up strongly for nearly 30 years. [The reader may note that the designation of dual qualifiers prior to 1983 was done much after the fact and that only those results from 1983 onward reflect designations that are contemporary with performances in the classics. – Frank Mitchell]

The Controversy Surrounding Dosage

Anyone even remotely familiar with modern Dosage is aware of the controversy it has spawned. The source of the controversy is problematic at best and often results from a gross misinterpretation of Dosage's purpose and intent. As stated at the outset, contemporary Dosage is simply a pedigree classification technique. It is not, as some have claimed, a breeding theory. It is not, as still others maintain, a handicapping system. However, the information Dosage provides may be used in both breeding and handicapping. The way people use it depends on how it addresses their particular needs. Those who apply it to the breeding of racehorses and who feel comfortable with the result are perfectly free to do so. If Dosage affords a better idea of the type of foal a mating might produce, then it has served its purpose. Those who believe it can help identify the potential winners of races are equally free to use it in that manner. If Dosage can increase the horseplayer's chances of cashing a ticket, who is in a position to deny him the opportunity? The only measure of Dosage's validity is if its application enhances one's understanding and if it provides insights one wouldn't have without it.

The most obvious source of negative reaction to Dosage may be that it represents a threat to those heavily invested in traditional ways of interpreting Thoroughbred pedigrees. The perception of a threat from Dosage may be enhanced by the fact that it is constructed within the context of rigorous statistical analysis. For the most part, traditional pedigree interpretation is anecdotal in character. There are many misconceptions and false principles espoused as truth that are based on subjectivity and intuition rather than real data or solid facts. One such

TABLE 15 - DUAL QUALIFIERS (DQs) IN TRIPLE CROWN RACES SINCE 1973

Years	Derby	Preakness	Belmont	All
2000-2002	3 races	2 races	1 race	6 races
	0 winners (0.0%)	1 winner (50.0%)	1 winner (100.0%)	2 winners (33.3%)
	11 DQs (20.4%)	5 DQs (26.3%)	3 DQs (15.0%)	19 DQs (23.2%)
	54 starters	19 starters	9 starters	82 starters
	IV = 0.00	IV = 1.90	IV = 6.67	IV = 1.44
1990-1999	9 races	9 races	10 races	28 races
	5 winners (50.0%)	6 winners (60.0%)	6 winners (60.0%)	17 winners (56.7%)
	39 DQs (25.7%)	19 DQs (19.2%)	21 DQs (20.0%)	79 DQs (22.2%)
	152 starters	99 starters	105 starters	356 starters
	IV = 1.95	IV = 3.13	IV = 3.00	IV = 2.55
1980-1989	10 races	10 races	10 races	30 races
	8 winners (80.0%)	2 winners (20.0%)	5 winners (50.0%)	15 winners (50.0%)
	33 DQs (19.3%)	13 DQs (13.8%)	14 DQs (13.5%)	60 DQs (16.3%)
	171 starters	94 starters	104 starters	369 starters
	IV = 4.15	IV = 1.45	IV = 3.70	IV = 3.07
1973-1979	7 races	7 races	7 races	21 races
	7 winners (100.0%)	5 winners (71.4%)	4 winners (50.0%)	16 winners (76.2%)
	18 DQs (19.8%)	15 DQs (26.8%)	11 DQs (20.4%)	45 DQs (21.8%)
	96 starters	56 starters	54 starters	206 starters
	IV = 5.05	IV = 2.66	IV = 2.45	IV = 3.50
1973-2002	29 races	28 races	28 races	85 races
	20 winners (69.0%)	14 winners (50.0%)	16 winners (57.1%)	50 winners (58.8%)
	102 DQs (21.6%)	52 DQs (19.4%)	49 DQs (18.0%)	200 DQs (20.0%)
	473 starters	268 starters	272 starters	1013 starters
	IV = 3.19	IV = 2.58	IV = 3.17	IV = 2.94

TABLE 16 - NON-DUAL QUALIFIERS (NON-DQs) IN TRIPLE CROWN RACES SINCE 1973

Years	Derby	Preakness	Belmont	All
2000-02	3 races	2 races	1 races	6 races
	3 winners (100.0%)	1 winner (50.0%)	0 winner (0.0%)	4 winners (66.7%)
	43 non-DQs (79.6%)	14 non-DQs (73.7%)	6 non-DQs (66.7%)	63 non-DQs (76.8%)
	54 starters	19 starters	9 starters	82 starters
	IV = 1.26	IV = 0.68	IV = 0.00	IV = 0.86
1990-99	9 races	9 races	10 races	30 races
	4 winners (44.4%)	4 winners (44.4%)	4 winners (40.0%)	13 winners (43.3%)
	113 DQs (74.3%)	80 non-DQs (80.8%)	84 non-DQs (80.0%)	302 non-DQs (79.3%)
	152 starters	99 starters	105 starters	381 starters
	IV = 0.60	IV = 0.55	IV = 0.50	IV = 0.55
1980-89	10 races	10 races	10 races	30 races
	2 winners (20.0%)	8 winners (80.0%)	5 winners (50.0%)	15 winners (50.0%)
	138 non-DQs (80.7%)	81 non-DQs (86.2%)	90 non-DQs (86.5%)	309 non-DQs (83.7%)
	171 starters	94 starters	104 starters	369 starters
	IV = 0.25	IV = 0.93	IV = 0.58	IV = 0.60
1973-79	7 races	7 races	7 races	21 races
	0 winners (0.0%)	2 winners (28.6%)	3 winners (42.9%)	5 winners (23.8%)
	77 non-DQs (80.2%)	41 non-DQs (73.2%)	43 non-DQs (79.6%)	161 non-DQs (78.2%)
	96 starters	56 starters	54 starters	206 starters
	IV = 0.00	IV = 0.39	IV = 0.54	IV = 0.30
1973-2002	29 races	28 races	28 races	85 races
	9 winners (31.0%)	15 winners (53.6%)	12 winners (42.9%)	36 winners (42.4%)
	371 non-DQs (78.4%)	216 non-DQs (80.6%)	223 non-DQs (82.0%)	810 non-DQs (80.0%)
	473 starters	268 starters	272 starters	1013 starters
	IV = 0.40	IV = 0.67	IV = 0.52	IV = 0.53

misconception is the notion of a direct correlation between a horse's characteristics as a runner and its ability to transmit those same characteristics to its descendants. Such a correlation can obviously exist in individual cases, but it is not predictable with any degree of certainty. If it were, then Kingmambo, a miler by a sprinter and sire of sprinter-milers and out of a champion miler, would hardly be a candidate to sire classic distance types. Yet he does. Similarly, we would not expect Slewpy, a Grade 1 winner at a classic distance by a classic sire and out of a producer of middle-distance horses, to have been predominantly a sire of sprinters. Yet he was. In fact, Dosage avoids the trap created when the emphasis is on an ancestor's racing performance rather than its actual performance at stud. That doesn't make Dosage a superior method, just an alternative one. Nevertheless, there are legitimate questions raised about Dosage methodology that should be answered.

Perhaps the most sensitive issue is that of *chef-de-race* selection. Many critics insist that the list of *chefs-de-race* should comprise only those sires worthy of inclusion based on their overall excellence at stud or those that have achieved a level of recognition within the breed that elevates them far beyond the ordinary. That would be fine if the *chef-de-race* list were a roster of great sires – a stallion hall of fame, so to speak. But it isn't. A suggested requirement for stallion greatness in a *chef-de-race* candidate parallels Varola's selection philosophy discussed earlier. However, contemporary Dosage methodology seeks the most accurate possible aptitudinal interpretation of a pedigree. If a strong case can be made for a less than stellar sire, yet one that is successful enough to generate sufficient data from his descendants to confirm aptitudinal prepotence, he becomes more important to an interpretation than the leading sire with no evidence of such prepotence. Those who are most concerned with honoring stallions will be served best by other systems of pedigree analysis. We will stay with demonstrated prepotence for type as the driver behind the selection process.

The critics of Dosage usually come out in force when an individual horse's performance contradicts its Dosage figures, particularly in high-profile races. Rarely do those same critics acknowledge the validity of Dosage when conventional analysis falters and Dosage prevails. Of course, these isolated examples have no bearing on the issue anyway. As the reader has no doubt noticed, Dosage is presented as a tool for developing statistical studies on large populations of Thoroughbreds in order to facilitate the observation of aptitudinal trends within the breed. Insistence that every individual conform to an arbitrary standard is a pointless exercise. Within large populations, especially those involving biological systems, we will always find a broad distribution range of characteristics. If, however, Dosage can statistically differentiate one subgroup from another even in the face of broad distributions within each group, then it has achieved its purpose. For example, as noted earlier, Dosage can confirm that the pedigrees of seven-furlong stakes winners are configured differently from those of eight-furlong stakes winners. Nevertheless, within each group there will be individuals with Dosage figures more suited to five furlongs or to 12 furlongs. Their presence in the subgroups has already been accounted for in the statistical analysis that showed the seven- and eight-furlong winners were indeed dissimilar in terms of pedigree construction. Whenever one deals with distributions within large populations, one must always consider the probability that an individual's traits will conform to those of the general population. A reasonable analogy may be the five pack-a-day smoker who lives to be 100 years old. Most people who smoke five packs a day will expire long before their 100th birthday. But such hardy individuals certainly might exist. Their survival against the odds does not in any way bring into question the validity of the demographic studies done on smoking and life expectancy. The same is true of individual horses with Dosage figures that fail to conform to those of the majority of the group they populate.

In this context, it is noteworthy that the critics of Dosage have never been able to deny the accuracy of the data. For the most part they ignore it and don't try. They probably don't try because, as the reader has seen, the correlations are so strong and so compelling that it would be fruitless to do so. If one finds Dosage a waste of time, that determination will result not from the data that support it but from a philosophical barrier.

In retrospect, much of the controversy could have been avoided had the subject matter been presented not as a continuation of Dosage theory but as a separate study of the effects of inherited speed on performance. The terms speed profile and speed index seem far less intimidating than Dosage profile and Dosage index. In truth, the current studies have only a marginal association with the historical aspects of Dosage theory. They do borrow the concepts of ancestral prepotence and aptitudinal type, but in a context very different from that proposed by either Vuillier or Varola. Latter day *chefs-de-race* are less icons of racing greatness than they are centers of inherited speed within a pedigree. Vuillier emphasized the class of the pedigrees that were populated with his *chefs-de-race*. Varola also emphasized class, but within a sociological framework of aptitudinal type and by taking great pains to dissociate type from specific performance traits. The latest iteration of Dosage concerns itself only with the relationship between aptitudinal type and racing performance. Sires are considered not for their place in Thoroughbred history but for the characteristics of speed and stamina they may consistently pass along to their descendants. Those who think about modern Dosage in this way and who appreciate the value of a pedigree classification system as a research tool should find the material not the least bit controversial.

About the Author

Steve Roman earned his Ph.D. in Organic Chemistry from Columbia University. He is the author of over 60 scientific publications and U.S. patents in the area of agricultural and animal health chemical products and processes. His 30-plus years of hands-on involvement with horses includes the breeding, raising, training and exhibiting of Morgan and Pinto show horses as well as the ownership of Thoroughbred racing and breeding stock. Although recognized primarily for the development of contemporary Dosage theory, Dr. Roman's research also focuses on the details of Thoroughbred performance. He has been a Thoroughbred breeding and racing advisor for over two decades and has been involved in the racing careers of many prominent horses including champions and Grade 1 winners Thunder Gulch, Yankee Victor, Favorite Trick, Marlin, Victory Speech, Tipically Irish, Eloquent Minister and others.

CHAPTER 12

Female Family Inbreeding

Ever since the early days of the Thoroughbred when the magic formula seemed to be the mating of Eclipse and his sons to the daughters of Herod, breeders have sought out special systems to enhance their likelihood of success. Over the past two hundred years, various methodologies including affinity patterns, Dosage formulation and biometrics have evolved and enjoyed their own following.

Another sometimes controversial approach to the way in which a racehorse's pedigree might be constructed has been the concept of inbreeding. Here, the primary focus is on the ancestors that both sire and dam have in common.

> "The object of inbreeding is to increase the influence of the ancestor to whom we inbreed. It is the process of taking two dips into the same well of parental ingredients."

> Sir Charles Leicester
> Bloodstock Breeding, 1957

While the overwhelming majority of breeding literature has always focused on the much more common occurrence of inbreeding patterns to male progenitors, there is the growing belief that more demonstrable good may be gained through the practice of duplicating the Thoroughbred's female influences.

Female Family Inbreeding (FFI) occurs when an individual's sire and dam contribute complementary strains of the same female ancestor (within a stipulated number of generations). In other words, the inbreeding occurs through (at least) two of her offspring.

Recent Hall of Fame inductee, Serena's Song, for example, demonstrates inbreeding to the great matriarch, Almahmoud 5X5 through her daughters, Cosmah and Natalma.

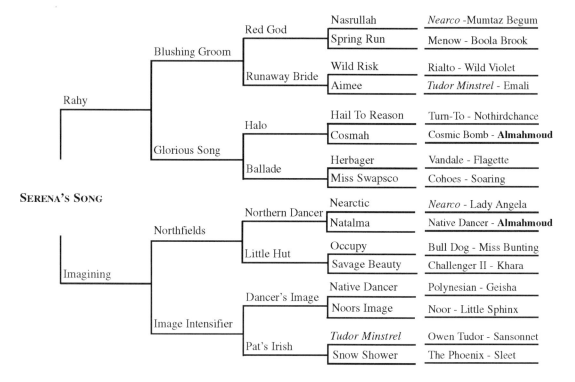

SERENA'S SONG

The actual practice of female family inbreeding far preceded its documentation as a suggested or preferred method of mating.

Since the onset of the breed, whether deliberate or not, inbreeding to great broodmares and their immediate families has been apparent in a remarkable proportion of the breed's finest runners, sires and dams. This has taken place, despite the fact that the majority of Thoroughbreds have normally lacked such pedigree patterns (within a comparative number of generations). One would, indeed, find it difficult to review the accomplishments of very many of history's top breeders and not find a significant degree of FFI in evidence.

The first known reference to FFI as a favored concept was not until 1964 when breeding theorist Dennis Craig highlighted it in his book, *Breeding Racehorses*.

> "My final conclusion, then, is that bloodstock breeders should take yet another and closer look at the classic methods of mating practiced by their successful forebears, as discussed in detail in this book: **inbreed, not to the same stallion, but to the same (foundation) mare within three to five generations** ..."

Unfortunately, the Craig book failed to receive the interest and support it deserved. In the years to follow, breeding analysis in books and journals continued to ignore, or at least underplay the influence of female family inbreeding.

It would be several decades before the true value of FFI reemerged in a number of Leon Rasmussen's Bloodlines columns carried in the *Daily Racing Form*. Rasmussen would later solidify his observations and conclusions at an important breeding symposium held in Sydney, Australia in 1993, where his address was entitled "Inbreeding to Superior Females through Different Individuals." Soon thereafter, *Owner-Breeder* magazine began referring to this phrase as the Rasmussen Factor.

In the years to follow, Leon and I worked together on a comprehensive review of the impact FFI has had on the Thoroughbred, from its origins to the present, over a broad range of racing nations. Our book, *Inbreeding to Superior Females*, published in 1999, is the best current text to expand upon this chapter.

Forms of Female Family Inbreeding

The RASMUSSEN FACTOR (RF) occurs when there is duplication of a female ancestor, between the individual's sire and dam, within five generations (5X5 or closer). The RF notes the presence of relatively close female family inbreeding in an individual's pedigree. As will be shown, it can be used to measure the relative level of FFI in collections of Thoroughbreds under review. Individuals who demonstrate the Rasmussen Factor may be referred to as "RFs" or as demonstrating the RF.

The Rasmussen Factor is not synonymous with female family inbreeding since it fails to identify and/or measure any FFI beyond five generations. It should, therefore, be emphasized that valuable FFI patterns do exist in individuals beyond RF criteria.

Table 1 lists the ten most prevalent patterns of female family inbreeding in America today.

TABLE I

THE TOP TEN FFI PATTERNS IN THE U.S. TODAY

1) Inbreeding to the family of **ALMAHMOUD** and her daughters, **NATALMA** and **COSMAH** is the most common, as well as the most successful pattern of FFI in the world today. Crossing the different strains of Almahmoud, the grand-dam of both Northern Dancer and Halo, has, indeed, led to an astonishing number of the world's most celebrated racehorses.

2) Inbreeding to the family of **LA TROIENNE** as well as her daughters and grand-daughters, particularly **STRIKING, BIG EVENT, GLAMOUR** and **BUSANDA** has produced the second largest collection of superior runners with FFI in the U.S. during the past decade.

3) Inbreeding to the family of **IMPERATRICE** and her daughter, **SOMETHINGROYAL** can be noted in an exceptional number of top runners, both in the U.S. as well as the rest of the racing world. The family's two most common strains are through Somethingroyal's sons, Secretariat and Sir Gaylord.

4) Inbreeding to the family of **MUMTAZ BEGUM** has been a very successful pattern throughout the 1980s and 90s. It represents the third consecutive generation of inbreeding to the 9-c family of Lady Josephine (1912). This is a strategy that has produced a remarkable share of the century's fastest Thoroughbreds.

5) Inbreeding to the family of **LALUN** can be observed in the pedigrees of a significant number of major U.S. stakes winners, particularly on turf. Additionally, it has become the second most frequently occurring pattern among European Group winners.

6) Inbreeding to the family of **LAVENDULA** has been a valuable breeding strategy for the last two decades. She is the dam of Ambiorix and the grand-dam of Turn-to and My Babu.

7) Inbreeding to the family of **BOUDOIR II** and her grand-daughter, **FLOWER BOWL** was the seventh most prolific FFI pattern during the 1990s. Boudoir II was the ancestress of a good number of influential stallions including Graustark, His Majesty, Majestic Prince and Secreto.

8) Inbreeding to the family of **THE SQUAW II** and her grand-daughter, **POCAHONTAS** has been another successful American FFI pattern. This clan, developed by Claiborne Farm, produced Ack Ack, Tom Rolfe and Chieftain.

9) Inbreeding to the family of **GREY FLIGHT** has manifested itself by crossing complementary strains of such sires as What A Pleasure, Sovereign Dancer and Time For A Change. This is another family tree developed at Claiborne Farm whose branches have certainly been worth duplicating.

10) Inbreeding to the family of **ROUGH SHOD II** and her daughter, **THONG** is another FFI pattern that has had particularly good results among grass runners. This, as previously noted, is the family of Nureyev and Sadler's Wells.

Two distinct structural forms of the Rasmussen Factor worthy of note are the Formula One and Delta Patterns.

The Formula One Pattern is constituted, when the individual's sire and dam both descend in tail-female line to the same superior matriarch. Quiet American, a Grade One winner and sire of Kentucky Derby champion Real Quiet, is a good example of this pattern.

Quiet American's pedigree shows both his sire, Fappiano, and his dam, Demure, both descended from the important producer, Cequillo.

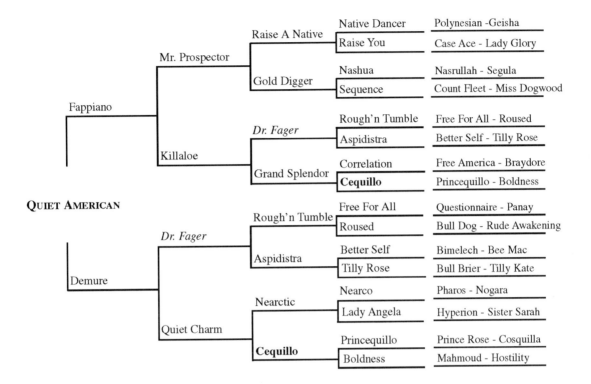

QUIET AMERICAN

Fappiano
- Mr. Prospector
  - Raise A Native
    - Native Dancer — Polynesian - Geisha
    - Raise You — Case Ace - Lady Glory
  - Gold Digger
    - Nashua — Nasrullah - Segula
    - Sequence — Count Fleet - Miss Dogwood
- Killaloe
  - *Dr. Fager*
    - Rough'n Tumble — Free For All - Roused
    - Aspidistra — Better Self - Tilly Rose
  - Grand Splendor
    - Correlation — Free America - Braydore
    - **Cequillo** — Princequillo - Boldness

Demure
- *Dr. Fager*
  - Rough'n Tumble
    - Free For All — Questionnaire - Panay
    - Roused — Bull Dog - Rude Awakening
  - Aspidistra
    - Better Self — Bimelech - Bee Mac
    - Tilly Rose — Bull Brier - Tilly Kate
- Quiet Charm
  - Nearctic
    - Nearco — Pharos - Nogara
    - Lady Angela — Hyperion - Sister Sarah
  - **Cequillo**
    - Princequillo — Prince Rose - Cosquilla
    - Boldness — Mahmoud - Hostility

I first introduced the Formula One Pattern in an article published in the March 1995 issue of *Owner-Breeder*. Other recent representatives include Grade or Group One winners, Priolo, Thirty Six Red, Dolphin Street, Startac and Gaviola.

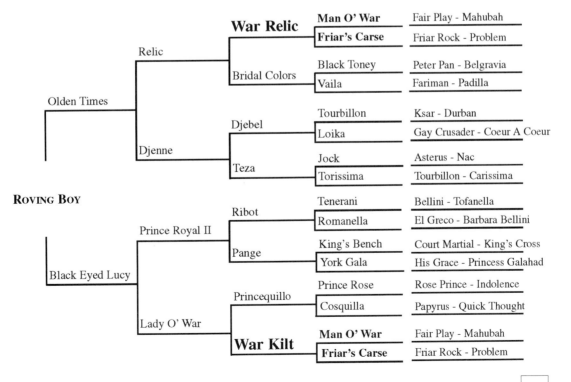

ROVING BOY

Olden Times
- Relic
  - **War Relic**
    - **Man O' War** — Fair Play - Mahubah
    - **Friar's Carse** — Friar Rock - Problem
  - Bridal Colors
    - Black Toney — Peter Pan - Belgravia
    - Vaila — Fariman - Padilla
- Djenne
  - Djebel
    - Tourbillon — Ksar - Durban
    - Loika — Gay Crusader - Coeur A Coeur
  - Teza
    - Jock — Asterus - Nac
    - Torissima — Tourbillon - Carissima

Black Eyed Lucy
- Prince Royal II
  - Ribot
    - Tenerani — Bellini - Tofanella
    - Romanella — El Greco - Barbara Bellini
  - Pange
    - King's Bench — Court Martial - King's Cross
    - York Gala — His Grace - Princess Galahad
- Lady O' War
  - Princequillo
    - Prince Rose — Rose Prince - Indolence
    - Cosquilla — Papyrus - Quick Thought
  - **War Kilt**
    - **Man O' War** — Fair Play - Mahubah
    - **Friar's Carse** — Friar Rock - Problem

For the Delta Pattern to be constituted, the sire and dam must trace in tail-male and tail-female line, respectively, to full siblings. The brilliant, but ill-fated, Roving Boy serves as a good example of this.

Roving Boy was the 1980 U.S. Champion Juvenile Colt. His pedigree shows War Relic, his paternal great grand-sire and War Kilt, his third dam, were brother and sister. This is the nature of the Delta pattern: the crossing of tail-male and female lines which carry full siblings.

I first introduced the Delta Pattern in an article published in the August 1994 issue of *Owner-Breeder*. Recent representatives include Grade or Group One winners, Habibti, Rosefinch, Lando and River Bay.

Pedigrees demonstrating the Delta or Formula One patterns have occurred in an extremely small fraction of the total Thoroughbred population. Nevertheless, over the years, they have presented themselves in a remarkable number of important pedigrees.

How can Female Family Inbreeding be applied?

1) to explain much of the development of the Thoroughbred: its male and female lines

2) to provide a mating strategy without necessarily increasing the cost of breeding a better racehorse

3) as a handicapping tool

Throughout much of Thoroughbred history, the most successful male and female lines have often followed pathways in which distinct patterns of female family inbreeding have occurred.

For example, Table 2 demonstrates the continuous weave of FFI patterns along the surviving male line of the Godolphin Arabian. Individuals inbred to female ancestors within five generations (within RF criteria) are noted in bold. Inbreeding to families of sires who appear along the tail-male line of the Godolphin Arabian is noted in capital letters.

Students of pedigree analysis are encouraged to look at other dominant male or female lines to verify the common trace of important FFI patterns. The duplication of genetic material from key maternal ancestors appears to be one of the fundamental ways in which the breed has been shaped and then continually reshaped since its origins.

It's interesting to note that the Spanker Mare, described in Chapter 8 (Nicking) as the Thoroughbred's "Ancestral Mom" was, herself, the product of a most intense FFI pattern. Her sire was bred to his own dam!

TABLE 2
FEMALE FAMILY INBREEDING ALONG THE VIABLE MALE LINE OF
THE GODOLPHIN ARABIAN

THE GODOLPHIN ARABIAN

	FFI Inbreeding Pattern:	Inbreeding to the Family of:
CADE		
MATCHEM	Spanker Mare 5X4	CADE
CONDUCTOR	Sister to Mixbury 4X5X5	Partner
TRUMPATOR	Brown Farewell 4X5	MATCHEM
SORCERER	Brown Farewell 5X6X5	MATCHEM
COMUS	Daughter of Soreheels 6X6	Highflyer
HUMPHREY CLINKER	Diomed & Fancy 4X5	Diomed
MELBOURNE	Termagant 4X4	HUMPHREY CLINKER
WEST AUSTRALIAN	Evelina 4X6 /Termagant 5X5X7	HUMPHREY CLINKER
AUSTRALIAN	Evelina 5X7X5	HUMPHREY CLINKER
SPENDTHRIFT	Whalebone, Whisker & Web 6X5X6X4X5	Whalebone
HASTINGS	No additional female family inbreeding	
FAIR PLAY	Pocahontas 5X5	Stockwell
MAN O' WAR	Pocahontas 6X6X7X7X7X7X8X7	Stockwell
WAR RELIC	Fairy Gold 3X3	FAIR PLAY
INTENT	No additional female family inbreeding	
INTENTIONALLY	Fairy Gold 5X5X5	FAIR PLAY
IN REALITY	Fairy Gold 6X6X6X6X6	FAIR PLAY

Aside from the many historical examples, female family inbreeding can often serve as a valuable strategy in the selection process of broodmare and stallion matings. The objective is the identification of those potential partners who carry complementary family strains to the sire or broodmare in question.

For whatever it's worth, there also appears to be some situations where the use of FFI might serve as a novel pedigree angle for handicapping purposes.

For example, a $2 win bet on all Kentucky Derby entrants demonstrating the RF over the past 25 years would have cost $64 (33 starters, an average of about 1 1/3 starters per year). Four big longshots (Gato Del Sol, Unbridled, Sea Hero and Charismatic) have returned $160 for a 250 percent profit.

A $2 win bet on all RF starters in the 20-year history of the Breeders' Cup (1984-2003) would have cost $214 (107 starters in 145 races) and has returned $275 for a 35 percent profit (including longshots, Last Tycoon, Unbridled, One Dreamer and Cash Run).

How can Female Family Inbreeding be evaluated?

1) Examining the Stallion

2) Examining the Broodmare (and her family)

3) Population Studies

By analyzing the extended pedigrees of a stallion's top runners, one can often observe a remarkable share of individuals demonstrating female family inbreeding.

To be more accurate, one can study the pedigrees of the stallion's entire progeny to assess the influence of FFI.

Take, for example, the sire record of the highly influential Mr. Prospector stallion, Fappiano (1977-90). Table 3 shows ratios of his best offspring comparing those individuals who demonstrated the Rasmussen Factor with the majority that did not.

TABLE 3 - FAPPIANO'S SIRE RECORD

	FOALS	STAKES WINNERS	GRADED SWs	G1 WINNERS
TOTAL	417	47 (11.2%)	24 (5.8%)	12 (2.9%)
Non-RFs	400 (95.9%)	43 (10.8%)	20 (5.0%)	9 (2.3%)
RFs	17 (4.1%)	4 (23.5%)	3* (17.6%)	3 (17.6%)

* Unbridled, Cahill Road & Quiet American

Of Fappiano's 417 total offspring, 17, or 4.1 percent, demonstrated FFI within five generations. Of these, three (17.6 percent) became Graded SWs, compared to 5 percent of the non-RF population.

Interested pedigree buffs are encouraged to uncover similar positive returns with the application of FFI in a remarkable proportion of stallions, both from yesteryear as well as the present.

Fappiano's four percent rate of producing offspring demonstrating the RF is just about what we have found as the current average among the overall population of North American Thoroughbreds.

The likelihood (opportunity) of a stallion producing RF progeny is usually signaled by the number of superior matriarchs in his pedigree who are capable of finding complementary strains in the pedigrees of his mares.

Bull Lea (1935-64), one of America's best mid-twentieth century stallions, had at least five different female families in his pedigree with which to inbreed. As demonstrated in Table 4, this created a particularly high rate of RFs among his progeny.

TABLE 4 - BULL LEA'S SIRE RECORD

	FOALS	STAKES WINNERS	SWS earning > $100,000
TOTAL	377	57 (15.1%)	27 (7.2%)
Non-RFs	305 (80.9%)	42 (13.1%)	18 (5.6%)
RFs	72 (19.1%)	15 (20.8%)	9 (12.5%)

Of Bull Lea's 377 total foals, 72 or almost one-fifth were RFs. As indicated, his rate of siring black type earners of over $100,000 was more than twice as high when issuing RF progeny as compared to the rest.

BULL LEA'S STAKES WINNERS DEMONSTRATING THE RASMUSSEN FACTOR

		FFI Pattern	Earnings	
TWILIGHT TEAR	f. 1941	Amie 5X5	$202,165	Horse of the Year at 3, Champion at 2, 3 & 4
HARRIET SUE	f. 1941	Mavourneen 5X5	$64,175	Arlington Matron H., Ashland S., etc.
TWOSY	f. 1942	Cerito 4X4	$101,375	Colonial H., Carroll H., etc.
FAULTLESS	c. 1944	Plucky Liege 3X4	$304,945	Preakness, Blue Grass S, Withers S, etc.
TWO LEA	f. 1946	Cerito 4X4	$309,250	Santa Margarita H., Hol. Gold Cup, Vanity H., etc., Champion at 3 & 4
THE FAT LADY	f. 1946	Mavourneen 5X5	$39,957	Royal Oak S., 2nd Kentucky Oaks
DELUXE	c. 1946	Colonial 3X5	$56,875	King Phillip H., Narragansett Special
MARK-YE-WELL	c. 1949	Colonial 3X5	$581,910	American Derby, Santa Anita H., San Antonio H., etc.

PERFECTION	f. 1950	Amie 5X5	$30,600	Playa Del Rey S.
SPINNING TOP	f. 1950	Plucky Liege 3X4	$67,155	Black Eyed Susan S., Vineland H.
MIZ CLEMENTINE	f. 1951	Cerito 4X4	$267,100	Hollywood Oaks, Calif. Derby & Oaks, Cinema H, etc.
AMORET	f. 1952	Colonial 3X5	$153,860	Beverly H., Columbiana H., Black Helen H.
MISS ARLETTE	f. 1952	Plucky Liege 3X4	$53,770	La Centinela S.
TRENTONIAN	c. 1952	Plucky Liege 3X4	$126,380	El Camino H., Golden Gate Futurity, etc.
IRON LIEGE	c. 1954	Plucky Liege 3X4	$403,919	Kentucky Derby, Jersey S., etc.

It's also important to note there are some stallions whose best offspring almost never demonstrate female family inbreeding (within five or six generations). Usually, these sires simply lack the superior families in their own immediate ancestry to be inbred to. Occasionally, these types become successful sires in their own right. In these cases, they should probably be considered the kinds of prepotent stallions whose qualities and abilities at stud simply transcend this form of pedigree analysis. In other words, female family inbreeding cannot account for any of their success.

One can also evaluate female family inbreeding by focusing on the broodmare, as well as her family at large. This process begins with the identification of those male alliances that create FFI with a particular broodmare. With computer assistance, the dam's produce record can be analyzed by examining the extended pedigrees of all of her offspring. Questions to be answered include, which, if any, of her offspring demonstrate FFI? Were they her most important? This type of analysis can be practiced with the 'Stakes Winners" sections of racing periodicals.

Family Tables are necessary for the proper evaluation of tail-female lines. The definitive text of Thoroughbred family structure, "Family Tables of Racehorses" was compiled by Kazimierz Bobinsky and was first published in 1953. More recently, Toru Shirai updated the work in "Family Tables of Racehorses Vol. III," which is complete through the racing year of 1988. Volume IV is due out in 2004. There is no stronger source of evidence for female family inbreeding's impact on the breed than these reference texts. By evaluating the pedigrees of individuals along key female lines, one begins to appreciate consistent patterns of FFI among the branches that not only survived but flourished.

A third way to evaluate the benefits of FFI is through population studies. Here, a specified collection of individuals are followed to see if the lot demonstrating female family inbreeding (the RF) go on to collectively outperform the remainder of the group.

One illustration of this is an examination of the annual roster of three-year-olds nominated to the American Triple Crown. Since 1996, a complete list of these sophomores, with their connections and pedigrees, has been published in the *Daily Racing Form* during the first part of February.

In 1996, soon after the list's release, I was given the opportunity to write an article for the Racing Form which highlighted those nominees who demonstrated the Rasmussen Factor. The study showed that of the 354 hopefuls, 19 carried the RF.

Early in 1997, after the group's three-year-old season, a follow-up feature piece in the 'Form reviewed how this lot performed, relative to the others. The results are summarized in Table 5.

TABLE 5
1996 VISA TRIPLE CROWN NOMINEES DEMONSTRATING FEMALE FAMILY INBREEDING WITHIN 5 GENERATIONS (THE RF)

	TOTAL	Gr. SWs (%)	Gr. 1 SWs (%)
Total	354	40 (11.2%)	12 (3.4%)
Nominees without the RF	335	32 (9.6%)	9 (2.7%)
Nominees with the RF	19 (5.4%)	8 (42.1%)	3 (15.8%)

	Auction price	Career Earnings	Class Level	FFI Pattern
ARJUN	HOMEBRED	$0	Unplaced	Almahmoud 5X5
GATOR DANCER	HOMEBRED	$138,880	Grade 2 Winner	Grey Flight 5X4
LOUIS QUATORZE	HOMEBRED	$2,054,434	CLASSIC WINNER	Grey Flight 3X5
NEVER TO SQUANDER	HOMEBRED	$88,216	G3 placed	Romanella 5X4
PLAYING FOR ASHES	HOMEBRED	$73,987	Winner	Big Hurry 5X5
SEACLIFF	HOMEBRED	$456,300	Grade 3 Winner	Up The Hill 4X5
ZIGGY'S AFFAIR	HOMEBRED	$42,168	Stakes Winner	Misty Morn 4X4
		$2,853,985		
A.V. EIGHT	$20,000	$217,740	Grade 3 Winner	Past Eight 4X5
ALYROB	$50,000	$81,916	G3 placed	Baba Kenny 5X5
BEST GO	$9,500	$77,572	Stakes placed	Rare Perfume 5X4
DEVIL'S HONOR	$35,000	$801,940	Grade 3 Winner	Cosmah 3X5
GAMEEL	$95,000	$73,904	G3 placed	Grey Flight 5X4
HONOUR AND GLORY	$125,000	$1,202,942	GRADE 1 WINNER	Big Event 5X5
MORE ROYAL	$90,000	$295,141	Grade 2 Winner	Aimee 4X4
SNOW TOWER	$42,000	$81,180	G3 placed	Bold Irish 5X4
STRAIGHTAWAY	$28,000	$80,343	Stakes Winner	Almahmoud 4X5
SUNNY A	$275,000	$25,700	Stakes placed	Kerala 3X4
TAX AMOUR	$4,200	$45,622	Winner	Rough Shod II 5X4
WILL'S WAY	$95,000	$954,400	GRADE 1 WINNER	Two Lea 5X5
	$868,700	$3,938,400		
Total Earnings		$6,792,385		

I think it's fair to say the results from this crop were quite remarkable. While 9.6 percent of the non-RFs went on to become graded stakes winners, eight of the 19 RFs, or 42.1 percent, reached that class level. Indeed, the numbers were even more striking at the Grade One level (15.8 percent to 2.7 percent).

Of these 19 RFs, seven were homebreds. They returned more than $2.85 million in purse money including a victory in the Preakness.

The other 12 were purchased at public sales for a total of $868,700. This dozen went on to earn more than $3.9 million. Not accounted for in here is the tremendous residual stallion value several of these colts would also enjoy. Honour and Glory and Louis Quatorze have already gotten off to quite promising starts at stud.

In turn, Table 6 summarizes the Triple Crown nominees with the Rasmussen Factor from 1996 to 2003. Over these eight years, a total of 3,179 three-year-olds were nominated to the VISA Triple Crown Challenge. Of these, 227, or 7.1 percent, demonstrated the RF.

TABLE 6
SUMMARY OF VISA TRIPLE CROWN CHALLENGE
NOMINEES WITH THE RF (1996-2003)

Year	Total Nominated	# of RFs	% of total	RF Graded/Group Stakes Winners
1996	354	19	5.4	(8) A.V. Eight, Devil's Honor, Gator Dancer, **Honour and Glory, Louis Quatorze**, More Royal, Seacliff, **Will's Way**
1997	368	25	6.8	(5) Accelerator, Acceptable, All Chatter, Rojo Dinero, Unite's Big Red
1998	384	28	7.3	(4) Allen's Oop, Da Devil, **Golden Missile**, Rock and Roll
1999	396	31	7.8	(6) Certain, **CHARISMATIC**, Desert Hero, Patience Game, Euchre, **The Groom is Red**
2000	387	26	6.7	(5) **Best of the Bests, Cash Run**, City on a Hill, **Hal's Hope**, Mr. Livingston
2001	439	42	9.6	(8) **King Charlemagne, Minardi, Mozart**, No Excuse Needed, **Noverre, Sligo Bay, Outofthebox, Startac**
2002	405	29	7.2	(3) **Johar**, Quest Star, Savannah Bay
2003	446	27	6.1	(6) **Southern Image**, Evolving Tactics, Max Forever, Statue of Liberty, Strong Hope, Van Nistlerooy
1996-2003	3,179	227	7.1	(45) 18 Grade/Group 1 Winners in bold

From these 227 RFs, 45, or 20 percent have become Graded or Group Stakes winners. Eighteen, or 7.9 percent of these have become Grade or Group One winners including 1999 Horse of the Year, Charismatic.

The most valuable breeding strategies are those that have been properly tested over time and have shown to outperform their collective opportunities. The only method that has demonstrated measurable success across the broad spectrum of Thoroughbred lines since the origin of the breed is female family inbreeding.

Of course, given enough opportunities, any method of breeding will eventually produce a superior racehorse.

The question really is: "How many coins must one place in a slot machine before a jackpot finally appears?"

TABLE 7
TEN FUTURE INBREEDING PATTERNS
TO LOOK FORWARD TO

1) **NUMBERED ACCOUNT** was the 1971 U.S. juvenile filly champion. Her pedigree demonstrated the Formula One pattern, 4X5 to La Troienne. She has become the matriarch of a large and distinguished family of stallions highlighted by Private Account, Polish Numbers, Rhythm, Not For Love and Mutakddim. It will take another equine generation or two (10-20 years), but inbreeding to this superior mare figures to become a valuable strategy.

2) **GOLDEN BEACH** is the ancestress of Clever Trick, Alydeed and Ascot Knight. Crossing two complementary strains of this successful family could very well lead to a higher rate of superior individuals.

3) **FALL ASPEN** has all the ingredients of a taproot matriarch: a Grade One winner who produced an astounding eight Group or Graded stakes winners. For good measure, the 1994 Broodmare of the Year was inbred to Selene 5X5. As new as her family is, it's not hard to project successful results in decades to follow with the duplications of Fall Aspen's strains.

4) **HIDDEN TALENT** is the ancestress of several influential stallions, including Broad Brush, Capote and Baldski. Successful inbreeding patterns to Hidden Talent have just begun. Among the first dozen attempts at this cross has been Grade One winner Include and his G3 winning full sister.

5) **COURTLY DEE** produced seven Graded stakes winners in becoming 1983 Broodmare of the Year. Her family, which has only gotten stronger with each succeeding generation, has already issued the stallions Twining and Green Desert. Inbreeding to Courtly Dee should eventually prove quite productive.

6) **WEEKEND SURPRISE**, a multiple Graded stakes winner and 1992 Broodmare of the Year, was inbred to Somethingroyal 2X4. She is the dam of A.P. Indy, Summer Squall and Honor Grades. It will take a while to manifest itself but this inbreeding pattern appears most promising.

7) **GRAND SPLENDOUR** is the ancestress of several influential stallions including Fappiano, Ogygian and Honour and Glory. Inbreeding to her dam, Cequillo, has already shown to be a successful pattern in producing superior individuals.

8) **KAMAR**, herself a stakes winner, was 1990 Broodmare of the Year. She is the maternal source of a growing number of potentially influential stallions including Fantastic Light and Cape Town.

9) **BALLADE** was 1992 Broodmare of the Year. She is the matriarch of Rahy, Devil's Bag and Saint Ballado, among others.

10) **CRIMSON SAINT**, a Graded stakes winner, has forged a family that includes Storm Cat, Pancho Villa and Royal Academy. Given enough time and eventual opportunities, inbreeding to Crimson Saint represents yet another promising pattern in the future.

CHAPTER 13

The X Factor Theory

When discussing the qualities of a winner, horsemen mention both tangible and intangible traits like conformation, speed, will, and heart. "Heart" encompasses both — it is not only a winning attitude but also an organ that plays a critical role in the success of a racehorse.

Extraordinarily large hearts have been found in racehorses when they were cut open for burial of the heart. In 1932, the heart of the legendary Australian racehorse Phar Lap was found to weigh 14 pounds, a discovery that set off an investigation by Australian scientists into what larger hearts meant in the line of performance. Other scientists around the world joined in the research. The 1989 revelation of Secretariat's 22-pound heart, which no other horse has yet matched, and later the 18-pound heart of his rival, Sham, set off a pedigree search for the genetic trail of the large-heart characteristic. It was found that both horses trace to another large-hearted horse, Princequillo. It was also discovered that the pedigrees of large-hearted horses can be traced back to Eclipse and to the mare Pocahontas, who carried the gene from Eclipse's great heart on both the top and bottom of her pedigree.

The large-heart gene, which became known as the X Factor, was later determined to be passed along on the female X chromosome.

The Meaning of a Great Heart

In her 1997 book, *The X Factor: What It Is and How to Find It*, author and pedigree researcher Marianna Haun reported on her findings. She wrote of the discovery of Secretariat's huge heart: "Recalling the autopsy, University of Kentucky pathologist Thomas Swerczek said, 'I had noticed a difference in heart size in horses during autopsies before we did Secretariat. I had picked up the difference in the male and female hearts and noticed that some were bigger than others. But I didn't pay much attention until Secretariat came along. He was completely out of everybody's league. Looking back to what he had done, it was easy to put a connection to it. The heart was what made him able to do what he did. It explained how he was able to do what he did in the Belmont — a mile and a half race. You would have to have a large heart to do what he did. It would be almost impossible for a horse with a small heart to do that.'"

In the 1950s, Dr. James Steel began measuring horses' heart size using electrocardiograms (ECGs). Steel, a professor of veterinary medicine at the University of Sydney in Australia, studied the racehorses of Australian trainer Maurice McCarten, as well as horses at other racing stables. His original intent was to explore heart disease in racehorses. During the ECG tests he found that a top racehorse, Prince Cortauld, had an unusually wide QRS complex compared with a less successful racehorse, Momote. A QRS complex is shown as a wave on an ECG printout. A larger heart has a longer activation time and thus a wider QRS complex and can pump more blood with each beat and per minute. Steel used the term "heart score" to show the correlation of heart weight, stroke volume, cardiac output, and aerobic power. The ECG analysis put Prince Cortauld's heart score at 130 and Momote's at 86.

Steel developed a heart score ranking system that placed male horses with a heart score of 120 or more (116 or more for fillies and mares) in the large-heart category; between 103 and 120 in the medium- or normal-sized category; and 103 or less in the small-heart category.

According to Haun, Australian veterinarians began to work with Steel and adopt his methods of equine cardiology, including the use of heart score. It became a valuable tool for judging performance potential in equine, human, and greyhound athletes. Dr. Anthony Stewart, another Australian cardiology expert, said the frequency of large heart scores among top racehorses points to the advantage of a large heart in racing performance. He determined that heart size makes up 23 percent of a racehorse's quality, taken along with other traits such as soundness and conformation.

"Guarded support has also come from Physick-Sheard and Hendren, studying Standardbreds in Canada. In the United Kingdom, Leadon, Cunningham, Mahon and Todd reported a significant correlation between heart score and Timeform ratings in 71 three-year-olds, but not in 70 two-year-olds; yet, strangely, both correlation coefficients (r-0.359 and 0.320, respectively) statistically seemed to be highly significant," said Stewart, as quoted in *The X Factor*.

Stewart said a U.S. study by Gross, Muir, Pipers and Hamlin recognized no correlation; however, the study used the heart scores of only 12 Thoroughbred yearlings. A horse's heart isn't mature until age three, so a measurement taken before then is only an estimate of adult heart size.

In her early research, with the help of Dr. Fred Fregin and Dr. Gus Cothran, Haun determined that the large-heart characteristic could be a sex-linked codominant genetic trait on the X chromosome. Heart size was possibly passed to fillies on either their dam's X or their sire's, or both, while the colt's X came from his dam. Later research determined that the heart expressed by an individual horse was

The Genetic Heart-Line Pedigree

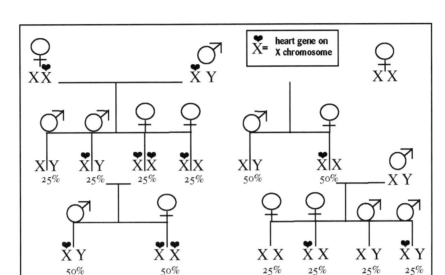

determined by the X expressed from either side of its pedigree. There was no indication of blending of the two sizes from sire and dam.

While a filly inherits her X chromosomes from her sire and her dam and will express one X and carry the other as a recessive, it is different with a colt. He will inherit one of his dam's two Xs, and that X will be both his expressed heart and the one he gives to his daughters.

Stewart said that horses with lower heart scores "do not perform as well or consistently in high-class racing as do horses with high heart scores, and a guarded prognosis should be made when the heart score is medium-low." He felt that a horse with a normal-sized heart should not be overlooked when it has other desirable attributes, such as excellent conformation, that make up for its heart size.

Heart Score, Heart Weight and Stroke Volume

Heart Score (msec.)	Heart Weight (kg)**	Stroke Volume (litres)	Cardiac Output (L/min. at max exercise) #
100	3.0	0.5	100
110	3.8	0.75	150
120	4.6	1.0	200
130	5.4	1.25	250

Estimated by Steel (Unpublished data, 1977)   ** kg.=2.2 lbs.
 # Assuming a heart rate of 200 beats per minute

Steel created a table of averages that relates heart score to heart weight, with a heart score of 100 being equal to a weight of three kilograms.

Stewart said that the difference between a heart score of 100 and one of 120 may be greater than 20 percent, due to the difference in stroke volume and cardiac output between the two heart sizes. "One should expect very different exercise performance from the horse with the large heart, with an estimated stroke volume of a liter or more, compared with the horse with a smaller heart, estimated to pump only half a liter or so," according to Stewart.

Due to the high oxidative metabolism of a racehorse's skeletal muscle fibers, a large heart with its greater stroke volume and cardiac output is better able to fulfill the oxygen requirements of a running horse.

The Nielsen and Vibe-Petersen study of Danish trotters and their ECGs found that 41 stallions with heart scores above 115 earned more than twice as much as 81 stallions with heart scores below 115. Mares with heart scores below 95 raced rather well compared with mares with higher heart scores. But the small group of eight mares with heart scores above 115 had average stakes earnings that were considerably higher than the 45 mares with lower heart scores.

Stewart estimated the heritability of heart score at 38 percent. "In studies conducted by Steel and Stewart in 1977 on the inheritance of heart scores in racehorses, an average heritability of 0.4 was estimated based on inheritance from sire to progeny," Haun wrote in The X Factor. "Within this study there was a smaller group of Thoroughbreds in which the heart score of the offspring and both parents had been determined. The group comprised 16 stallions with an average heart score of 123, 51 mares with an average heart score of 115, and 87 progeny — 42 colts with an average heart score of 118 and 45 fillies with an average heart score of 116.

"The regression coefficients (statistical method for seeking predictive relationships) obtained between the heart scores of parents and offspring averaged 19 percent from sire to progeny and 59 percent from dam to progeny. Thus the total of the parent contribution to the heart scores of their progeny was 78 percent.

"Since this total could possibly include non-genetic influences from the mare to her foal, the purely genetic heritability is based on her contribution being equal to the sire, i.e., $0.19 + 0.19 = 0.38$. This estimate of 38 percent is remarkably close to Cunningham's previous estimate of 35 percent for the inheritance of track performance.

"The regressive coefficient from sire to son was 0.06, or statistically zero. From sire to daughter it was 0.32. From dam to son it was 0.78, and from dam to daughter it was 0.40. The regression coefficients in the Australian study could be even higher if it is a recessive gene, since the daughters could have the heart gene and not express it. They would be carriers, with the gene on one X chromosome and not on the other. If the X chromosome without the large heart on it was dominant, the mares would not express the characteristic but would still have a 50-50 chance of passing it on to their sons and daughters."

A double-copy or homozygous mare with the heart gene on both X chromosomes would probably express the large heart and could pass it on to both male and female offspring. Secretariat's daughter, Weekend Surprise, carried the large-heart characteristic on both X chromosomes, as did her dam, Lassie Dear, daughter of another large-hearted sire, Buckpasser. Weekend Surprise's classic-winning sons, A.P. Indy and Summer Squall, received the great heart of Princequillo passed down from Secretariat and his half-brother, Sir Gaylord, and they, in turn, are passing the gene to their daughters.

A Complementary Theory: The M Factor

In his 1996 book, *Genetic Heritage*, bloodstock consultant Ken McLean, a specialist in Thoroughbred genealogy and amateur geneticist, writes about studying the importance of mitochondria in cells. He also wrote about the X Factor theory and the research of Steel, Stewart, and others, as well as Marianna Haun's 1994 *Thoroughbred Times* article on the X Factor.

McLean gave a layperson's explanation of mitochondria: "Mitochondria are tiny organelles within the cytoplasm that surrounds the nucleus of living cells . . . Their function is to provide the cell with its energy, which they do by taking energy from the bonds holding food molecules together and transferring that energy to so-called high energy phosphate groups which can then be shunted around the cell to various locations . . . Biologists discovered three surprising things about mitochondria: 1) They possess their own DNA with its slightly different genetic code. Mitochondrial DNA is independent, and Non-Mendelian. 2) Mitochondria are passed on to the next generation solely by the mother, who hands on some of her mitochondria in the cytoplasm of the egg. 3) The rate of evolution of Mitochondrial DNA appears to be approximately 10 times faster than that of Nuclear DNA (i.e. DNA found in the nucleus of cells)."

In 1994, McLean received a letter from geneticist Jacinta Flattery of the University of New South Wales, in response to his request for information. "In a post-script . . . she wrote: 'Are you aware of the function of mitochondria? They are sites at which oxygen is converted to water with the concomitant production of energy. It may be that horses that have 'better' mitochondria can perform better . . . ???'"

Flattery included data entitled, "Organelle Genes Are Maternally Inherited in Many Organisms," of which McLean quoted a passage: "'In higher animals, the egg cell always contributes much more cytoplasm to the zygote than does the sperm, and in some animals the sperm may contribute no cytoplasm at all. One would expect mitochondrial inheritance in higher animals to be uniparental or, more precisely, maternal.'"

Since mitochondrial DNA is passed along from mother to daughter, McLean investigated what he calls "the M-factor." "Perhaps some racehorses inherit far superior mitochondria from their dams in direct female-line descent. This might explain why some families can produce a consistent number of stakes winners," he wrote in *Genetic Heritage*.

Mitochondrial DNA may help explain the presence of elite mares in the stud books. "Famous stakes producers probably inherit special mitochondrial DNA values from their direct female line, and if coupled with any sex-linked advantages via X chromosomes carrying the genes for large heart size, can become consistent dams of high-class performers on the racetrack," wrote McLean.

He went on to say that, "It is conceivable that great mares which helped shape the breed . . . such as Old Bald Peg, Tregonwell's Natural Barb Mare, and The Vinter Mare possessed better mitochondrial DNA than perhaps all other mares entered in Volume One of the *General Stud Book*. Their female lines represent numerically the greater percentage of the overall gene pool after 200 years of Thoroughbred breeding. Incredible, yes?

"Their genetic codes have become widespread in pedigrees of the modern racehorse, and their influence via non-Mendelian mtDNA (mitochondrial DNA) is transmitted via their direct female line for generations. Elite mares possess superior mitochondria to transmit to all their female descendants; and thus, these females probably transmit 'better' energy levels to their progeny.

"If we knew which mares possessed the X chromosomes for a large heart, plus the M-factor, we could with confidence select foundation mares for a racing and breeding program. The only way one can judge is to guess, using pedigree information at hand, and details of the family's ability to produce stakes winners. This information is available on computers from the Jockey Club's EquineLine Services, from Bloodstock Research, or other research-oriented organizations."

The X Path in Pedigrees

After Secretariat's and Sham's deaths and the discovery that large-hearted Princequillo was on both of their pedigrees, Haun initiated a pedigree research project built on Australian researchers' discoveries about large hearts plus the possibility the characteristic was a sex-linked trait.

Dr. Gus Cothran, a geneticist at the University of Kentucky's Maxwell Gluck Equine Research Center, said if the Australians' findings on sex linkage were correct, the large-heart trait was probably a genetic mutation from a single source and wouldn't change for hundreds of years. The gene that gave Eclipse, foaled in 1764, his large heart could very well be the same gene that gave Secretariat, foaled in 1970, his large heart.

Haun's search led to a link along the X path of two stallions through the mare Pocahontas, foaled in England in 1837. Pocahontas produced for 20 years and died in 1870 at age 33. She is thought to have been a double-copy mare. She traces to Eclipse through his daughter Everlasting, on both the top and bottom of her pedigree. Haun said this is likely why Pocahontas was the main source for the passage of Eclipse's large heart along the pedigrees of all large-hearted horses that were researched, including Australian champions like Phar Lap.

Two U.S. universities began searching for the genetic marker for the trait, led by Cothran at the University of Kentucky and by Dr. Fred Fregin, a top equine cardiologist and Director of the Marion duPont Scott Equine Medical Center at Virginia Tech in Leesburg, Va. Fregin, author Marianna Haun and Cothran pooled their respective talents in the X Factor study, with Cothran supplying the genetics knowledge, Fregin conducting ECG measurements, and Haun comparing the data with horses identified through pedigree research.

Fregin has measured more than 1,000 racehorses using ECGs. He had met Dr. Steel of Australia and uses the same method of measuring hearts. Blood samples have been taken from each horse to be used in the DNA research for the genetic marker. The research goal has been to document a genetic characteristic and establish a pattern of inheritance. Through heart measurements, specific large-heart lines from sire to daughter to son have been traced, and consistent heart sizes have been found along each line.

According to Cothran in *The X Factor*, "The initial findings on the heart scores would suggest that the genetic characteristic is probably co-dominant. That means there is a difference between no copy, one copy, and two copies . . . If we find what we think we will, and identify the genetic marker, then it will be a matter of a simple blood test to know if an individual has this inheritable characteristic," said Cothran.

A single-copy mare will pass on either the large-heart X or the small- or normal-heart X. Whichever X is dominant is the one she herself expresses. A double-copy mare will express the large heart, as well as pass it on. Double-copy mares can receive the two large-heart X chromosomes from a single line, such as Princequillo, or from different lines, such as Princequillo and War Admiral.

A single-copy mare may express a large heart and do well in races but carry a small-heart gene on her other X chromosome. Winning Colors is an example. This Kentucky Derby winner received her large heart from her maternal grandam Miss Carmie, who carried the Blue Larkspur X; she also carried a gene for a small to normal-sized heart from her sire, Caro. If Winning Colors was bred to a sire with a heart size other than large, the odds of the foal having a small to normal-sized heart increase.

Breeding for the X Factor

The genetic mutation for the large heart has been passed down for more than 200 years through Thoroughbreds, as well as Standardbreds and Quarter Horses. The reason for this is that due to the traditional practice of breeding the best to the best; breeders unknowingly were maintaining the large-heart characteristic. A large heart won't guarantee a champion, but it does make up a quarter of the desirable qualities.

Understanding how the X chromosome works can help breeders ensure that they take full advantage of the X Factor. Since the large-heart characteristic comes from the female line, large-hearted champion stallions aren't always able to produce champion sons. Instead, they may produce good daughters that produce good sons, and then the stallion becomes known as a great broodmare sire. For best results, a large-hearted stallion should be bred to a good mare that also has a large heart. Also, the bottom of the mare's pedigree should be explored as well as the top, since the large-heart trait on the X chromosome passes along the female line on either side.

Notable stallions that were successful broodmare sires by passing the large-heart X to their daughters include Secretariat, Omaha, Citation, Whirlaway, and Alysheba. Through his daughter Terlingua, Secretariat produced a great sire in Storm Cat. A speed sire, Storm Cat has been bred to mares with large hearts and produced champions like Tabasco Cat, Sardula, and Desert Stormer.

Man o' War was bred to the mare Brushup, whose heart was larger than his, and was able to produce an excellent son: Triple Crown winner War Admiral. Brushup was by Sweep, whose large heart came from Domino through his daughter Pink Domino. Sweep also passed his great heart to Dustwhirl, the dam of Whirlaway.

The War Admiral heartline is among four of the largest heartlines that have been identified in today's pedigrees. The other three are the heartlines of the Thoroughbred stallions Mahmoud, Blue Larkspur, and Princequillo. Triple Crown winner Seattle Slew, his champion grandson Cigar, and Kentucky Derby winner Silver Charm all raced with the War Admiral heart.

A double-copy mare obviously can help increase the chance of producing a large-hearted winner. The previously mentioned Weekend Surprise, who died after foaling a daughter in 2001, had the Princequillo heart on both X chromosomes, carrying one from her sire Secretariat as a recessive, and expressing the other from his half-brother, Sir Gaylord. Her heart score was 137 to 140, reflecting the Sir Gaylord heartline. With Princequillo on both of her Xs, her sons like Horse of the Year A.P. Indy and millionaire Summer Squall also inherited the Princequillo X. Both have produced excellent daughters and, when mated with large-hearted mares, excellent sons.

In his book, *Genetic Heritage*, Ken McLean said of Princequillo: "There was a genetic affinity between Princequillo with Nearco and his best sons Nasrullah and Royal Charger. It produced many Group 1/Grade 1 winners. Did this 'nick' have anything to do with the inheritance of sex-linked genes via the X chromosomes carrying the large heart factor? Is it worthwhile designing matings with two or three examples of this nick? I notice successful use of the nick has already been used in the pedigree of Grand Lodge (Chief's Crown - La Papagena, by Habitat), winner of the Dewhurst Stakes Gr-1, St. James's Palace Stakes Gr-1, and runner-up in the English 2,000 Guineas Gr-1. This nick comes via Secretariat and Habitat's sire Sir Gaylord.

"By coincidence (or is it?) Grand Lodge happens to be line bred to Nogara, dam of Nearco and Niccolo dell'Arca, carries influence from Ajax's son Teddy via Sir Gallahad III and Bull Dog, and has Tracery coming via a doubling of Princequillo, via Petition's dam Art Paper, plus Nearctic's dam Lady Angela. Grand Lodge was rated English champion two-year-old colt and was ranked second-best three-year-old miler on the International Classification. Alan Porter, a pedigree consultant, rightly points out that Chief's Crown has done exceedingly well with mares carrying the strain of Somethingroyal (by Princequillo), dam of Secretariat and Sir Gaylord."

Heart scores are one indicator of which heart X is being passed. For example, the Sir Gaylord heart score of 137-140 has been on the X line of his descendants, including Shelter Half. This heart score also was found by Dr. Fregin when he measured fillies and colts at The Meadow, birthplace of Secretariat. It was discovered in a daughter and a grandson and has been found throughout several years of measurements.

Tracking the Double-Copy Mare

As mentioned earlier, Pocahontas was an outstanding double-copy mare who had the same source — Eclipse, through his daughter Everlasting — for the large-heart trait on both of her X chromosomes. Another great double-copy mare, La Troienne, also traces back to Everlasting and Eclipse on both Xs. La Troienne has links to Pocahontas but instead traces to Everlasting through Sterling via her sire Teddy and her dam.

Sterling (1868) was out of a mare named Whisper (1857) who was by Flatcatcher. Flatcatcher's dam Decoy (1830) was out of Finesse (1815), who was out of Violante, by John Bull, whose dam Xantippe was by Eclipse. Violante was out of a daughter of Highflyer simply known as Highflyer mare, that was out of Everlasting, by Eclipse.

Whisper's dam was Silence (1848) by Melbourne, who was out of a daughter of Cervantes, out of Evelina, by Highflyer. The Cervantes daughter was out of a Golumpus mare out of a Pavnator mare out of a St. George mare. St. George was out of a daughter of Eclipse.

Silence's dam Secret (1841) has as her fourth dam Cobbea, by Skyscraper, who is by Highflyer and out of Everlasting, by Eclipse. La Troienne's pedigree is a good example of the importance of the tail-female line in passing on genetic traits like the large-heart X.

Seattle Slew's dam, My Charmer, is another superb double-copy mare. On her X lines, she traces to two daughters of War Admiral out of daughters of Bubbling Over, who, like War Admiral, was a source for the transmission of Sweep's heart. There is a strong resemblance among daughters of Seattle Slew and Desert Secret that express the My Charmer X, such as similar body type, large feet, and reactive personalities.

Marianna Haun wrote in her 2001 book, *Understanding the Power of the X Factor*, "When it comes to identifying double-copy mares, it is important to look at the pattern of performance in their produce . . . [A]n excellent guide is to look at the male offspring of mares. When considering younger mares that have no offspring, then [their] pedigree, conformation, and performance record must be your guide.

"It is important to measure your broodmare (by ECG) so you know for sure what kind of heart she is carrying and capable of passing on to half of her offspring. It is hard to identify double-copy mares without years of measuring offspring unless they are by a sire whose heart score you already know and they express the bottom side of their pedigree. This is always seen as a gift. It is that recessive or hidden X that is so hard to identify."

Physical Characteristics

Haun expounded on physical clues to the large heart — resemblances among equine families that appear to accompany the large-heart trait. "In the past six years

DOUBLE-COPY THOROUGHBRED MARES *

Adoryphar	Courtly Dee	Lovage	Sharon Brown
Alcibiades	Crimson Saint	Mah Mahal	Shayne McQuire
Alluvial	Cue	Maplejinsky	Shenanigans
Almahmoud	Dry North	Miesque	Shy Dawn
Althea	Duty Dance	Milan Mill	Sissy's Time
Araucaria	East of the Moon	Millicent	Six Crowns
Aspidistra	Emerald Reef	Minnette	Soaring Softly
Aura of Glory	Escena	Miss Carmie	Solar Slew
Baby League	Eternally	Miss Zigby	Somethingroyal
Bathing Girl	Fairy Garden	Misty Morn	South Ocean
Bee Mac	Falconese	Moccasin	Soviet Problem
Be Faithful	Fall Aspen	Moscow Tap	Special
Bel Sheba	Flaming Page	Moscow TV	St. Adele
Belthazar	Flanders	Mumtaz Begum	St. Diva
Betty's Secret	Flitabout	Mumtaz Mahal	Strawberry Reason
Bird Flower	Flower Bowl	My Charmer	Strike a Balance
Black Helen	Fly North	My Dear Girl	Striking
Bloodroot	Forever After	My Flag	Sun Colony
Blue Banner	Gaga	Myrtlewood	Sun Princessa
Blue Denim	Gana Facil	Natalma	Sunline
Boat	Gay Missile	Naval Orange	Sunset Wells
Bonnie's Poker	Gertruc Mc	Never Hula	Sweet Tooth
Boudoir II	Glorious Song	Never Knock	Surfside
Bramalea	Golden Ballet	Noble Lassie	Talamanca
Bright Candles	Happy Holme	Northern Sunset	Tale of Two Hearts
Broadway	Heaven Knows Why	Numbered Account	Teleran
Broadway Boogie	Hopespringseternal	Passing Mood	Tamerett
Brushup	Image of Glory	Personal Ensign	Teresa Mc
Busanda	Imperatrice	Planting Time	Terlingua
Busher	In Prime Time	Plucky Liege	The Last Red
Businesslike	Inside Information	Political Favor	Time to Plant
C'est Moi Cheri	In the Curl	Prayer Bell	Toll Booth
Cadillacing	Jancy	Pure Profit	Torelia
Cap and Bells	K D Princess	Quickly	Trifecta Box
Carriette	Katambra	Raise an Heiress	Wac
Chalk Box	Kerala	Rare Mint	Wavy Navy
Chapel of Dreams	Key Bridge	Relaxing	Wayage
Charette	Key Witness	River Fairy	Weekend in Seattle
Charming Lassie	Killaloe	Romanella	Weekend Surprise
Cheerily	Lady Angela	Rough Shod II	Welcome Surprise
Christmas Bonus	Lady Josephine	Saintly Manner	Won't Tell You
Con Game	Lady's Secret	Secrettame	Work the Crowd
Cosmah	Lady Winborne	Selene	
Cosquilla	Lassie Dear	Sequence	
Count the Votes	La Troienne	Sewing Lady	

* This list is not complete but serves as a guide to mares of the past and present that are found in pedigrees that have passed the tests of time or measurement and are considered to be double-copy mares.

of research on the X Factor by myself and Fregin," she wrote in *Understanding the Power of the X Factor*, "it is hard not to notice family-line characteristics that seem to follow the X line. The most notable of these, which was first noticed by Secretariat's breeder Penny Chenery, is that small ears seem to follow the big heart."

Haun reported that Chenery first noticed a resemblance between Secretariat's small curly ears and those of The Last Red, the twin used in the breeding research by Haun. "Both horses express the Princequillo X chromosome, Secretariat from his dam Somethingroyal, a daughter of Princequillo, and The Last Red from her sire Moscow Ballet, who gets it from his second dam Milan Mill, another daughter of Princequillo. In photo comparisons with the two horses, one can see that they do have the small curly ears associated with Princequillo. In addition, they have a similar hip, eye, and nostrils.

"Chenery made this observation while being interviewed for my first book on the X Factor, *The X Factor: What It Is and How to Find It*. Subsequently, we have started following the ears of different lines and have found this method to be amazingly accurate. If a horse inherits a specific ear, he gets the same heart score. Dr. Cothran of the University of Kentucky believes that the ears are a physical marker for a genetic trait on the X chromosome inherited by the horse."

Haun said that while it is not always easy to see the differences among ears, the small, rounded ear of the Mahmoud heartline stands out. She described it as having a distinctive leaf-like quality when viewed from the front. Northern Dancer, Halo, Spectacular Bid, and Machiavellian, who stands in England, are examples of this Mahmoud X ear. Kentucky Derby winner Fusaichi Pegasus inherited these ears from Halo, the sire of his maternal grandam Rowdy Angel, along with Mahmoud's great heart.

With Approval, whose dam Passing Mood has Mahmoud and Buckpasser in her pedigree, received the Mahmoud X and has the small round ears and a body that looks very much like Mahmoud's. Another son of Passing Mood received her Buckpasser X and resembled the stallions of the War Admiral line, with the medium sculptured ears and body type like those of War Admiral.

Man 'o Sheba, the Alysheba colt out of The Last Red, has Man o' War's ears with a distinctive notch and his front end with its distinctive withers. Haun wrote in *Understanding the Power of the X Factor*, "In looking at conformation shots of Man o' War and his descendants that express his X chromosome, there is a striking resemblance in the front end and withers of these horses. Man o' War had high, pronounced withers with a rounded appearance that reminds me of a 'dowager's hump.' His front end had an upright appearance, although he was by no means straight-shouldered. It was a powerful shoulder and very distinctive. When comparing conformation photographs of Man o' War, his dam Mahubah, her sire

Rock Sand, and Man o' War's daughters, as well as other descendants such as Spotted Bull, Hempen, Spy Song, and Coup de Cas, there is a very strong family resemblance. The Man o' War front end and rounded withers are easy to spot and obviously follow the X chromosome trail."

Haun said, "It has become a shortcut — and an amazingly accurate one — for us in measuring horses to check the ears and compare the heart score after the horse has been measured. Just as humans look for family resemblances in their offspring, seeking physical similarities in foals is a clue to which X has been expressed."

Performance Patterns

According to Haun, in the pursuit to breed superior racehorses, breeders should learn about the genetic equipment in the horses they work with. Which horses pass a large heart? Which pass speed? Which pass both?

Where an ECG measurement isn't available, clues can be found in pedigrees and track records. Look for a pattern of performance on the X line of pedigrees in the stud book, Haun suggested, particularly the dams' produce. A mare that has produced 10 runners and 10 winners, for example, could be a double-copy mare. Ten runners and five winners is the pattern of a single-copy mare. Sometimes injury, finances, poor training, or other factors can keep a mare's offspring from racing well or at all; so there will be double-copy mares that had, for example, 10 runners and eight winners. However, Haun wrote, "as a rule of thumb a good produce record indicates a pretty good X being passed."

When looking at a sire, look at his daughters. When looking at the females in the bottom of his pedigree look at their sons; if there are outstanding performers among the sons, that is a good sign.

Look at the sire's track record. A sprinter that had more success with sons than daughters could be a speed sire. A mare with a good heart, as well as speed, should be bred to a speed sire so that their offspring are able to "go the distance." The same kind of mare should be bred to a sire with a large heart that has done well at classic distances, to maximize the options.

"Because there is no way of controlling which X comes out of a mating, it is important to cover your bases in terms of the choices," wrote Haun. "It's like developing your own recipe where you combine particular ingredients in hopes of producing an award-winning entrée. You fold in the heart, but don't forget to add a dash of speed. You consider body types. There is the classic long, elegant type that is associated with distance racing and the shorter-coupled more muscular type that is aligned with sprinters. The ideal should be a combination of the two like Secretariat, who had great length of stride, powerful muscles, amazing speed, and the world's greatest heart.

"It isn't easy to find the correct combination because so often they seem to be one or the other — distance or speed. If you take a top stallion with one or the other features, you have to provide a mare that can make up what is missing."

Breeders should keep in mind that a large heart alone does not guarantee a horse will be a champion. A large, powerful heart can help, but success requires a variety of traits working together. For example, if a horse has a large heart but crooked legs, unless it has developed a strong will and a way of running to compensate for the incorrect conformation, it may not win races despite having the large heart. The biomechanics of the horse — stride length, body weight, and power — and how well those factors are balanced play an important role in its racing ability. So do conformation, training, and health.

In *Genetic Heritage*, McLean wrote, "Heart size is just one of the components needed in the racing machine we call a stakes performer. There are many other vital factors needed for a superior athlete."

The X Factor theory intrigued Dr. G. Frederick Fregin, a leading equine cardiologist and director of the Marion du Pont Scott Equine Medical Center. He correlates heart score and ultrasound measurements. He is quoted as saying,

"'I have a number of combinations where we've looked at the dam and found normal heart score, yet when you look at her offspring, she is producing some outstanding runners with large hearts. So, if the mares have got the right X chromosome and they are passing it on, that's what's important. It doesn't matter if she expressed the characteristic herself.'

"We study individuals in the breed and make assumptions based on what we see, hear, and smell. Taking heart scores of a mare only shows what she is generally able to express — it doesn't indicate hidden recessive genes which lie waiting to be exposed in the mare's foals. This helps explain how valuable genes which aid in the production of a stakes winner might 'skip a generation.' The mare with one of her two X chromosomes carrying the large heart size factor is a 'carrier,' and while she may never have won a race, she can still transmit to 50 percent of her foals the large heart size characteristic. Naturally courage must accompany a large heart or big heart score, for without the will to win, it doesn't mean a lot; but strength of a heart's walls (lining) might be very important."

McLean also believes that filly foals from weak female lines can be upgraded for racing performance providing, he said, they are by a stallion whose dam carries the important large-heart factor, which he also refers to as X(H). "Continued use of stallions with the X(H) factor (that is, stallions which are sons of powerful mares) will create gradual upgrading of performance, and previously weak female lines can begin to produce stakes winners. The reverse is true, too. Fillies from strong female lines can be downgraded for racing performance if their sire's dam carries the X(h) average heart factor. Perhaps this answers why female lines rise and fall. There is nothing more disconcerting than to buy a daughter of a Graded stakes winner which proves to inherit below average ability on the racetrack, and worse still, fails to produce a stakes winner."

Heartlines

The most successful large-heart lines in today's pedigrees are those of Princequillo, War Admiral, Mahmoud, and Blue Larkspur. Other large-heart lines trace to Eclipse as well.

Besides passing his heart to Princequillo, Papyrus also passed it to Favorite Trick, Ribot, Star Kingdom, and Forli. John Henry, Quarter Horse champion Sgt. Pepper Feature, Mari's Book, and Congaree all got the Double Jay heart.

Man o' War's heart is passing along the lines of Peaks and Valleys, Sandpit, Green Dancer, Hempen, and Spy Song, among others. The Damascus heart passed to Dixieland Heat, Coronado's Quest, Ghazi, Red Ransom, Shadeed, Marlin, and other progeny.

Domino is passed through Stalwart, as well as War Admiral. Haun said that Political Favor may have one of the largest hearts she, Fregin, and Cothran have come across in their project. Domino, through Stalwart, was the only source for a heart that size in Political Favor's pedigree.

Native Dancer, the broodmare sire of Northern Dancer, is still present in today's pedigrees. Haun believes that Louis Quatorze is among those passing along this heart size.

Following are lists of horses that pass along the heartlines of Princequillo, War Admiral, Mahmoud, and Blue Larkspur, compiled by Haun. They present a broad range of contemporary sires carrying important lines. There are many other horses carrying large hearts that trace back to Eclipse in other ways that are not included, such as those mentioned above.

Photo courtesy of The Thoroughbred Times

WAR ADMIRAL HEARTLINE STALLIONS

Acceptable
Academy Award
Affirmed
Allen's Prospect
Alphabet Soup
Alysheba
American Chance
Behrens
Believe It
Better Self
Broad Brush
Bupers
Buckpasser
Cape Canaveral
Cape Town
Cherokee Run
Chester House
Crafty Admiral
Cryptoclearance
Cure the Blues
Deerhound
Desert Secret
Dr. Fager

Dubai Millennium
Easy Goer
El Gran Senor
Evansville Slew
Fappiano
Fast Play
Golden Missile
Great Above
Hoist the Flag
Housebuster
Irish Open
Judge TC
Key to the Kingdom
Lear Fan
Lemon Drop Kid
Lomond
Miner's Mark
Mining
Mutakddim
Our Emblem
Personal Flag
Plugged Nickle
Polish Navy

Polish Numbers
Private Account
Quiet American
Rare Performer
Real Quiet
Roar
Romanov
Seattle Slew
Seeking the Gold
Silver Charm
Slew o' Gold
Stephanotis
Stormin Fever
Stormy Atlantic
Swaps
Top Account
Torrential
Touch Gold
Truckee
Wavering Monarch
Wild Rush
Will's Way
Woodman

MAHMOUD HEARTLINE STALLIONS

Arazi
Bucksplasher
Demon's Begone
El Prado
Flying Continental
Fusaichi Pegasus
Gallant Man
Gilded Time
Graustark
Halo
Harlan
His Majesty
Homebuilder
Lord Avie
Machiavellian
Majestic Prince
Mickey McGuire

Northern Dancer
Pine Bluff
Rahy
Rainbows for Life
Skip Trial
Silver Deputy
Silver Ghost
Southern Halo
Spectacular Bid
State Dinner
Tasso
Tossofthecoin
Waquoit
What a Pleasure
Wild Again
With Approval

BLUE LARKSPUR HEARTLINE STALLIONS

Alleged	Never Bend
Alydar	Nijinsky II
Alydeed	Opening Verse
Bahri	Personal Hope
Banker's Gold	Prince John
Bates Motel	Red Ransom
Batonnier	Relaunch
Big Spruce	Riverman
Blushing John	Roberto
Boldnesian	Saint Ballado
Bold Reason	Scatmandu
Cat Thief	Seattle Song
Caveat	Skywalker
Cohoes	Slewpy
Cozzene	Smile
Damascus	Stalwart
Dayjur	Subordination
Devil's Bag	Tiznow
Fly So Free	TV Lark
General Meeting	Two Punch
Grey Dawn II	Victory Speech
Holy Bull	Wagon Limit
Little Missouri	Zanthe
Lure	

PRINCEQUILLO HEARTLINE STALLIONS

Ack Ack	Mill Reef
Afleet	Miswaki
Al Mamoon	Moscow Ballet
A.P. Indy	Mountain Cat
Becker	One for All
Bold Bidder	Party Manners
Boone's Mill	Pleasant Colony
Chief's Crown	Quack
Corporate Report	Roben des Pins
Danzig Connection	Sham
Diplomat Way	Sir Gaylord
Dixie Brass	Skip Away
Dr. Blum	Smart Strike
Farma Way	Somethingfabulous
Galileo	Successor
Gone West	Summer Squall
Grand Slam	Swain
Honor Grades	Sword Dance
Indian Charlie	Tiger Ridge
Key Contender	Vicar
Key to the Mint	Western Fame
Kris S.	Western Symphony
Lion Cavern	Yarrow Brae

"Of the four major super hearts in today's pedigrees, War Admiral is probably the most successful," said Haun. "His great heart, which came to him through his broodmare sire Sweep, who probably inherited it from the legendary Domino, has fueled countless racehorses, including three Triple Crown winners — War Admiral himself, Affirmed, and Seattle Slew. If you count the source, Sweep, then there are four Triple Crown winners, including Whirlaway, who, like War Admiral, was out of a daughter of Sweep."

Silver Charm and Real Quiet raced on War Admiral's heart. So did the storied Cigar, who tied Citation's great record of 16 victories in a row.

She noted that the War Admiral X carries a very large heart, great amplitude and a large heart score, and also seems to come with tenacity and an unwillingness to be headed, as evidenced by War Admiral's successful descendants.

In addition to a large heart and racing tenacity, War Admiral had a high level of energy. Tom Harbut, son of Man o' War's famous groom Will Harbut, compared War Admiral's behavior with the antics of 2001 Preakness and Belmont Stakes winner Point Given, who frequently went airborne, occasionally losing his rider while on the Triple Crown trail. "Every time you got on War Admiral he would give three huge jumps," said Harbut. "You always had to remember there would be a third jump or you were in trouble. You didn't relax until he did all three. Then he was fine."

Harbut said War Admiral wasn't a big horse at 15.2-1/2 hands but was refined and full of fire. "He had plenty of heart."

War Admiral is an example of the size of a colt coming from the dam instead of the sire. In size he was unlike his big sire Man 'o War, who stood at 16.2. He was built more like his broodmare sire Sweep. War Admiral had a beautifully-shaped head featuring medium-sized sculptured ears, large eyes, plenty of space in between his jaws, and a fine muzzle with oversized nostrils. He also had prominent withers with a beautifully sloped shoulder, long forearms and short cannons. His aristocratic head with its small muzzle and large nostrils and wide space between his jaws is seen in his descendants expressing his X chromosome. Haun noted that when comparing the heads — especially from the front — of Escena, Lemon Drop Kid, Tale of Two Hearts, Desert Secret, Affirmed, Surfside, Seattle Slew, Silver Charm, and Cigar, among others, a striking family resemblance can be seen in the shape and expression of the head and face.

In measuring the four lines, the heart scores for Princequillo-line stallions were consistently the largest ones found. The largest heart score found by Dr. Fregin during this project was in champion Key to the Mint, whose dam, Key Bridge, had the unique pedigree that contained three of the largest heartlines: Princequillo, War

Admiral, and Blue Larkspur. Based on performance and heart score, Key to the Mint had the Princequillo heart. It is the third-largest heart after those of Secretariat and Sham.

Blue Larkspur's line will long be remembered for his daughters, which have kept his heart alive through lines of production that have resulted in horses like Nijinsky II, Boldnesian, Alydar, Damascus, Prince John, Stalwart, Alydeed, Mr. Prospector, Bold Reason, and many others. When Blue Larkspur daughters were bred to War Admiral and the resulting foal was a filly, the mating produced mares like Busanda, dam of Buckpasser, who has had a profound effect on large-hearted maternal grandsons.

Mahmoud's line also is a distinguished one. This great sire and broodmare sire gave his large heart to the likes of Northern Dancer, Holy Bull, Halo, Spectacular Bid, Arazi, and many more successful horses. Mahmoud's pedigree is closely allied to that of Nasrullah, another large-hearted sire. They both share the same maternal grandam, Mumtaz Mahal.

In the project, the large Mahmoud heart was found in Northern Dancer daughters. Northern Dancer had an ECG taken of his heart when he was 23 that revealed he had a very large heart with a heart score of 150, consistent with the size found in his daughters and other Mahmoud descendants on the X-chromosome lines.

If an owner has purchased, or is considering the purchase of, a horse with a large-hearted champion like War Admiral in its pedigree, the owner should not assume that his horse has received a large heart from its famous ancestor. The large heart is not passed to all descendants. If an owner or a prospective buyer is curious about a horse's heart size, he or she should explore the top and bottom of the horse's pedigree for other large-hearted ancestors, have an ECG or ultrasound examination performed to determine heart score, and look for physical clues to the large-heart trait such as ear shape and conformation that are similar to those of large-hearted ancestors.

"There is still much to learn about the genetic trail along the X line," said Haun. "But the recurring patterns of specific traits, in addition to specific hearts, following certain Xs is hard to ignore."

Marianna Haun is a member of the National Turf Writers Association. She has covered the racing industry as a writer and photographer for the past 11 years, first for the Thoroughbred Times *and later for the Associated Press. She is the author of* The X Factor: What It Is and How to Find It *and* Understanding the Power of the X Factor: Patterns of Heart Score and Performance. *Currently, she is a pedigree and breeding consultant. She continues to be involved in the X Factor research project with Drs. Fregin and Cothran.*

Ken McLean was born in Sydney, Australia. He and his wife Carla are bloodstock consultants in Lexington, Kentucky. McLean became interested in genetics when he was seven years old and is now a specialist in Thoroughbred genealogy. He took a trolley ride in search of genetic knowledge about the racehorse and never applied the brakes. He is the author of Quest for a Classic Winner, *in which he discusses the Elite Mares, and* Genetic Heritage.

CHAPTER 14

Bruce Lowe and the Numerology of Pedigrees

Numerology, the study of numbers and their influence on human life, has held great significance at various times. As an element of Christian theology, numerology has significance in the more mystical interpretations of scripture, especially with regard to the number three. Any eminent Victorian would have been familiar with some aspect of numerology, and Bruce Lowe, working purely with pedigrees, became aware of some general trends and patterns as he tabulated the numbers of English classic winners.

Lowe traced the winners of the English Oaks, Derby, and St. Leger through their female families back to the first registered mare found in the English Stud Book. This line of descent, the tail-female line, had been investigated rather little in the 18th and 19th centuries. Generally, the attention of major breeders, most of whom were gentlemen of family, was concentrated on the male lines of pedigrees.

As part of his researches, Lowe found that some families had produced many more classic winners than others. The family that had produced the most classic winners at that time, Tregonwell's Natural Barb Mare, he labeled the Number 1 Family; the family with the second-highest total was the Number 2 Family and so forth. The families studied by Lowe eventually numbered a total of 43.

He did not live to put his book, *Breeding on the Figure System*, through the press, however. That fell to William Allison, who became the leading proponent of Lowe's conjectures about breeding racehorses with this method.

Not surprisingly, this approach to breeding had an immediate and international appeal. It combined history, romance, and mathematics into a pretty good framework for telling the story of a pedigree or a mating, and Joe Estes observed "that there was no one so foolish but that he could grasp the main plot."[1]

The Figure System had enough complexity that it intrigued breeders, and the outcome a century ago was that the numerology of pedigrees became the predominant method of assessing value in a family. In the *American Thoroughbred Stallion Register* compiled by Treacy & Walker in the 1920s, in addition to the immensely valuable six-cross pedigrees, family notes, and race records that they include in the volume, the compilers also list the Bruce Lowe families "with additions from the British Thoroughbred" by Allison. By this time, he had added to Lowe's families, increasing the list to 50.

The notes from the *American Thoroughbred Stallion Register* say of the No. 1 Family: "This is essentially a running, as distinguished from a sire line. It is very prominent as a winner of the three classic events (fifty-two) -- (eighteen Derbies, twenty Oaks, fourteen Legers." The notes for the No. 15 Family, Royal Mare, conclude that "It is very evident that the members of this family do not come early, or else are not partial to short courses, for I cannot find a winner of either the 1,000 or 2,000 Guineas, and this is corroborated by the fact that its St. Leger winners are out of proportion to the Oaks and Derby."

As these notes suggest, a minority of the families were categorized as sire families, or as running families. The first five families are running lines, and the No. 3, 8, 11, 12, and 14 families are sire lines. The No. 3 Family has the distinction of being both a running and sire line.

The Method

Since Lowe didn't actively survive to explore the uses of his research, his followers have had differences of opinion about the most effective ways to use it. The most common tenets, however, follow.

The family number is traced through descent of the female family line to the original mare in the *General Stud Book*. Regardless of the fact that the sire contributes half of the genetic material, the number follows from the mare's line. This has the positive factor of making breeders more aware of their female lines but is suspect as an interpretation of genetics.

As a result, each horse in the pedigree has a family number. This means that in a five-cross pedigree, there would be 32 families recognized, and in a six-cross, there would be 64. Obviously, there would be duplications, and the repetitions and alternation of family numbers was given great significance by those who used the Figure System to breed their horses.

The interpretation of the pedigree of a foal or prospective foal is arrived at by assessing these female family numbers, and usually there is mention of balancing the running elements with the sire elements. Some families are also reputed to work better in conjunction with others, creating almost a nick in the female line.

Practical Applications?

About 13 minutes of semi-reflective thought brings some problems to mind on the question of actually using the Figure System in breeding racehorses. For one thing, it is essentially a listing of historical performances. This wouldn't be much of a problem if the performances were moderately recent, but a horse with no stakes winners in his last five dams still may belong to the No. 1 Family.

This is so because the numbers are traced through the tail-female line of the pedigree, and regardless of the stock grafted on top of the bottom line, the resulting individual's family number remains the same.

Clearly, modern events do not agree completely with historical precedents. And if they do not in the affairs of men, why should they do so with our horses? As the family numbers generated by Lowe became a monolithic force in pedigree circles, those who were researching the facts about breeding found the Lowe family numbers to be an obstacle of outrageous difficulty. Many breeders wanted to believe in the numbers because they had the allure of science and gave the breeders a tangible goal to strive for.

In the face of obvious fact, some people went on searching for a way to make the family numbers fit. This obviously frustrated Joe Estes, who said that a top racehorse can be condemned by breeders because "he does not come from a 'sire family,' a sire family being a myth invented by Bruce Lowe."[2] Estes's companion at *The Blood-Horse*, Joe Palmer, also fired a few good mortars at the Figure System, noting that "the monumental work of Bruce Lowe should be at every breeder's fingertips, and a careful application of its principles will enable him to avoid such stud failures as Cyllene, Fair Play, Star Shoot, Fairway, Highflyer, and others, these being from families which do not produce either sires or racers."[3]

Both Fair Play and Star Shoot were from the No. 9 family, and some people were daft enough to believe they weren't good sires. Cyllene, one of the great sires in England and the paternal grandsire of Phalaris, was allowed to be exported to Argentina, at least in part because his family number wasn't good enough. The Argentines took him gladly, and the grand animal became a cornerstone of their breed.

Estes's work with statistics showed that the Figure System was actually a classic case of opportunity. The most populous female families were, in general, the most successful. The families with the larger numbers of classic winners were the same families who accounted for the larger proportion of the breed. And their success was in proportion to their representation. A family might account for 12 percent of the breed through the tail-female line, and its members would have won 12 percent of the classics, more or less.

Furthermore, the Lowe families from first to least, for instance, also follow their rankings in having the largest number of claiming race winners. The rankings, in the final estimation, are a measure of quantity but not quality.

Lowe's work was interesting because it urged breeders to take more thought about the bottom lines in their breeding plans, but the theory was not thought out with an understanding of statistics and opportunity. As a result, it would have little use for any practical breeder today.

The Figure System and Mitochondrial DNA

In a process wholly funded by Gainsborough Stud Management Ltd., E.W. Hill and others produced a study of mitochondrial DNA from a sample population of 100 Thoroughbreds and attempted to trace their ancestry back to the original tap-root mares, which are also the basis of Lowe's figure system. The researchers published their resulting documentation in Animal Genetics in 2002, and their conclusions fairly rocked the foundations of the figure system.

Although their small sample did not include horses from all the Lowe female families, the researchers did find that there was significant variation in the expected attribution of lines to particular mares. Some lines previously treated as distinct families showed indication of common ancestry, and a few others showed that there were not the marks of common ancestry expected, indicating that there may be errors either in the stud books or in the genetic data used to infer relationships.

For instance in a case of likely common ancestry, Family 4 (the Layton Barb mare), Family 11 (the Pet Mare), and Family 13 (the Sedbury Royal mare) could well descend from a single source, according to the investigators. As the writer in the research paper noted, these families had conjecturally been thought to stem from a common ancestor, and the mitochondrial DNA research gives this line of thought further substance.

The researchers go so far, however, as to propose that perhaps only a dozen animals created the 19 lines studied in the survey.

Considering the social and economic roots of the Thoroughbred, however, this too isn't terribly peculiar. Most of the best stock that contributed to forming the breed was held by the monarchy or by members of the aristocracy, and I would expect that considerable sharing of valued family heirlooms (in this case, horses) was the norm rather than the exception.

Although this information is rather fascinating historically, what is its value to a modern breeder? None. The stud book is not going to go back, even if the data were specific and conclusive and unquestionable, with a black marker and disqualify particular horses or lines from registry. They have proven themselves of value to the breed over the past 200 years, and breeders will continue to judge their worth by the results they get on the racetracks of the world.

Nor do the individual names from this time have any significance to breeding a horse today. The genetic recombinations have made the Thoroughbred horse today a significantly different beast from his ancestors of even the 19th or early 20th centuries. And the evidence from the racetrack and the breeding farms from the last two, three, or four generations is the guide for establishing what is significant and valuable for a breeder today.

The notes following were condensed largely from Treacy & Walker.

No. 1 Tregonwell's Natural Barb Mare

This is essentially a running, as distinguished from a sire, line. It is very prominent as a winner of the three classic events (52) – 18 Derbys, 20 Oaks, 14 St. Legers. The No. 1 family has figured more largely than any line as a winner of the 1,000 and 2,000 Guineas, and the fillies have proved themselves high-class, prolific broodmares. The earliest horses of note in the family were Old Snap, and his Goldfinder, never beaten. Very few great sires have sprung from this line in proportion to its winners. The best are Partisan, Melbourne, Bay Middleton, Glencoe, Whalebone, and Whisker. Minting is from this line, also his sire Lord Lyon, Silvio, Craig Millar, and Trumpeter. The above, except Whalebone and Whisker (both good all-round horses), are mostly esteemed through their female progeny. The members of the family possess great quality, brilliancy, and good looks as a rule. To this family trace such as: Prince Palatine, Cicero, Wrack, Gay Crusader, Chelandry, Neil Gow, Celt, Voter, Bend Or, Meddler, Spinaway (1872 by Macaroni and winner of the 1,000 Guineas and Oaks), Jest, Black Jester, Cap and Bells, Spearmint, Swynford, and High Time. [Clearly, the notes above were written well before the importance of either Swynford or Phalaris was evident to breeders, English or otherwise.]

Modern descendants: Abdos, Admiring, Searching, La Troienne, Bimelech, Sea Hero, Glowing Tribute, Affectionately, Personality, Priceless Gem, Allez France, Afleet, Altesse Royale, Alycidon, Ambiorix, Arts and Letters, Blenheim, Buckpasser, Dr. Fager, Queen Hopeful.

No. 2 Burton's Barb Mare

Burton's Barb mare family, like its great rival, is a very valuable dam strain and has furnished a large contingent of Oaks winners. Forty-eight classic events have fallen to its share (nine Derbys, 19 Oaks, 20 St. Legers). In St. Leger winners, it nearly doubles No. 1, which would point to its being better staying blood, though it is somewhat behind No. 1 as a Derby winner (strain).

As a sire line it is distinctly ahead of its great rival, and though not in the front rank by a long way, many celebrities may be counted amongst its members. Prominent are Whiskey, Blacklock, Sir Hercules, Voltigeur, and Lord Clifden in England. It was never strongly represented in America in early days, except through Yorkshire and Hurrah, but of recent years, frequent importations of the family have filled up this gap. While successful sires sprang from this family, they were either got by horses which were in sire families, or won their successes by being mated with dams from the sire families, thus showing their dependence on sire blood. To this family trace such as: Himyar, Keystone, The Tetrarch, Peter Pan, Cremorne, Rosedrop, Gainsborough, Clarissimus, William the Third, Hurry On, Carbine, Sundridge, Ajax, Mother Goose, Priscilla Ruley, and Mars. Alcide, Alleged, Aureole, Ballymoss, Bold Lad (64 out of Barn Pride), Candy Spots, Cannonade, Cosmah, Northern Dancer, Almahmoud, Halo, Feola, Round Table, and Forty Niner.

No. 3 Dam of Two True Blues

This is perhaps the most valuable family in the Stud Book because it possesses the dual qualities of both a running and a sire line. Its descendants have won 44 of the three great races (15 Derbys, 15 Oaks, 14 St. Legers). It has produced more Derby winners than No. 2 and nearly as many winners of the Oaks, and the fillies are both prolific and successful as dams. As a sire line it stands nearly, if not quite, at the top of the tree and mates well with all the other families, being very pliable in its nature and improving every other strain of blood it is crossed with. It is only necessary to mention the following names to show how prolific of winners its sons have invariably been when put to stud work: Sir Peter Teazle, Buzzard (by Woodpecker), Tramp, Velocipede, Lanercost, The Flying Dutchman, Stockwell, Sir Hercules, Musket, Galopin, King Tom, Isinglass, American-bred Eclipse, and Rayon d'Or.

To this family trace such as: Kizel Kourgan, La Fleche, Memoir, John o' Gaunt, Endurance by Right, Polymelus, Radium, Qu'Elle Est Belle, Brown Prince, Fifinella, Irish Lad, McGee, Cleopatra, and Pompey. Beau Pere, Blandford, Bold Bidder, Caro, Caveat, Dancing Brave, Jolypha, Dante, and Davona Dale.

No. 4 The Layton Barb Mare

This family is prolific both in numbers and classic winners – 33 have fallen to its share, nine Derbys, 12 Oaks, and 12 St. Legers. The family comes from a pure Barb source and is distinctly feminine in character. No great all-round sires have sprung from this family, though many of them have been highly valued through their fillies, to wit: Matchem, Thormanby, Bona Vista, Goldfinch, Iroquois, and notably Wenlock, whose daughters are veritable gold mines.

To this family trace such as: Hourless, Le Sancy, North Star III, Sir Visto, Bruleur, Prestige, Rock Sand, Man o' War, Whisk Broom II, The Finn, Uncle, Artful, Ladkin, Wise Counsellor, Chance Play, Crusader, and Epinard. It's in the Air, Amour Drake, Aryenne, Quest for Fame, Assault, Bella Paola, Canonero, Gallant Bloom, Marguerite, and Ribot.

No. 5 Daughter of Massey's Black Barb

Twenty-nine classic events have been entered to No. 5, in the proportion of 12 Derbys, 10 Oaks, and seven St. Legers. The horses of this family which stand out conspicuously are Gladiateur, Hermit, and Doncaster.

As a running line it is most valuable, and from its pliability mates with most of the strains, preferring sire blood. Great sires in the family are few and far between, i.e., as compared with sire lines.

To this family also trace such as: Sunstar, Princess Dorris, Minoru, Grand Parade, Knight of the Thistle, Galtee More, Ard Patrick, White Eagle, Marie Stuart, Elf, and Flying Ebony.

Moccasin, Apalachee, Thong, Nureyev, Sadler's Wells, Thatch, Bold Lad (64 out of Misty Morn), Reviewer, Brown Berry, Avatar, Capot, Quick as Lightning, Inside Information, Educated Risk, and Native Dancer.

No. 6 Old Bald Peg

This family played a conspicuous part in the early and middle ages of classic racing. To Diomed, one of its members, was accorded the honor of winning the first Derby, run in 1780. Diomed was imported to America, where his blood was highly esteemed, seeing that his stock (through Lexington principally in the male line) was dominant for many years on the American turf. That the blood is only valuable as dam blood is now generally recognized by American breeders.

No. 6 has always been a poor sire family. The best horse it ever produced was Priam, and his failure in America was mainly owing to being bred back to his own family descendants from Diomed. The paucity of Oaks winners indicates the decadence of the line.

No line had better chances, as it attracted attention in early racing days through Flying Childers, Young Giantess, Eleanor, Julia, and Priam. To this family also trace such as: Corcyra, Plenipotentiary, Old Man (Argentine), Ogden, Old Rosebud, Worth, Sansovino, Teresina, Blue Tit, Tranquil, Polemarch, and Cherry Pie.

[The writer mentions the importance of Diomed's blood to American racing through Lexington, leaving a bit of an impression that the latter great sire is from this family also. Not so, Lexington comes from family No. 12, but he also was one of the primary "taints" that allowed the English Jockey Club officials to rule most American-breds "half-bred" for exclusion to the *General Stud Book* through most of the first half of the 20th century. In a bit of particularly venomous logic, the writer concludes that Priam failed due to matings that carried the Diomed blood, but how is this such a problem when the lines of descent are counted through the dam? Really, isn't this history being read so that it agrees with preconceived ideas?]

Alibhai, Big Game, Hyperion, Sickle, Pharamond, and Matatina.

No. 7 Black Legged Royal Mare

This line is familiar to pedigree men through West Australian, its best representative. Like No. 6, there is a preponderance of Derby over Oaks and St. Leger winners, which would seem to point to its fillies being, as a general thing, wanting in feminine character and not over good producers.

To this family trace such as: Caligula, Flying Fox, Persimmon, Diamond Jubilee, Semolina, Donovan, and American Flag.

Arazi, Bering, Coaltown, and Wistful.

No. 8 Bustler Mare (Dam of Byerly Turk Mare)

This line is one of the most valuable sire families in the Stud Book, not excepting No. 3. Not only have many great sires come directly from the line, such as Marske, Orville, Sultan, Newminster, Cain, Humphrey Clinker, etc., but there is a marked tendency to leave equally great sons and sires behind them.

Marske begot Eclipse, a greater sire than himself; Orville was inferior as a racehorse and sire to Emilius his son; Bay Middleton was more esteemed than his sire Sultan, as was Melbourne than his sire Humphrey Clinker; while few will be found to dispute the fact that great as Newminster proved to be at turf and stud, he was outclassed by both Lord Clifden and Hermit in these respects.

To this family belong Sun Briar, Constancy, Maskette, Perth, Melton, Ayrshire, St. Serf, Sweep, Novelty, Eternal, Pennant, Black Servant, John P. Grier, and Bubbling Over.

Alcibiades, Menow, Assert, By My Guest, Bewitch, Bikala, Blue Larkspur, Bold Ruler, Storm Cat, Damascus, El Gran Senor, Nijinsky, and The Minstrel.

No. 9 The Old Vintner Mare

If any proof were wanting to show that families retain their original characteristics, even though they carry much contemporary blood in their veins, the history of this family affords strong evidence of the fact. Though not so high on the roll of winners as many of its rivals, it makes a goodly show and contains the names of such remarkable racehorses as Mercury, Dick Andrews, Barefoot, Peter, and Bendigo, and in Australia, Navigator, Trident, Camoola. Despite this, it would be a difficult task for the warmest believer in the family to point to one really high-class sire in its ranks.

This is the more remarkable because of the proportions of St. Leger winners over Derby and Oaks, showing how really stout its sons have been, as witness Peter and Bendigo. The three Australian horses mentioned above were noted for their staying powers; also Commotion (by Panic), winner of the St. Leger (and two champion races, three miles, under 5 min. 27 sec.), yet a pronounced stud failure.

To this family also belong Fair Play, Friar Rock, Omar Khayyam, Sir Martin, Sir Barton, Star Shoot, Sysonby, Cyllene, Winkfield's Pride, Dark Ronald, Upset, Bramble, Billy Kelly, Mumtaz Mahal, Nellie Morse, and Princess Doreen.

[The writer's comments about the "sire qualities" of this family is the sort of pristine horse manure rarely found in stables. If some of the stallions in the paragraph above weren't enough to make breeders discard this theory, just think about some of the modern animals below.]

Alydar, Abernant, Ack Ack, Alzao, Asmena, Asterus, Bet Twice, Bold Forbes, Cicada, Clever Trick, Corrida, Mahmoud, and Zafonic.

No. 10 Daughter of Gower Stallion (Dam of Childers' mare)

This line came to the front early in its career by winning the sixth Derby with Aimwell, a son of Marc Antony. After this, winners were returned at rare intervals, and the family never assumed any importance until Blink Bonny appeared upon the scene and accomplished Eleanor's hitherto unrivaled performance of winning the double of Oaks and Derby.

The line cannot be included amongst the high-class running lines. As a sire line, it has been successful when backed up with plenty of sire and running blood, as witness Blair Athol, Petrarch, Hampton, and Fireworks. It will be found that many of the outside (obscure origin) families have blazoned into notoriety after years of silence, and this has been brought about in nearly all cases by striking combinations of the running lines 1, 2, 3, 4, and 5, which have been grafted on to the parent stems of the outside lines.

To this family also belong Bayardo, Lemberg, Tristan, Beldame, Bonnie Scotland, Black Toney, and Picaroon.

Bed o' Roses, Canadiana, Deputy Minister, Marquetry, and Riverman.

No. 11 The Sedbury Royal Mare

This family includes many illustrious names that have helped to make the English stud famous. The first prominent horses of the family were Squirt and Regulus, and more recently Birdcatcher and Faugh-a-Ballagh kept up its prestige. (Orme, Love Wisely, Great Scot, and Rightaway have done well in recent years.) St. Simon hails from its ranks. In America, the name "Australian" will long be treasured, while in the Antipodes, Marvellous claims the honor of siring Marvel, probably the fastest mile horse ever saddled in Australia and the conqueror of Carbine over that distance of ground.

To this family also belong Tanya, Royal Hampton, His Highness, Spinaway (1878 by Leamington and important American producer), and Plack.

Aunt Edith, Dickens Hill, Eight Thirty, and Honest Pleasure.

No. 12 Royal Mare (Dam of Brimmer Mare)

This line affords an instance of one of the anomalies of breeding, for whereas the Oaks winners are out of all proportion to the solitary and fluky Derby winner Cadland (and two St. Leger winners) and would thereby lead one to the conclusion that it is effeminate in its nature, experience shows it to be the stoutest and most masculine in the stud book all the way up from Eclipse. To the name of Eclipse we can add a larger number of good sires from this family than any other now existing, except No. 3. Some of the best-known names are Conductor, Voltaire, Sheet Anchor, Weatherbit, Edmund, Oxford, Sterling, Scottish Chief, Marsyas, Prince Charlie (and his son Salvator), Ethelbert, Restitution, Adventurer, Kingston (1849 by Venison and sire of Oaks winner Queen Bertha), Springfield, Lexington, and some of the males of the Levity family. It is also a line that stands inbreeding to itself. This is more noticeable in America, where there has been a great deal of inbreeding to the Levity family and with good results. Salvator was the result of a cross of Prince Charlie (12), onto Salina of the same family; and what is more remarkable, Prince Charlie is himself inbred to 12, and Salina is by Lexington of the same line. It will, however, be found that in all cases of inbreeding the 12 line to itself with success, it was accompanied by a strong return to the running families as well (through collateral branches), to insure the requisite amount of racing vitality to the offspring.

To this family also belong Mimi, St. Maclou, Cantilever, Amphion, Ornament, Duke of Montrose, King James, Stimulus, and Coventry.

Bally Ache, Bramalea, Roberto, Challedon, Delta Judge, and Ivanjica.

No. 13 Royal Mare (Dam of Mare by Darcy's White Turk)

The first horse to give any prominence in this line was the unbeaten Highflyer. Stella (Oaks), in 1784, was the first classic winner, then Fyldener won the St. Leger in 1806, and we find nothing classical again till Ellis won the St. Leger in 1836. Then appeared the sensational Orlando, and after this winners cropped up every now and again.

To this family also belong Galliard, Hamburg Belle, Shotover, Beadsman, Kingston (1884 by Spendthrift and leading American sire), Pillory, Grey Lag, and Pharos.

Akarad, Akiyda, Acamas, Baldric, Colonial Affair, Dahlia, Gold Digger, Mr. Prospector, Natashka, and Ivory Wand.

No. 14 The Oldfield Mare

As a classic winner, this family does not take high rank. Taking into consideration the inferior figure it cuts as a classic winner, one would hardly look to its ranks for great sires if one followed the orthodox plan of "using only running families." On the one side, we require stout masculine breeding, combined with strong individuality, symmetry, and ability to race, if possible, and on the other soundness of constitution with an accumulation of vitality only to be acquired by close inbreeding to Nos. 1, 2, 3, 4, and 5. The first sire of any note in the 14 line was Trumpator. Then came Touchstone, a horse that has made himself a great name for all times, The Libel, Touchet, Buccaneer, Saraband, Carnival, and Saccharometer. Also Leamington, imported to America, destined to sire Iroquois.

To this family also belong Pretty Polly, St. Amant, Craganour, Rabelais, Ballot, Ultimus, Tetratema, and Pot au Feu.

Alydaress, Balidaress, Desirable, Barathea, Brigadier Gerard, Coronation, Hard to Beat, and Rainbow Quest.

No. 15 Royal Mare (Dam of Old Whynot)

It is very evident that the members of this family do not come early, or else are not partial to short courses, for I cannot find a winner of either the 1,000 or 2,000 Guineas, and this is corroborated by the fact that its St. Leger winners are out of proportion to the Oaks and Derby. This paucity of good females would indicate its gradual extinction, and such appears to be the case, though it has come again with a spurt in the shape of Foxhall and Harvester. As a sire family it has always been a pronounced failure. To this family also belong Hanover, Alarm (1869 by Eclipse [1855] and sire of Belmont winner Panique and Domino's sire Himyar), and Chaleureux. [Hanover, from this family of pronounced stud failures, led the American sire list four times and was probably the best stallion in the U.S. in the years between Lexington and Domino.]

In my brief search for contemporary representatives, this is the first family that came up blank. Their numbers are obviously small, as with almost all the "outside" families, but this one may be getting very scarce.

No. 16 Sister to Stripling by Hutton's Spot

Up to the time St. Gatien (1884) ran a dead heat for the Derby with Harvester, the line had been absolutely silent as regards classic winners, though many fair racehorses (and sires) came from its ranks, notably Tibthorpe, Brown Bread, etc. The line is better known to the breeding and sporting world as the "Agnes family." The gradual building up of the Agnes family is one of the most interesting problems in the annals of breeding.

There is no pedigree in the stud book with so much concentrated vital force as this of Lily Agnes.

To this family trace Broomstick, Sceptre, Spanish Prince, Sardanapale, Ormonde, Kendal, Zinfandel, Desmond, Buchan, Pommern, Papyrus, St. Germans, and Craig an Eran.

Plucky Liege (her sons Sir Gallahad III, Bull Dog, Admiral Drake, and Bois Roussel), Petition, Carnauba, Chateaugay, Primonetta, Detroit, Fair Salinia, Green Dancer, Herbager, Holy Bull, and Slip Anchor.

No. 17 Byerly Turk Mare (Dam of Wharton Mare)

The family is best known in England through Pantaloon, in Australia by Yattendon, and in America by Sir Modred and Cheviot, his brother, sire of Rey el Santa Anita. Pantaloon's blood has always been esteemed highly and should be more bred to than it is, considering how well it blends with Touchstone, Blacklock, Stockwell, and Melbourne. The 17 line, though not a prolific line, has turned out a few really high-class sires. There is no question that good individuals of this family are valuable acquisitions to any stud.

To this family trace such as Negofol and Macdonald II.

Danzig Connection, Pine Circle, Lyphard, Nobiliary, Jacola, and Johnstown.

No. 18 Daughter of Old Woodcock (Dam of Daughter of Old Spot)

Though a slightly larger classic winner than three of the preceding lines, Nos. 14, 16, and 17, I have placed it behind them in order of merit, as it appears to be on the decline. Most of its victories were won in the early and middle days.

To this family trace such as: Roamer, Trenton, Rose Tree, and Percentage.

April the Fifth, Durban, and Strawberry Road.

No. 19 Daughter of Davill's Old Woodcock

The descendants of this line have been singularly unfortunate as regards the higher classic races, considering the number of phenomenal horses the family has produced. Only one Derby and four St. Legers can be placed to its credit. Sir Hugo, in 1892, was the first Derby winner for the family. No. 19 has produced no Oaks winners and, indeed, very few mares of high-class racing form (if we except Plaisanterie and one or two others), though they develop into good dams. In spite of its want of success in classic events, a glance at some of the celebrated horses descended from its rank shows how valuable the blood is: Isonomy, Vespasian, Monarque, Vedette, Plaisanterie, Alarm (1842 by Venison and winner of the Ascot Gold Cup), Sabinus, Clearwell, Surefoot, Gorgos, Electra, Cambuscan, Lowlander, Count Schomberg, Hammerkop, Llangibby, Sailor Prince, Childwick, and Gallinule. The sons have not only been good racehorses but good sires as a rule.

To this family trace Colin, Spion Kop, Tracery, Trap Rock, and Salmon Trout.

Lalun, Never Bend, Bold Reason, Bolkonski, Crepello, Kooyonga, and Kotashaan.

No. 20 Daughter of Gascoigne's Foreign Horse

The line is an effeminate but improving one, and more largely represented today in the last volume of the stud book than Nos. 15, 16, 17, 18, and 19. Traducer (exported to New Zealand) proved to be a high-class sire.

To this family trace such as: Tagalie, St. Florian, Friar Marcus, Le Sagittaire, Virgil, Henry of Navarre, and Sarazen.

Alysheba, Blue Peter, Comtesse de Loir, Miesque, Lady Pitt, and Olden Times.

No. 21 The Moonah Barb Mare of Queen Anne

A family well known to pedigree students through that excellent horse Sweetmeat. Like the 20 line, it runs mostly to good fillies. The members of the family are evidently not early beginners or sprinters, as none of the shorter classic races have fallen to their share. In America the line is well and favorably known through imported Tranby (by Blacklock), whose name appears in so many good pedigrees across the water, where he undoubtedly helped to lay the foundation of Levity's greatness. It is worth noting that the triumphs of this family have been mainly owing to its association with the No. 2 line. I would infer that the fillies of this family should be put to sires closely inbred to Blacklock through the 2 and 3 lines to give their progeny the necessary running qualities. To inbreed 21 to itself or to 14, 15, 16, 17, 18, 19, and so on, is only excusable where there is some intense inbreeding to Nos. 1, 2, 3, and 4 on both sides and in the first two or three removes. Where these conditions do not exist it is clearly a step backward in breeding.

To this family trace Hastings, Plaudit, Bachelor's Button, Lonely, The White Knight, Prudery, and Bachelor's Double.

Bride Elect, Broad Brush, Decathlon, Doyoun, In Reality, and Lost Soul.

No. 22 Belgrade Turk Mare (Dam of Bay Bolton Mare)

Gladiator has made this family famous for all time, and evidence is forthcoming that the family is by no means dead (despite the poor figure it has cut in the Derby, Oaks, and St. Leger), as St. Blaise and Merry Hampton testify. Up to the time St. Blaise won in 1883, the line had not been fortunate enough to win a Derby. It is no exception to the rest of the outside families in requiring the aid of running lines and is decidedly feminine in its character.

To this family trace Your Majesty, Our Lassie, St. Frusquin, Omnium II, Captain Cuttle, and Manna.

Awaasif, Snow Bride, Lammtarra, Blushing Groom, Éclair, Khaled, Flying Paster, Korveya, Lady's Secret, and Mill Reef.

No. 23 Piping Peg (Dam of the Hobby Mare)

Well-known stallions of this family that deserve mention are Solon and his son Barcaldine, Hagioscope, Pepper and Salt, Miguel, and in America, Duncombe and all the "Gallopade" family. This family is a valuable one and assimilates easily with the best running blood.

To this family trace Ethelbert, Signorina, Signorinetta, Domino, Yankee, Correction, Blackstock, Edith Cavell, Florence Nightingale, and Zev.

Twilight Tear, A Gleam, Bardstown, Affirmed, Best Turn, Chief's Crown, Chris Evert, and Dance Smartly.

No. 24 Helmsley Turk Mare (Dam of Rockwood Mare)

If this line were judged by classic wins, it stands very low, only a solitary St. Leger by The Baron. Yet some of the males of the family have been such excellent sires that it almost deserves the rank of a sire line. The sons of this 24 line have, in two cases (Camel and The Baron), earned imperishable fame as the sires respectively of Touchstone and Stockwell.

To this family trace such as: Firenze and Hindoo.

Carry Back.

No. 25 A Brimmer Mare (Dam of Old Scarborough Mare)

There are two Derby winners and one Oaks, viz. Selfton (D), Azor (D), and Zinc (Oaks). This filly won the 1,000 Guineas, as did also Zeal and Arab from this family. Other notable horses are Young Melbourne, Comus, and Slane.

To this family also trace: Planet, Handspring, and Ballyhoo Bey.

Hatoof and Mrs. Penny

No. 26 Daughter of Merlin (Dam of Mare by Darley Arabian)

There is no plea (save its unfitness) for this family being so low on the list of classic winners (two Derbys, two Oaks, and one St. Leger) because few lines got such an excellent send off consequent upon King Herod's success as a racehorse sire.

To this family trace Orby, Rhodora, The Commoner, Nasturtium, Glenelg, Longfellow, and Ten Broeck.

De La Rose, Dunette, Lyric Fantasy, and Park Top.

No. 27 A Spanker Mare (Dam of Byerly Turk Mare)

One Derby and one St. Leger, viz. Pero Gomez (L) and Phosphorus (D), while Firebrand, the Selim filly, and May Day won the 1,000 Guineas in 1842, 1815, and

1834. Enthusiast (winner of the 2,000 Guineas), Arbitrator, Cherry, and Saunterer come also from this family, which has not singled itself out by any specialty and like all the outside lines is wholly dependent upon the more favored ones.

To this family also traces Star Hampton.

By the time we get this low on the Lowe Family rankings, the numbers of representatives for these families are extremely low. It isn't that all the descendants are claimers; there simply are none . . . or are very scarce in most cases. Except for families No. 29 and 42, I found no modern representatives in my quick survey. Doubtless some good horses out there were overlooked.

No. 28 Daughter of Place's White Turk (Dam of Coppin Mare)

Emilius has made this family famous, but nothing else of note has spring from its ranks except Wings, Imperator, Actauon, Dalesman, Barillon, etc. Emilius is the only high-class sire in the line, which is evidently going to the wall.

To this family also trace Camilla and Chouberski.

No. 29 A Natural Barb Mare (Dam of a Bassett Arabian Mare)

This family is apparently dying out. In Australia it is known as the Lady Emily family; Reprieve, Pardon, and Queen's Head, by Yattendon, brought the line into prominence a few years back. Le Noir also comes from this family.

Lucero.

No. 30 Daughter of Duc de Chartre's Hawker

Stamford and Delpini are the best known of a line which is poorly represented today. Stamford was a full brother to Archduke and Paris, the three being from Horatio by Eclipse, and she was bred for 10 years consecutively to Sir Peter. There was an interval of five years between the two Derby winners, Paris being the 10th foal by Sir Peter.

No. 31 Dick Burton's Mare (Sometimes called a Barb mare)

If this line really had a pure origin, it has failed to fulfill expectation. The only classic winners are Ruler (St. Leger) in 1780 and Fazzoletto (2,000 Guineas) in 1856. It will be recognized of late years by Cape Flyaway, King of the Forest, Kilcock, Bellerophon, and that good mare Canezou (1,000 Guineas) by Melbourne (No. 1), dam by Velocipede (3), he by Blacklock (2).

To this family also traces Chicle.

No. 32 A Royal Barb Mare (Dam of Dodsworth)

It is very evident (as in the case of 31) that the pure origin availed nothing in this case for we find only one Oaks winner, Nike by Alexander, and Challacombe, winner of the St. Leger in 1905. The line will be better identified by horses of a later date – The Caster Barbarian, Fitz-Gladiator, and Arthur Wellesley.

It is quite probably that Nos. 29, 31, and 32 were not of pure Eastern descent at bottom. It has been a loose fashion from all time to designate a filly of first cross by an Arab stallion as "an Arab" amongst men who do not breed to race and attach no value to pedigrees, and in early days the mistake might easily have crept into records unwittingly.

To this family also trace Mandy Hamilton, Highball, Roseben, Oiseau, Whistle Jacket, and Supremus.

No. 33 Sister to Honeycomb Punch

This line can only claim a solitary Derby winner, Sergeant, in 1784. Dungannon is from this line, which has almost died out.

No. 34 Daughter of Hautboy (Dam of Coneyskin's Mare, progenitor of Hutton's Daphne)

Antonio in 1819 and Birmingham in 1830 placed two St. Legers to the credit of this family, not otherwise distinguished.

The foregoing numbers include all the classic winners of the Derby, Oaks, and St. Leger, excepting the first St. Leger, Allabaculia, whose pedigree is not given in the stud book. There are a few well-known English, American, and Australian horses from families that have never produced a classic winner in England, though they trace to the English Stud Book, and for this latter reason I have included them in a non-classic list to follow, so that the horses of the line may also be identified by a figure.

No. 35 Daughter of Bustler (the dam of the grandam of the Byerly Turk and Bay Bolton mares)

It is quite possible this Bustler mare is identical with the "Daughter of Bustler, dam of the daughter of the Byerly Turk" forming tap root of the No. 8 line, but in the absence of actual proof they must be classed as separate families. The prominent horses of this family are Haphazard, Bustard, Newcourt, Consul, Battledore, and Le Marechal.

No 36 Daughter of Curwen's Bay Barb

From this mare Economist descends. Economist and the great colonial racehorse and stallion Lochiel are the only horses of note in the family, showing once more that the outside lines must be crossed with No. 1, 2, 3, and 4 to insure success. Great Scot also comes from this family.

No. 37 Sister to Old Merlin

Bourbon (St. Leger winner), Dr. Syntax, and Little Red Rover trace to this mare, but the family is gradually getting extinct.

To this family also trace descendants of Melrose, including Purchase, Eon, Eole, St. Saviour, etc.

No. 38 Thwait's Dun Mare

I find no horses of any note, save Pot-8-os, in this line, which speaks volumes for the potency of Eclipse as a sire. Few better horses than Pot-8-os ever carried a saddle.

No. 39 Bonny Black (From a Daughter of a Persian Stallion, Dam of Cyprus Arabian Mare)

Splendora, imported to Australia, and her descendants, including a high-class horse, Dagworth, by Yattendon.

Aside from Val d'Or and Vanicius, I know nothing from this family that attained any prominence in England during this century.

No. 40 A Royal Mare (Dam of Brimmer Mare)

Boston, sire of Lexington, traces to this mare.

No. 41 Grasshopper Mare (Dam of Daughter of Hartley's Blind Horse)

From this mare came Bagot and Portrait.

No. 42 A Spanker Mare (Dam of Mare by Pulleine's Arabian, Fourth Dam of Bolton's Patriot Mare)

Rowton (St. Leger), Oiseau, Cetus, Berrill, and Theobald are from this line.

Czaravich.

No. 43 Natural Barb Mare (Presented by Emperor of Morocco) (Great-grandam of Cardigan Colt)

Balfe and Underhand come from this family.

In addition to the Bruce Lowe families, the following are noted in the *British Thoroughbred Horse* (Mr. W. Allison):

No. 44 – Bustler Mare. No winners; no sires.

No. 45 – Young Cade Mare. Maid of Ely (Stud Book, vol. II, p. 121)

No. 46 – Babraham Mare. Matchem Mare (sister to Gordon) (Stud Book, vol. I, p. 124)

No. 47 – Spectator Mare. No winners; no sires.

No. 48 – Shield's Galloway Mare.

No. 49 – Whitenose Mare.

No. 50 – Miss Euston.

Bibliography Notes

[1] J.A. Estes, *A Quarter Century of American Racing (The Blood-Horse),* 1941, p. 7.

[2] J.A. Estes, *The Blood-Horse,* December 6, 1941, p. 744.

[3] J.A. Estes, *The Blood-Horse,* February 10, 1940, p. 256.

CHAPTER 15

Quantification of Racing Performance in the Research of Harry Laughlin

Working independently of the traditional methods of analyzing pedigrees and racing performance, Dr. Harry Laughlin attempted to quantify what makes a racehorse fast and what probability lies in particular matings.

His results were important to the development of research into breeding horses because they showed that a consistent program could produce good results and that inheritance of racing ability through planned matings was not just a matter of luck.

Laughlin's research, largely unknown to breeders for nearly three-quarters of a century, is presented in considerable detail in the following assessment.

Finding Harry Laughlin

Tucked away on the parklands of Keeneland Racecourse in Lexington, Ky., is the Keeneland Association Library. The library's collection includes rare and valuable manuscripts on the lineage, breeding, history, and tradition of the Thoroughbred. Some items in its collection are priceless.

Open to the public, the decor of fine paneling, polished hardwood bookcases, stuffed furniture, and Oriental carpets suggests the tradition, pageantry, and quality of the Thoroughbred itself. It is a special place for anyone fascinated with the Thoroughbred.

Here, I first learned of Dr. Harry Laughlin. Graciously allowed to explore some uncataloged boxes of papers and other materials neatly stacked in the library's storage room, I found the first of Laughlin's papers.

Laughlin (1880 - 1943) was a geneticist employed by the prestigious Carnegie Institution of Washington at its Cold Spring Laboratory in Cold Spring Harbor, N.Y., from 1910 to 1940. Laughlin was interested in human genetics, and his thoughts on this subject are available at major public libraries. To advance his theories about human genetics, he conducted extensive research and experiments on the breeding of Thoroughbreds. Information on his Thoroughbred research is much more difficult to come by, but I set out to learn more about Laughlin's research on breeding Thoroughbreds. Over time, I searched for his papers in libraries around the country. There were many dead ends. Finally, through a combination of detective work and plain good luck, I found the mother lode: Laughlin's unpublished correspondence, notes, and papers in the Pickler Memorial Library at Northeast Missouri State University in Kirksville, Mo.

These materials offer valuable insights into how and why Laughlin came to study Thoroughbreds. As part of understanding how Laughlin came to conduct genetic research on the Thoroughbred, one must first understand eugenics.

The publication of Charles Darwin's *The Origin of the Species* in 1859 spurred a worldwide interest in genetics. In 1869, Darwin's cousin, Francis Galton, published *Hereditary Genius*. It contained the results of Galton's studies of the pedigrees of successful men as evidence that "it would be quite practical to produce a highly gifted race of men by judicious marriages during several consecutive generations."

From these studies Galton, in 1883, coined the term "eugenics," which can be defined as "the science that deals with the improvement of races and breeds, especially the human race, through the control of hereditary factors."

Dr. Charles B. Davenport, Laughlin's superior at the Carnegie Cold Spring Harbor Laboratory, described eugenics as, "The science of the improvement of the human race by better breeding."

In practical terms, however, eugenicists believe that abstract values in humans are inherited in the same way that eye color, stature, and skin color are inherited. These inherited values may be those which either are admired or scorned. Among these values which eugenicists believe are inherited are the work ethic, honesty, morality, integrity, criminal type, sexual deviation, and similar items which fall under the broad heading of "character." Persons not exhibiting admired "values" were collectively labeled as "feeble-minded" or by less generous terms such as "moron" and "idiot."

The eugenics movement enjoyed widespread popularity in the first half of the 20th century. It emerged as a respected scientific field, and prominent institutions like Carnegie devoted substantial resources to its study.

As part of the growing interest in eugenics, in 1904 Charles Davenport became the founding director of the Carnegie Institution Station for Experimental Evolution at Cold Spring Harbor. In 1910, Davenport persuaded Mrs. E.H. Harriman, widow of the railroad tycoon, to contribute $500,000 to establish the Eugenics Record Office (ERO) at the Cold Spring Harbor Laboratory. The Carnegie Institution took over the ERO in 1918 and operated it until 1940. Laughlin was hired as the superintendent of the ERO in 1910.

The mission of the ERO was to collect the pedigrees and family records of selected "feeble-minded." The idea behind the project was to prove that feeble-mindedness — as defined by the eugenicists — was a hereditary condition. Mrs. Harriman wrote to Galton in 1910, advising that "we have a plot of ground of 80 acres near New York City, and a house with a fireproof addition for our records. We have a superintendent, a stenographer and two helpers, besides six field workers . . . We have a satisfactory income . . . and have established very cordial relations with institutions for imbeciles, epileptics, insane and criminals."

The troubling part about Laughlin is not his work on Thoroughbred genetics but rather his politics. Laughlin was a racist, pure and simple. Under the cloak of science, Laughlin, Davenport, and other prominent eugenicists were able to persuade the Congress, the Supreme Court, the governors of the majority of the states, and even the President to embrace policies that were clearly racially and ethnically biased.

Laughlin believed that the positive qualities of a work ethic, morality, and intelligence were more likely to be found in the Western European stock or, as he called it, "the Nordic race." Non-Western European whites — and Jews in particular — were believed to be "inferior stock," as were all blacks, Orientals, and "mulattos."

To further his inquiries into eugenics, Laughlin needed to conduct research to better understand how certain qualities were transmitted from generation to generation. The qualities he sought to "transmit" in humans, of course, were abstract ones, things like "the work ethic" and "character" and the "desire to achieve."

Perhaps his concentration on these abstract qualities led him to become interested in the Thoroughbred, since the qualities which make up a champion racehorse, in many ways, are also abstract.

Searching for a sponsor for his wider research in eugenics, Laughlin met Walter Salmon, a successful New York real estate developer who also was an owner and breeder of Thoroughbreds. His Mereworth Farm near Lexington, Ky., raced the Preakness Stakes winner Display and bred his son Discovery. The latter was a heroic weight carrier while racing for Alfred Vanderbilt in the 1930s, and Discovery is the broodmare sire of both Native Dancer and Bold Ruler.

Mereworth, a perennial presence among the leading breeders in North America, was most notable for quantity of its produce, as the farm led the list of breeders by number of winners repeatedly. The noted speed sire Ariel was one of the farm's most successful stallions.

Merely interested in breeding better Thoroughbreds, Salmon apparently had no interest in Laughlin's politics. In 1923, quite early in Salmon's career in horses, he began funding Laughlin's research on Thoroughbreds. Between 1923 and 1932, Salmon contributed $75,762 directly to Carnegie and unknown additional amounts given directly to Laughlin as reimbursement for travel expenses. From 1924 to 1928, Salmon allowed Laughlin to carry out studies on his Thoroughbreds at Mereworth. The horses resulting from matings during this time began racing in 1926, and it was Laughlin's dream (and Salmon's hope) to develop a mathematically pure formula by which a breeder could predict the probability of a fast horse resulting from a particular mating.

Laughlin eventually did develop a formula which he published under the title of "*Racing Capacity in the Thoroughbred Horse.*" The supporting reference tables which would have made the Laughlin theory practical for breeders to use were scheduled for publication in two volumes by the Carnegie Institute in the late 1930s but never saw print, possibly because Laughlin's work in eugenics had become an embarrassment to the Carnegie Institute, due to the political use that Adolf Hitler was making of arguments based on eugenics.

For breeders, however, Laughlin's formula is intriguing because he developed an objective means to measure Thoroughbred success, and during the time he had input on matings for the Mereworth broodmare band, the farm produced a number of successes, most notably with the breeding of Discovery.

-Russell L. Meerdink

Measuring Thoroughbred Performance

Geneticists know that two basic principles must be followed when seeking to breed superior livestock:

1. A standard of the ideal animal must be established.

2. An objective means of measuring must be devised to determine how an individual animal compares with the ideal.

Defining the ideal animal is not simple.

All Thoroughbred breeders seek to breed a good horse. But what is it that a Thoroughbred must accomplish to be universally regarded as good. What is the standard against which Thoroughbreds are judged? Either distance or time should be the item measured. In racing, said Federico Tesio, "distance is measured by the stop watch, not the tape measure." If one were to believe Tesio, the index for Thoroughbred performance should be only time. This is not necessarily the case.

The difficulty with establishing a standard or index for Thoroughbred performance is complicated by the varying distances the horses are asked to run, the different ages at which the horses are asked to run and the varying weights which each horse is assigned to carry.

A Thoroughbred which cannot win at a mile has the option of being entered into races which are either longer or shorter. A Thoroughbred that cannot win carrying 126 pounds may do better carrying only 116 pounds. A horse that cannot win as a two-year-old may achieve success at three years of age. How does one go about evaluating and indexing the relative worth of Thoroughbred racing performance over an infinite combination of distances, ages and weights?

Thoroughbred breeders have long understood the importance of established indexes or benchmarks against which a horse's performance may be judged. The complicating factors of age, weight and distance have resulted in Thoroughbred performance being evaluated on the basis of money won. The item measured is money. At the end of the year, a horse either won more or won less than the average of all other Thoroughbreds for that year. The horse with the greater earnings is deemed to be the better horse. What is measured is not the underlying quality or performance of the horse, but rather the market value of the quality or performance.

Selecting Thoroughbred breeding stock on the basis of monies earned misses the mark. How much money a particular horse wins may point to nothing more than good or bad management. A good effort in a race with a small purse counts for less than a mediocre effort when a large purse is at stake. A single rich purse can skew the numbers and make relatively slow horses appear good.

Before Laughlin could attempt to develop a formula for breeding better Thoroughbreds, it was necessary for him to establish a means by which he could measure racing performance. A scientist must have some basis for measuring progress. In other words, before he could undertake the job of breeding a better horse, he first needed to understand what qualities resided in a horse generally recognized as good. He needed some standards against which he could judge horses.

Laughlin thought that five factors weighed in on the performance of every Thoroughbred and that these could be measured objectively. Sex, age at the time of performance, weight carried, distance run, and speed attained.

All these factors work together in defining a good horse. Take for instance, the impact of age in assessing Secretariat and John Henry. Secretariat was a champion of such stature that he was Horse of the Year at two and three. As winner of the Triple Crown, he was nearly invincible as a racehorse among horses of classic caliber. John Henry, on the other hand, had a good but not distinguished two-year-old year. At age three, he dropped into the claiming ranks, and it was not until midway through his fourth year that his goodness began to emerge. He continued winning major races through his ninth year.

Which is the better horse? If money won is the basis of comparison, the nod must go to John Henry with his $6.5 million of winnings compared to Secretariat's $1.3 million. But if the comparison is made on the basis of racing worth at an age eligible to win the Triple Crown, the nod clearly goes to Secretariat.

The truth is that racing worth or the ability to win races of distance over quality competition emerged at different ages for these two very good horses.

Nor is race time any more certain a measure of a horse's superiority. Clearly the horse which runs the race in the shortest time is the winner regardless of any other factor. But measuring speed is not as simple as it may appear. The configuration of the track, the radius of its turns, the depth of its surface, and whether it is grass or dirt will all have a bearing on the speed attained. All these conditions vary, but the time it takes a horse to cover a particular distance is the very essence of horse racing.

In Laughlin's estimation, to create an index, he had five variables to measure and for which compensation must be made before an index of performance can be developed. Laughlin also struggled with this problem and eventually came up with an index of his own.

To create his index, Laughlin said that each race the horse runs must be measured by a definite figure called the quality of performance. All these must be properly coordinated and correctly stressed in order to determine just how good a racehorse is and certify his biological handicap.

To compute his equation, Laughlin tried to weigh his factors and arrive at the probability of a successful breeding from mating Thoroughbreds. Thoroughbred breeders have always had a problem with selecting matings and choosing breeding stock. What is the probability that a particular mating will result in a foal with the speed that can win races? Even the dice players at the Las Vegas craps tables can predict the probability that a particular roll of the dice will add up to seven.

Until Laughlin's attempt, Thoroughbred breeders had no way to predict whether a particular mating would have one chance in 10 of producing a winner or whether the odds were even.

Even today, major breeding theories avoid the issue of probability. Dosage advocates point to the fact that most classic winners have a particular Dosage profile and a center of distribution within a specific range. That's fine for the winners. What these advocates ignore is that slow, losing horses have similar profiles. Breeding on the basis of Dosage gives no indication as to the probability of breeding a winner. One can have a stable full of horses with good Dosages and not have a winner in the bunch.

Quality of Performance: The Mathematical Formula

Like any good academician, Laughlin came up with many more formulas and postulates than answers. To gauge the quality of performance in racehorses, he came up with a formula that compared standard mean seconds per furlong by the actual mean seconds per furlong. If a racer's actual speed (measured in average seconds per furlong) met the projected average time per furlong, the horse made par for that race. If he did better, he beat the par figures. Clearly, not many horses were going to beat par often.

Laughlin wrote that "If such handicapping were an exact science, and the 'quality of performance' of the individual horse were never variable, then all horses in the particular handicap race would cross the finishing line at the same instant. But, as a matter of fact, actual quality of performance is subject to great variability. This is an important factor which must be considered in the measure of racing capacity. Some horses show little range in quality in their successive best races; they are 'reliable.' Others are erratic, sometimes running very superior races, while at other times they are disappointing."

The realization that racehorses did not produce the same form race to race caused Laughlin to propose a second formula. He computed this by taking the mean quality of performance from a horse's best races, giving the animal the benefit of the doubt, and arriving at a biological handicap for the animal's career.

Biological Handicap (B.H.) = (716 QP) −585

Laughlin believed these equations measured the inherent ability of a racehorse, "sex, age, weight-carried and distance-run being duly considered."

In his own assessment of this research, Laughlin said that, "If two things (for example, distance and weight) are each independent functions of the same third thing (for example, speed), then these first two things (distance and weight) are, for each specific value of this third thing (that is, speed) unique functions of each other. The principle of added functions, by the mathematical models shown in Fig. 1, illustrates this very fundamental principle quite clearly."

Following this reasoning, Laughlin was assured that he could describe the mathematical value of a racehorse's ability. He didn't bother with no-name critters, either. In his conclusion to the first part of his *"Inheritance of Racing Capacity,"* he discussed nothing less than Man o' War.

He noted that "We know that Man o' War was a chestnut colt, by Fair Play, out of Mahubah by Rock Sand, that he raced in his two- and three-year-old forms, that in all he ran 21 races carrying from 115 to 130 pounds, for distances from five to 13 furlongs, that he won 20 of these races and was second in the one race which he lost, that he 'crossed par' nine times, and that he established many records. We know that Snowflake was a chestnut filly, by Mad Hatter, out of Snowdrop by Cicero, that she raced in her two-, three- and four-year-old forms, that she ran in all 30 races, carrying from 103 to 126 pounds, for distances ranging from 4 1/2 to 11 furlongs, that she won seven races, was second once, and that she 'crossed par' three times. We also know the sex, age, weight-carried, distance-run, speed (mean seconds per furlong), track condition and 'trueness of the race' for each of these individual performances. Although these two horses are of different sex, and never ran at exactly the same age, for the same distance, carrying the same weight, the new yard-stick for measuring the inborn racing capacity of the Thoroughbred horse rates, on the same scale, Man o' War at 139.25 and Snowflake at 127.31."

In Laughlin's estimation, this appraisal of Man o' War and the little-known Snowflake showed that racing ability could be quantified. This reasoning led him to declare that, "We are now in possession of a reliable yardstick for the measure of racing capacity in the Thoroughbred horse. We are, therefore, now ready for the next stage of these researches which will seek the mathematical rules by which nature governs the inheritance of racing capacity."

In beginning to ascertain the mathematical formula for the transmission of racing capacity, Laughlin noted that horse breeders of skill and experience had been trying to find out the answer for upwards of 300 years. They had spent time and considerable money trying to find the best way to breed Thoroughbreds. He wrote that earlier "studies have supplied a wealth of material, but too many of them have assumed a theory of some sort at the start, and then proceeded to bolster it up by selected evidence — the method of special pleading but not of scientific investigation."

As a result, Laughlin set out to put the inquiry on a firm scientific foundation. He considered the biological and mathematical elements that made up the horse and said that, "The only points upon which all investigators — biological and mathematical, practical and theoretical — have agreed are that racing capacity is a very complex quality, that it tends strongly to run-in-the-family, and that care and training of an exacting nature are necessary to bring out inborn capacity . . . Accordingly the present investigation will not begin with any theory. It will first seek only the most accurate mathematical picture which can be found for the behavior of Nature in transmitting racing capacity from one generation to another."

In attempting to quantify racing ability, Laughlin correctly interpreted the demands that had to be met by the animal in training. It had to have the mental and physical well-being to undergo training and profit from those stresses. This requires an interrelation of many different systems within the animal, and Laughlin observed that "racing capacity, far from being a 'thing present or absent,' or based upon a single gene, is, in its hereditary aspect, more probably based upon the developmental interaction of many thousands of genes.'"

Laughlin and associated researchers investigated the genetics of the horse, as well as they could nearly 80 years ago, and he asserted that "Practical breeding has contributed substantially to determining the essential genetic nature of racing capacity." He tried to develop a prediction formula for heredity in the Thoroughbred, and he concluded that a "functional quality like racing capacity in the Thoroughbred horse, far from being based upon a single or a few Mendelian genes, is, as we have seen, doubtless the developmental end-product of a great many — possibly a thousand or more — genes. In the course of development these genes interact, some accelerating their fellows, others canceling what otherwise would be high plus-effects in the individual. The resultant is that, keeping environment constant, the pre-selected individual offspring will possess the particular quality in an end-value somewhere on a scale ranging from very low to very high. Although such a quality may be definitely measurable, its constituent nature is vastly too complex to be attributable, in Mendelian fashion, to the additive combination of a few genes. Geneticists cannot yet dissect a single complex quality, much less any whole animal organism, into its constituent Mendelian genes. In such a dissection each gene would have to stand for a definite part played in the development of a quality - good or bad, structural or functional - of some sort. Doubtless, with a very few exceptions, each quality of use in practical breeding is based upon many genes, and each such gene, in turn, contributes, in some manner, to a great many - possibly hundreds - measurable structures and functions."

So Laughlin gave up the idea of describing the racehorse in the fashion of Mendel, with a small set of factors each responsible for a particular function. In this conclusion, he is in accord with the findings of geneticists and researchers over the following three-quarters of a century.

But Laughlin was a determined character and developed a formula for inheritance of racing ability in the Thoroughbred. According to Laughlin's researches, "racing capacity ranges continuously in different horses from B.H.=0 to B.H.=140 - the latter just a trifle above Man o' War's rating. Granted that racing capacity in the individual horse depends upon the working out of a vast group of genes in the course of development, and that the quality of racing capacity is highly hereditary, the formula for the inheritance of racing capacity must read: 'The Probability that the preindicated or random-selected foal of a particular sire and dam will develop a racing capacity within definitely named limits, as a function of the prediction index.' In general terms the formula is P=f (PI, OCR)

In this P = Probability; PI = Prediction index; and OCR=Offspring-class-range. Thus the task narrows down to 'Just what prediction-index, just what offspring-capacity-range, and just what function?'"

Laughlin, one of several gifted mathematicians and statisticians to undertake analyses of the Thoroughbred (others include Phil Bull and Joe Estes), used a Cartesian coordinate system to define his predictions of racing ability.

In describing his system, Laughlin said, "One of the three Cartesian coordinates — fore and aft — represents the prediction-basis, another — right and left — the center of the offspring-class-range predicted, and the third — the upright coordinate — represents the probability that, when the selected value of the prediction-basis is used, the offspring will fall into the selected offspring-class-range. Set one of the model-pointers over the selected prediction-basis; set the other over the mid-offspring-class-range 'predicted.' Then adjust the two arms so their points will meet on the surface of the model. Then swing one arm-point to the vertical coordinate-scale; the point-height thus measures the probability that the selected value of the prediction-basis and the selected offspring-class-range will, in actual breeding, fall together."

The result of this predictive model was called the futurity index or FI, and it is "composed entirely of racing capacity values of a group of the nearest blood-kin antecedent to the foal whose racing capacity is predicted. Each near blood-kin constituent of the prediction-basis is stressed or weighted the proper amount, determined by experience to give the most consistent series of predictions."

In his discussion of this procedure, Laughlin stresses the assessments of the immediate ancestors, according to their quality of performance and its influence on the biological handicap. He has, in essence, taken a rather statistically cumbersome route around to saying, "Breed the best to the best." He wrote that, "Experience has shown that the nearest blood-kin — direct and collateral — constitute a sounder basis of prediction for racing capacity in the foal than can be worked out by tracing descents along a few dilute ancestral lines."

Working out the mathematical implications of his research with great intensity, Laughlin also suggested something now commonly called "regression to the mean." By this scientists describe the tendency of any population to return to a mean average, or standard, of the breed for particular characteristics.

But a regression implies outliers, which are exactly what happen in breeding, and they are the subject of much comment in most breeding theories, as good horses produce moderate offspring, and no-name horses produce occasional champions.

Laughlin was aware of this factor, and he wrote that, "Practically it happens, and theoretically it is by the present findings expected to happen, that almost any quality of Thoroughbred sire and dam will on occasion produce almost any racing capacity in the offspring. But, depending on the racing capacities of the foal's near-blood-kin, the probability that inborn racing capacity of a certain quality will be possessed by a pre-selected future foal is many times the probability that the same foal will possess a certain other inborn racing capacity."

In Laughlin's calculations into the probability of inheritance, he found horses with high racing class and their close relatives had the highest probability for producing those characteristics. Likewise, horses who were less related to good racehorses in their immediate families had a lesser probability.

His comments on the models he used in deciphering these studies are useful to other Thoroughbred researchers searching for guidance in judging which results are significant. Laughlin said, "In the mathematical model of any specific formula of heredity, steepness and narrowness in general shape, and an axial trend which gives the minimum overlapping, indicate good prediction. If, on the same scales, a model shows much overlapping and a sprawling flatness in shape, it means that the investigator has not succeeded very well in finding a good prediction-basis. But experimental re-stressing of prediction-units can seek a better prediction basis without destroying the element of truth already found."

Laughlin concluded that there was no contradiction between a Mendelian analysis of genetics "and that procedure of genetic analysis which here supplies the specific formula of heredity, by the technique here called 'ogive-regression-probability.' If with the latter type of analysis the investigator will build the mathematical model for the particular formula, he will be aided substantially in the genetic analysis of his problem. For instance, a cross-section of the model in its lower prediction-values (but still, in the present model, substantially above the mean of the breed) will show a tall, steep slope, while another section with a still higher prediction-basis (i.e., still further above the mean) will show a lower, flatter slope. This indicates that heredity-prediction is better among the lower plus-values of racing capacity, for the strain under consideration, than among the upper plus-values.

"Again consider the upper breed-values represented by the blood found in the leading breeding farms for the Thoroughbred horse. Among such superior strains, the present evidence indicates that the Thoroughbred horse is less pure-bred or more variable, in Mendelian terms more heterozygous, for the higher plus- than for the lower plus-values of racing capacity of the antecedent near-in. As further evidence in using the general formula of heredity as an aid of Mendelian interpretation, we find that, based on the shape of the present mathematical model, the lower plus-values in racing capacity depend upon relatively more recessive phases of the more important constituent genes for this quality than do the higher plus-values. In this, and doubtless in many other ways, the Mendelian interpretation, and the formula of heredity or analysis by ogive-regression-probability, may aid each other. If they are the only two ways of looking at the truth, and each presents a true picture, the two pictures must be consistent.

"In the analysis of the more complicated qualities, genetics needs to attack the problem from many directions. It may be interesting, therefore, to compare the uses and limitations of the technique of gene-analysis with analysis by ogive-regression-probability. We find that Mendelian or gene-genetics predicts the nature of the offspring by qualitative classes or categories, determined by one gene or by the additive combination of a few genes. Its principal strength is that it is often able to tie-up its breeding predictions with the underlying chromosome mechanics. Its main weakness is that it can offer no satisfactory genetic analysis or prediction for those more complex traits which are definitely hereditary, and which constitute the main materials with which practical breeders and students of embryology and evolution are constantly working.

"Ogive-regression-probability as here outlined presents a general or pattern formula of heredity, the specific application of which also predicts offspring values. The basis of such prediction is a measured or quantitative range-of-value for a single complex trait, rather than for a combination of segregable qualitative or unmeasured traits. For the 'thing-predicted' ogive-regression-probability establishes arbitrarily selected but definitely measured offspring class-ranges. It deals with those qualities which result from the developmental interaction of a great many genes. Its main virtue is that, in its attack on genetic analysis, it can produce an accurate offspring-prediction for certain very complex measurable structural or functional entities. Its main weakness is that it cannot analyze such traits into their constituent genes; it can indicate only their relative number and potencies. But for the more complex qualities which definitely run-in-the-family neither has gene-analysis made much headway in specific gene-determination. Each within its own sphere, these two types of genetic analysis are equally accurate in offspring-prediction, while each has its own kind of strength and its own kind of weakness. The type of problem, and the 'favorableness of the material,' determine which technique will probably prove the more profitable. Doubtless in some cases the two methods working together will be more successful in the discovery of the truth about genetic problem than either one by itself.

"In keeping with current developments in the physical sciences, probability-mathematics comes in for ever increasing usefulness in the biological sciences also. This is true whether the investigator is making an early reconnaissance and seeking a hint of 'how it is,' or whether the particular study is well developed and he is seeking to defend the theory and to check it critically against experimental facts."

Conclusions

Laughlin asserted, that as part of his studies, he developed a measure for Thoroughbred racing ability, that this capacity was a hereditary quality, and that it could be abbreviated as a formula

P sel. BH (2.5 = f(FI,BH).

This means that P is the probability that a potential foal, with a given FI or complex of racing capacities among its antecedent direct and collateral near-kin, will, if such foal races, possess a Racing Capacity within the range BH.

In summing up Laughlin's work, it is important to note that his work was more fully developed and applied by Joe Estes. But Laughlin's primary realizations are important to thinking about breeding horses. First test the animal for the quality of its performance, then assess the likelihood that it can transmit those qualities. Breeders today are still working on the best and most effective ways to solve those puzzles. In essence, he was saying "breed the best to the best" because the result of using his criteria is culling, both for racing ability as horses come off the track and then for pedigree strength in terms of the racing quality of immediate relatives.

CHAPTER 16

Evaluating Breeding Theories – Looking for the Real Patterns Underpinning Tesio's Greatness

The separate racing worlds of the Thoroughbred, Quarter Horse and Standardbred have always had many theories on the subject of how to breed the best racehorses. Why are there so many theories in racehorse breeding? In cat breeding, the genetics of color inheritance are well worked out, and virtually everyone accepts the prevailing theory. The ratios of various colors to be expected in a litter are known. The lottery of mating means that the results in any particular litter may not come out anything like the expected ratio, but no-one doubts the theory.

That's not how it is in breeding to race. Outsiders can't believe it. Surely someone's theory should eventually achieve the best results, i.e. prove itself, and be accepted? Well, not so far — the success of racetrack stars as sires is still unpredictable, and no single theory has proven itself so successful in explaining what happens that it has been accepted universally. Nor have I ever heard or read anything by any professional or academic geneticist that can fully explain the genetics of the racehorse.

Abram S. Hewitt, in his wonderful book *The Great Breeders and Their Methods* (1982), expressed it this way: "Will some learned geneticist please come forward with an explanation that any layman can understand?"

Professor John James at the University of NSW published a paper on the mystery of racehorse genetics as recently as 1996. In the absence of any scientific understanding, a multitude of theories have flourished.

Why hasn't one theory been proved by simple empirical results, and the rest disproved? Because of the quicksand. There is intellectual quicksand everywhere in assessing breeding theories. Intellectual quicksand is sneaky stuff. It looks like firm ground, but it gets a grip of you while appearing to give you complete freedom of movement. You move about a lot but you aren't really going forward. Some people spend a lifetime in one pit or another and never know they are trapped. Sometimes we can see they are in a bog hole, even if they can't. But we can never be certain we are not in one ourselves. You have to listen very carefully to anyone who suggests you are in an intellectual quicksand pit — because they might be right.

So I'll start with some rules that I believe can help to spot quicksand, and those deceived by it.

Staaden's approach to evaluating breeding theories (as systems for planning matings):

(1) Have sound rules for evaluating breeding theories

There is an in-built lottery in genetics, so small numbers of results have little meaning in assessing breeding theories. One champion does not a theory prove. The racing ability of the foal from any particular mating is unpredictable. This lottery is inescapable and operates in each and every mating. An enthusiast could buy one mare, mate her to three different stallions on the basis of some theory — such as the first letter of the stallion's name has to be the same as the first letter of her name for the first foal, second letter of her name for second foal, etc. — and find great success. The enthusiast might breed three out of three stakes winners through sheer good luck. Someone who had a realistic, soundly-based mating plan could breed three horses and have all non-winners, through sheer bad luck.

Indeed it is such a lottery that the results from even quite large numbers, say 100 horses bred, still contain a large element of luck. Nothing is absolutely certain, only highly probable. In the assessment of breeding theories, there is quicksand everywhere. One of the problems in assessing breeding theories for the racing breeds is that very few individuals can afford to breed large enough numbers for any high degree of certainty about conclusions.

How many results are enough? That depends on the degree of apparent success or failure. It's not the number of champions and stakes winners alone; it's the percentage of champions and stakes winners that helps determine if the result was a fluke or a representative result.

It is hard not to be impressed if someone is introduced as the breeder or theoretician who produced 10 stakes winners. But is it impressive if they got that number from 1,000 foals? Definitely not. That is only one percent stakes winners, way below average for any racing country I know of. But it is impressive if they got that number from 100 foals? Ten percent stakes winners is very good going over largish numbers.

But even then there can have been some role for good old Lady Luck. There is even a tiny chance that the fabled Italian Thoroughbred breeder Federico Tesio's results were due more to luck than to his approach to the planning of his matings. How's that for heresy? The breeder of Nearco and Ribot, two of the greatest racehorses of the century, just lucky? No, not JUST lucky but with Tesio's approach to matings, whatever it was, for the exact same list of matings (at least 200), luck may decide whether he gets zero, one, two, three or four such outstanding horses. If Tesio's best horse had been Donatello II, usually considered his third-best horse, you would never have heard of him.

So what is the proof? Well, one stakes winner out of one foal bred proves very little, even though that is 100 percent stakes winners. Three out of three looks suspiciously good. Six out of six looks like a proven certainty, and with small numbers. The trouble is a breeder never gets six out of six. They might get two out of three, but as the numbers of foals rise, we get numbers more like three out of 30. Is that proof? Ten percent stakes winners on 30 foals to race is looking pretty good, but the next crop could add 30 more runners and no extra stakes winners.

There is no hard and fast set of figures that prove a theory. There are only probabilities. The larger the number of foals and the higher the percentage of stakes winners, the greater the probability the breeder had something more than luck in obtaining their results.

(2) If a deluded idiot with a theory plans the matings of sires and dams who did well on the racetrack, he will have above average success. This will not prove his theory.

There is a definite, well-proven tendency for the horses that performed very well on the racetrack to produce more top offspring than poorly performed racehorses. It is a bit freaky, with some top track horses doing very badly at stud, but on average, top track horses produce more winners of high-class races. So, a super-wealthy enthusiast, who buys only stakes-winning mares, could have the nuttiest breeding theory on earth, but if they only breed from top track sires and stakes-winning mares, they may well produce a champion, even several. They may top the breeder's table, win the awards, and their theory will look pretty good. However, with such breeding stock, it would be difficult NOT to get above average results.

(3) If a deluded idiot with a theory plans the matings of sires and dams who have already produced winners, he will have above average success. This will not prove his theory.

Once again, there is a definite, well-proven tendency for the horses that have already performed well in the stud to continue to produce top offspring.

(4) Improving or upgrading low-class stock does not necessarily prove a particular breeding theory is a good one.

It is easy to improve low-class stock. So if you mate a sire to a non-winning dam, on the basis that their star signs are perfect for each other, the result will most likely be superior to the dam. Does that mean your astrologer's star sign theory is right? No, it was the most probable outcome no matter what your theory was.

Similarly, if you use low-class mares to test a theory that good sires should have 16 doses of Stockwell in their sixth remove, your sire will mostly produce off-spring much better than the mares, i.e. he will "move them up." Does it prove your theory? No, it only shows, once again, that it is easy for a stallion to "move up" low-class mares.

Many a one-mare breeding theorist in Canada, America and Australia has bent my ear with a "proven" theory, where the proof was that he or she got several good foals from a low-grade mare. They are quite certain they'd breed champions if they could afford to apply this theory to high-class stock. The mare and/or the sire were chosen because they had a double cross of Hoot Owl or whatever, but the improvement had a high probability of happening anyway.

(5) Failing to improve or upgrade top-class stock does not necessarily prove a particular breeding theory is a bad one.

If you buy 100 stakes winning mares, and mate them to proven top level sires, will you get 100 percent stakes winning foals in one crop? No, you'll be lucky if you get 15 percent stakes winners, more likely five percent. Once again, this "poor" result is due to the tendency for matings of top-class animals to produce offspring more towards the population average. Scientists call this "a tendency to fall back to the mean."

The average of this crop will be well below the average of their dams, though still above the overall population average, but not by any huge amount. However, a few outstanding stakes winners may still be enough to win some breeders' awards. But — on at least one table at the awards — there will be someone saying, "He hasn't a clue, doesn't understand breeding — didn't move the mares up."

The main point here is that the offspring of really outstanding parents will, on average, be below the standard of those parents. The outstanding proven sires will have "moved down" most of the dams mated to them. Why? Because no matter what theory is used to decide the matings, due to the lottery and the "fall back to the average" phenomenon, the overall result will appear to be a failure if the "moved up the mares" criterion is applied. No sire of any racing breed has gotten 100 percent stakes winners from his stakes winning mares over large numbers – that I have ever heard of anyway.

Never forget that it is easy to improve low-class stock but hard to improve high-class stock.

(6) Any theory that plans matings by pedigree alone, or ranks pedigree above major physical traits, is suspect. No, I'll go further than that – it is dangerous rubbish.

Let me explain why. Two full sisters can have completely different temperaments, racetrack performances, faults and strengths. Yet they have identical pedigrees. Let's say the first one has shortish thick legs, buck-kneed, with a very strong hindquarter, and her only wins were at 1,000 meters (five furlongs). The second is more of the gangly type, weaker in the hindquarter, somewhat back at the knee (calf-kneed), and had a few wins at around 1,600 meters (about one mile). People who breed by pedigree alone will choose the same sire to breed to both these mares!

What if that sire has shortish thick legs? From the mare with shortish thick legs, there is a high probability you could breed a hippo! You might, if luck and the lottery are with you, breed a champion, but there is a vastly greater chance of a hippo. What if the sire is a tiny bit back at the knees — from the calf-kneed mare there is a high probability you could breed a horse that simply wouldn't stand up to training — let alone racing. A horse that would break down — that is why I would call such a totally pedigree-based theory dangerous rubbish.

Chosen on some pedigree breeding theory, this sire is supposed to be the best mate for both mares, yet NO one sire can be the best mating prospect for two such physically different mares.

(7) The genes of the two parents ALONE determine the traits of the offspring, not the "blood" of mysteriously "prepotent" ancestors.

For simple traits, consider two chestnut horses born of brown, bay or black parents. When these two chestnuts are mated, they can only have chestnut offspring. It does not matter how many ancestors in however many previous generations were black or brown or chestnut, the offspring can only be chestnut. It does not matter if an outstanding, prepotent bay stallion occurs six times in the first four removes. The offspring will not be bay. They will all be chestnut.

For complex traits, with many genes involved, the outcome of the combinations of the parents' genes become very varied. Then the trait values of the previous one or two generations can be a useful guide, especially to the range of variation in the trait.

(8) The further back into the pedigree a theory has to go, the more likely it is rubbish.

I will quote Alan Porter, on page 225 of *Patterns of Greatness*, when he is trying to shoot down rival mating services based on male line nicks:

"When . . . male line nicks are expressed in terms of sons or grandsons of a particular sire working with mares by sons or grandsons of a particular sire, this type of analysis is rendered virtually useless. If we consider Northern Dancer for example, his 'male line' might be represented by say Lyphard or by Nijinsky, two horses of vastly different physical types."

With every generation, the influence of a particular ancestor is halved. More importantly, in every mating, it is a different half, a different subset of the great ancestor's genes, a different group of chromosomes handed down. A sire passes different traits to different offspring, and especially to different grand-offspring. His sons, for example, have at least half of his genes for every trait, but their offspring may get none of the grand sire's genes for a particular trait.

(9) First-generation Male Line Nicks are real but not all apparent nicks are real.

A first-generation male line nick is a higher than expected success rate of the offspring from the crossing of one sire on the daughters of another sire. Note that it is not just a higher than average success rate. It has to be a higher rate of success than the track performance and breeding performance of the stock would lead you to expect. Sire Z might appear to nick with the daughters of sire Y, but it might just be that Y has a lot of high class daughters, and the class of their offspring is just what you would expect. Remember also that it will be easy to upgrade low-class mares. Remember it will be difficult to move up high-class mares. Remember the quicksand.

The numbers in nicking studies are always low, so there will be many lucky and unlucky results, results that are not truly representative of the potential of that cross, but when a nick produces good results, you can hardly go wrong repeating it. As they say — why not drill for oil where oil has already been found? The most difficult thing is to say when a cross is a failed nick (sometimes called an anti-nick), i.e. one that will get a lower than expected percentage of winners and stakes winners, etc. After five offspring without a good one? After 10? After 20?

(10) Because of the genetic lottery, nicks are very seldom passed on.

(Another indictment of breeding by pedigree alone)

(11) Beware of theories that use vague terms like "bringing together," "balancing," or "concentrating" the "blood" or "the strains" of Mythic, etc.

These are not genetic terms; they are airy-fairy warm fuzzies. Genes are not blood. Blood is not genes. When Foal A inherits some genes from the great Mythic, five removes back on both sides of its pedigree, it might get some genes for nose shape, some for rib spring, some for fast-twitch fibers in its deep gluteal muscle. Because traits are decided by the interaction of at least two genes, Foal A is, even then, unlikely to have Mythic's exact nose, rib spring or fast-twitch percentage in the deep gluteal muscle.

Foal B also inherits some genes from the great Mythic, but it is a different subset. Foal B might get some of Mythic's genes for hoof wall thickness, pastern angle, length of back and fast-twitch percentage of its longissimus dorsi muscle. The chances of reconstructing Mythic from his very own genes are astronomically small, about one divided by the number of stars in the Milky Way.

(12) Beware of hindsight

A lot of glowing praise for a mating that produced a particular outstanding horse means nothing unless the author can give plausible reasons for the success of that mating. And by reasons, I don't mean warm fuzzies like "brilliant mating because Pocahontas occurs in the fourth remove on one side and the fifth on the other side." We never hear why the studmaster paired the sire and dam, which may well have been on physical type, Pocahontas having not entered the studmaster's mind. Individual crosses of a mare and stallion rarely have more than a few offspring; so it is hard to evaluate them.

Is There a Place for Pedigrees?

Absolutely, particularly the first two generations, but mainly as a way of determining if there are likely to be any surprises in complex traits or overall ability. For example, a champion on the track is more likely to breed champions if his parents were champions than if they were average horses.

In complex traits, what you see in parents is only a rough guide to what you will get in the offspring because so many traits "jump around." Short parents tend to have short children, but some of their children might be surprisingly tall. Knowing what the grandparents were like can improve your ability to predict trait outcomes. If all the grandparents were short, you can expect the grandchildren to be short with less variation in height. If, however, all the grandparents were tall, the outcome could be very unexpected, and the offspring very varied in height.

Similarly, if you are trying to breed a horse to win the English Derby (1½ miles) or the Kentucky Derby (1¼ miles) it would be useful to look at the optimum distance of the parents and grandparents. If you had a mare who could stay all day, i.e. whose best distance was too far, then you might want a sire whose best distance was right on Derby distance or a bit short of Derby distance. But you should check to see if his sire and dam in turn were not all-day stayers, because if they were, you increase the chances of again throwing a horse whose best distance is too far.

Evaluating the Existing Theories

Vuillier's Dosages. A mathematical illusion made successful by the high quality of the stock and the trainer.

At any time, many of the top horses in a breeding pool will have a similar list of famous ancestors in their pedigree. Breeding to arrive at the same "dosages" of these ancestors will not produce above-average results unless done with above-average stock.

There are a number of reasons why many of the top stock of a particular era will have a similar list of top ancestors of previous years. One reason is simply the large number of offspring of the best sires. Once a sire gets some really outstanding stud results, he gets about 60 to 100, even 200 well-bred mares a year. Well-bred mares at the time will be offspring of the previous generation of successful stallions. In a smallish, largely isolated breeding pool like England's Thoroughbreds of the 1800s and the early part of the 1900s, the result is that a large proportion of the most successful animals on the track have similar "doses" of certain prominent ancestors.

Another factor which produces similarity of "dosages" of great ancestors in pedigrees is nicking. If a nick produces some very good horses, it will be repeated a lot of times, so a very large number of good horses will have similar pedigree patterns and hence "dosages."

So, the appearance of "dosages" arose from breeding proven sires to well-bred, well-performed, and proven mares. To attempt to get top racehorses by selecting sires and dams so that the offspring will end up with similar "dosages" will only achieve above-average success if those individual sires are proven at stud, and the dams are well bred and/or well performed. The success of dosage matings will be according to the class of sire and dam, rather than the dosages.

I believe Vuillier was successful because he had top stock, paid for by the Aga Khan, and "vetted" by a top trainer of his day, Frank Butters. From what I have read, I believe Butters' role in choosing the stock and training them was more important in making the Aga successful than was Vuillier's Dosage system.

(NOTE: Dr. Steve Roman's Dosages for the stamina rating of horses in the Kentucky Derby operate through a different mechanism and are different to breeding by Vuillier's Dosages.)

Two crosses of a great ancestor

Many theories involve two crosses of a great ancestor, one on either side of a pedigree, e.g. Alan Porter's *Patterns of Greatness*, Highflyer International, London, 1992.

In the foreword, it is claimed Alan Porter does not promote a system to follow; however, on page 224 he says, "One constant is the occurrence of inbreeding or linebreeding to superior ancestors and to their near relatives. In matings contrived by such as Tesio . . . the deliberate attempts to reinforce superior strains are clearly evident."

I will quote Alan Porter, on page 225 of *Patterns of Greatness*, on male line nicks:

"When . . . male line nicks are expressed in terms of sons or grandsons of a particular sire working with mares by sons or grandsons of a particular sire, this type of analysis is rendered virtually useless. If we consider Northern Dancer, for example, his 'male line' might be represented by say Lyphard or by Nijinsky, two horses of vastly different physical types."

Also I will quote Dewey G. Steele. This man was regarded as one of Kentucky's most eminent authorities in the field of horse genetics. Nelson Nye, the Quarter Horse writer, quotes him in *Speed and the Quarter Horse* (1973 page 49). Steele compared two extreme groups, the stakes winners of 1935, 1940 and 1941 with last horses in the last races on Thursday or Friday afternoons of the same years. He used some statistical analysis. Inbreeding in the two groups was compared, including the relationship to various ancestors, St. Simon, Bend Or, Domino, etc.

". . . There did not appear to be any significant differences between the two groups. It was apparent that the poors trace rather quickly to the same ancestry as do the best performers. The greatest ancestral difference between these two extreme groups was in the first generation. It declined rapidly in each of the succeeding generations . . ."

"Evidence from these studies indicates that pedigrees should be judged primarily upon the basis of the first and second generations and that ancestors beyond the third generation may for all practical purposes be ignored."

The famous racing writer Joe Estes came to a similar conclusion, due to his research published in *The Blood Horse*.

Members of this "two crosses" group usually claim that Ken McLean, in his book *Tesio: Master of Matings*, showed this was the secret of Tesio's success. When I read the book, it was hard to find a conclusion of any kind, yet everywhere in conversations with breeding enthusiasts, I encountered the belief that Ken McLean believes Tesio used inbreeding to achieve his great results.

Let's examine the evidence for the claim that Tesio used two crosses of a great ancestor. The evidence for this is weak, if not downright contradictory to the claim.

Nowhere in Tesio's writings (he wrote a book on racehorse breeding called *Breeding the Racehorse*) nor in quotes of him by others that I have seen, has Tesio ever written, talked, or even hinted of any such inbreeding theory. Still, he may have deliberately and deviously written a book to throw everyone off the scent.

McLean himself says on page one of *Tesio: Master of Matings*, "He had no single style or method. Instead, it appears he utilised matings based on inbreeding, linebreeding, and outcrossing." This suggests to me that Tesio was not looking back past the first few generations and was not much concerned with remote pedigree beyond two removes.

In *The British Racehorse* of September 1958, Franco Varola, a racing journalist and author, wrote, "Tesio did not plan his matings on paper very much, but relied mostly on his visual impression of the individuals concerned." McLean says when he quotes this passage in his book on Tesio (page 65), "I feel it is totally out of order and far from the truth . . . Franco Varola has tried to mislead us, I think. Tesio used the Split-Pedigree book on a constant basis." It should be remembered, however, that pedigrees serve as "physical fault" maps to some conformation experts.

Tesio was famous for frequent trips across Europe from his base in Italy to look at horses in France and England. He visited stallions before using them. He inspected horses before buying them. This sounds to me like someone who took a lot of interest in physical type.

Tesio was an ex-jockey and a trainer. I wrote a book on racehorse trainers, after interviewing 36 in depth. I found that trainers become very aware of the weaknesses of individual horses and their close family. Through the disappointments and frustrations of breakdowns, they become very attuned to physical weaknesses. When they become breeders, they, like — for example — Wayne Lukas, tend to mate horses to avoid creating or increasing weaknesses.

Nearco (1935), Tesio's finest breeding product, a champion on the track and an all-time great sire (sire of Nasrullah, and grandsire of Northern Dancer), **has no double crosses in his first three generations**. In his fifth generation back, he has St. Simon on both sides of his pedigree. By this time in England, it was hard to find horses without St. Simon in the back of their pedigrees. Five generations back he has St. Simon twice more and Brown Bess on both sides.

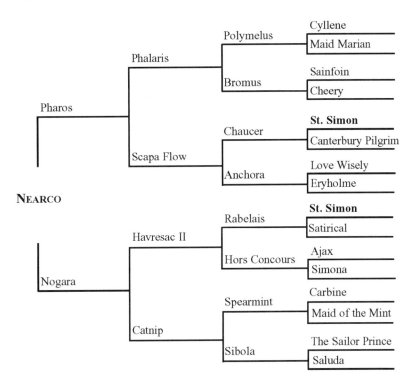

Ribot (1954), Tesio's finest racing product, twice winner of the Prix de L'Arc de Triomphe, unbeaten in 16 starts on the racetrack, champion of Europe and Britain, and considered one of the greatest racehorses of the century as well as a success as a sire, **has no double crosses in his first four generations back**. Five generations back, he has Sunstar occurring twice in his dam side. Six generations back, St. Simon occurs five times, and there are multiple appearances of three others.

Marco Luigi Poli, overcome by hero worship and hindsight, is quoted by McLean (page 91): "Ribot can be said to be fully representative of everything that Tesio learned in his 60 years of study . . . Only Tesio would have thought of mating the fragile and temperamental Romanella with the dour Tenerani . . . What secret did Romanella hold that only Tesio knew? Was it because her dam was a daughter of Papyrus from whom Tesio had obtained Sanzio; and that Papyrus was by Tracery for whom Tesio had such high regard? Or was it because the maternal grandsire of Barbara Burrini was by Buchan, a son of Sunstar who was the sire of Tesio's first international winner, Scopas?"

However, if Tesio had some grand insight, and thought Romanella and Tenerani would produce something special, why were Romanella's first eight matings (while Tesio was still alive) to five different stallions? Why wasn't the mating to

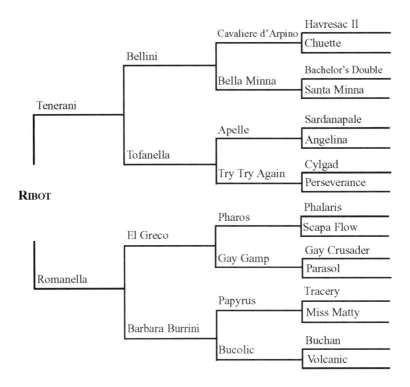

Tenerani repeated a third time until 1957, when Tesio was dead (Tesio died in 1954) and Ribot had just completed his sensational four-year-old year on the track?

The fact is, mating the fragile and temperamental Romanella with the dour Tenerani sounds like mating opposite faults, nothing to do with pedigree.

Donatello II (1934), generally considered Tesio's third-best horse, **has no double crosses in his first four generations**.

One of the most important people to have questioned Tesio was Abram S. Hewitt, later the author of *The Great Breeders and Their Methods*. I say important because Hewitt, in his books and in one very long phone conversation I had with him, appeared to have a very open, intelligent, and inquiring mind about things. He did not go around trying to fit results to some preconceived theory. He was a student of racing from his days at Oxford University, and later was an owner and breeder, associated with the likes of Ksar, sire of Tourbillon.

What did Hewitt discover about Tesio's methods? On page 371 of his book, he says Tesio made the following points in 1938:

"He sent his mares outside Dormello to be bred, as this gave him the widest possible selection in mating to obtain the characteristics needed by each mare as

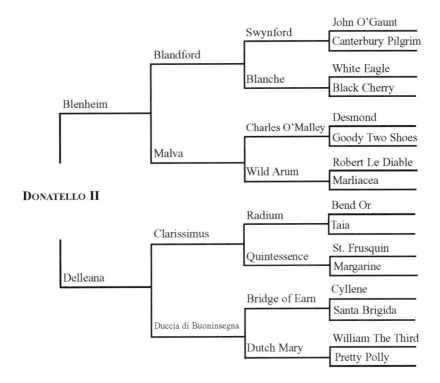

DONATELLO II

to conformation, constitution, distance capacity, nervous energy, early or late maturity, gameness, etc." This was Hewitt's first point, and it is a classic complimentary mating program.

Is there any mention of inbreeding? In his point eight, Hewitt says, "There are very few examples of inbreeding in the Tesio pedigrees . . . He once inbred to Havresac II 3x2."

Is there any mention of double crosses? In point five, Hewitt says, "His favorite strain was that of St. Simon (Tesio said he had curby hocks), and he tried to pile up as much St. Simon as he could get, but, as he said, 'Not close up.' Inasmuch as we were talking in 1938 and St. Simon had been foaled in 1881, it was already a little hard to get the name 'close up.'"

Clearly Tesio did like to have St. Simon piled up in the rear of a pedigree, but the first thing Hewitt lists is the complimentary mating. If Tesio put piles of St. Simon ahead of the complimentary mating, he could have simply gone to the same sire rich in St. Simon every year for any mare. But he didn't — he went to a large variety of different sires — usually a sign that someone needs different sires for different mares.

Summary:

Evaluation Rule 1:

Only count stakes winners. Winners help, but the real money is in stakes winners and champions.

Evaluation Rule 2:

The higher the percentage of stakes winners, the more likely the theory works.

Evaluation Rule 3:

The higher the number of runners that percentage is from, the more likely the theory works.

Evaluation Rule 4:

Almost any theory, applied using top-class race-proven sires and dams, will produce above-average results. That does not prove the theory.

Evaluation Rule 5:

Almost any theory, applied using sires and dams who have already produced top-class offspring, will produce above-average results. That does not prove the theory.

Evaluation Rule 6:

Getting better offspring from low-class mares does not necessarily prove a theory.

Evaluation Rule 7:

Getting a lower average class of offspring from high-class mares does not necessarily disprove a theory.

Evaluation Rule 8:

Any theory that plans matings by pedigree alone, or ranks pedigree above major physical traits, is suspect.

Evaluation Rule 9:

The further back into the pedigree a theory has to go, the more likely it is rubbish.

About the Author

Ross Staaden, BVSc., Ph.D. has been working on the mystery of racehorse genetics for more than 25 years. A practicing veterinarian in Australia, he has a Ph.D. in Exercise Science for his studies in energetics, oxygen uptake and cardiac output of greyhounds at race speed. In 1991 he authored the book Winning Trainers - Their Road to the Top. *Dr. Staaden enjoys testing observed facts against theory, especially in the realm of breeding. He and his wife reside in Perth, Western Australia.*

Index

About the Author

Frank Mitchell is a freelance writer and bloodstock consultant living near Lexington, Ky. Turning away from an academic career as a college professor, Mitchell began writing full time in the horse business in 1991 and joined the staff of *Daily Racing Form* in 1993. In addition to being deputy bloodstock editor at *Daily Racing Form* for several years, Mitchell continues to write a weekly column for the *Form* covering bloodstock and pedigrees. His other contributions have appeared in *The Thoroughbred Times*, *The Blood-Horse MarketWatch*, *MidAtlantic Thoroughbred*, *Florida Horse*, *Owner-Breeder* and other publications.

In addition to writing, Mitchell has worked with several industry professionals to understand the practical facets of racing and breeding. To this end, he has become well-acquainted with the techniques of appraising and valuing breeding and racing stock, as well as judging conformation and conditioning. Having owned and bred Thoroughbreds, Mitchell is familiar with the many trials and pleasures relating to our great sport and the most fascinating pastime and occasionally rewarding endeavor that horse breeders undertake.